Collaboration in
Psychological Science

Collaboration in
Psychological Science

BEHIND THE SCENES

Richard L. Zweigenhaft

Guilford College

Eugene Borgida

University of Minnesota

worth publishers
Macmillan Learning

New York

Vice President, Editorial, Social Sciences: Charles Linsmeier
Executive Editor: Christine Cardone
Editorial Assistant: Melissa Rostek
Marketing Manager: Katherine Nurre
Director of Content Management Enhancement: Tracey Kuehn
Managing Editor: Lisa Kinne
Project Editor: Edward Dionne, MPS North America LLC
Senior Production Supervisor: Paul Rohloff
Director of Design, Content Management: Diana Blume
Cover Design: Diana Blume
Permissions Manager: Jennifer MacMillan
Text Design: Kevin Kall
Composition: MPS North America LLC
Printing and Binding: RR Donnelley
Cover Art: Vernon Wiley/Getty Images

Library of Congress Control Number: 2016944173

ISBN-13: 978-1-4641-7574-9
ISBN-10: 1-4641-7574-8

First printing

Worth Publishers
One New York Plaza
Suite 4500
New York, NY 10004-1562
www.macmillanlearning.com

DEDICATION

To Irene Zweigenhaft and Karl Scheibe, both of whom saw the best in us, even when we were young and foolish.

ABOUT THE EDITORS

Courtesy of Sasha Maslow

Richard L. Zweigenhaft is the Charles A. Dana Professor of Psychology at Guilford College. He received a BA from Wesleyan University, an MA in social psychology from Columbia University, and a PhD in personality and social psychology from the University of California, Santa Cruz. He has taught at Guilford since 1974, where he has served as the chair of the psychology department (many times), as the chair of the social science division, and as the director of the interdisciplinary minor in communications. He is the author and coauthor of many articles, and the coauthor (with G. William Domhoff) of a series of books on the American power structure, the most recent of which is *The New CEOs: Women, African American, Latino, and Asian American Leaders of Fortune 500 Companies* (2014).

Eugene Borgida is a professor of psychology and law at the University of Minnesota, and a Morse-Alumni Distinguished Professor of Psychology. He is also adjunct professor of political science and founding codirector of the Center for the Study of Political Psychology. He received his BA from Wesleyan University and his PhD in psychology from the University of Michigan. Borgida has served as associate dean and executive officer of the College of Liberal Arts and as chair of the Psychology Department. He received the Distinguished Teacher Award from the College of Liberal Arts and the systemwide Morse-Alumni Award for Outstanding Contributions to Undergraduate Education.

Steve Niedorf

tion. He is a fellow of the Association for Psychological Science (APS) and the American Psychological Association (APA) and an elected fellow of the American Association for the Advancement of Science (AAAS). He has served on the board of directors for the APS and the Social Science Research Council (SSRC). Borgida has published extensively in social psychology, law and psychology, and political psychology, and his research has been supported by the National Institute of Mental Health (NIMH), National Institutes of Health (NIH), National Science Foundation (NSF), and The Pew Charitable Trusts. He is coauthor of four books, the most recent of which (with John Bargh) is the *APA Handbook of Personality and Social Psychology: Attitudes and Social Cognition* (2015).

CONTENTS

PART IV COLLABORATION WITH INSTITUTIONAL AND COMMUNITY PARTNERS

PART V CONCLUSION: BEST PRACTICES IN COLLABORATION IN PSYCHOLOGICAL SCIENCE

LIST OF CONTRIBUTORS

Dominic Abrams
Professor of Social Psychology
Director, Centre for the Study of Group
    Processes
University of Kent

Ellen Berscheid
Regents Professor of Psychology Emerita
University of Minnesota

Eugene Borgida
Professor of Psychology and Law
Morse-Alumni Distinguished Professor
    of Psychology
University of Minnesota

Steven J. Breckler
Former Executive Director for Science
American Psychological Association

Nancy Cantor
Chancellor
Rutgers University–Newark

Geoffrey L. Cohen
Professor of Psychology
James G. March Professor of Organizational
    Studies in Education and Business
Stanford University

John F. Dovidio
Carl Iver Hovland Professor of Psychology
Yale University

Peter Englot
Senior Vice Chancellor for Public Affairs
    and Chief of Staff to Chancellor
Rutgers University–Newark

Susan T. Fiske
Eugene Higgins Professor of Psychology
Professor of Psychology and Public Affairs
Princeton University

Samuel L. Gaertner
Trustees Distinguished Professor Emeritus
Department of Psychological and
    Brain Sciences
University of Delaware

Steven W. Gangestad
Distinguished Professor of Psychology
University of New Mexico

Julio Garcia
Consulting Research Scientist
Graduate School of Education
Stanford University

Jeff Greenberg
Professor of Psychology
University of Arizona

Elaine Hatfield
Professor of Psychology
Universty of Hawaii

Miles Hewstone
Professor of Social Psychology and
    Public Policy
Director, Oxford Centre for the Study
    of Intergroup Conflict
University of Oxford

Michael A. Hogg
Professor of Social Psychology
Chair, Social Psychology Program
Claremont Graduate University

James S. Jackson
Former Director, and Research Professor
Institute for Social Research
Daniel Katz Distinguished University
    Professor of Psychology
University of Michigan

Deborah Roedder John
Professor and Curtis L. Carlson Chair
    in Marketing
Carlson School of Management
University of Minnesota

Charles M. Judd
Professor of Distinction
Department of Psychology and
    Neuroscience
University of Colorado Boulder

Shinobu Kitayama
Robert B. Zajonc Collegiate Professor
of Psychology
Director, Center for Culture, Mind,
and the Brain
University of Michigan

Barbara Loken
David C. McFarland Professor of Marketing
Carlson School of Management
University of Minnesota

Hazel Rose Markus
Davis-Brack Professor in the Behavioral
Sciences
Stanford University

Robin Martin
Professor of Organisational Psychology
Alliance Manchester Business School
University of Manchester

Mario Mikulincer
Professor of Psychology
Provost, Interdisciplinary Center (IDC)
Herzliya, Israel

Richard E. Nisbett
Theodore M. Newcomb Distinguished
University Professor
Department of Psychology
University of Michigan

Allen M. Omoto
Professor of Psychology
School of Social Science, Policy,
and Evaluation
Claremont Graduate University

Bernadette Park
Professor of Psychology
Department of Psychology
and Neuroscience
University of Colorado Boulder

Tom Pyszczynski
Distinguished Professor
Department of Psychology
University of Colorado Colorado Springs

Lee Ross
Stanford Federal Credit Union Professor
of Humanities and Sciences
Department of Psychology
Stanford University

Phillip R. Shaver
Distinguished Professor of Psychology,
Emeritus
University of California, Davis

Steven J. Sherman
Emeritus Chancellor's Professor of
Psychological and Brain Sciences
Indiana University

Mark Snyder
McKnight Presidential Chair in Psychology
University of Minnesota

Sheldon Solomon
Professor of Psychology
Skidmore College

John L. Sullivan
Emeritus Regents Professor of Political
Science
University of Minnesota

Shelley E. Taylor
Distinguished Research Professor
Psychology Department
University of California, Los Angeles

Gary L. Wells
Distinguished Professor of Psychology
The Wendy and Mark Stavish Chair in
Social Sciences
Iowa State University

Richard L. Zweigenhaft
Charles A. Dana Professor of Psychology
Guilford College

PREFACE

Collaboration in Psychological Science: Behind the Scenes includes 21 chapters written by social scientists who have collaborated extensively during their careers. They peek behind the curtain and generate insights about the process of collaboration, and, along the way, insights about the pros and cons, the challenges and the benefits, and the practical and the ethical dilemmas that are part of working collaboratively. We believe that they will be of interest to readers in at least four ways. First, the stories that they tell are inherently interesting. Second, they highlight the lessons to be learned from collaborating, both in terms of the benefits and pitfalls. Third, they help to shed light on the nature of an increasingly crucial aspect of professional socialization in the field (e.g., what do we explicitly teach young psychologists about collaboration in the field, and what is communicated less directly?). Finally, the chapters provide some broader lessons about the nature of scientific work and the norms of collaboration that define scientific work in psychology as it is done today. Moreover, as we argue in our concluding section, these lessons and best practices apply not only to social psychologists doing collaborative work but also to the work of all psychological scientists working collaboratively. In fact, we suspect and suggest that these are lessons that pertain to all academic collaborative work, not only in psychology.

These four sets of issues are related to many questions that are addressed in the chapters (not every one addresses every question, however). Among these are the following:

1. What considerations motivated the collaboration?

2. What about the collaboration made it work better?

3. What about the collaboration made it work less effectively?

4. Could any one of the collaborators have conducted equally good research on the topic on his or her own?

5. Does the substantive domain in which the collaboration occurs shape the nature of the collaboration (e.g., if social issues research or interdisciplinary research questions take on larger-scale problems, then does the broader scope of the research questions involved necessitate a "team" science approach?)

6. How have advances in technology made it easier to collaborate?

7. How was it determined who was to be included as an author and the order of authorship?

8. When it came to tenure and promotion, or nominations for research awards, how did coauthored articles or books affect the decisions made?

9. Are there particular issues that arise for students collaborating with faculty members, or faculty members collaborating with students?

Acknowledgments

We have many people to thank, for this was very much a collaborative project. We, of course, are indebted to the 35 contributors to the 21 chapters in the book. They sent us their chapters and were good-natured when we asked for revisions, and they were patient with us as the project took longer than we initially anticipated. In short, they were a total pleasure to work with. We are also indebted to Heidi Wolff and Alex Van Dyke at the University of Minnesota for their invaluable assistance as we sought to put the 21 chapters into a consistent APA format (headings, references, margins, you name it). Our wives, Lisa Young and Susan M. Wolf, not only encouraged us throughout the project but at times also offered inspirational guidance and spot-on correctives. Finally, we wish to thank our wonderful editor Chris Cardone. Chris was enthusiastic about this project from the beginning, and her editorial savvy and her good judgment have made this a much better book than it otherwise would have been.

As the coeditors of a volume on collaboration, it seems only fitting that we should explain how we came to collaborate on this project, and the nature of our own collaboration. In the summer of 2011, Richie Zweigenhaft, while reading a book titled *Mentor: A Memoir* (Grimes, 2010),[1] began to think about his own academic mentor and the collaborative work that they have done together over many decades. He realized that a volume on collaboration might be interesting and useful to graduate students and faculty alike. He spent the next month or so writing a working draft of an essay about his own experiences with collaboration, as well as a working draft of a book prospectus. He then sent it to Gene

Photo taken by Lisa Young.

The editors, at Wesleyan University, in the fall of 1989.

Borgida, an old friend, asking for feedback. Borgida liked the idea and had lots of thoughts about how it might happen and what it might include, and the two decided to collaborate on this volume.

Over the next year, we traded e-mails about this putative project. Then, in June 2012, while Gene was visiting Duke University to collaborate with a former colleague at Duke's School of Law, Richie, who lives an hour from Duke, drove over for an afternoon of planning. As a result of that session, we sent invitations to about 30 social psychologists known to have done important collaborative research, describing the project and inviting them to write essays for the proposed anthology. All seemed to like the idea, and almost all agreed to contribute to the volume (the few who said no liked the idea but were swamped with other commitments). Here, Borgida's considerable social capital in social psychology was invaluable.

How did we know each other in the first place? In early 1972, as Richie was in the midst of his second year as a graduate student at the University of California, Santa Cruz (UCSC), Gene, who had finished college 6 months earlier, was looking for a job. After having spent some time in France, he was staying at his parents' house in Silver Spring, Maryland, planning to work until he started graduate school at the University of Michigan in the fall. On a whim, he went by the office of the American Institutes for Research (AIR), a nearby research organization that did applied psychology, and dropped off a résumé and an application.

As it turned out, Richie's mother, Irene Zweigenhaft, worked at AIR, which was a fairly buttoned-down place, where the men wore jackets and ties. She took one look at Gene (dressed—how should we say this?—quite casually, and with pretty long hair), and her first thought was that it was unlikely that AIR would hire him. However,

---

[1] Tom Grimes. *Mentor: A Memoir.* Portland, OR and New York, NY: Tin House Books, 2010.

when she looked at his résumé, she saw that he had gone to Wesleyan University, from which Richie had graduated, and that Gene had listed Karl Scheibe, Richie's favorite psychology professor, as a reference. She decided to interview him, was charmed, and, based on her recommendation, AIR hired him. Gene and Irene became close friends. She told Gene about Richie, and she told Richie about Gene. Years later, at a meeting of the International Society of Political Psychology in Washington, D.C., they met, not knowing at the time that they would eventually collaborate.

Irene would be delighted by this collaboration. We dedicate the book to her, and to Karl Scheibe.

FOREWORD

A little more than 30 years ago, I was interviewing for my first faculty position in a department of psychology. Like those of you who have shared this experience, I remember those interviews—for better or for worse—quite well. There was the time when my job talk was interrupted by a hostile questioner after I had uttered only one sentence. I began my talk by saying, "Today, I am going to discuss *the self.*" This very senior member of the faculty quickly raised his hand and asked, "Peter, do you take a California view of the self or a New England view of the self?" I had no idea what he was talking about. I still don't. Let's just say the talk went downhill from there. At another university, my initial interview was with the chair of a department whose very first question to me—before he even had welcomed me to the department and well before I had presented my talk—was simply, "How does $24,000 sound for a starting salary?" My response: "Are you offering me a job?" He said, "No, I just wanted to know if the pay—should we offer you a job—sounds good enough to you." As it happens, I am still waiting to hear back from that department.

Well, we all have our job interview horror stories, and I guess I have mine. But the interview that most sticks in my mind is the one where nearly every member of the faculty asked some version of the question, "Why is it that your publications always have several authors?" and "Where are your single-authored publications?" For the first time, I was struck by the fact that some people do not view collaboration positively. Years later, the same questions were asked again when I was considered for promotion to tenure.

Quelle surprise! I had always thought that the very best work in our field was accomplished by investigators with complementary interests and talents working together to produce something of greater impact than they could have generated individually: Amos Tversky and Daniel Kahneman, Richard Nisbett and Lee Ross, Lester Flatt and Earl Scruggs. OK—that last one is from the domain of my other passion, bluegrass music. But the point is the same—by working together, beautiful things are possible. But ours is a discipline that sometimes overvalues individual achievement, to the detriment of those who enjoy and appreciate working with others.

For whatever reason, other fields of scholarship and research have figured this out. When was the last time a physicist conducted an experiment by himself or herself concerning—let's say—the properties of the Higgs Boson, using the Large Hadron Collider as a tool? I suspect the answer to this question is "never," and, in fact, research articles in particle and high-energy physics often include dozens and dozens of coauthors. Our colleagues in the life sciences tend also to work in largish groups, and it is unusual when the senior member of the team (usually a tenured faculty member) isn't listed on a publication as the final author, not the first one.

But in the psychological sciences, we are just a little leery of collaboration. Why is this? Is it a carryover from more than a century ago, when psychology was a subfield of philosophy? Does it reflect an insecurity about the nature of our contribution to knowledge, such that we believe our impact is diluted by the number of investigators responsible for it?

All I can say is that most of the psychological science in which I have been involved—from laboratory studies of human emotion to field research on health communications—has involved collaboration with others, often undergraduate and graduate students. And in my view, these programs of research are better for it.

The idea of *emotional intelligence*, for instance, originated in a collaboration with Jack Mayer, who was then on the faculty at SUNY–Purchase and is now at the University of New Hampshire. Jack is a student of human intelligence with a special interest in ideographic approaches to personality, and I consider myself a student of human emotion with a more nomothetic orientation. It was through arguing with each other—conversations that began when Jack helped me paint my living room in 1987—that we thought of the idea that people might differ in the skills that they used to discern the information contained in their own and others' emotions. The most important lesson in that partnership? Well, it turns out that collaboration is simply a lot more fun that toiling alone.

After reading through this remarkable collection, skillfully shepherded by Richie Zweigenhaft and Gene Borgida, I hope you will agree.

Peter Salovey

President, Yale University

New Haven, CT

March 25, 2016

PART I

Introduction: Behind the Scenes

Richard L. Zweigenhaft

Guilford College

Eugene Borgida

University of Minnesota

This book is long overdue. Over the past four or five decades, major changes have taken place in the ways that psychologists do research. Although many psychologists continue to write articles and books on their own, more and more research in the field is coauthored, sometimes by teams of researchers, and coauthored works are cited more frequently than solo-authored works

(Hegarty & Walton, 2012). The increase in collaborative research has been a trend not only in psychological science, but also in other fields, for quite a while now—so long, in fact, that there are journals dedicated to "scientometrics" ("what we know about the structure and dynamics of collaboration"; Beaver, 2001, p. 365), there is an international organization whose members share a common interest in scientific collaboration (Beaver, 2004, p. 399), and there is a field called "the science of team science," which studies the "circumstances that facilitate or hinder the effectiveness of team science initiatives" (Stokols, Hall, Taylor, & Moser, 2008, p. S78; see also Cooke & Hilton, 2015; Hall et al., 2012). So many researchers now work with what is called Big Data (or Big Science) that there are dozens of programs at colleges and universities in data science (Miller, 2013). Moreover, as federal funds for research have decreased over the past decade or so (for example, since 2003, the National Institutes of Health [NIH] has seen its budget decrease by 25% in inflation-adjusted value), there has been more and more pressure to do collaborative team research (Baskin, 2015). Collaboration in psychology, therefore, is part of a trend that encompasses the biological and physical sciences and the social sciences—one that is interdisciplinary or transdisciplinary, as well as international.

In an analysis of the Thompson Reuters Web of Science publication data, Wuchty, Jones, and Uzzi (2007) found that 52% of the articles published in the social sciences between 1996 and 2000 were coauthored. This percentage was higher than for articles in the arts and humanities (10%), but lower than for the material sciences and engineering (80%). Social psychology, experimental psychology, and biological psychology were the fields with the highest rates of coauthored articles (77%, 78%, and 85%, respectively). This trend has continued: Voosen (2013), reporting on a more recent Web of Science study, reports that the percentage of single-authored articles in the social sciences dropped from 72% in 1981 to 38% in 2012, and single-authored articles were even less frequent in economics and business, math, and the sciences. In microbiology, only 2% of the published articles in 2012 were written by a single author (see also King, 2013).

Collaboration in psychological science is also especially likely to be interdisciplinary. A 2005 study of more than 1 million journal articles published in the year 2000 found that psychology is one of seven "hub sciences"—that is, those areas of inquiry with the most interdisciplinary linkages (Boyack, Klavens, & Borner, 2005). Former president of the Association for Psychological Science (APS) Walter Mischel referred to this as "scientific bridge building," noting that "[b]ridge-building opens phenomena that lie at the intersections among multiple disciplines, play out at multiple levels, and cannot be seen within the boundaries of any single discipline or captured in the work of any single investigator or lab" (Mischel, 2009, para. 14).

Not only are more articles coauthored, the number of authors per article has increased. In a study of all the articles published in the *Journal of Personality and Social Psychology* (*JPSP*) between 1965 and 2000, the authors found that the average number of authors per article increased steadily, from 1.91 between 1965 and 1974, to 2.16 between 1975 and 1984, and finally 2.49 between 1985 and 2000. As the authors concluded back in 2004, "Gone are the days of the 18th- and 19th-century science, when individuals working alone conducted much of the scientific research" (Quinones-Vidal, Lopez-Garcia, Penaranda-Ortega, & Tortosa-Gil, 2004, p. 449).

Moreover, there is evidence that coauthored articles are more scientifically influential than single-authored articles—at least, they are cited more frequently. In a study of the citations to 1,133 articles published in nine leading psychology journals between 1996 and 2005, Hegarty and Walton (2012) found that coauthored articles were significantly more likely to be cited than single-authored articles (see also Bornman & Daniel, 2008, and Wuchty et al., 2007). As Professor John Cacioppo of the University of Chicago concluded in 2007, "It is clear that the most influential research in psychology and in the sciences more generally is now more likely to be the product of a scientific team than of a solitary scientist" (Cacioppo, 2007, para. 11).

There is also reason to believe that some colleges and universities have come to encourage collaboration among their faculty and to encourage them to collaborate with nonacademic residents of the community (see, for example, the chapter in this volume by Cantor and Englot, and the one by Cohen and Garcia). Chase F. Robinson, the president of the Graduate Center of the City University of New York, argues that his school has been able to attract eminent scholars from prestigious schools because of the promise of collaboration. Here's how he put it in a May 2014 article in the *Chronicle of Higher Education* titled "Trouble Recruiting Top Faculty? Promote Collaboration":

> Scholars respond to opportunity and, increasingly, to the promise of collaboration. Interdisciplinarity can be overhyped, but we have put in place structures that transcend and complement departmental organization, placing students, postdocs, and junior and senior faculty members together in research-driven seminars. So what we've been building are not buildings, but communities and partnerships.... Exceptionally talented academics also have choices, and they make them in ways that maximize their odds for success. The promise of both intellectual ferment and broad impact is one choice. (para. 9, 11)

Moreover, some schools dedicate money and space to allow and encourage their faculty to work collaboratively. For example, at the University of North Carolina, Chapel Hill, the Center for Faculty Excellence (CFE), working with the Institute for the Arts and Humanities in the College of Arts and Sciences, created a Summer Writing Group to support scholarly productivity and interdisciplinary collaboration. Using before-and-after measures for the 62 participants from 13 academic departments in the College of Arts and Sciences and from 9 of the university's 11 professional schools, it was quite clear that "faculty members are thirsty for this kind of support," and that "they want to live as writers in community rather than isolation" (Muller, 2014, p. 38).

So, too, is the federal government encouraging and providing support for collaborative efforts. The Behavioral Research Program at the National Cancer Institute has developed Grid-Enabled Measures (GEM), an online resource that uses crowdsourcing to explore difficult topics and to encourage consensus on the use of common assessment techniques in collaborative research studies. As Moser and Coa (2015) explain:

> This process can be seen as a "bottom-up" approach to gaining consensus on measures that is different from other efforts that use more of a "top-down," expert-driven approach to achieve consensus. The wiki aspect of the tool encourages collaboration, as users enter (and potentially edit) information about the existing constructs and measures, including definitions and other meta-data. (para. 8)

Therefore, psychologists today engage in a good deal of collaboration, collaborative research is likely to generate the most frequently cited works in the field, and some scholars and some institutions very much encourage collaboration. Ironically, however, little has been written about the complicated behind-the-scenes process of working with others to design research, to gather and analyze data, and to write reports, articles, or books. Undergraduate and graduate methods courses largely ignore the rationale for (let alone the nuts and bolts of) collaborative research. Moreover, even less has been written on the reasons behind the rise of collaborative research in psychology. Is it because of the rise of interdisciplinarity more generally? Is it because of the emergence of Big Data and Big Science, with their emphasis on, and need for, collaborative teams? Or are researchers banding together to maximize their likelihood of being funded by public and private agencies struggling with drastically reduced budgets?

About the Authors

With these issues and questions in mind, we encouraged those who wrote chapters for this volume to tell us how they came to collaborate and the nature of their interactions while collaborating. Traditionally (that is, in the old, pre-Internet days), when psychologists decided to collaborate with one another, they knew each other personally, sometimes as friends who met in graduate school (see, for example, the chapter by Greenberg, Pyszczynski, and Solomon or the one by Nisbett and Ross), sometimes when one person was a graduate student and the other a faculty member (see, for example, the chapter by Dovidio and Gaertner), sometimes when one was an undergraduate and the other a faculty member (see, for example, the chapter by Fiske and Taylor), sometimes as colleagues who work or worked at the same school (see, for example, the chapters by Abrams and Hogg, Hatfield and Berscheid, Hewstone and Martin, Judd and Park, Sullivan and Borgida, and Loken and John), and sometimes as colleagues who work at different schools (perhaps in different countries) and decided to collaborate because of shared research interests (see, for example, the chapter by Shaver and Mikulincer).

As you'll see, Phil Shaver and Mario Mikulincer at times stand next to one another, with one at the keyboard composing sentences and the other critiquing those sentences, although they also do most of their collaborative work when they are on different continents (Shaver lives in California, Mikulincer in Israel). Mark Snyder and Allen Omoto, who both live in the United States but in different time zones, tell us, parenthetically, that "we are, at this very moment, sitting in the same room at separate tables tapping away on separate computers writing separate sections of this chapter." Abrams and Hogg tell us that when they wrote their first book, "often we sat side by side at the same computer," but they then go on to assert that this was "not the most efficient way to write!" Susan Fiske tells us that any tensions in her relationship with Shelley Taylor were overcome by their communal shared interests, which included "food, wine, art, and dancing." When Dick Nisbett and Lee Ross got together to work on collaborative projects, they sometimes stayed up late into the night, talking and debating political, literary, and existential matters. Some of the collaborations that you will read about in this volume, however, have been done by people who have conducted their research having never, or only rarely, met face-to-face.

Although so much work in psychology is collaborative, readers typically see only the final product. Because that product has gone through a demanding gatekeeping process that includes editing, more editing, copyediting, proof-reading, and the many other steps that occur before peer-reviewed research sees the light of day, the published version appears to be (and hopefully is) smooth and tightly woven together. Rarely, if ever, does one encounter self-reflection on the collaborative process.

Hence, in this volume, we examine the heretofore unasked question: "What did it take to get here?" Because these chapters expose underlying processes that are part of collaboration and help to identify emerging norms of collaboration, we have used the image "behind the scenes" in our subtitle. Our contributors have written chapters that generate insights about the process of collaboration. Their insights also cover the joys and frustrations of collaborative work. Perhaps most important, as we discuss in the concluding chapter, this material generates invaluable advice on the "best practices" when it comes to collaboration. Anyone who does collaborative research or is thinking about doing so would benefit enormously from the wisdom conveyed in these writings.

Landmarks in Collaboration

Collaboration in psychological science has a number of landmarks, and we have organized the 21 chapters in the next three sections of this collection around three of these landmarks: collaboration within psychological science, collaboration with other disciplines, and research collaboration with institutional and community partners. Part II, "Collaboration Within Psychological Science," includes 10 chapters, beginning with one by Elaine Hatfield and Ellen Berscheid, longtime collaborators on relationship science and romantic love. They met as colleagues in the summer of 1965, when they were both in marginal positions at the University of Minnesota; as they note, "in the University at large, and in the discipline of Psychology," they were not allowed to eat at the "hushed, elegant, airy, and well-upholstered" all-male Faculty Club. Their chapter, with its discussion of their 50-year collaboration and the lessons they have learned, leads to the varied experiences and conclusions drawn about the collaborative process within the discipline in the next nine chapters in this part of the book.

Part III, "Collaboration and Interdisciplinarity," includes five chapters, all of which explore the process of psychological scientists working with researchers from other disciplines. This section includes a chapter by John L. Sullivan and Eugene Borgida (a political scientist and a social psychologist, respectively); Richard Zweigenhaft (a psychologist), who describes his work with G. William Domhoff (a psychologist-turned-sociologist); and three more chapters by psychologists who routinely have crossed disciplinary lines in the work they have done over the course of their careers (Steve Gangestad, Jim Sherman, and Gary Wells).

Part IV, "Collaboration with Institutional and Community Partners," includes six broad-ranging chapters. These include a discussion and analysis of the collaborative work by psychologists with other social scientists in the national policy process (Steve Breckler); with various groups in the local community (Nancy Cantor and Peter Englot), and in the schools (Geoff Cohen and Julio Garcia); with those who work with community organizations on HIV/AIDS prevention (Mark Snyder and Allen Omoto); and those who work with businesses in the corporate community (Barbara Loken and Deborah John). Finally, James Jackson's chapter explores the use of team science to study health and well-being in racial and ethnic communities.

In their chapter titled "The Academic Marathon: Controlling One's Career," which appears in *The Compleat Academic: A Career Guide* (second edition), Shelley Taylor and Joanne Martin (2004) caution both younger and older academics (those who have entered the ranks of "professor and beyond") to choose carefully which projects and tasks to take on. If you decide to edit a book, they claim that "you may have to do a lot of intellectually undemanding and often unpleasant work (nagging, editing) to get it out." After discussing the pros and the cons, they conclude that "if you do edit a book, make sure it is a good one" (p. 372).

For the two of us, editing this book entailed very little intellectually undemanding or unpleasant work. We did, at times, have to nag—but, thankfully, not all that much. We did in fact edit all the chapters, but we found that task neither intellectually undemanding (quite the contrary, actually) nor unpleasant. And we are quite sure that the book is a good one. We hope that you enjoy it.

▓ REFERENCES ▓

Baskin, P. (2015, March 9). Team science: Research cooperation grows as federal money tightens. *Chronicle of Education*. Retrieved from http://chronicle.com/article/Team-science-Research/228175/

Beaver, D. D. (2001). Reflections on scientific collaboration (and its study): Past, present, and future. *Scientometrics, 52*(3), 365–377.

Beaver, D. D. (2004). Does collaborative research have greater epistemic authority? *Scientometrics, 602*(3), 399–408.

Bornman, L., & Daniel, H. D. (2008). What do citation counts measure? A review of studies on citing behavior. *Journal of Documentation, 64*, 45–80.

Boyack, K. W., Klavens, R., & Borner, K. (2005). Mapping the backbone of science. *Scientometrics, 64*(3), 351–374.

Cacioppo, J. T. (2007, October). The rise in collaborative psychological science, *APS Observer, 20*(9). Retrieved from http://www.psychologicalscience.org/index.php/publications/observer/2007/october-07/the-rise-in-collaborative-psychological-science.html

Cooke, N. J., & Hilton, M. L. (Eds). (2015). *Enhancing the effectiveness of team science.* Washington, DC: The National Academies Press.

Hall, K. L., Stokols, D., Stipelman, B. A., Vogel, A. L., Feng, A., Masimore, B., ... Berrigan, D. (2012). Assessing the value of team science. *American Journal of Preventative Medicine, 42*(2), 157–163.

Hegarty, P., & Zoe W. (2012). The consequences of predicting scientific impact in psychology using journal impact factors. *Perspectives on Psychological Science, 7*(1), 72–78.

King, C. (2013, September). Single-author papers: A waning share of output, but still providing the tools for progress. *ScienceWatch.* Retrieved from http://sciencewatch.com/articles/single-author-papers-waning-share-output-still-providing-tools-progress

Miller, C. (2013, April 11). Data science: The numbers of our lives. *The New York Times*, Education Life. Retrieved from http://www.nytimes.com/2013/04/14/education/edlife/universities-offer-courses-in-a-hot-new-field-data-science.html?_r=0

Mischel, W. (2009, January). Becoming a cumulative science. *APS Observer, 22*(1). Retrieved from http://www.psychologicalscience.org/index.php/publications/observer/2009/january-09/becoming-a-cumulative-science.html

Moser, R. P., & Coa, K. I. (2015). Grid-Enabled Measures (GEM): A crowdsourcing tool to support team science [blog entry]. Retrieved from https://www.teamscience toolkit.cancer.gov/public/ExpertBlog.aspx?tid=4

Muller, E. L. (2014). Developing the faculty as a writing community. *Academe, 100*(6), 34–38.

Quinones-Vidal, E., Lopez-Garcia, J., Penaranda-Ortega, P., & Tortosa-Gil, F. (2004). The nature of social and personality psychology as reflected in JPSP, 1965–2000. *Journal of Personality and Social Psychology, 86*(3), 435–452.

Robinson, C. F. (2014, March 24). Trouble recruiting top faculty? Promote collaboration. *Chronicle of Higher Education.* Retrieved from http://chronicle.com/article/Trouble-Recruiting-Top/145495/.jobs__topjobs-slider

Somaiya, R., & Cohen, N. (2014, April 11). Journalists who broke news on N.S.A. surveillance return to the U.S. *The New York Times*, p. B3.

Stokols, D., Hall, K. L., Taylor, B. K., & Moser, R. P. (2008). The science of team science: Overview of the field and introduction to the supplement. *American Journal of Preventative Medicine, 35*, S77–S89.

Taylor, S. E., & Martin, J. (2004). The academic marathon: Controlling one's career. In J. M. Darley, M. P. Zanna, & H. L. Roedigger III (Eds.), *The compleat academic: A career guide* (2nd ed., pp. 363–392). Washington, DC: American Psychological Association.

Voosen, P. (2013, November 11). Microbiology leaves the solo author behind. *Chronicle of Higher Education.* Retrieved from http://chronicle.com/article/A-Science-Leaves-the-Solo/142903/

Wuchty, S., Jones, B. F., & Uzzi, B. (2007). The increasing dominance of teams in production of knowledge. *Science, 316*(5827), 1036–1039.

PART II

Collaboration Within
Psychological Science

Chapter 1: In Research, as in Love, One Is the Loneliest Number

Elaine Hatfield

Professor of Psychology
University of Hawaii

Ellen Berscheid

Regents Professor of Psychology Emerita
University of Minnesota

Why Did We Collaborate? The Causal Conditions

When we began our collaboration, conditions for women in the academy were very different from those enjoyed today. For example, most psychology doctoral programs did not admit women at all. Each of us was fortunate to have successfully jumped that hurdle. Moreover, we were extremely fortunate to have jobs—such as they were—because most psychology departments would not hire a woman even if she had managed to earn a doctorate. Elaine got her job in the Student Activities Bureau primarily because her mentor, Leon Festinger, who thought her brilliant and was chagrined when she was passed over by all the psychology departments she applied to, called his old friend, the university's dean of students, who created a job for her. Ellen, who was preparing to retire, unexpectedly got a temporary appointment in the university's business school (at that time all male—both faculty and students) to teach their graduate students "how to do research." She got the position both because she knew how to do research and because a man with comparable skills would have been in high demand and would have scoffed at the business school's offer of a temporary job for little money.

Both of us were given courtesy "adjunct" appointments in the psychology department. Then, such appointments meant next to nothing. With our adjunct appointments, the chair told each of us to consider the psychology department our "spiritual home." Although meant in a kindly way, the subtext was clear: "Your spirits are welcome here, but park your minds and faces elsewhere." Elaine remembers that he also cautioned her that, being a woman, she would not be allowed to eat lunch in the posh Campus Club on the top floor of Coffman Union, overlooking the Minneapolis skyline and the Mississippi River. The club at that time was hushed, elegant, airy, and well upholstered; the tables were covered with pristine white linen, and there even was a separate section on the mezzanine that provided napping rooms for male faculty who, exhausted from their labors by midday, might need a little lie-down after lunch. "But not to worry," he continued, "faculty women (along with secretaries, students, groundskeepers, and other university supernumeraries) can eat in the Union's delightful Café." He professed that he actually wished that he could eat there because the food was better and it was more efficient—but, alas, he was condemned to eat with his fellow faculty in the Campus Club. The Café, Elaine shortly discovered and Ellen knew well, was a large, self-service cafeteria down in the bowels of the Union, where steam tables filled the room with damp and heat and the clattering of tin trays on the metal tables and the scraping of the metal chairs ricocheted off the hard surfaces of the tile ceilings, concrete walls, and linoleum floor, on which there was always a smattering of trash. Some time later, the Campus Club was opened to female professors, but only on the condition that we not shock male sensibilities by wearing pants. So on our rare skirt-wearing days, we'd eat lunch in the Campus Club—but *not* at the famous "psychology table" reserved in the main dining room for the all-male faculty of the psychology department; we received a soul-withering rejection—with the sting felt to this day—when we once attempted to join them.

This was the backdrop of the fateful summer afternoon when Elaine came into the lab as Ellen was cleaning out her desk in the graduate student "bullpen" (as Elliot Aronson referred to it) to move her books and papers to the business school. After chatting about the uncertain state of the lab, Ellen was about to leave when Elaine said, "You can take that office over there. I'm going to take this one." Shocked by Elaine's suggestion that they be squatters in the lab, Ellen feebly protested that they would be summarily thrown out should they be discovered. Elaine just waved her hand dismissively and said, "Oh, they won't notice." Apprehensive, but ever docile and easily led (at that time, at least), Ellen moved her books to her new lab office, not to the business school. Elaine turned out to be right—"they" didn't notice (although we now suspect that the chair of the psychology department was engaging in what government policy analysts call "benign neglect" of messy problems better left alone).

When we are asked to reveal how our collaboration came about (and this has not been an infrequent query over the years), Ellen says, "We found ourselves cowering together in the same foxhole." Elaine agrees that there is truth to that. Both of us were in marginal positions in our places of employment, in the university at large, and in the discipline of psychology. We were outside looking in at what others who were similar to ourselves (other than that they possessed a Y chromosome and we didn't) were enjoying. But now there were *two* of us who had our noses pressed against those windows, and that made all the difference.

In his classic memoir of his life in the theater, Moss Hart, the celebrated playwright who famously collaborated for many years with George S. Kaufman (on such noteworthy plays as *The Man Who Came to Dinner*), observed that "collaboration is an infinitely more pleasurable way of working than working alone. Most human beings fear loneliness, and writing is the loneliest of professions" (1959, p. 305). (Those engaged in dissertation research, required to be a wholly individual product, would not agree that writing takes first prize in the loneliness contest; they'd claim that designing, conducting, analyzing, and writing research all by oneself is the hands-down winner.) Hart goes on to say, "Collaboration cuts this loneliness in half. When one is at a low point of discouragement, the very presence in the room of another human being, even though he too may be sunk in the same state of gloom, very often gives that dash of valor to the spirit that allows confidence to return and work to resume" (1959, p. 306).

And so it was with us. Each of us could understand what the other was experiencing, could empathize and sympathize and reassure each other, as we frequently did—"You're not crazy; *they* are!"—and quickly get on with our lives and our work. Or, as Solomon Asch famously demonstrated, two outcasts are enormously better than one in resisting the majority opinion and the negative sanctions that go along with dissent. Strong and enduring bonds are often forged in such daily struggles, some of which rise to the level of combat.

In addition to our positions in the academy, there were other similarities that augured well for our research collaboration prospects, had we ever consciously thought about it—which we didn't. (Others did, however, as we shall shortly discuss.) In retrospect, perhaps the most important of these similarities was that we both came out of the same strong Lewinian research tradition— Leon Festinger having been Kurt Lewin's student and Aronson having been Festinger's student. As a consequence, there was much that was unspoken but understood and little that generated argument (or even discussion and clarification) when it came to the mechanics of research.

Also important, we realize in retrospect, our pariah positions allowed us to escape the suffocating influence of the colleagues we didn't have, especially their conventional prejudices about what was important and suitable for psychological research (e.g., "behaviorism" was in its heyday). We were free to pursue our own intellectual interests, and these most definitely were not in the mainstream of the elite departments of psychology at the time (e.g., romantic and passionate love, sex, the importance of physical appearance, equity in close relationships, and so forth). We also avoided their imperialistic attempts to proselytize us into working on their oh-so-important projects, as sometimes happens to junior faculty even today. (At that time, women psychology students who married their professors hoping for a career in psychology often found themselves working in the shadows for the great men, receiving at best a footnote—and usually not even that—for what was actually a collaborative product.) Looking back, we now understand that along with our marginalization came intellectual freedom and the opportunity to exercise it, which are rare commodities in the academy at any time.

In addition to our similarity of low status in the cosmos and our similarity of research training, we were a mutual admiration society; each thought the other was extraordinarily intelligent, kind, courageous, and exceedingly funny. Elaine describes Ellen's humor as "mordant and iconoclastic," and Ellen describes Elaine's as "wicked in the extreme." In other words, we appreciated each other's wit (whereas many others, then and later, didn't). Our collaboration was filled with laughter at the absurdities and idiocies strewn along our professional path. For example, when the chair of the psychology department heard a rumor at lunch (in the aforementioned Campus Club—no doubt at the "psychology table") that we were asking our male subjects in Ford Hall to go down the hall to the men's room and piddle in a cup, he rushed back to his office, picked up the telephone, and, in a chewing-the-rug apoplectic rage, ordered us to cease *immediately*! End of conversation. No explanation permitted (in this case, we were running an aggression experiment that required cortisol assay). The fact that our tears of frustration could so often be turned into sidesplitting hilarity was perhaps our most precious gift to each other.

Our collaboration developed so quickly and naturally that, as previously mentioned, we never thought about it, and we certainly never spent time questioning our choice of collaborator. But others did. One eminent social psychologist and founder of an important scholarly society (which, again, was initially males only) asked an acquaintance of ours if we were lesbians! He added that because we seemed to enjoy each other's company so much, there was "bound to be gossip." The fact that each of us was happily married to a man apparently was not pertinent to his analysis of our sexual orientation. (Elaine notes that misogynistic men often view women who enjoy another woman's company as "one of the 10 'tells' of an LGBT lifestyle.") Another example of a gratuitous, if unintended, comment on our collaboration came when Ellen, visiting Elaine at the University of Wisconsin, where she later worked, just a short train ride away, encountered an eminent psychologist in the hall who briskly brushed by her, saying, "You here again?!" More easily intimidated then than now, she chose to make that her last visit. Yet another important psychologist warned Ellen that because Elaine was academically more experienced than she was, all her good ideas would be attributed to Elaine. And so it went. Because our collaboration was happy, productive, and time-consuming, this meant that we were not available to collaborate with others, who, by this time, might have thought it would be profitable for them if we did. Even now, one does not know how to otherwise interpret the hostility that the fact of our continued collaboration sometimes encountered.

The Process of Collaboration

"I have always been more than a little puzzled by the fascination that the mechanics of collaboration hold for most people," Hart (1959, p. 304) claims. He is right; people *are* interested, especially other professionals. According to Ellen, the linchpin of the mechanics of this collaboration is easily identified: It was Elaine. She explains that Elaine was the spark plug, the Energizer bunny that just kept going and going and going. Moreover, Elaine always knew her worth—she knew what she deserved, and what she deserved was a position in what she called a "real" psychology department. Not only was she determined to achieve that aim, but she was also confident that she would. Ellen, on the other hand, had no such aspirations. She was resigned to retirement. "No psychology department is going to hire a woman" was her reply when Aronson asked about her plans before he left to teach at the University of Texas. Aronson knew that her "no jobs for women" assertion was not amenable to debate, so he nimbly changed the question to "Well, what would you *like* to do?" After pausing to think of something halfway realistic, she said, "Well, I'd like to be John Darley's research assistant" (they had collaborated during their graduate years, he had just gotten a good job in a "real" psychology department, and she knew that he was clever enough to find a way to hire her). Aronson was aghast. After a moment of grim silence, he said, "*Well!* I think you might aspire to something higher than *that*!" Oh really? He forgot Lewin's aspiration theory, which predicts that no goal will be attempted, no matter how desirable, if the perceived probability of reaching it is zero.

Dissimilarities Between Collaborators, or Can the Hare and the Tortoise Collaborate Harmoniously?

When Ellen appeared in her lab office, Elaine would ask, day after day after day, "Have you written up your dissertation for publication yet?" Ellen had no intention of wasting her time writing up what she considered to be a dreadfully boring experiment in which no one with half a grain of intelligence could be interested. But Elaine was (and still is) a world-class nagger; finally, just to stop the hare from tap-dancing on her tortoiseshell back every day, Ellen did write it up. To her amazement (but it came as no surprise to Elaine), it was immediately accepted—without revision—for publication in social psychology's premier journal.

It is, of course, one of the functions of collaborators to keep reminding each other of obligations and impending deadlines. In our collaboration, the role of nagger (and worrier) gradually became balanced, primarily because Elaine, in her boundless enthusiasm, inexhaustible energy, and voracious curiosity about human behavior, always had a terrifyingly long to-do list. That list not only detailed current commitments but also new projects that we were to undertake ASAP. The length of the list made Ellen nervous. She was horrified, for example, when she heard Elaine promise that they would speak at an upcoming conference about the results of a study that had not yet been fully designed, much less conducted. When she voiced her concerns, Elaine calmly reassured her "not to worry"; they would be able to get it done in time, "easy-peasy." It did get done, but it definitely was not easy-peasy.

Elaine also would become impatient with Ellen's slowness to write up a study for publication. When she asked each day about how the latest work was coming along, Ellen's response often was the same as that of early television's tightwad Jack Benny. When a mugger confronted him, demanding "Your money or your life!" Benny stalled, saying, "I'm thinking, I'm thinking." Finally, Elaine would cheerily present Ellen with a piece of paper and say, "Well, what do you think of these first few paragraphs I've written?" Ellen would take one look, think, "Oh good grief, this won't do," and off she'd go, writer's block magically removed. After this happened repeatedly, Elaine (no fool she) could write the equivalent of nonsense syllables at the top of a page to get Ellen going.

Eventually, of course, Ellen learned to write without such priming from her muse, but, touchingly, Hal Kelley, with whom she was collaborating on one of his last papers, did not know this. Having agreed to write the first draft, Ellen was surprised to receive from Kelley a couple of opening paragraphs; she was puzzled until she read the accompanying note, explaining that he had heard somewhere that Elaine always provided her with a little something to get her started. (Her reaction to Kelley's effort was the same as those to Elaine's years earlier—"Good grief! This won't do"—and it had the same galvanizing effect.)

Moss Hart claims, "It [collaboration] requires no special gift except the necessary patience to accommodate one's own working method harmoniously to that of one's collaborator" (Hart, 1959, p. 305). He is right again. It is patience—supported by respect for the talents, opinions, eccentricities, and quirks (including differences in metabolism)—that allows even a hare and a tortoise to work together harmoniously and productively.

Not All Collaborations Are Felicitous

We were fortunate that our collaboration with each other early in our careers was pleasant and productive. Not all collaborations are, which each of us later discovered. We learned that although in a good collaboration, 1 + 1 can equal 4 or more; in a bad collaboration, 1 + 1 usually equals −2 or even less. We have probably collaborated with at least 50 other scholars in our professional lifetimes. Most of these have been enjoyable, and the quality of the products was many orders of magnitude higher than if we had undertaken the projects alone. But we have learned to examine carefully the teeth of a gift horse volunteering to collaborate with us and to recognize the omens of disaster. Next, we itemize just a handful of signs that flash "RUN!"

Surprise! You Didn't Know You Were Collaborating, but There You Are

We once crafted a paper in which the various sections were introduced with an apt quote. We'll call the editor of our paper "Professor Cuckoo Bird" because lazy cuckoos lay their eggs in another bird's nest, and when their offspring hatch, they eat the food meant for the real mother's hatchlings. Professor Cuckoo redlined all our quotes, indicating in the margin that, since "by chance" he happened to be writing a chapter on the very same topic and "amazingly" had chosen to employ our format (as well as the exact same quotes) in *his* paper, we must delete ours. We didn't.

Few editors are thieves, but many view themselves as collaborators. Not a few, usually those editing a book to which they themselves are contributing, expect you to have written the paper that they would have written if they only had the time. But they didn't, so they proceed to change (or maybe *mutilate* is a more accurate word) your paper to better conform to their vision or their position on a controversial issue. One of us submitted an invited chapter to a book, and many, many months later, received back an unrecognizable, garbled, reorganized (e.g., whole paragraphs moved and scattered here and there, and some missing altogether) Frankensteinian creation that substantially changed our position on an important issue to one more compatible with the editor's own stance (and undoubtedly expressed in the editor's own forthcoming chapter). We had to threaten to withdraw the paper before this editor finally relinquished the chop-and-paste job (which the editor professed to have "worked so hard on") and reluctantly accepted the original.

Some editors, however, are wonderful, unsung collaborators on the order of the legendary Maxwell Perkins, the editor who succored the likes of Fitzgerald, Hemingway, and Thomas Wolfe at Scribner's publishers (Berg, 1978). Such editors play the role of superb but anonymous collaborators. Beyond their formal editing, they buck up depressed spirits, cajole and threaten, encourage and praise, suggest and arrange, and, in the end, transform a lump of coal into a sparkling gem, all the while recognizing, as Perkins did, that the "book belongs to the author." But talented editors are few and far between; incompetent (but not necessarily malicious) editors are overrepresented in our bad collaborator category.

Beyond incompetence, there is another, fortunately infrequent, problem with editors. One of us once collaborated with another scholar on a chapter on people's motives for engaging in sex. To our amazement, not long afterward the editor came out with a paper that quoted vast chunks of our paper without attribution; he had lifted not just a phrase or two, but major ideas and paragraphs. This posed a dilemma, but finally, we decided to overlook the theft. Why? We realized that it was entirely possible that this editor truly just forgot where he got the material; when you edit a paper and read it again and again, the contents tend to get engraved on your brain.

We sometimes worry that we will have the same Doris Kearns Goodwin moment this editor had. (Goodwin, an eminent historian, was accused of plagiarizing portions of works that she had unknowingly committed to memory.) But so far, Elaine has only been guilty (to her knowledge) of stealing Ellen's felicitous phrases, of which "[t]he bluebird of happiness is an elusive fowl" is a favorite. But plagiarism by others—whole paragraphs, if not entire pages, of our books, chapters, or articles—is another matter, especially because one usually doesn't know of the theft until it appears in print. Only a particularly savvy editor or reviewer, who knows the content area well, can recognize the true source of plagiarized material. One such editor recognized that an ambitious and (formerly) rising young social psychologist had purloined a significant portion of one of our previous writings, and informed us about it. His paper was rejected, of course, and the excoriating chastisement in the editor's letter and the spreading knowledge of his dishonesty irrevocably damaged his reputation.

How Can You Believe Me When I Say I Love You When You Know I've Been a Liar All My Life?

When a potential collaborator says, "Why don't you write the first half of the article? I'm just swamped right now, but next year…," don't do it. It doesn't matter whether they are (a) going to Europe, (b) planning a new class, (c) training a puppy, (d) recovering from the bubonic plague, or (e) almost anything else because you will discover that the personality theorists are right—there is consistency in personality. If they are busy in Year 1, they will be even busier in Year 2, but by then, you will have invested so much work in the article that you will have no choice but to write the rest.

We once spent a year working with a delightful colleague who entertained us with creative excuses as to why he couldn't actually do any work. "Not right now," he'd say, "but I'll get to it later." After a year, and just before we picked him up at the airport, we resolved to each other: "He's not going to charm us this time. Not this time. He is going to sit down and do some work. No excuses." Alas, when he got off the plane, he announced, "So sorry. I have to run. I'm on my way to get married." We finished the article ourselves.

In 1968, one of us collaborated with others on a study designed to test divergent hypotheses of anthropologists, sociologists, and psychologists concerning the antecedents and consequences of incest. Scanning the data, we saw that we had some interesting results, but the analyses, given 25 hypotheses, turned out to be extraordinarily complex, especially before the magic of computers. A sociologist friend listened sympathetically to our plight and then graciously offered to collaborate. He'd be happy, he said, to analyze the data using some new data-crunching techniques that would "knock the socks off sociologists." We delivered the stacks of data to him and waited…and waited…and waited. As we said, that was in 1968. Every few years since then, we would write him a piteous letter. Please, please return our data. We are happy to continue to collaborate, we said, and, in fact, he could be first author if he just would return the data. "No, no," he would reply, "I'm eager to conduct the analyses—it'll be fun and I have a sabbatical coming." We kept waiting. Finally, 2 years ago, he died. We asked his widow if there were any boxes stored in their basement. We are still waiting.

The "He Speaks Like John Gielgud but Writes Like Snooki" Problem

Some engaging and seemingly intelligent people speak beautifully but write badly. We have spent untold hours reviewing papers from colleagues and students who simply can't write. Elaine believes that they "just somehow fall apart" once they pick up a pen. Ellen thinks she knows why. She believes that a silver tongue sometimes masks a muddy mind. She believes that people who can't write clearly can't think clearly, so it is unlikely they are speaking clearly either. This is why some of us would rather read another's ideas than hear them orally, where a charming and attractive manner can mask a mediocre mind. The opposite is also often true; a shy and painfully hesitant oral presentation may mask a brilliant mind that is revealed only on paper. For most of us, the most reliable signal that we aren't thinking clearly comes when we have difficulty setting our ideas down on a piece of paper. Of course, we must have the capacity to notice that what we have written is nonsensical gibberish. Not all people do.

One of us spent a year trying to divine what a collaborator was trying to say with a text that we were writing, even drawing her spouse into the process to decipher. Every time the spouse was handed a new chapter to "translate," he would moan and bang his head on the table at the opacity of the prose (sad, but all marriages require sacrifice). Unfortunately, the collaborator thought that he was a master of clarity, so it was embarrassing to raise difficulties with him, especially because his wife would drop by and say that her husband was working day and night on the book and it was taking a toll on their marriage. She obviously was vaguely resentful that we—the other collaborators—had it so easy. When the albatross of a book was finally published and we held it in our hands, the clueless collaborator exclaimed, "Wow! This turned out great. Let's do a sequel! Next time, you can be first authors." That offer has become a source of merriment for all involved in the production of the book. After some particularly horrendous experience, one of us has only to say, "Why not do it again? This time, you can be first author," to induce fits of giggling.

Conclusions

In 2012, we were named recipients of the William James Award from the Association for Psychological Science (APS) for our "distinguished achievements in psychological science"—its highest award. Informed separately, we later discovered that each of us had the same reaction: Our minds immediately flew back to all those years ago when we first collaborated in the lab and continued to collaborate actively several years afterward. Details of those early years—both good and bad—are easily remembered by each of us even now, especially the names of so many in the discipline who gave us support when we desperately needed it. Heading the list are Leon and Elliot, who gave us our chance and continued to support us, but an entire paper could be written about so many others who stretched out their hands to save us when we were about to sink.

At the APS symposium honoring our work (Finkel, 2012; Reis, Aron, Clark, & Finkel, 2013), we were stunned to hear that things we did as a matter of course or necessity were being described as "important" or "seminal." At the time, we could not have imagined that anyone would ever think what we were doing was worthy of notice, let alone honor. We were just having a good time doing research on questions we were interested in, a privilege that too few scholars have today. Universities now expect their faculty to bring in revenue in the form of grants or other moneymaking activities. Like Willie Sutton, who, when asked why he robbed banks, answered, "Because that's where the money is," young researchers (and old researchers, too) when asked why they are working in a particular area could (if they were honest) answer, "Because that's where the federal government money is."

We were blessed. We didn't know it then, but we know it now. Would that all collaborations were as happy and productive as ours and that all researchers could be as free from constraints as we were then. In succeeding years, we both continued, individually and often with others, to follow the lines of research we had begun earlier, with Elaine focusing more on the multicultural and sexual side of love and attraction and Ellen looking more at the close relationship side. This leads us to what we view as the "takeaway lesson" of the story of our collaboration: A young scholar's initial collaborations are of great importance, for they erect a platform for later work. A misguided decision to collaborate with the wrong person or persons in the fragile early career stage can be truly disastrous for young scholars because they often cannot afford to lose the time and energy that they devoted to the failed enterprise and, discouraged, may not regain sufficient enthusiasm to start again. Collaboration, in other words, is a serious business at all stages of one's professional career, but even more so at the beginning. The right collaboration, however, can make the process of discovery and report joyous—as ours did.[1]

▦ REFERENCES ▦

Berg, A. S. (1978). *Max Perkins: Editor of genius*. New York, NY: Dutton.

Finkel, E. J. (2012, May 25). *Legends and legacies: The continuing influences of Berscheid and Hatfield in the science of interpersonal attraction*. Paper presented at the annual meeting of the Association for Psychological Science, Chicago, IL.

Hart, M. (1959). *Act one*. New York, NY: Random House.

Reis, H. T., Aron, A., Clark, M. S., & Finkel, E. J. (2013). Ellen Berscheid, Elaine Hatfield, and the emergence of relationship science. *Perspectives on Psychological Science*, *8*, 558–572. Retrieved from http://pps.sagepub.com/content/8/5/558.abstract doi:10.1177/1745691613497966

---

[1] After all these years, the same collaboration process asserted itself with this chapter, despite Ellen's hope that it would be a more leisurely process than in the past because it was not due for a while. However, Ellen happened to find the Hart quotes on collaboration and sent them to Elaine so they would not be forgotten. Her accompanying note emphasized that that they need not even *begin* to think about this chapter for 4 or 5 months—at the earliest! However, the very next week, Elaine sent back the title to the chapter and a full first draft! A month or so later, the editors needed an abstract, so Elaine sent Ellen a rough draft, suggesting that it needed revision. It did. Ellen sent a revised abstract to the editors and extracted a promise from them that before proceeding further, they should wait for a revision of the first draft of the chapter (which Elaine already had sent them when they wanted to know the gist of what their authors were doing). Ellen then revised Elaine's first draft to conform to the format instructions received in the interim, massaged some of the prose, added a few things and subtracted some others, and then sent the manuscript back to Elaine. Elaine immediately made a few minor changes and pronounced the script "finished." Ellen incorporated the changes and made some more, wrote this footnote, and sent it back to Elaine for "storage" until the chapter was due. Today is July 31. This manuscript is due December 31. Once again, the hare had her way! And, as usual, the tortoise is very glad she did.

Chapter 2: Building Bridges: A Story of Collaboration Across Three Continents

Dominic Abrams

Professor of Social Psychology
Director, Centre for the Study of Group Processes
University of Kent

Michael A. Hogg

Professor Social Psychology
Chair, Social Psychology Program
Claremont Graduate University

Our collaborative partnership can be described in three phases—meeting, developing, and generating. Above all else, it has always been enormous fun—conspiratorial boozy meetings late into the night in gloomy dives around the world, and more exotic plotting venues in Australian coastal towns and under the California sun. And, as the saying goes, we have always "had each other's back."

Our first meeting was inauspicious. Picture a disoriented doctoral student being introduced to a globetrotting quasi-hippie, with instructions that within a few days, it would be their collective responsibility to carry forward the reputation of a world-renowned center of social psychology.

How We Got Together: Bristol

Let us back up a little. The scene is 1983, 8-10 Berkeley Square, Bristol, England. A large beech-paneled office two floors up overlooked a pretty Georgian square at the foot of the Clifton district of Bristol. This was where Henri Tajfel, and his students, John Turner, the orchestrator of self-categorization theory, and Howie Giles, the promulgator of ethnolinguistic vitality theory, had forged what became the social identity approach to intergroup relations and group processes. Margaret Thatcher was in power, inflation was high, U.K. academia was in the throes of major cutbacks, grant funds had withered, there were no academic jobs, and those few who did have academic positions faced bleak prospects. Tajfel had died in the summer of 1982, Turner had left the United Kingdom to take up a chair at Macquarie University in Australia, and Giles had been on sabbatical at the University of California, Santa Barbara (UCSB) and was poised to accept an offer of a full professorship there. In short, social psychology at Bristol, which was often referred to as the *Bristol school of social psychology*, was on the brink of extinction.

In the summer of 1983, Howie's last efforts, literally while simultaneously packing up his office and booking international flights, were to ensure that the courses in social psychology, communication, and intergroup relations, as well as the department's commitments to its graduate and undergraduate dissertations in these areas, could be covered, at least for the coming year.

Mike Hogg was already at Bristol. He had arrived in October 1978 by way of his undergraduate years at Birmingham University, where he worked with Michael Billig (one of Tajfel's recent PhDs) and Ray Cochrane. After that, he spent a year traveling around the Americas. He was one of John Turner's doctoral students and had been appointed in 1981 as a lecturer (assistant professor) to teach some of the classes usually taught by Tajfel, Turner, and Giles. In 1983, he and the Bristol social psychology program needed help, as everyone had left or was leaving. In particular, some of Howie's classes had to be covered.

So Howie phoned Rupert Brown (another of Tajfel's former PhDs), at the University of Kent, to inquire whether he had any graduate students that might be up to the task. As it happened, Dominic was one of these "Rupert's students," with only a few months of his 3-year PhD program left, and was looking for work. Howie invited him to come to Bristol for an interview. This turned out to be quite a hectic meeting on a hot day in an office filled with packing cases, and it involved a brief introduction to a couple of graduate students, the department secretary, and John Brown, the department head.

So, on October 1, 1983, Hogg (his contract renewed for another 9 months) and Abrams (with a 9-month teaching contract) had inherited what remained of the social psychology program—a couple of graduate students, the 3-year undergraduate program in social psychology, communication and developmental psychology, a quarter of the department's undergraduate theses to supervise, and a social psychology colloquium series to run. Hogg was installed in Giles's office, which also had a small annex that was occupied by John F. Edwards, a sabbatical visitor from Francis Xavier University in Nova Scotia. Abrams was installed in a small room up a maze of rickety stairs—the rickety stairs are important, as you will soon discover.

The two temporary faculty had more in common than they might have suspected. It turned out that both had a widowed mother living in Bristol, within a mile of one another. Both were proud owners of slightly funky and very "retro" old cars with sunroofs—Hogg a horrible brown Citroen 2CV (think the classic film *The Pink Panther*) with bits of bodywork stuck together by duct tape and Abrams an anemic blue Morris Minor (think *Herbie the Love Bug*). Both were partial to the occasional pint of Courage Director's bitter. Both were broke; both had little idea what was in store for them. That year set the scene for what was to become a lifetime of collaboration.

Our MO: Morning and Afternoon People

A typical week would run like this. Mike would arrive at the office fairly early on Monday morning, typically around 9:30 a.m. (why that was "early" will become apparent) and full of energy and enthusiasm. Dom would join him, and they would meet to plan the week, particularly to make plans for the visiting colloquium speaker and to meet with the graduate students and the final-year undergrads to discuss their research projects. Mike would spend most of the morning consuming five or six cups of strong coffee while pacing around the large meeting table in his office and vigorously deliberating over how to extract the most fun out of these prospects. Dom, who was finishing writing his PhD (by hand), would spend the morning patiently listening to Mike, hammering out the logistics and practicalities while also contemplating such great questions as how to repair his car, what time lunch would be, and what his next lecture would be about.

These morning sessions were frequently graciously attended by the laconic, pipe-smoking John Edwards, who would generally find them greatly amusing. John spent most of his time typing his latest book on a manual typewriter in his annex but would occasionally interject in the sessions by offering small (often vital) insights and extremely witty observations. Judging by the amount of time we devoted to "wittering," he reckoned that it would be Christmas before either of us could make a decision about anything.

Most days, the afternoon signaled a marked change of gear as Mike's energy and enthusiasm waned and Dom's ramped up. Mike would retreat to his tiny flat in Clifton to work. Meanwhile, Dom would typically be in the library writing lectures, and they would reconvene, finally in synch, sometime after supper to their evening office—most often the local pub. The local pub was actually a gloomy bar in the basement of a nearby building, but it had two great advantages. First, very few other people went there, and second, it stayed open much later than it was legally entitled to. This, then, was the venue for plot hatching, document drafting , and sharing of both joy and misery. It was also where Dom would often prepare his lecture for the next day. Most of the time, such work was aided by the consumption of two or three (or sometimes as many as six or seven) pints of Courage Director's. At least two or three evenings a week, we were accompanied by our friends and students.

Our Bristol in the Early 1980s

It is hard to convey the buzz and excitement of this period. In the United Kingdom, final-year psychology students have to complete an empirical thesis. Each faculty would supervise one or two students each year. The whereabouts of the rest of the department was a mystery, but between us, we had fourteen students to supervise, as well as two or three graduate students. These students, along with John Edwards and one or two others, would join us each week to receive a distinguished, and often senior or international, academic who had been invited to present to the social program. Colloquia were held in Tajfel's office. During Tajfel's time, the speaker would deliver his or her presentation while he sat behind his desk at the far end of the room, opening mail, receiving international phone calls, and so forth. Tajfel's students and colleagues would be expected to fire devastating questions (along the lines of "Why are you purveying this reductionist nonsense?" or "What does it all mean anyway?"), leaving each visitor either in a state of shocked realization that his or her research was pointless or as a convert to the truth (i.e., social identity theory).

This combative approach reflected the raging metatheoretical debates of the 1980s. European social psychology was involved in a direct confrontation with North American social psychology, the battle being over how society itself should be incorporated into theory and research. We have discussed this debate in some detail in Abrams and Hogg (2004), but the essence of it was whether phenomena such as stereotyping, prejudice, discrimination, social influence, social protest, crowd behavior, and social communication could be explained solely by treating people as independent individuals or, rather, if they required a higher level of explanation—one that addressed the question of how these phenomena become coordinated and systematized across sets of individuals.

Really, the issue was what process makes people become *psychologically* interdependent, even when they are not materially interdependent and may have no direct relationship with one another. The driving metatheory, then, was what we called the *social identity approach* or *social identity perspective* (Abrams & Hogg, 1990a; Hogg & Abrams, 1988). The approach embodied both the social identity theory of intergroup relations (Tajfel & Turner, 1979) and the theory of group processes, later enshrined in self-categorization theory (Turner, Hogg, Oakes, Reicher, & Wetherell, 1987). The social identity guns were aimed directly at any ("traditional" or "North American") theory or theorist seeking to explain group phenomena in terms of socially decontextualized individual psychology—for example, in terms of individual differences in prejudice, social cognitive biases, interpersonal exchange, or motives for personal gain (namely, almost all mainstream social psychology).

Although this approach was sustainable in Tajfel's time, we, as rather lowly officers suddenly placed in the front line of this battle, were conscious of two things. First, having traveled a little, we realized that elsewhere, public trial and the threat of intellectual execution was not the normal way to receive academics, or indeed to win friends and influence people. We also realized that distinguished visitors might regard such treatment as insulting (or perhaps worse, laughable) if administered by two down-at-their-heels recent PhDs who drove a dilapidated 2CV and a Morris Minor. Second, it struck us that some of our visitors might actually have very interesting things to say, which we might learn from. We therefore adopted a different approach (namely, to learn and have fun). At the very least, this meant entertaining our visitors to an evening out—a visit to our local pub, followed by enjoying a spicy vindaloo on nearby Park Street and then returning to the pub, usually accompanied by at least half of our students. At best, it meant establishing new relationships and potential collaborations that would provide a basis for exciting new opportunities.

Our (First) Book

One is never more on top of a body of literature than when one is at the point of completing a PhD. Both of us were in that situation, having benefited from being taught by John Turner, Michael Billig, Hilde Himmelweit, Rupert Brown, and Geoffrey Stephenson. We also both had to prepare extensive lecture series covering a wide range of topics in social psychology. At some point in the year, encouraged by Dom's mother, Sonia Jackson, and by John Edwards, we reflected on how all this effort could fruitfully be directed to some larger product or outcome. Our students complained that trying to understand social identity theory was like unraveling spaghetti. At that time, there were several edited collections (e.g., Tajfel, 1978; Turner & Giles, 1991) that contained summaries of different elements of the approach, but these made for dense reading, and the theory as a whole was hard to assimilate. Moreover, within Europe, there were undercurrents of dissent about what social psychology should really look like. On the one hand, Moscovici's work on minority influence and on social representations (e.g., Moscovici, 1981) strongly framed the "European" perspective, while, on the other hand, new approaches such as discourse analysis seemed to be challenging all positivist approaches to social psychological issues. With the exception of Tajfel's (1970) article in *Scientific American*, there was almost no exposure to social identity theory in North American journals, and just a few scholars from the United States were interested (Marilynn Brewer had spent a sabbatical in Bristol in the late 1970s, shortly after Mike got there—but that is a story for another time).

Driven more by passion than logic, we decided it would be a magnificent (if *awesome* had been used then as it is now, that would be the appropriate word) idea to distill our understanding and knowledge of social identity theory into a book. This would help us both organize our own thinking, and lay out what this field had to offer social psychology. Our aim was to set out the metatheory of the social identity approach, showing how the theory as a whole could be used to organize and conceptualize a raft of phenomena that were central to social psychology. Neither of us had ever dealt with publishers before, and we racked our brains to think whom to approach about this project. One of the things that we had both enjoyed as children, and secretly still enjoyed, was reading Tintin books. They were published by Methuen. So, on the somewhat shaky premise of what was good enough for Tintin, Snowy, and Captain Haddock would be good for us and for science, we contacted Mary Ann Kernan, a senior editor with Methuen, to discuss the project. She came to visit us in Bristol, and to our shock and delight, she was cautiously enthusiastic and, after offering some helpful guidance (deadlines, length, audience), she offered us a contract for what was to become *Social Identifications* (Hogg & Abrams, 1988).

Other Projects

The remainder of our year together in Bristol passed quickly and eventfully. Remember those rickety stairs mentioned earlier? Well, at one point, Dominic fell, very loudly and with a mastery of an Anglo Saxon that even

Chaucer would be impressed by, down the stairs outside Mike's office. Peter Powesland (Giles's former advisor) kindly, and we believe very sensibly, offered Dominic a glass of his finest sherry following the tumble. But despite Dominic requiring a plaster cast and crutches for six weeks, the department gave him no relief from teaching duties, and he could be seen navigating the five flights of stairs to his office most days of the week and being driven around in Mike's old, beat-up 2CV.

Meanwhile, research and ideas flowed at a hectic pace. With our students, we designed and conducted a suite of studies that ultimately were translated into published articles on topics ranging from stereotypes of homosexuality (Abrams, Carter, & Hogg, 1989) to language switching in Switzerland (Hogg, Joyce, & Abrams, 1984) to the effects of numerical distinctiveness on gender identity (Abrams, Thomas, & Hogg, 1990). We also published early papers from our doctoral research on group cohesion/social attraction (Hogg & Turner, 1985) and self-regulation as a group member (Abrams, 1985), and worked on one of our most heavily cited collaborative articles, on the role of self-esteem and self-enhancement in social identity theory (Abrams & Hogg, 1988).

More important than individual writing projects was the process of getting to know one another's way of thinking. We found that we enjoyed hammering out ideas together—all the more so if we started with different perspectives or opinions. Mike would sometimes assert some point, Dom would assert the opposite, and the game was on, with the ultimate goal of finding a meeting point. Such discussions might well start toward the end of a morning and would not conclude until very late into the night at some pub or other. It was always fun, and criticism and disagreement were never taken personally or seen as anything other than a collaborative process of scientific inquiry and development.

A second aspect of learning to collaborate was that we discovered we could appreciate (and criticize) one another's writing. We found each other's ideas and observations sometimes puzzling and mysterious but always interesting. Often, we would work through examples or metaphors together to work out what would be the most vivid and accessible way to convey a point. We shared the belief that accessibility was important and that complex ideas did not have to be communicated complexly. On page 179 of *Social Identifications* (Hogg & Abrams, 1988), you will find our example of the way context frames group prototypes, illustrated by the meat-eater/vegetarian/vegan categories. It is perhaps ironic that by adopting a new approach to social identity theory, we were busy placing ourselves in the theoretical equivalent of the vegetarian situation—vulnerable to rejection from two different metatheoretical perspectives on opposing extremes. Another aim was to provide a coherent and systematic account of the theory itself, such as the table on page 55 of this same book, which set out predictions that followed from the theory's account of the effects of group status and the legitimacy of the strategies that group members would adopt to sustain their social and personal identity. We are very proud of this table—it took forever to design (and probably shortened each of our lives by a full decade).

Split Asunder: Scotland, England, Australia, and California

By the early summer of 1984, the university had agreed to replace Giles's position with a (tenured) position in social psychology, and we knew that at least one of us would need to seek a position elsewhere. In fact, given that Miles Hewstone was in the running for the position, we were pretty certain that both of us would need to move on. With a certain degree of irony, we both applied for the position and submitted each other's application. It was no surprise, however, when Miles was offered the post. Dominic's contract was extended until the end of the year, and by that time, he had secured a position at the University of Dundee; meanwhile, Mike accepted a postdoc with John Turner at Macquarie University in Sydney.

Finishing Our Book: Melbourne

So, at the start of 1985, Dominic headed north to Scotland and Mike headed south to Australia. Even though we were now on opposite sides of the planet, we continued to collaborate. E-mail was in its infancy (accessed via computer terminals that displayed in either orange or green type on 12-inch screens), and the 11-hour time difference did not help, but we each took responsibility for the first drafts of different chapters of our book, and then we used Dominic's sabbatical leave in Melbourne (Mike had moved to a lectureship at the University of Melbourne in early 1986) as the opportunity to stitch it all together and finalize the text. This involved close readings and collaborative redrafting of each chapter, as well as forging the overview that framed the entire book.

Often, we sat side by side at the same computer—not the most efficient way to write! In the morning, Mike would range around the department to drag Dominic back from entertaining the office staff; lunch was spent gorging on ice cream (Dom) and downing espresso (Mike) on Melbourne's Lygon Street; afternoons involved Dom tracking Mike down from socializing to get him back to the office; and evenings were spent, once again in synch, in bars avoiding the book and planning new research commitments instead. So, the "Bristol" pattern of working had reemerged quickly, and we were able to complete the book on time. It felt like a huge step.

The book, deliberately not called "social identity theory," but rather *Social Identifications: A Social Psychology of Intergroup Relations and Group Processes*, took 3 years to write, but it achieved the integrated account that we believed was necessary to make the social identity metatheory and the specifics of social identity theory accessible to readers around the world. First published in 1988, the book has remained in print continuously to this day and has, according to Google Scholar, been cited 2,500 times.

Life After *Social Identifications*

Encouraged by this success, we began to recognize why the book held value—it had opened doors to others who had previously regarded social identity theory as arcane, and as a rival or competing perspective. We had helped show

how it could complement and enhance other approaches. Around that time, we decided to work on this more-inclusive approach more directly. First, we edited a book titled *Social Identity Theory: Constructive and Critical Advances* (Abrams & Hogg, 1990a), published by Harvester Wheatsheaf/Springer Verlag under the experienced editorship of Farrell Burnett. Our aim for that book was to attract and welcome critical views of social identity theory, particularly from outside the social identity "in-group."

The book included our revised analysis of the role of motivation in intergroup relations, which we had initially set out in the now highly cited article mentioned previously (Abrams & Hogg, 1988). This was also the starting point for uncertainty identity theory (Hogg, 2000, 2007, 2012), which we developed in our next edited book, *Group Motivation* (Hogg & Abrams, 1993).

Dom moved 400 miles south to the University of Kent in 1989, and Mike moved 1,000 miles north to the University of Queensland in 1991—so now we were arguably fewer miles apart. During this period, the critique of traditional social psychology spawned by Tajfel and Moscovici developed a new and much more radical direction—discourse analysis. That approach (e.g., Potter & Wetherell, 1987) challenged the entire positivist apparatus of psychology and set its sights firmly on experimental social psychology as a way to argue its case. The perspective was a new and distinctive one that was well received in the United Kingdom by sociologists and researchers in communication, culture, media, and literature. It quickly gained purchase among the newest generation of social psychologists too. At the same time as we were seeking to put forward a social identity perspective internationally, we now also found ourselves defending the value of traditional empirical methods and articulating what we felt were important limitations of the discourse analytic perspective. Mike was at a safe distance, and other experimental social psychologists in the United Kingdom maintained a low or diplomatic profile, but Dom was very much in the firing line, such as at conferences and colloquia, where he argued the case for an inclusive approach. We articulated this vision in a paper (Abrams & Hogg, 1990b) that was also graciously reprinted in a collection edited by Ian Parker (2002).

We then pursued the idea of linking with North American social psychology more explicitly in our third edited volume, *Social Identity and Social Cognition* (Abrams & Hogg, 1999). This book was famously conceived in a cellar bar in Washington, D.C., at the legendary 1995 joint meeting of the Society of Experimental Social Psychology (SESP) and European Association of Social Psychology (EASP)—legendary because Yasser Arafat was in town and staying in the conference hotel (and also perhaps because we completely emptied Mike's minibar!).

Whereas the new cognitive approach in social psychology could be viewed as inherently reductionist, our aim was to invite those who were leading that field to consider how their work was connected with social identity processes. In our 1993 and 1999 edited volumes, we see the beginnings of important new theoretical work, such as intergroup emotions theory (Smith, 1999). But the more important aspect of this project was that we created social and intellectual relationships beyond our own work. We began to widen the scope a little further to consider not just intragroup and intergroup relations, but the broader question of the nature of exclusive and inclusive social relationships in our subsequent book, *The Social Psychology of Inclusion and Exclusion* (Abrams, Hogg, & Marques, 2005). Here, we sought to bridge more directly to work on interpersonal relations, again with the aim of showing how theories and evidence at different levels of analysis could be mutually informative for a broader framework for understanding problems in social psychology.

The Journal: *Group Processes and Intergroup Relations*

Along with these editing projects, our other major project was developing the idea for a journal, *Group Processes and Intergroup Relations* (*GPIR*). We had relatively little experience as editors, but the scheme as a whole was hatched following a British Psychological Society meeting in Cambridge in 1994, where Dominic was explaining to a junior editor at Sage UK his deep concerns that academic publishing in social psychology seemed very split between U.S. and European readerships. In particular, social identity research papers were being published almost exclusively in the British and European journals of social psychology, whereas the rest were appearing in the *Journal of Personality and Social Psychology* (*JPSP*) and the *Journal of Experimental Social Psychology* (*JESP*). It seemed that the constitution of the editorial boards of these journals signaled a perpetuation of this unconstructive and now archaic schism. The editor's response was—why not do something about it?

Almost immediately, we devised a plan and proposal to launch the journal, and we peddled this plan to a number of publishers, memorably at the EASP meeting in Gmunden, Austria, in 1996. The plan was that it should directly embrace work from both sides of the Atlantic, that it should explicitly link intergroup and intragroup processes, and that it should create a new space for research that embraced the links between them. We were thrilled that Dick Moreland, Diane Mackie, Jack Dovidio, Scott Tindale, and Anne Maass enthusiastically signed up to be our inaugural associate editors. This team was substantially more experienced than ourselves, and their encouragement and advice proved invaluable for the success of the journal, which was first published in 1998 and is now in its 18th year.

Over the years, we have worked with a fabulous series of associate editors and editorial assistants (most of the latter are former graduate students who are now faculty at various universities around the world). When we set the scene at the launch of the journal (Abrams & Hogg, 1998), we were optimistic that the fields of group processes and intergroup relations would both strengthen and begin to cross-fertilize. After 10 years, our optimism had only increased (Abrams & Hogg, 2008), supported by empirical evidence (Randsley de Moura, Leader, Pelletier, & Abrams, 2008). The cross-linkage between these two areas, as well as the multilevel approach (Abrams & Christian, 2007) emerge conceptually from the social identity perspective, and are focuses that we have always promoted (Abrams, Wetherell, Cochrane, Hogg & Turner, 1990). It continues to gather momentum in terms of the focus and scope of research, aided greatly by advances in methodology and data analysis.

Onward Into Our Fourth Decade

Dominic has remained in the United Kingdom and is now the director of the Centre for the Study of Group Processes at the University of Kent, and Mike moved partially to California in the early 2000s and fully in 2006, to chair the social psychology department at Claremont Graduate University in Los Angeles. So, little by little, we are drifting closer geographically—on a good day, it's now less than a 10-hour flight.

Since launching *GPIR*, our collaborative work has focused largely on continuing to promote and explain the value of the social identity metatheory. We have written a number of handbook chapters, reviews, and papers on this theme. As coeditors in chief, we collaborate closely on *GPIR* and have developed the journal by embracing regular special issues edited by guest editors, focusing particular attention on specific topics and problems. Our independent lines of research continue to connect closely in various areas, such as influence and leadership, extremism, and uncertainty, and across the continents, we have occasionally cosupervised graduate students. Overall, we have a shared passion for understanding how differentiation within groups is shaped by and plays out in identity processes and intergroup relations.

We are in regular contact and have occasional FaceTime meetings, as well as getting together whenever a conference or other event allows. We retain our enthusiasm for the grander project of linking social psychology to major real-world issues in a way that is inclusive and illuminating, and we both remain committed to supporting our wonderful graduate students.

What next? Well, as well as doing our best to promote the relevance of group processes and intergroup relations research through small conferences, presentations, and articles with our colleagues and students, working across a wide range of domains, we are looking forward to 2017, when we will celebrate the 20th anniversary of the launch of *GPIR* by guest editing a special issue of the journal, taking stock of the state of and future direction of group research in social psychology.

We have come a long way since first meeting in the psychology department in Bristol in 1983—and it is not lost on us that 30 years later, in 2013 and 2014, Mike became president of SESP and Dom president of the Society for the Psychological Study of Social Issues (SPSSI).

How Has It All Worked?

Our collaboration has been a product of many factors, including shared adversity and challenges, wonderful mentoring and support by our more experienced colleagues, and the shared motivation to work toward a vision that is larger than our own work. Where our collaboration has succeeded, this often reflected the willingness of others (editors, colleagues, employers) to take a gamble on projects or ideas that we offered. This serves as a reminder that it is vital to remain open to such initiatives by others too.

If we have advice to offer others, it is that collaboration involves recognizing the different and complementary strengths of one's collaborators and being open to criticism and willing to learn and improve from feedback. Sustaining a collaborative relationship also means accepting that there is a "long game"—it is not just about the next paper or chapter; rather, it is about a bridge of trust and support that does not have to encompass everything one does but that can be mutually sustaining over time. If such collaboration goes well, it should offer a model that can serve others by including them and by showing how collaborative work can produce something that is greater than the sum of its parts.

At the risk of sounding syrupy, a successful, productive, and enduring collaborative relationship is like any other successful relationship. There has to be shared vision and shared interests, some complementarity of expertise and behavioral style, and a feeling of confidence that, come what may, you each have each other's professional back. Above all, it has to be fun.

■ REFERENCES ■

Abrams, D. (1985). Focus of attention in minimal intergroup discrimination. *British Journal of Social Psychology, 24*, 65–74. doi:10.1111/j.2044-8309.1985.tb00661.x

Abrams, D., Carter, J., & Hogg, M. A. (1989). Perceptions of male homosexuality: An application of social identity theory. *Social Behaviour, 4*, 253–264. Accessed from http://psycnet.apa.org/psycinfo/1990-14580-001

Abrams, D., & Christian, J. N. (2007). A relational analysis of social exclusion. In D. Abrams, J. N. Christian, & D. Gordon (Eds.), *Multidisciplinary handbook of social exclusion research* (pp. 211–232). Oxford, England: Wiley-Blackwell. doi:10.1002/9780470773178.ch12

Abrams, D., & Hogg, M. A. (1988). Comments on the motivational status of self-esteem in social identity and intergroup discrimination. *European Journal of Social Psychology, 18*, 317–334. doi:10.1002/ejsp.2420180403

Abrams, D., & Hogg, M. A. (Eds.). (1990a). *Social identity theory: Constructive and critical advances*. London, England: Harvester-Wheatsheaf (also published New York, NY: Springer-Verlag).

Abrams, D., & Hogg, M. A. (1990b). On the social psychological relevance of discourse analysis. *Philosophical Psychology, 3*, 219–225. doi:10.1080/0951508900857300

Abrams, D., & Hogg, M. A. (1998). Prospects for research in group processes and intergroup relations. *Group Processes and Intergroup Relations, 1*, 7–23. doi:10.1177/1368430298011002

Abrams, D., & Hogg, M. A. (Eds.). (1999). *Social identity and social cognition*. Oxford, England: Blackwell.

Abrams, D., & Hogg, M. A. (2004). Metatheory: Lessons from social identity research. *Personality and Social Psychology Review, 8*, 98–106. doi:10.1207/s15327957pspr0802_2

Abrams, D., & Hogg. M. A. (2008). *Group Processes & Intergroup Relations* ten years on: Development, impact, and future directions. *Group Processes and Intergroup Relations, 1*, 419–425. doi:10.1177/1368430208095397

Abrams, D., Hogg, M. A., & Marques, J. M. (Eds.). (2005). *The social psychology of exclusion and inclusion*. New York, NY: Psychology Press.

Abrams, D., Thomas, J., & Hogg, M.A. (1990). Numerical distinctiveness, social identity, and gender salience. *British Journal of Social Psychology, 29,* 87–92. doi:10.1111/j.2044-8309.1990.tb00889.x

Abrams, D., Wetherell, M., Cochrane, S., Hogg, M. A., & Turner, J. C. (1990). Knowing what to think by knowing who you are: Self-categorisation and the nature of norm formation, conformity, and group polarisation. *British Journal of Social Psychology, 29,* 97–119. doi:10.1111/j.2044-8309.1990.tb00892

Hogg, M. A. (2000). Subjective uncertainty reduction through self-categorization: A motivational theory of social identity processes. *European Review of Social Psychology, 11,* 223–255.

Hogg, M. A. (2007). Uncertainty-identity theory. In M. P. Zanna (Ed.), *Advances in experimental social psychology* (Vol. 39, pp. 69–126). San Diego, CA: Academic Press.

Hogg, M. A. (2012). Self-uncertainty, social identity, and the solace of extremism. In M. A. Hogg & D. L. Blaylock (Eds.), *Extremism and the psychology of uncertainty* (pp. 19–35). Oxford, England: Wiley-Blackwell. doi:10.1002/9781444344073.ch2

Hogg, M. A., & Abrams, D. (1988). *Social identifications: A social psychology of intergroup relations and group processes.* London, England: Routledge.

Hogg, M. A., & Abrams, D. (Eds). (1993). *Group motivation: Social psychological perspectives.* London, England: Harvester Wheatsheaf.

Hogg, M. A., Joyce, N., & Abrams, D. (1984). Diglossia in Switzerland? A social identity analysis of speaker evaluations. *Journal of Language and Social Psychology, 3,* 185–196. doi:10.1177/0261927X8400300302

Hogg, M. A., & Turner, J. C. (1985). Interpersonal attraction, social identification, and psychological group formation. *European Journal of Social Psychology, 15,* 51–66. doi:10.1002/ejsp.2420150105

Moscovici, S. (1981). On social representations. In J. P. Forgas (Ed.), *Social cognition* (pp. 181–209). New York, NY: Academic Press.

Parker, I. (Ed.) (2002). *Critical discursive psychology* (pp. 172–180). New York, NY: Palgrave-Macmillan.

Potter, J., & Wetherell, M. (1987). *Discourse and social psychology: Beyond attitudes and behaviour.* Newbury Park, CA: Sage.

Randsley de Moura, G. R., Leader, T. I., Pelletier, J. P., & Abrams, D. (2008). Prospects for group processes and intergroup relations research: A review of 70 years' progress. *Group Processes and Intergroup Relations, 11,* 575–596. doi:10.1177/1368430208095406

Smith, E. R. (1999). Affective and cognitive implications of group membership becoming part of the self: New models of prejudice and of the self-concept. In D. Abrams & M. A. Hogg (Eds.), *Social identity and social cognition* (pp. 183–196). Oxford, England: Blackwell.

Tajfel, H. (1970). Experiments in intergroup discrimination. *Scientific American, 223,* 96–102.

Tajfel, H. (Ed.). (1978). *Differentiation between social groups: Studies in the social psychology of intergroup relations.* New York, NY: Academic Press.

Tajfel, H., & Turner, J. C. (1979). An integrative theory of intergroup conflict. In W. G. Austin & S. Worchel (Eds.), *The social psychology of intergroup relations* (pp. 33–47). Monterey, CA: Brooks/Cole.

Turner, J. C., & Giles, H. (Eds.). (1991). *Intergroup behaviour.* Oxford, England: Blackwell.

Turner, J. C., Hogg, M. A., Oakes, P. J., Reicher, S. D., & Wetherell, M. S. (1987). *Rediscovering the social group: A self-categorization theory.* Oxford, England: Blackwell.

Chapter 3: Living What We Learn: Dual Identity and Collaboration

John F. Dovidio

Carl Iver Hovland Professor of Psychology
Yale University

Samuel L. Gaertner

Trustees Distinguished Professor Emeritus
Department of Psychological and Brain Sciences
University of Delaware

Our collaboration is a longstanding and productive one. We began working together over 40 years ago, and we have coauthored over 140 books, articles, and chapters. The collaboration began as a graduate student (Jack)/faculty advisor (Sam) relationship, and it has evolved over time with experience and as the focus of our work has shifted. In this chapter, we begin by recounting the origins of our collaboration and the development of our collaborative interests. We then discuss the principles that have guided and sustained our collaboration over the years. We consider what some may view as challenges of distinguishing our contributions for professional recognition and formal evaluation (e.g., for tenure and promotion decisions) but what we see as the advantages of complementary perspectives, skills, and interests. Throughout the chapter, we reflect upon how our collaboration has helped to shape the topics we have studied and how our research has provided new perspectives on our collaboration.

The Origins of Our Collaboration

Sam Gaertner, an assistant professor at the University of Delaware, a new PhD from the City University of New York Graduate Center in 1970, had been working on the topic of aversive racism, a contemporary and subtle, but insidious, manifestation of racial bias. His work on this topic began with his PhD dissertation, which contained a serendipitous and provocative finding. The study (Gaertner, 1973) involved the willingness of registered Liberal and Conservative Party members in New York City to help a Black or White motorist whose car had broken down on a local highway. Confederates, who were identifiable as Black or White on the basis of their dialects, made telephone calls, claiming to have been wanting to dial their mechanic's number from a public telephone along the highway. The callers explained that they now needed the respondent's help to call a mechanic because they used their last coin for this wrong-number call.

Conservative Party members discriminated by helping Black callers less frequently than White callers, whereas Liberal Party members did not discriminate in terms of helping. Surprisingly, however, Liberal Party members discriminated in a different way. Although Liberals helped Black and White callers equally when they knew their assistance was needed, they terminated this encounter more readily for Black than for White callers prior to learning fully of the callers' need for their help. These latter results were initially puzzling but became more understandable in the context of the notion of aversive racism (Kovel, 1970). This perspective suggested that liberals may be unconsciously biased and engage in subtle rather than blatant discrimination.

In 1973, Jack Dovidio, following the advice of his undergraduate advisors, came to Delaware as a graduate student after earning his BA at Dartmouth. He came with a range of interests, including altruism and nonverbal behavior, but with a primary personal interest in intergroup relations and prejudice. After about two years, our own group-based boundaries as faculty advisor and graduate student disintegrated, and we became a research team and have been close personal friends ever since.

The Evolution of Our Collaborative Research

Our collaboration was fueled by our individual interests in the topic of contemporary racism. These interests emerged from different, but not totally unrelated, experiences. Both of us are first-generation college students from blue-collar backgrounds. As a boy, Sam's family lived in a Jewish-Italian neighborhood in the Sheepshead Bay section of Brooklyn, New York, which contained few Blacks. This relatively homogeneous White community basically shielded him from directly experiencing anti-Semitism or other forms of prejudice and discrimination. Sam's interest in prejudice was initiated when he read his parents' copy of John Hersey's (1950) book, *The Wall*, which described in vivid detail the horrors suffered by Jews during the Holocaust. Sam remembers weeping convulsively while reading sections of Hersey's book. Learning about those horrific experiences of people with whom he shared a common religious identity emotionally sensitized him to the cruelty and injustice of anti-Semitism and to prejudice and discrimination, more generally.

Sam also remembers a duality in his mother's reactions to Blacks that as a boy he found confusing—but which made more sense to him many years later as a graduate student upon reading Joel Kovel's (1970) *White Racism: A Psycho-History*. Kovel first introduced ideas about aversive racism existing among people who endorsed a liberal ideology and who regarded themselves as non-prejudiced. For example, Sam recalls his mother remarking that she participated in the first large March on Washington for civil rights in the 1950s. However, he also remembers walking with his mother when he was younger and how she would squeeze his hand more tightly while pulling him closer to her whenever they were approaching a Black man.

Jack's interest evolved from experiences growing up outside of Boston during a period of recent immigration followed by racial tensions arising from movements for racial equality that emerged in the 1960s and, later, discontent and local conflict over busing to achieve racial balance in primary and secondary schools. The composition of the community in which he grew up was shifting from predominantly Irish-American to one with a rapidly increasing representation of Italian-Americans. Irish-Americans felt threatened by this demographic shift and, as a consequence, engaged in often not-so-subtle forms of bias, in open expression and action, toward Italian-Americans. Jack experienced that bias directly.

At the same time, the Italian-American community joined with other White ethnic groups around Boston to resist the possibility of rapid racial integration, in schools and residentially, by Black Americans. The experience of seeing both sides of bias clearly, as a victim, on one hand, and as part of a perpetrator group, on the other hand, made a deep and enduring impression on him. It gave Jack some unique insights about the dynamics of prejudice and about how apparently good people can readily discriminate, justifying their actions in ways to prevent others and themselves from recognizing the role of bigotry in their actions.

In 1974, with support from the Office of Naval Research, we began a series of studies to explore predictions derived from the aversive racism framework. The fundamental premise of this research on aversive racism was that many Whites who consciously support egalitarian principles, endorse a liberal political ideology, and believe themselves to be nonprejudiced also harbor negative attitudes about Blacks and other historically disadvantaged groups. These unconscious negative feelings and beliefs develop as a consequence of normal, almost unavoidable, and frequently functional cognitive, motivational, and social-cultural processes. As a consequence, whereas old-fashioned racists exhibit a direct and overt pattern of discrimination, aversive racists may appear more variable and inconsistent in their actions. At times, they discriminate (manifesting their negative feelings), and at other times they do not (reflecting their egalitarian beliefs). Specifically, we hypothesized that aversive racists discriminate against Blacks mainly when norms in a situation are weak or ambiguous such that aversive racists' behavior is difficult to judge as inappropriate or when they can justify or rationalize their negative behavior on the basis of some factor other than race. Thus, discrimination occurs without challenging their nonprejudiced self-image.

Over the next decade, we conducted a number of collaborative projects studying race and helping, which not only provided support for the aversive racism framework but also contributed to an emerging literature on bystander intervention. This line of research led to a collaboration with Jane Piliavin and Russ Clark that resulted in the book *Emergency Intervention* (Piliavin, Dovidio,

Gaertner, & Clark, 1981), which attempted to explain why bystanders might intervene in the problems of other people. In the version of the Arousal: Cost-Reward Model presented in this volume, we explained how bystander intervention could be motivated by a desire to reduce the unpleasant arousal elicited by witnessing an emergency, while weighing the rewards and costs associated with various alternative actions for reducing this arousal. Moreover, we identified "we-ness" between the bystander and the victim as playing a central role in influencing a bystander's willingness to intervene in an emergency.

The *Emergency Intervention* project was especially critical to shaping our theoretical perspective and creating a conceptual foundation for what we came to call the "Common Ingroup Identity Model" (Gaertner & Dovidio, 2000, 2012). Over the 3 years that we worked on revising the Arousal: Cost-Reward Model, our focus became riveted on the value of "we-ness," particularly among virtual strangers, in a context in which one of them needed the assistance of the other. Our interest in the importance of the social connection between individuals expanded our perspective to consider more fully the nature of *intergroup* processes beyond the intrapsychic processes, such as the ambivalence between the conscious egalitarian values and the unconscious bias on which we had been focusing in the study of aversive racism.

As we presented our research on aversive racism to various audiences, we were frequently asked about what can be done to combat aversive racism and its adverse effects on Black Americans. Aversive racists are unaware of their personal biases; they believe that they are nonprejudiced. In addition, the basis of their negative feelings was hypothesized to be rooted in normal, often functional processes, such as favoring members of one's own group over other groups. These questions stimulated our next major collaborative set of studies, which formed the foundation for the development of the Common Ingroup Identity Model (Gaertner & Dovidio, 2000, 2012).

Various seeds of the ideas that formed the basis of the model appeared in our studies of race and helping (e.g., Gaertner & Dovidio, 1977) and prosocial behavior more generally (Piliavin et al., 1981), as well as in our research about identifying and combating subtle racism (Gaertner & Dovidio, 1986). In the concluding chapter of our edited volume, *Prejudice, Discrimination, and Racism* (Dovidio & Gaertner, 1986), we wrote that "the research challenge is to discover techniques and strategies that induce members of separate groups to conceive of the aggregate as one entity, and then to examine whether this perception facilitates cooperativeness, acceptance, and personalized interactions" (p. 326).

The ideas coalesced into the initial formal presentation of the theoretical framework by Gaertner, Dovidio, Anastasio, Bachman, and Rust (1993), which was published in the *European Review of Social Psychology*. We later described the model and the support for it more fully in a monograph called *Reducing Intergroup Bias: The Common Ingroup Identity Model* (Gaertner & Dovidio, 2000). The Common Ingroup Identity Model assumes that social categorization that delineates members of one's own group (the ingroup) from members of other groups (outgroups) forms the psychological foundation of intergroup bias. People respond more favorably to others whom they perceive as belonging to their group than to those in different groups (Dovidio & Gartner, 2010), and they are motivated to see their group as better than other groups, sometimes achieving greater status for their group by discriminating against other groups (Tajfel & Turner, 1979). These biases are exacerbated by perceptions of competition between the groups.

From the perspective of the Common Ingroup Identity Model, the goal is to change perceptions from two different groups to incorporating others into a common superordinate identity (e.g., through cooperative interaction). A common identity can be created through interventions, such as cooperative interdependence, personalized interaction, and common goals, identified by the Contact Hypothesis as requisite conditions for improving intergroup attitudes (Allport, 1954; Pettigrew & Tropp, 2011). Once outgroup members are perceived as ingroup members, we hypothesize that they would be accorded the benefits of ingroup status. Thus, upon recategorization, there would likely be more positive thoughts, feelings, and behaviors toward these former outgroup members by virtue of categorizing them now as ingroup members.

One of the more recent developments in our work on the Common Ingroup Identity Model has been greater emphasis on another form of recategorization—in addition to recategorization within a single superordinate identity—that maintains a recognition of original subgroup identities but as elements within an overarching superordinate identity—like "two groups working together as a team." We termed this a "dual identity." For example, we believe that it is possible for members to conceive of two groups (for example, parents and children) as distinct units within the context of a superordinate (i.e., family) identity. Thus, the development of a common ingroup identity does not necessarily require each group to forsake completely its less inclusive group identity.

This development in our work on the Common Ingroup Identity Model has an additional meaning in our collaboration. Although we had worked closely together for almost 30 years by the time our ideas about a dual identity crystallized, we see in retrospect that the elements of that formulation were consistently operating in our collaboration.

Collaboration and Our Dual Identity

At the very beginning of Jack's graduate career, he had a meeting with Sam that helped define the nature of their work together. It specified an advisor's expectations of a student generally, but it also established two important principles of their long-term collaboration. First, with respect to the content of the research, Sam listed the topics he was interested in and asked Jack to do the same. Then Sam said, "Now my task is to get you interested in what excites me, and your task is to get me interested in what excites you." He succinctly identified one key element to a successful collaboration—pursuing topics that both investigators are not simply interested in but instead are truly excited about.

As we noted earlier, upon reflection, we can now see parallels between the dynamics of our collaboration and the focus of our collaborative research.

From the perspective of the Common Ingroup Identity Model, intergroup interactions that involve common goals, cooperation, and close interaction promote the development of a shared superordinate identity. Having our collaboration revolve around topics that we were both passionate about and committed to ensured that we had a common goal that involved close interaction and cooperative effort. It helped to forge our individual identities in a common, superordinate collaborative identity.

At that meeting early in Jack's graduate career, Sam also explained, at some length, the importance of understanding the most current statistical techniques for successful research. The details of his argument were less important than the way he ended it. Sam concluded it by saying, "And so understanding statistics well is critical. I don't, so you have to." Sam, of course, understated his own proficiency in statistics, but he did so to make an important point. Research is complex and requires a broad range of knowledge and skills. The value of collaboration is, thus, that individuals can bring different expertise to the joint enterprise. When individuals have a commitment to a shared enterprise and see themselves as collaborators (a common identity), each person bringing different skills, ideas, and perspectives is valued, not threatening. These differences form the basis of cooperative interdependence rather than competition. In essence, 25 years before we developed the Common Ingroup Identity Model, Sam articulated the value of dual identities, recognizing and appreciating the different qualities that each of us could bring to our team research effort.

Having a sense of common identity while recognizing the distinct nature of our contributions has been a primary element of our collaboration over the years. Common identity fosters positive attitudes—and indeed, we have maintained a close personal friendship for over 40 years—but it also promotes trust and generosity. People show increased trust for those they perceive as part of the ingroup, are particularly concerned about fairness and procedural justice with respect to ingroup members, and are more likely to disregard the faults and attend to the strengths of ingroup members (for a review, see Dovidio & Gaertner, 2010). These processes represent the "social glue" for successful collaborations. When people share a common identity, they are more receptive to new ideas from members (Kane, Argote, & Levine, 2005) and place higher value on the different expertises of others (Dovidio, Gaertner, & Validzic, 1998). These processes are valuable at every creative and technical stage of a research project.

In the kind of collaboration that we have had over the past 40 years, it becomes increasingly difficult to distinguish the common and distinct elements of our dual identities. We teach each other what we know in our collaboration. However, we are still able to recognize distinctive contributions that each of us has made in our collaborative journey. Sam brings unusual creativity and scholarly vision to our work. Certainly, as we described earlier, our research on aversive racism was stimulated by serendipitous findings in his dissertation work. In addition, in the 1980s, during a period in which social cognition was dominating U.S. psychology, Sam recognized the promise of social identity theory (Tajfel & Turner, 1979) for understanding and addressing the kinds of subtle biases associated with aversive racism. Rather than chasing the "hot" topic or technique in the field, Sam has a rare independence of thought and strong intellectual curiosity. These qualities have been a guiding light in our collaborative work. In addition, his deep passion for studying social issues scientifically has sustained our work through both the tedious and frustrating parts of our research. Not all studies work out, and sometimes it appears that we might be facing a dead end. Sam, however, is dogged in his pursuit of answers and innovative in his approach.

One of Sam's scholarly strengths has been his talent for developing "kitchen sink" interventions that are strong and ecologically valid but do not necessarily have the purity of disentangling the contributing factors (at least initially). He reminds us that it is important to find out if an effect exists before doing the fine-tuning of the specific components of the effect. In addition, he demonstrates the high priority of our collaborative research in his life. It is not unusual to get an e-mail containing his revisions of a manuscript, his interpretation of complex and unexpected findings, or his thoughts about a new project at 4 a.m. (when he sent it, not when I [Jack] read it), or while he is on a cruise ship in the Caribbean. His enthusiasm and passion have helped sustain a vital collaboration.

Jack is the type of colleague—who, if I (Sam) telephoned him at 4 a.m. with a research idea, when the initial shock of being awakened subsided and he learned why I called, would become engaged in the conversation as though it were 10 a.m. (although he would never see this as an accurate description of himself). Jack's calm emotional disposition allowed our collaboration to move forward through such difficulties as facing inconsistent results across studies or responding to editorial criticism of our methods or interpretation of findings. In terms of addressing inconsistent results, Jack's flexible, penetrating mind allowed him to devise plausible, testable moderators that could help resolve the apparent inconsistency.

Jack's theoretical and methodological interests have generally been broader and more varied than Sam's. While Jack's interests in nonverbal and prosocial behaviors became distinct and intrinsically interesting domains of scholarship for him, Sam found these behaviors interesting primarily because of their potential to inform us of something important about intergroup relations, and specifically about prejudice, discrimination, and racism. So we often approached our collaborative work with different viewpoints as to why, individually, we found the work intellectually stimulating. The other's interests, however, reciprocally ignited our mutual passion for our work.

If you ever had the good fortune to listen to Jack deliver a paper at a professional conference or colloquium, you could not help but recognize his exquisite oratorical skills (usually punctuated with a keen sense of humor), capable of clearly describing complicated patterns of findings or conflicting theoretical perspectives so as to make them understandable, even to nonexperts. Rather than treating these disparate findings or theories as completely separate entities, the organization of Jack's presentation would lead listeners to anticipate the integrative understanding that he was about to propose. These presentational skills were even sharper and more nuanced in his writing, which suffered only from a nontouch-typist's slow, two-finger poking at a typewriter or computer keyboard. Jack also possesses exceptionally strong technical and statistical expertise, which is so crucial for sophisticated experimental paradigms or analyzing mountains of nested data.

Dual Identity and Team Science

We were able to keep in frequent contact even after Jack received his PhD from Delaware and began his first faculty position at Colgate University (in 1977). We did this with frequent phone calls and visiting each other on occasion with our families. The advent of the Internet, however, helped solidify our collaborative relationship. The phone was—and still is—an effective way of brainstorming, bouncing ideas off one another, or discussing particular thorny issues in a research project. However, while its effects are largely taken for granted today, the Internet revolutionized the way we collaborated. It replaced the costly and inefficient exchange of drafts by U.S. mail. We could write, revise, and comment on manuscripts or on protocols for new studies immediately, often while we talked on the phone. Being able to communicate asynchronously (e.g., with Sam sending e-mails at 4 a.m. while Jack reads them at 8 a.m.) allowed us to communicate fresh ideas and insights as they occurred. Having the Internet helped us sustain our collaboration at a time— the transition from graduate school to a new job—when students and mentors typically part ways professionally.

However, another way that the Internet benefited our collaboration was that it allowed us to develop a network of scholars to expand our collaborative activities. While thinking in terms of a common identity has many benefits for social coordination within a group, it can enhance the delineation between members of the ingroup and outgroups—who is "we" and who is "they" (Kessler & Mummendey, 2001). However, unlike material resources that are zero-sum, common identity has a symbolic value that can extend freely to others, once they become identified as an ingroup member. This quality has allowed our "circle of inclusion" to expand over the years. Our collaboration has expanded by association, with our students and other collaborators becoming incorporated in the research identity that we forged around aversive racism and the Common Ingroup Identity Model.

Social networking over the Internet is taken for granted today. However, even in its earliest, crude forms, computer-mediated interaction allowed us to get to know new potential collaborators. It allowed us to meet and form personal and close professional relationships with each other's students. Although we might have limited opportunity to meet with them personally and they might be reluctant to contact us by phone, we (Sam and Jack) were able to develop true relationships with each other's graduate or postdoctoral students, incorporating them within our common ingroup identity.

In addition, developments in computer-mediated communication greatly facilitated our collaborative connections with international scholars. Whereas working with people in time zones 5 to 7 hours apart had been a major obstacle to sustaining collaborative relationships internationally by phone, the Internet made it a strength. A collaborator in Europe could work on a manuscript for several hours and send it to us at the end of the day, and it would arrive as we began our workday, doubling the amount of time devoted to a manuscript in a 24-hour period. The permeability of the group boundary defined by our collaborative common identity thus has allowed us to extend our work with others substantially across time and space. At the beginning of this chapter, we mentioned that we have coauthored over 140 writings together. Those publications also included 90 other coauthors.

Challenges of Collaboration

Although we have concentrated in this chapter on the virtues of collaboration, there are certainly challenges, some of which are internal. Collaborations are relationships, and like all relationships, there are ups and downs. We often disagree or express different opinions, expectations, or interpretations. The trust, understanding, and mutual respect that we have developed over the years have made these disputes only small bumps in the road. While we disagree at times, we have yet to exchange an angry word with one another. In fact, we have found differences of opinion to be a valuable source of creativity, motivating each of us to look at issues differently. Our various perspectives have also stimulated us to adopt a multimethod approach to attack common problems or hypotheses using different methods, designs, and tools. Within a solid relationship of trust and common purpose, disagreements can be appreciated as creative tensions that stimulate new insights and levels of understanding.

The more substantive challenges to our collaboration have been imposed externally. The field encourages researchers to establish an identity as productive, independent scholars. Consistent collaboration with another scholar can raise questions (including formal ones in tenure decisions) about one's independence as a scholar. When those collaborations are with one's PhD advisor, those questions are even more likely. Questions arise about whether a junior faculty member is simply "riding the coattails" of his or her advisor (or vice versa). Tenure and promotion deliberations are often about giving someone a job for life. They are serious and cautious deliberations. Thus, there were professional risks (particularly for Jack, but for Sam too), which we recognized.

In our case, the benefits far outweighed the risks because of the quality of the work and the productivity of the collaboration. The fact that Jack was at a liberal arts college without graduate students and with a limited subject pool also figured into the calculus. Our collaboration provided him intellectual and professional support in social psychology that was less readily available at his home institution, as well as the resources necessary for conducting programmatic research at an appropriate pace. One hallmark of our collaborative relationship, which has helped sustain it, is that it is not an exclusive relationship. We also work with other people, independent of each other. This is particularly valuable for an untenured faculty member to demonstrate his or her scholarly independence to a department or tenure committee.

The issue of how collaborative relationships are perceived also needs to be considered, beyond implications for tenure, but more generally in terms of professional reputation in the field. Scholarly reputations are earned by making distinctive theoretical contributions. Many a journal rejection letter includes the explanation that the work "did not make a sufficiently novel theoretical contribution." Thus, the prevailing pressure is to differentiate one's contribution from the work of others. Successful collaboration in some ways requires the opposite—placing team achievement above individual recognition. Internally, collaboration based on a dual identity can satisfy the needs to have one's unique contribution valued while promoting collective accomplishment. However, public recognition in the profession depends on first-authored publications.

The strength and longevity of our collaboration has recognized these pressures. We decided that if the goal of our profession is to produce scholarship of the highest quality, bringing our different strengths but common goals to bear upon the same projects is the best way to make quality contributions. In addition, if we publish more research collectively than we would individually and distribute first authorship equitably, then there is no disadvantage. Being first author on five papers and coauthor on another five based on collaborative work represents a stronger scholarly contribution than being first author on only five individually published papers. Moreover, the mutual stimulation in our collaboration and the new ideas, energy, and perspectives offered by others included in the common identity offer vitality and creativity to our collaborative relationship.

Conclusions

Collaborating is like dating. Many people look really attractive across the room, but after only a brief interaction, we can determine that, despite their apparent virtues, we would never want a relationship with them. Also, like dating, it is hard to know in advance which relationships, once initiated, will develop and deepen, and which will be only short-term "flings." However, for a limited number of times, mutual interests and passions can sustain the relationship, often for a lifetime. When the relationship works, you know it. And the security of the relationship allows differences—in perspectives, academic strengths or interests, and appetites for new directions or new colleagues—to be strengths that maintain the vitality and productivity of the relationship.

There are a number of different forces within the profession to establish distinctive reputations that make sustaining long-term collaborative relationships difficult. However, one of the most attractive aspects of an academic career is being able to select projects that one feels deeply committed to and passionate about, and having the freedom to pursue these projects in the way that one wants. Our collaboration has helped us maintain that motivation over our long careers, and each of us makes the other's work better and fuels our passion for new projects and directions. Having the primary common goal of addressing important social problems through psychological research has made the decision to sustain our collaboration an easy one.

▨ REFERENCES ▨

Allport, G. W. (1954). *The nature of prejudice*. Cambridge, MA: Addison-Wesley.

Dovidio, J. F., & Gaertner, S. L. (Eds.). (1986). *Prejudice, discrimination, and racism*. New York, NY: Academic Press.

Dovidio, J. F., & Gaertner, S. L. (2010). Intergroup bias. In S. T. Fiske, D. Gilbert, & G. Lindzey (Eds.), *Handbook of social psychology* (Vol. 2, pp. 1084–1121). New York, NY: Wiley.

Dovidio, J. F., Gaertner, S. L., & Validzic, A. (1998). Intergroup bias: Status, differentiation, and a common in-group identity. *Journal of Personality and Social Psychology, 75*, 109–120.

Gaertner, S. L. (1973). Helping behavior and racial discrimination among liberals and conservatives. *Journal of Personality and Social Psychology, 25*, 335–341.

Gaertner, S. L., & Dovidio, J. F. (1977). The subtlety of White racism, arousal, and helping behavior. *Journal of Personality and Social Psychology, 35*, 691–707.

Gaertner, S. L., & Dovidio, J. F. (1986). The aversive form of racism. In J. F. Dovidio & S. L. Gaertner (Eds.), *Prejudice, discrimination, and racism* (pp. 61–89). Orlando, FL: Academic Press.

Gaertner, S. L., & Dovidio, J. F. (2000). *Reducing intergroup bias: The Common Ingroup Identity Model*. Philadelphia, PA: Psychology Press.

Gaertner, S. L., & Dovidio, J. F. (2012). Reducing intergroup bias: The Common Ingroup Identity Model. In P. A. M. Van Lange, A. W. Kruglanski, & E. T. Higgins (Eds.), *Handbook of theories of social psychology* (Vol. 2, pp. 439–457). Thousand Oaks, CA: Sage.

Gaertner, S. L., Dovidio, J. F., Anastasio, P. A., Bachman, B. A., & Rust, M. C. (1993). The Common Ingroup Identity Model: Recategorization and the reduction of intergroup bias. In W. Stroebe & M. Hewstone (Eds.), *European review of social psychology* (Vol. 4, pp. 1–26). New York, NY: John Wiley & Sons.

Hersey, J. (1950). *The wall*. New York, NY: Alfred A. Knopf.

Kane, A. A., Argote, L., & Levine, J. M. (2005). Knowledge transfer between groups via personnel rotation: Effects of social identity and knowledge quality. *Organizational Behavior and Human Decision Processes, 96*, 56–71.

Kessler, T., & Mummendey, A. (2001). Is there any scapegoat around? Determinants of intergroup conflict at different categorization levels. *Journal of Personality and Social Psychology, 81*, 1090–1102.

Kovel, J. (1970). *White racism: A psychohistory*. New York, NY: Pantheon.

Pettigrew, T. F., & Tropp, L. R. (2011). *When groups meet: The dynamics of intergroup contact*. New York, NY: Psychology Press.

Piliavin, J. A., Dovidio, J. F., Gaertner, S. L., & Clark, R. D., III. (1981). *Emergency intervention*. New York, NY: Academic Press.

Tajfel, H., & Turner, J. C. (1979). An integrative theory of intergroup conflict. In W. G. Austin & S. Worchel (Eds.), *The social psychology of intergroup relations* (pp. 33–48). Monterey, CA: Brooks/Cole.

Chapter 4: Collaboration: Interdependence in Action[1]

Susan T. Fiske

Eugene Higgins Professor of Psychology
and Professor of Psychology and Public Affairs
Princeton University

Shelley E. Taylor

Distinguished Research Professor
Psychology Department
University of California, Los Angeles

What relationship can provoke all of the following emotions? Awed. Annoyed. Delighted. Amused. Frustrated. Excited. Embarrassed. Satisfied. Ashamed. Proud. Disappointed. Afraid. Hopeful. Pleased. Angry. Thrilled. Guilty.

In collaborations, most of us have felt all the above-mentioned emotions, and more, on multiple occasions. Interdependence, as close-relationship researchers teach us, opens us up to a variety of emotions (Berscheid, 1983). Collaborations on work are no exception to the emotion-provoking rule of interdependence. The term *interdependence* describes situations in which people need each other to facilitate their goals (Kelley et al., 1983). If one of us wants to write a paper, what she may lack—in expertise, time, ideas, data, or resources—can come from someone else, who sees that she can supply some of the qualities that the other person may lack.

When two people (or more) depend on each other for outcomes that matter, such as research publications, they may indeed facilitate each other's goals, causing pride, contentment, and satisfaction. Or they may hinder each other's goals, causing annoyance, frustration, and disappointment. Or they may aid each other in unanticipated ways, causing awe, delight, and pleasure. The publicity of these joint products can be thrilling or embarrassing. One's own role in helping or hindering the collaborator can be the cause of guilt and shame or pleasure and pride.

[1] Dedicated to collaborators, near and far, with deep appreciation.

Let's take some hypothetical examples, and then examine some structures of collaboration, borrowed not from interdependence theory, but from another Fiske's relational models theory (Fiske, 1992, 2004). This chapter closes by examining how an interdependence approach, seen through the lens of relational models, may address some common collaboration issues.

Hypothetical Examples: Any Resemblance to Persons, Living or Dead, Is Mere Coincidence

Dr. Elder invites Ms. Younger to work on an invited paper. Dr. Elder will retain first authorship, but it rapidly becomes apparent to Ms. Younger that she will do all the work for less of the credit. Ms. Younger can decline, fearing for her future, or accept, feeling angry about being exploited but possibly proud of the outcome. Dr. Elder will probably feel hurt and offended if she declines or magnanimous and pleased if she accepts.

Dr. Boss offers to pay Mr. Subordinate in the same circumstances. If Mr. Subordinate agrees, fewer feelings will probably be involved, but Mr. Subordinate's career will not be advanced much, except as a consultant.

Dr. Compulsive and Dr. Relaxed agree to collaborate on a project. Given their stylistic mismatch, will they hatch mutual homicide plots, or will each protect the other from their own worst impulses?

Dr. Peer and Dr. Littermate agree early on to collaborate on virtually everything they publish, adding each other as coauthors even on papers they have barely read. Both achieve fame and tenure at a tender age.

Dr. Colleague sees that Dr. Contemporary's career could use a boost and offers involvement in a new project; they collaborate effectively, and Dr. Colleague cedes first authorship to Dr. Contemporary, who needs it more. Both achieve recognition.

Dr. Quick and Dr. Slow agree to collaborate and proceed to drive each other crazy. They either should (1) never have agreed to work together, (2) set up realistic expectations for deadlines, or (3) consult Drs. Compulsive and Relaxed about undetectable murder methods.

Dr. Idea and Dr. Critic agree to collaborate, with Dr. Idea's job being to talk and Dr. Critic's role to say, "No…no…no…yes!" They achieve great things and lasting friendship.

Dr. Balanced and Dr. Sensible agree on who will do what, deliver on time, provide thoughtful feedback, and revise without being defensive. They also achieve great things and a lasting friendship.

Relational Models of Collaboration

Are there general principles beyond the interdependence–emotion linkage that pertain to and generate insights into collaboration? People have expectations about the nature of their collaborative relationships, which work best if both people have the same framework in mind. What happens if rational Dr. Balanced tries to work with relational Dr. Contemporary? Dr. Balanced sees collaboration through an exchange lens, but Dr. Contemporary sees collaboration communally, as each responding to the other's needs (Clark, Mills, & Powell, 1986). What about Dr. Elder and Ms. Younger, in a power relation, or Dr. Boss and Mr. Subordinate, in a consulting deal?

Some answers may come from a theory describing different forms of relationships, applied to collaboration. Alan Fiske's relational models theory (Fiske, 1992, 2004) describes a theoretically innate human predisposition for four types of relationships, varying with context but universally identifiable. Professional collaborations can take any of these forms, as discussed in what follows.

Collaborators can relate according to what they have in common: communal sharing. Families exemplify this mode, but so do a variety of other tribes, including sometimes the tribe formed by sharing a psychological field's age cohort. As a result of such tribal ties, Drs. Colleague and Contemporary share on the basis of need.

Collaborators can relate on the basis of ordered hierarchy: authority ranking. Dr. Elder and Ms. Younger are embedded in such a hierarchy, as would be Dr. Advisor and Mr. Student, who progress through graduate training, with collaboration initially driven more by the advisor and eventually more by the student. However, advisor-advisee collaborations also carry elements of professional family and communal sharing, as when an advisor shares with an advisee more credit than the work itself may deserve, or vice versa.

Drs. Peer and Littermate, coauthoring everything they do before tenure, are equality matching, engaging in additive balance: one for me, one for you. Turn taking may occur within labs or other ongoing collaborative structures, such as by alternating first-authorship.

Finally, collaborators may relate according to ratios of input and output: market pricing. Dr. Boss, who hires Mr. Subordinate, does so with the mutual understanding that certain investments will be made on both sides, mostly dollars in exchange for hours of effort and expertise.

Each of these four models may apply, or there may be a mixture. Collaborations doubtless work best when both partners share the same internal model of how the collaboration will operate. As a case of mixed but shared models, consider one decades-long, successful collaboration that happens to be close to our hearts and minds.

Fiske and Taylor's Collaboration as a Case Study: Interdependence in Action

Relying on the vocabulary of interdependence theory and relational models theory, consider this case study of collaboration in terms of several common issues of collaboration. Specifically, focus on an early and long-running collaboration between Shelley Taylor, who taught at both Harvard University and University of California, Los Angeles (UCLA), and Susan Fiske, while she worked with her at Harvard, and then long distance from Carnegie Mellon University, the University of Massachusetts at Amherst, and Princeton University.

The collaboration was overdetermined. At first, undergraduate senior Fiske wandered into first-year assistant professor Taylor's office. Fiske wanted some research experience (her goal in seeking the interdependent relationship); she was also seeking a role model, and Taylor, as a young female professor, seemed a good candidate to meet that goal. On her part, Taylor was happy to have a for-credit research assistant (RA) to help run some studies that she had in mind. Taylor had been told, in effect, "If you plan it, they will come," and show up Fiske finally did, along with other students. Taylor and Fiske ended up conducting studies that worked as hypothesized, and this excited Fiske, so she applied for a graduate spot, and the research continued into her graduate training. Fiske helped Taylor found her lab and kept Taylor on task to generate work fast enough to keep the eager Fiske engaged. In return, Taylor taught Fiske how to be a psychological scientist at the cusp of the social cognitive revolution.

They worked hard and played hard, which seemed to Fiske like a pretty good model for a career. The collaboration at that stage had elements of authority ranking (Taylor the professor, Fiske the student), communal sharing (they went clubbing together with a variety of friends), equality matching (they took turns hosting dinners with each other's partners), market pricing (Taylor paid Fiske to be an RA for 6 months after graduation), and communal sharing again (Fiske happily worked full-time for half-time pay and then volunteered part-time after Taylor's start-up funds ran out; Fiske's financial needs were minimal because her commune was a bargain).

After Fiske graduated, they finished and submitted some projects begun together in graduate school, as is often the case. Then, a couple years into her first job, Fiske's department head, Charles Kiesler, offered her a contract in his well-known social-psychology book series, to write an upper-level text on the then-emerging field of social cognition. Fiske was surprised that he had asked her, such a junior person, and was also surprised when he offered her the chance to do the book with or without Taylor. Of course, she wanted Taylor's expertise and collaboration, although she knew that she was supposed to be working without her advisor at that stage in her career. Taylor consented because she saw a chance to define a newly emerging field. In addition, both Fiske and Taylor were teaching social cognition seminars that needed a textbook.

The collaboration has always worked well in many respects. Fiske credits Taylor with making the collaboration pragmatic, direct, fair, loyal, and fun. Taylor credits Fiske with bringing the project in and having the vision, at such a young age, to see the impact that it would have. Also, both of them were pretty poor at this stage of their lives, so the estimated royalties were an incentive (they were absurdly off base, reaping about 10% of what they foolishly thought the book would generate).

For the book, as in previous joint projects, they split up the work in a practical way, cocreating a table of contents based on their respective research interests and teaching experience, and then each choosing which chapters to do, agreeing on some deadlines, and assuming the overall authorship order.

They were direct with each other about who wanted to do what, and which chapters neither wanted to do but someone must; they took turns on the chores as well as the treats. They were direct with each other about what parts of the drafts worked, what didn't, why, and how to fix them. (Early on, this was mostly Taylor guiding Fiske, given their relative seniority and experience.)

They were fair with each other, sharing the workload. They were loyal, even when someone (Fiske) was always slower or needing to make more revisions. And they had fun, building in face-to-face meetings set to the backdrop of perfect Los Angeles weather and "Hotel California." Their goal was to be scholarly but entertaining, and those twin goals started with where and how they worked.

In addition to their respect and fondness for each other's methods and idiosyncrasies, the collaboration benefited from their commitment to the ideas. Indeed, it is hard to imagine a successful collaboration without devotion to the intellectual foundation of a project. At the time, social cognition was criticized within psychology—even within social psychology—as being too narrow, too cognitive, and overly based on artificial experiments with undergraduates. Both of them, however, believed fervently in the merit of the social cognitive perspective and defined their mission as showing why it was important. The subsequent growth of this field suggests that others shared this viewpoint.

Given their mutual understanding of their mixed relational models (authority ranking, equality matching, communal sharing, etc.), their interdependence functioned with few misunderstandings and few disappointments. Mostly, they facilitated each other's goals, resulting in much scholarly pride and mutual appreciation.

Nevertheless, every relationship hits bumps in the road. The age gap meant that Fiske had more to learn than Taylor, so there were doubtless moments, best forgotten, that annoyed each of them (Taylor can be particularly cranky). Any inadvertent failures at equality-matching arrangements were compensated by their communal-sharing relationship. Shared interests in food, wine, art, and dancing helped smooth any tensions.

The bottom line: Each of them probably could have written the book herself, but without Taylor, it would not have covered as much control motivation, positive illusions, or health psychology, and without Fiske, it would not have had as much stereotyping, impression formation, or political psychology. Without Taylor, it might not have dared to be impertinent, and without Fiske, as literary. Taylor improved Fiske's novice writing, and Fiske picked the outrageous red of the first-edition cover. (However, neither is responsible for the cover's dated 1980s wood-block prints that have not aged as gracefully as the authors like to hope they have.)

Nowadays, it's a whole lot easier to Dropbox the tracked-changed and revised chapter files than it was then to write the originals longhand on legal pads, cut-and-paste actual paper inserts, wait for the secretary to type the day's efforts, proofread the inevitable transcription errors, mail the manuscript across the country, scribble on photocopied drafts, mail them back, and revise/retype/ cut and paste accordingly. Admittedly, while they don't miss much from that paper-driven era, they do miss each other's occasional handwritten grateful or congratulatory little notes on half-size university letterhead. E-mail seems so much more fleeting.

When it came to tenure and promotion, the coauthored articles and book did affect the decisions that were made. *Social Cognition* (Fiske & Taylor, 1984, 1991, 2008, 2013) is the most-cited publication for each of the authors (at current writing, more than 10,000 citations on Google Scholar). Arguably, the book defined the field, seeing as it was reviewed favorably in *Science*, appeared in several languages, and continues to be republished in new editions. Nonetheless, despite having been invited by her department head to write the book, Fiske learned during her review that it had been a bad idea for tenure and promotion, both because it was written with her graduate advisor and because it was seen as a textbook. Fiske was granted a "terminal promotion," so she was required to move on, but with happier results, since she ended up in a better fit at the University of Massachusetts. Without rearguing an ancient case, Fiske has no regrets. Taylor had already failed to get tenure at Harvard, and by then happily settled at the University of California, Los Angeles, so these criticisms mattered less to her career. She also has no regrets about choosing this area of scholarship and, especially, this collaboration.

The collaboration benefited from each of them having a second field about which they were passionate (Fiske in intergroup relations, Taylor in health) which both fueled their social cognition research and writing and provided an intellectual and personal respite when there was the occasional period of stress or lapse in enthusiasm.

However, according to Taylor, Fiske saw the breadth implications of social cognition better than Taylor did. Recognizing now that social cognition provided much of the early scholarship base for behavioral economics, for example, reveals that failing to make connections like these early on was a missed opportunity.

Conclusions

With the right person, the right timing, and mutual appreciation, collaboration can be a joy, benefiting both career and friendship. We think interdependence is important to recognize, especially when experiencing the inevitable emotional ups and downs. Thinking about each person's relational expectations— communal sharing, equality matching, authority ranking, market pricing, and so on—may help avert misunderstandings. Collaboration profits from being explicit about expectations, direct about feedback, and forgiving about faux pas, along with celebrating early and often what the collaborators share as a scientific project. However framed, the collaborative synergy creates energy, intellectual and personal. Like any close relationship, when it works well, it's life-sustaining.

■ REFERENCES ■

Berscheid, E. (1983). Emotion. In H. H. Kelley et al. (Eds.), *Close relationships* (pp. 110–168). New York, NY: W. H. Freeman.

Clark, M. S., Mills, J., & Powell, M. C. (1986). Keeping track of needs in communal and exchange relationships. *Journal of Personality and Social Psychology, 51*(2), 333–338.

Fiske, A. P. (1992). The four elementary forms of sociality: Framework for a unified theory of social relations. *Psychological Review, 99*(4), 689–723.

Fiske, A. P. (2004). Relational models theory 2.0. In N. Haslam (Ed.), *Relational models theory: A contemporary overview* (pp. 3–25). Mahwah, NJ: Lawrence Erlbaum Associates.

Fiske, S. T., & Taylor, S. E. (1984). *Social cognition*. New York, NY: Random House.

Fiske, S. T., & Taylor, S. E. (1991). *Social cognition* (2nd ed.). New York, NY: McGraw-Hill. Translated into Chinese as S. T. Fiske & S. E. Taylor (1994). *Social cognition: How people understand self and others*. Translated by Zhang Qinlin & Chen Xingqiang.

Fiske, S. T., & Taylor, S. E. (2008). *Social cognition: From brains to culture*. New York, NY: McGraw-Hill. Translation into Italian by Apogeo Srl (Milan), 2009; into Korean by McGraw-Hill (Korea), 2011; in Chinese (short form) by McGraw-Hill Education (Asia), 2010; in French by Mardaga (2011); and in Spanish.

Fiske, S. T., & Taylor, S. E. (2013). *Social cognition: From brains to culture* (2nd ed.). London, England: Sage.

Kelley, H. H., Berscheid, E., Christensen, A., Harvey, J. H., Huston, T. L., Levinger, G., ... Peterson, D. R. (Eds.). (1983). *Close relationships*. New York, NY: W. H. Freeman.

Chapter 5: Psychology's Folie à Trois: 'Til Death Do Us Part

Jeff Greenberg

Professor of Psychology
University of Arizona

Tom Pyszczynski

Distinguished Professor
Department of Psychology
University of Colorado Colorado Springs

Sheldon Solomon

Professor of Psychology
Skidmore College

They say that three is a charm: the Three Stooges; the Three Musketeers; the Marx Brothers (no, Zeppo and Gummo don't count); Emerson, Lake, and Palmer; the Supremes; the Three Tenors; the Three Faces of Eve. And us. We are one of the few collaborative trios in psychology—and to our knowledge, the most enduring. We've coauthored over 100 journal articles, many chapters, and books as well. We've worked on numerous National Science Foundation (NSF) grants. We began working together back in 1978, and we're still collaborating on a variety of projects—including this one, in which we describe how our collaboration started, how it has persisted, and mainly what we have learned about the benefits of collaborating, as well as the challenges that arise. Hopefully doing so will be of value to young psychological scientists for their own current and future collaborations.

Origins of Our Collaboration: From the Beginning

We first began working together at the University of Kansas (KU) in 1978. Sheldon came to KU in 1975. Tom entered the program in 1976, and Jeff arrived in 1978 with a master's degree from Southern Methodist University. Jeff met

Tom at the start of the fall semester, and they bonded immediately because of their common interests in jazz and causal attribution. They shared an office with other social psychology graduate students, and Jeff would occasionally see one of them sleeping all afternoon, curled up in a blue bean bag chair (which currently sits in Jeff's lab). Tom told Jeff that this was a guy named Sheldon and that he was going to like him because "Sheldon thinks *everything* sucks." It turned out that "Rip Van Sheldon" was working nights in a dog food factory churning out tons of kibble. Eventually, Jeff caught Sheldon in one of his brief moments awake, and, shortly thereafter, a three-way collaboration was born.

We were all interested in the psychological underpinnings of prejudice and self-serving biases. We found that our ways of thinking about these issues were remarkably compatible but that we each brought unique ideas to our discussions. An optimal combination of intellectual compatibility with independent thinking is one of the most important ingredients for fruitful collaboration. We were also lucky to have been mentored by Jack Brehm, who placed more value on students developing their own ideas than following his own research agenda. That freedom and flexibility was invigorating but also a bit daunting, especially when we saw the travails that our more senior graduate student colleagues and postdocs experienced as they faced a job market that was becoming increasingly competitive. We were unnerved when one of our more senior graduate school colleagues was forced to consider a position in which his first task would be to figure out how few chocolate chips a cookie company could put into their cookies without consumers noticing. The scary prospect of spending our lives helping corporations fool consumers motivated us to redouble our efforts to build marketable CVs.

Our shared professional interests, goals, and fates were certainly part of what brought us together. But the foundation of our collaboration, and the most likely reason it has lasted so long, was the close friendship we forged in our time at KU. We shared a love of music, sports, altered states, and ethnic cuisine. We also shared a view of life as often absurd and unfair, as well as an increasingly skeptical view of the field that we were preparing to become part of. Social psychology in the late 1970s and early to mid-1980s was becoming increasingly dominated by perspectives that conceived of human beings as sophisticated information-processing machines, devoid of needs or emotions. One prominent leader of this movement told us that it was only a matter of time before advances in understanding the mechanisms of cognition would render concepts of motivation and emotion unnecessary distractions to the forward progress of cognitive science. Could it really be that the things that drew us to psychology were on their way to the trash bin of intellectual history?

Our disappointment with the direction the field was taking was tempered by the sense of humor regarding the many absurd aspects of life that we shared. It was surely no coincidence that our most prized weekly gathering centered on watching *Monty Python's Flying Circus* on our local PBS station. The Pythons' sense of absurdity, joy in skewering tradition and pomposity, and evolving comic way of confronting existential issues, as in their 1979 movie *The Life of Brian*, fit perfectly with our own emerging worldviews and showed us that humor and satire could be an effective way of illuminating even the most tragic life circumstances. So although we felt out of step with our chosen profession, our shared sense of humor and absurdity—along with the many other things we had in common—forged a strong bond that helped us persevere and eventually directed us to focus on the kinds of issues that brought us to the study of social psychology in the first place.

Our point here is that an enormously important reason that our collaboration has been successful and enduring is that it was—and continues to be—fun. We enjoy each other's company and the conversations, whether serious or silly, that inevitably start when we get together. Perhaps it's the way that the serious and silly often become intertwined in these discussions that provide the exhilaration that energizes our work. Although there are certainly times that it's necessary to bear down and focus on the intricate or mundane details of what needs to be accomplished, we're convinced that not taking life or ourselves too seriously and being able to see the humor in what we're doing is an important motivator for working together. We suspect that it may even increase the creativity of the ideas we generate. Research has shown that exposure to humor can indeed increase creativity (e.g., Ziv, 1976). This may be due to both the positive effects that humor generates and the fact that much humor involves stretching the boundaries of the thoughts and associations that a topic typically brings to mind—the very essence of creativity. It certainly seems to work that way for us. More generally, we are convinced that collaborations (indeed, most things in life) work better when they are enjoyable.

We also shared a deep admiration for our mentor, Jack Brehm, and a desire to emulate his characteristics as a psychologist and human being. Jack had a deep curiosity about the determinants of human behavior, but at the same time, he was wary of faddish or reactive research. He felt that it was generally a waste of energy to design studies in reaction to current research, especially if it was solely for the sake of piling up publications. Jack was skeptical of social psychologists' burgeoning preoccupation with cognitive information-processing models of human behavior unless they were situated within a motivational framework. Surely understanding how and what people were thinking about was important; but without also considering the fundamentally motivational question of *why* people were thinking at all and what needs their thoughts served, social cognitive approaches were descriptive rather than explanatory and seemed destined to miss much of what was most important and interesting about human nature. Jack's general approach to psychology provided a beacon that gave us hope and made us realize that, as both professionals and human beings, it was our own responsibility to find ideas that we felt were worth pursuing.

Jack was very nondirective in general. Certainly he never sat us down and explicitly told us that it was important for us to collaborate. However, he was a master of implicit influence, just by how he went about his science and directed our program. In his subtle ways, he conveyed to us that science is a fundamentally social and collaborative enterprise by encouraging the exchange of ideas (and critical scrutiny of them) in a playful and frank fashion, both in and out of the classroom. Seminars on campus and social gatherings at Jack's house were typically wide-ranging raucous and jocular verbal scrums. All ideas—from the sublime to the sublimely ridiculous—were encouraged and seriously considered. We still have fond memories of Jack being keenly attentive as earnest grad students (including us) made an impassioned case for their latest theoretical, empirical, or methodological insights, and then watching him bursting into convulsive laughter a few seconds or minutes later, followed by a thoughtful and patient explanation of why they were wrong, and why it's fine to be wrong, so long as you learn from your mistakes—echoing Sir Francis Bacon's 17th-century proclamation that "[t]ruth emerges more readily from error than from confusion."

We also admired the close connections that Jack maintained with his current and former students and colleagues, and were struck by Jack's genuine concern for their personal and professional well-being, regardless of whether they stayed in the academic world or moved on to applied or other vocational pursuits. We've tried to do the same. We are pretty sure, particularly in retrospect, that our years together at KU working with Jack had a tremendous influence on the nature of our collaboration thereafter. Mixing work and play, feeling free to study what truly interested us, batting ideas around (and often down) in the spirit of open inquiry, forging strong personal and professional connections to peers and students, and a commitment to theory-driven programmatic research—all of these are things we gratefully inherited from Jack, and we have tried to make central to our ongoing collaborations after graduate school and with our own students once we were scattered by the necessities of the job market.

All for One: The Value of Collaboration

When we started working together in graduate school, we really didn't plan on embarking on a 35-year collaborative project. But when we struck out on our individual academic careers, continuing the discussion we began at Kansas felt like the natural and obvious thing to do. We all had ideas of our own to pursue, but we all intuitively knew that talking with each other about them was the best way to move those projects forward. Usually just mentioning the general direction one of us was going with his thinking would lead to quick ideas about how this related to other ideas and past work, variations on the theme that took it in interesting new directions, ideas for operationalizing variables, and even ideas for clever titles for the papers that would hopefully emerge. We're pretty sure that each of us could have been successful on our own, but it was obvious that bouncing our ideas off of each other yielded high dividends in terms of improved ideas and strategies for pursuing them. And it continued to be fun. Back then, in the days before e-mail and the Internet, we spent enough time on the phone with each other to draw the ire of our department administrators. But it was clear that the discussion should and would continue.

What made us such good collaborators for each other? No doubt, the many interests, values, and attitudes that we held in common before we met set the stage. But our unique proclivities, talents, and quirks probably also played a role.

We think we bring a nice set of complementary strengths to our collaboration: one of us is particularly scholarly and a voracious reader, one is a very integrative thinker who enjoys thinking about how things that appear different often share similarities, and the third is the most analytic, adept at finding gaps in an argument, and the optimal design for assessing an idea. In our experience, collaborative relationships work best when there is an optimal level of shared perspective, unique approach, and complementary skills.

Along with providing complementary strengths, collaborators should offer critical evaluations of one's reasoning, thoroughness, and the quality of the project on which one is working. They provide the reality check that we all sometimes need. Everyone is at least somewhat myopic regarding their own ideas—collaboration provides the corrective lenses that enable us to better evaluate our own work. The critical eyes of a collaborator can save us from wasting time chasing down a flawed idea. It can also be invaluable when dealing with editors and funding agencies, especially after a rejection that seems, on first blush, to be unwarranted, unfair, or evidence of the evaluators' deeply rooted biases. We've saved each other the embarrassment—and later need to apologize—for more than a few hastily written letters to editors in response to rejected papers. It also sometimes happens that one's collaborators confirm one's initial inclinations and provide the impetus to go forward with a challenge to an editor, albeit usually in a more diplomatic and tactful way.

Another factor that can contribute to productive collaboration is the extent to which a problem or topic has generative potential. If the idea you're working on easily sheds light on a lot of related issues, it's a lot easier for a collaboration to blossom because there will be a lot of opportunities for all members of the team to contribute potentially useful and important pieces to the solution of the puzzle. And as these new directions and variations on the theme emerge, it provides both personal satisfaction and direction for empirical efforts to get the ball rolling. Generative theoretical ideas fuel creative research and interesting research findings fuel conceptual expansion of theories—it's a cyclical and reciprocal process, which feeds on itself. Fertile ground for collaboration makes it much easier for any collaborative effort to bear fruit.

Collaboration often leads to interesting findings and new ideas. It also validates one's thinking about the issues and ideas at hand and enhances one's sense of competence as a scientist. In the language of terror management theory, it validates one's worldview and enhances one's self-esteem, thus reducing anxiety and improving one's general sense of well-being; it's also very likely to strengthen the bonds within the collaborative team. Our point here is that successful collaboration helps psychologists meet the same needs that they study in people in general, and, for this reason, the success is likely to encourage further collaboration. To the extent that such validation increases the overall psychological equanimity of the team, it's also likely to facilitate creativity in their future endeavors.

A cohesive collaborative relationship is a form of collective identity that can help one weather the tough times that most of us face from time to time. The academic world can be a rough place in which to live: from facing the ever-competitive job market, to the constant stream of evaluations mandated by one's university, to the rigors of the peer-review process, unfriendly colleagues, political squabbles within departments, and balancing one's career with other aspects of one's life. A sense of collective identity also makes it easier to take risks with ideas, challenge accepted wisdom, and generally take a bolder approach to one's work. We were very much swimming upstream when we proposed terror management theory back in the mid-1980s. Our collaborative relationship provided the validation and confidence that encouraged us to persevere in our pursuit of these ideas in the face of skeptical colleagues.

The Hoi Polloi: The Nature of Collaboration in Science

Science is an inherently collaborative enterprise. New research is always based on a foundation of earlier theories and research. In addition, the training of new scientists involves mentoring, which we view very much as another form of collaboration. As experienced mentors, we of course know more than our students about the pragmatics of the field, such as how to write in "journalese," negotiate with editors, and so forth. However, we have always tried to treat our students as collaborators, with as much potential to contribute to the field as we have, if not more. One key aspect of this is encouraging our students to develop their own directions for research and following them on journeys that they lead. These are among the many things we learned from Jack Brehm. We are also gratified to say that virtually all of our former students are friends as well, and we have continued to collaborate with many of them on occasion as they have developed their own productive research programs.

Maintaining an extended family of colleagues and former students creates a community that is valuable in myriad ways. Perhaps most concretely, it creates a larger pool of ideas, insights, expertise, and knowledge from which one can draw. In a field as rapidly expanding and changing as our own, where it is increasingly difficult to keep up with the research literature in even relatively circumscribed areas, an extended scholarly family provides easy access to information and expertise that no one individual is likely to possess. Extended communities of like-minded but independent scholars also provide much-needed critical input on ideas and strategies that might elude any individual or small team, due to groupthink or other forms of irrational exuberance.

Over our careers, we have collaborated with well over two dozen current and former students and colleagues from around the globe. Of course, the cliché "Too many cooks spoil the stew" does have some validity; committee decisions are often ones that compromise toward mediocrity. But the key to avoiding that problem is to have a lead dog for each particular project, preferably a dog very open to input from team members, but also driven to keep the project moving forward in bold, creative directions. Collaborative projects, especially complex multifaceted ones, require that inputs and responsibilities be coordinated. It's all too easy to diffuse responsibility when there's a lot to be done. And given the busy schedules of most academics and multiple, changing responsibilities, it's usually a good idea to have someone take the reins and remind his or her partners to get their jobs done. Even the most highly motivated researchers can easily get overwhelmed or distracted—a person who takes responsibility for getting the project done can minimize these problems.

A lead dog can also facilitate decision making. We make virtually all really important decisions, especially about theoretical positions, by consensus, and rely on a majority vote in cases when an issue is not vital and consensus is just not going to happen—one particular advantage of a three-person team. But there are also issues for which our discussions don't lead to a single ideal solution on which we generally agree; and there are issues that are more matters of style and personal taste than logic and reasoning. In situations like these, it's good to have a person in charge who can make those final, tough, and often subjective decisions.

Reflections: Collaborating With the Dead and the Young...

In this section, we provide a few examples of how our collaborations have worked, not just among the three of us both also with the help of both older and younger generations. Two fundamental questions arose out of our discussions and research in grad school. First, why do people resort to such elaborate mental gymnastics—self-serving attributions, compensation, self-handicapping, and so on—to protect their self-esteem? Second, why do people have such a propensity to denigrate those different from themselves? These questions soon led us to the work of Ernest Becker (e.g., Becker, 1962, 1973, 1975) and the development of terror management theory (TMT; Greenberg, Pyszczynski, & Solomon, 1986; Solomon, Greenberg, & Pyszczynski, 1991). In a very real sense, we have been collaborating with Becker ever since.

After many discussions and some preliminary writing, the three of us formulated a concise synthesis of Becker's ideas, which we labeled *TMT*. This theory posits that the uniquely human awareness of death gives rise to potentially paralyzing terror that is assuaged through the construction and maintenance of cultural worldviews: humanly constructed beliefs about reality shared by members of a group that confer a sense that one is a person of value in a world of meaning (i.e., self-esteem) and, hence, is eligible for literal or symbolic immortality.

Perhaps not surprisingly, although we were enamored with TMT from the outset, our peers in experimental social psychology were quite skeptical and kept insisting that they would not take the theory seriously until we produced empirical evidence to support it. While we'll save the full story for our memoirs, some broad observations and specific examples from this journey of accumulating empirical evidence in support of TMT (and modifications of the theory that ensued in light of new findings) illustrate, among other things, how collaborating is really often (if not always) an enterprise of broad scope involving a lot of people in the scientific community and those in one's social sphere who may or may not appear as coauthors on one's publications.

For Becker, the unconscious fear of death is a constant, not a variable, making the testing of TMT particularly challenging. We arrived at the idea that if our synthesis of Becker's ideas was right, people should become more defensive of their worldview after being reminded of their mortality. Our first test of this hypothesis relied on collaboration with one of Jeff's students, an undergraduate named Deborah Lyon, who had returned to school to complete her degree. Jeff had agreed to work on a thesis with Deb, and she was interested in judges' decision making. Fortunately, she was dating a municipal court judge who could give us access to fellow judges. The general idea was to give the judges a packet of questionnaires that included some measures of personality aspects and have the judges decide a hypothetical case similar to the ones that municipal court judges in Tucson commonly preside over.

With her boyfriend's help, Deb came up with materials typical for setting bond for an alleged prostitute. Jeff suggested to Deb that we slip a reminder of death into half the packets, so we could see if that would increase the judges' desire to uphold the law and thus increase the bond they would set. The next question was how to remind the judges of their mortality, and Deb again came through in a big way. She had taken a class on death and loss and showed Jeff an exercise that the instructor gave to the students. We modified that for our purposes, and this became the now-classic mortality salience induction (Rosenblatt, Greenberg, Solomon, Pyszczynski, & Lyon, 1989), which has been used in hundreds of studies. To say this brief period of collaboration with Deborah (and her boyfriend, who shall remain nameless!) was pivotal to the development and ascendancy of TMT would be a gross understatement.

Here's another example. In the mid-1990s, some students with whom we collaborated were similarly central to developing a new laboratory measure of aggression, which has gained some popularity. Its genesis again illustrates the value of bringing in additional student collaborators. Jeff was working with an ambitious undergrad, Holly McGregor, who noted that although we had written about TMT explaining real-world aggression, we had not demonstrated in the lab that mortality salience increased aggression. So we set out to do so. At the time, Sheldon was visiting Jeff in Tucson from Saratoga Springs, and he, Jeff, Holly, and grad students Joel Lieberman, Jamie Arndt, and Linda Simon were sitting around Jeff's crowded office thinking about how we were going to do that. We rejected the shock paradigm because it might remind students of the Milgram paradigm. Sheldon came up with an idea inspired partly by all the Mexican food we had been eating during his visit and partly by a recent incident in New England in which a cook spiked the food of some cops with…hot sauce.

Once we had that idea of using hot sauce allocation as a measure of aggression, we researched the use of hot sauce for aggressive acts in the real world— for instance, it's not an uncommon instrument for child abuse—and collaboratively worked out a rather complex cover story, procedure, and set of materials that could allow us to see if mortality salience would indeed increase aggression against a critic of participants' worldviews. One person came up with the cover story of personality and food preferences. Another pointed out that the hot sauce needed to be painfully hot and that the participants needed to taste it so they could know that. Someone else pointed out that participants needed to know that the recipients of the hot sauce disliked spicy foods. Still others suggested that we needed the right kind of cup and spoon for the hot sauce, the right way to measure the amount allocated, the right way to attack participants' worldviews, and so on.

When all this was done, we found in a series of studies that mortality salience indeed increased aggression against the worldview critic (McGregor et al., 1998). Perhaps more important, since then, hot sauce allocation has been used to assess the effects of many variables on aggression, including frustration, social rejection, handling a gun, genes, testosterone, and misogynistic song lyrics (e.g., McDermott et al., 2009).

Grips, Grunts, and Groans

The challenges of collaborations vary with the nature of particular projects. We have found collaborating on research especially easy and exciting, and, as our examples illustrate, have usually brought in additional minds who have often added greatly to our research endeavors. Collaborating on the writing of research papers for journal publications has also almost always been very smooth and easy. Journal articles have a clear structure, and the goals and strategies for successful writing of this kind have always helped us "stay on the same page." Grant proposals are similarly straightforward. We have also found book coediting very straightforward.

However, as projects become less inherently structured, we have found them to become more challenging to write collaboratively. Without a clear road map, it's easy for different people to have very different visions of how a piece should be organized and the kind of writing style that should be used. Book chapters offer some challenge along these lines, but we have found this problem to be much more daunting for academic books, trade books, and textbooks (in ascending order of difficulty, with textbook writing the worst). There are so many different ways to write textbook chapters, so many choices, and no one "best" way to proceed with regard to writing style, examples, the order of presentation of the material, and what material to include and not include. This is the only form of collaboration in which we found ourselves unable to resolve differences in a fruitful way. Obviously, most textbooks are collaborative enterprises, so it can be done. But it didn't work for us. (Hey, even the Marx Brothers made a few bad films.)

Probably the most unique aspect of our three-way collaboration is how long it has lasted. Our knowledge of other well-known collaborative teams in social psychology is that the vast majority have a limited shelf life, with the partners eventually going their separate ways. From the perspective of advancing science, whether a collaborative team endures probably doesn't matter. They work until they don't, and then people move on to other, often reinvigorating collaborations. We suspect that sooner or later, resentments build up, egos clash, a sense of staleness sets in, partners get pulled in divergent directions, and grad students take over as new collaborations emerge. We've certainly felt some of these strains at times, but our friendship has always kept our partnership going, whether professionally for better or worse.

No Duck Soup, This Collaborating: Our Formula

Our overall recommendations for fruitful long-term collaborations are not too different from what we would suggest for long-term close relationships.

First, choose your collaborators wisely. As in all aspects of life, people who have unstable self-esteem, borderline personality tendencies, and other bases of cognitive rigidity are not generally good long-term partners, although they may be bright, creative, and skilled. The same goes for people who lack motivation or conscience. The optimal foundation for long-term collaboration is one of shared values, shared views of the field and of life, and shared questions. These commonalities help forge the friendship and mutual respect that are critical for enduring professional success as a team. Beyond that, complementary strengths can lead to particularly fruitful collaborations. In our case, as we noted earlier, one of us is particularly scholarly, one is a very integrative thinker, and the third is the most analytic.

Second, for each particular project, make sure that it's clear whom the lead person is, as that person will have the final say on that particular set of studies or paper. It may also be useful to set up particular role expectations for each collaborator, although we have found flexibility more important than precise role ascriptions. That is probably because none of the three of us has much need for structure. If collaborators are in great need of structure, more well-defined roles would likely work better.

Third, don't expect your collaborators to be perfect. No one is. Everyone has quirks, limitations, and blind spots. Disagreements about study designs, writing strategies, and theoretical positions will arise, albeit only occasionally if a partnership is going well. When such issues arise, two factors facilitate good solutions. First, there has to be a working consensus on who is the lead person for the particular project, and that the lead person has the final say. Second, clear and constructive communication is critical. If you're not the lead on a project but you disagree with something, make your case as respectfully and logically as you can. If the lead person wants the work to be as good as it can be, he or she should be open to reasoned arguments. If you're persuasive, great; if not, let it go. Many decisions are judgment calls, and there is often not one certain answer. The cliché "Pick your battles" is also a helpful hint for collaborating well. You don't want to question every step along the way, even if you would do things differently; some issues are more important than others.

When you have a strong friendship, it is generally easier to have open discussions over disagreements that end in optimal resolutions. Respecting your collaborators and recognizing your own and your collaborators' strengths and weaknesses also help a lot. For example, you might think that a certain operationalization or statistical analysis is best for a particular project, but if a teammate who is more adept with that particular skill or knowledge base thinks otherwise, deferring is usually the way to go.

Finally, bringing in fresh talent is very helpful for advancing research programs. New people bring new perspectives and ideas. While our trio has been relatively constant, many new students and colleagues have brought a great deal of freshness to the directions that our work has taken over the last 35 years.

We hope that these thoughts have some value to you as you think about and decide on your own collaborations. And we hope your collaborations are as long lasting, fruitful, and enjoyable as ours have been and continue to be.

▓ REFERENCES ▓

Becker, E. (1962). *The birth and death of meaning: An interdisciplinary perspective on the problem of man*. New York, NY: Free Press.

Becker, E. (1973). *The denial of death*. New York, NY: Free Press.

Becker, E. (1975). *Escape from evil*. New York, NY: Free Press.

Greenberg, J., Pyszczynski, T., & Solomon, S. (1986). The causes and consequences of a need for self-esteem: A terror management theory. In R. F. Baumeister (Ed.), *Public self and private self* (pp. 189–212). New York, NY: Springer-Verlag.

McDermott, R., Tingley, D., Cowden, J., Frazzetto, G., Johnson, D. D. P. (2009). Monoamine oxidase A gene (MAOA) predicts behavioral aggression following provocation. *Proceedings of the National Academy of Sciences, 106*, 2118–2123.

McGregor, H., Lieberman, J., Greenberg, J., Solomon, S., Arndt, J., Simon, L., & Pyszczynski, T. (1998). Terror management and aggression: Evidence that mortality salience motivates aggression against worldview threatening others. *Journal of Personality and Social Psychology, 74*, 590–605.

Rosenblatt, A., Greenberg, J., Solomon, S., Pyszczynski, T., & Lyon, D. (1989). Evidence for terror management theory I: The effects of mortality salience on reactions to those who violate or uphold cultural values. *Journal of Personality and Social Psychology, 57*, 681–690.

Solomon, S., Greenberg, J., & Pyszczynski, T. (1991). A terror management theory of social behavior: On the psychological functions of self-esteem and cultural worldviews. In M. P. Zanna (Ed.), *Advances in experimental social psychology* (Vol. 24, pp. 93–159). San Diego, CA: Academic Press.

Ziv, A. (1976). Facilitating effects of humor on creativity. *Journal of Educational Psychology, 68*, 318–322.

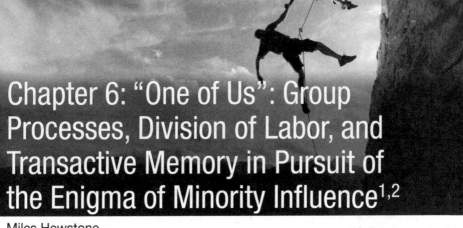

Chapter 6: "One of Us": Group Processes, Division of Labor, and Transactive Memory in Pursuit of the Enigma of Minority Influence[1,2]

Miles Hewstone

Professor of Social Psychology and Public Policy
Director, Oxford Centre for the Study of Intergroup Conflict
University of Oxford

Robin Martin

Professor of Organisational Psychology
Alliance Manchester Business School
University of Manchester

> *Every sin is the result of a collaboration.*
>
> —Seneca the Younger; ca. 4 BC–AD 65

> *The company makes the feast.*
>
> —Proverb, 17th century

The Odd Couple or a Band of Brothers?

One of us is English, middle-class, private-school-educated, and supports Arsenal, the stylish London-based football team; he also believes that English grammar matters. One of us is Welsh, working-class, state-school-educated,

---

[1] In all collaborations, it is important to openly acknowledge the extent of respective contributions. We have often joked that we would one day publish a paper with our respective contributions indicated by the font size in which each author's name appears. Given the nature of this volume, we were tempted to take the opportunity to do this. Instead, we simply note that any misattributed quotations are entirely the fault of the first author and that any typographical or grammatical errors are due to the second.

[2] Acknowledgments: Order of authorship was determined by an equation based on age, H-index, and weight (in kilograms).

and supports Arsenal's bitter rivals, Manchester United, the more successful team from the North of England; he asks, "What are English grammars?"
We do indeed make an odd couple. But as we relate herein, we have moved
beyond these surface-level differences; found common ground on deeper,
more research-related goals; and have collaborated over many years. As the
epigrams at the beginning of this chapter suggest, collaboration may have vic-
es as well as virtues. But our experience, all things considered, is that it has
been a distinctly positive, enjoyable, and creative experience. As we also relate,
this collaboration has functioned as a kind of "buffer" that has helped us to
keep going in the face of frustrating obstacles that almost inevitably block the
route forward to academic success (rejected papers or unfunded grant proposals, for example), especially when one is trying to challenge existing opinion.
We relate briefly how our paths came to cross, some key social-psychological
aspects of our collaboration, and why we believe that it has endured.

In the Beginning

We are not exactly sure when we first met. One of us recalls that he first heard of
the other's name in about 1982; he was then "a keen undergraduate student at
Plymouth." Some postdocs had gone to the British Psychological Society Social
Psychology Conference, and one claimed (evidently incorrectly) that "the new
wonder boy of social psych was someone named Miles Hewstone." Apparently
so in awe of his lofty presence, she even claimed that "he is the future of social
psychology, he's everywhere...." The other has no recollection whatsoever of
ever hearing of his erstwhile collaborator. He claims he was "under the influence" at the time they met, first collaborated, and first published.

One of us (evidently also under the influence) then wrote the other
(at that time in Paris, working under Serge Moscovici), asking if he would
supervise his PhD. The other wrote back (in longhand in those days), very
encouragingly, but explained why he was not the best man for that particular
job. One of us asked his supervisor if the other was a suitable PhD examiner,
only to be told, "He is too young, too much to prove, and would be difficult."
One of us has confirmed that, at that time, the assessment was right. In fact,
"the age thing" may not be an insignificant factor in our collaboration. We
are roughly the same age (although one of us insists that the 3-year difference distinguishes middle age from youth) and, for much of our collaboration time, we have occupied the same academic rank. This has made us
a team of equals, completely lacking in within-team competition for first-
authorships and the like.

This is not, of course, to say that collaborations with large age gaps don't
work. Of course they do, and we have many that we value greatly. But our
equal-age/equal-status collaboration in some ways frees us of the responsibilities of mentoring and simply allows us to sit back and enjoy the research.
Perhaps this rather hedonistic approach to research is further strengthened by
the fact that, for some time, our area of collaboration has not been the major
topic of research for either of us. It is simply a research area that we have

both long found fascinating; our joint work is intellectually stimulating, it is great fun, and every paper is a bonus. We have found this a joy in the world of academe that is increasingly dominated by outputs, H-index values, and so on. Our closeness in age and status has also meant that we have avoided R. K. Merton's (1968) "Matthew effect," whereby the better known of two collaborating scientists gets the lion's share of the credit for the work. (Although in our case, it might simply be that no one noticed the work in the first place.)

We first met when one of us had just begun his first teaching job at Bristol University (1985); we had a good meeting, and the elder citizen gave advice on doctoral research to the young scholar. Wilderness years ensued (we come to view these now as a happy interlude) before we met again at a conference in the 1990s, and then fate threw us together at the Department of Psychology of Cardiff University in 1995. The department was not a happy place. Social psychology was very much at the bottom of the hierarchy (somewhat below cognitive and neuropsychology, but a bit above the lab rats), with the consequence that several outstanding social psychologists went in (but unlike the lab rats) then out of the revolving door in the space of just a few years. We toughed it out, staying 7 and 4 years, respectively. We were lucky to be joined by an able PhD student, Antonis Gardikiotis, with whom we continue to collaborate. But it proved, ultimately, a time of ferment for our joint work; and perhaps our collaboration, and our friendship, grew because of, rather than despite, the unpropitious atmosphere of the department. It was not "me against the world"; it was the two of us (a numerical minority).

We have now been working together for nearly 20 years. We got our first joint grant in 1995, and put out our first joint publication in 1999. Together, we have published 15 articles in peer-reviewed journals, 12 chapters in edited books, and coedited one volume and counting. This output is nothing compared to that of many contributors to this volume, but recall that this has not been our main area of research; we have continued in this area because we believe that issues of social influence should remain at the heart of social psychology, and also because we so enjoy working together. We have organized numerous symposia at international conferences and a Small Group Meeting (at Oxford) supported by the European Association of Social Psychology (EASP). It was on this occasion that one of us expressed his thanks to the other for organizing the conference in the ancient historical buildings of New College, Oxford (founded 1379) by complaining that the floor sloped more than the graph in one of our recent articles. All of our joint work has been on social influence, with the main focus being on the development of a new theoretical approach to explaining when and how minority versus majority sources have a greater impact on attitudes (as discussed further later in this chapter). Our intention has been simple: to provide a theoretical framework for understanding the conditions under which people will process and be influenced by persuasive messages from a numerical majority or minority. This "simple" goal, as will unfold later, was made more complex by the multitude of different and often contradictory findings in the literature.

Influential Social Psychological Processes in Our Collaboration

Being a discipline about social processes, social psychology potentially has a great deal to contribute to the study of collaboration. Viewed from the standpoint of our own partnership, we have identified four key processes that help to explain the success (or at least the longevity) of our collaboration: need complementarity, motivation and coordination loss in groups, transactive memory, and social impact.

Need Complementarity

How do marital partners choose each other? In a famous analysis, Winch, Ktsanes, and Ktsanes (1955) claimed support for the hypothesis that husbands and wives selected each other on the basis of complementary needs. Among other aspects of "complementariness," they highlighted the assertive-receptive dimension and reported that high "assertives" tended to marry high "receptives." We don't think either of us is particularly high or low on this dimension, or that we are complementary on it, but we are complementary on many other dimensions.

One of us brings to the table a wide knowledge of the field of social psychology and injected ideas and methods from social cognition into our research from the outset. He loves designing studies, "polishing" a first draft, and, most of all, finding at least one suitable quotation, sometimes to round off the study and sometimes around which to base a study (it might even be suggested that, like Poo-Bah in Gilbert and Sullivan's *Mikado*, he views evidence as "merely corroborative detail intended to give artistic verisimilitude to a bald and unconvincing narrative").[3] Unfortunately, he also has a tendency to hibernate, especially from answering e-mail (neither of us, however, particularly likes to use the telephone for work; we are more "doers" than "discussers," and we move things forward by presenting each other with something written, which is to be edited, mauled, or ridiculed, as appropriate).

The other one brings an encyclopedic knowledge of theory and research on minority influence, and insights from organizational psychology. He loves data analysis (and is so much better at it than the other) and has heroic patience with this dark art; he is terrific at getting out a first draft.

We always decide early, however, who the lead author is; it is his responsibility to provide a full draft to the other. There may well be a few gaps, with requests (sometimes demands) for "[expletive deleted] input needed here," but unlike some other teams, we write together in series, rather than parallel, and we don't each appropriate particular sections of the paper that just do not feel right for us. We have found this mode of working to be very helpful. The road from conception of study to publication—often via endless redrafts, reanalyses,

---

[3] W. S. Gilbert and A. Sullivan, *The Mikado*, 1885 (Act 2).

rejections, and resubmissions—can be a long one, and when one of us flags, the other will rally us. Sadly, both of us are terrible with deadlines—ask this volume's editors! (We live our lives by that famous quotation "I love deadlines. I love the whooshing noise they make as they fly by.")[4] In an ideal world, we would find someone to turn our folie-à-deux into a ménage-à-trois; whoever joined us would have to have an impeccable record of punctuality in answering e-mail and delivering work on time.[5]

Motivation and Coordination Loss in Groups

From the perspective of group processes, we might consider co-researching as a prototypical group task (in this case, the group is a dyad). Building on Steiner's (1972) pioneering distinction between motivation loss and coordination loss in groups, group potential and actual group performance often diverge, due to process losses and process gains, both of which occur as a result of social interdependence and social interaction in groups. Hackman and Morris (1975) proposed the following formula:

Actual group performance = Group potential − process losses + process gains

For our research dyad to perform effectively, its members must make in-dividual contributions, and these contributions have to be coordinated. We consider here two types of process losses and gains: namely, coordination and motivation (for an excellent introduction, see Schulz-Hardt & Brodbeck, 2015).

In terms of coordination losses, by definition, coordination in groups can only lead to process losses, not to process gains. Coordination losses are said to occur if a group fails to coordinate the contributions of its individual members in an optimal manner. As we have said, we have organically evolved a division of labor and a diffusion of responsibilities in our research collaboration, which, together with a group size of only $N = 2$, appears to have restricted coordination losses. In terms of motivation, collaboration theoretically could result in either losses or gains because working in a group can lower or increase people's moti-vation to contribute to task performance.

Looking first at potential motivation losses, again our limited group size seems to have restricted the dangers posed by "social loafing," on the one hand (i.e., group members reducing their effort because their individual contributions to the group product are not identifiable), and the "dispensability effect," on the other (i.e., group members reduce their effort because their individual contribu-tion seems to have little impact on group performance).

Finally, our collaboration seems to have benefited by exploiting the potential for motivation gains in groups. Without going into details of poten-tial motivation gains, we believe that our collaboration concurs with the

---

[4] Attributed to Douglas Adams (1952–2001).

[5] The editors of this volume will confirm the need for this third party, and we thank them for their patience and good humor while awaiting the arrival of the muse somewhere between Oxford, Manchester, and Lord's Cricket Ground, London.

emphasis placed in this literature on the importance of group goals. We both view the group goal—ultimately to conduct and publish plentiful high-quality research—as highly important, and so neither of us underperforms. Indeed, the bond that we have developed over the years hopefully makes us overperform.

Overall, we know that production loss in interactive groups increases with group size (Mullen, Johnson, & Salas, 1991), and we feel that in our dyad, we just about get the best of all worlds. According to former Brisbane Lions Australian Football League player Robert Copeland, "[t]o get something done, a committee should consist of no more than three men, two of whom are absent." In our experience, we can do all right with the two of us. Unlike committees, we acknowledge that while we disagree often over issues concerning football, restaurant choices, and day trip activities at conferences, we have never disagreed about research issues. Regarding conferences, and even time off, we have a habit of taking our work everywhere, whether to long cricket matches or high up in cable cars; one of us even took Moscovici's (1985) monumental handbook chapter on social influence with him on a day trip to one of Australia's most beautiful beaches, Noosa. One of us also has a habit of shopping on such trips, where we disagree about appropriate choices and even sizes of garments to buy for our offspring, even resorting to accepting the kindly offer of staff to try on and model clothes in an attempt to resolve our increasingly disputatious mutual influence attempts.

Evidently, we are not alone as a (more or less) creative duo. Wolf Shenk (2014) has devoted a whole fascinating book to the basis of innovation in creative duos, and he argues that the pair is the primary creative unit and is the "most fluid and flexible" (p. xxii) of relationships. More to the point, perhaps, is that there is no hiding place in a dyad. As eminent sociologist Georg Simmel (1902) noted, the key characteristic of the dyad is that each of its two members must actually do something. Wolf Shenk proposes that there are three archetypal pairs: "the liquid and the container" (his example is John Lennon and Paul McCartney), "the star and the director" (Vincent and Theo van Gogh), and "the dreamer and the doer" (Pierre and Marie Curie).

Transactive Memory

Without ever discussing a division of labor, it was principally one of us who developed the core materials that we used in many experiments and who conducted extensive pilot research on the many topics of attitude change that we have used (legalization of cannabis, euthanasia, and so on); one of us who did the main data analysis; one of us who wrote most of the first drafts; and one of us who revised the drafts. This undoubtedly worked for us, and we suspect that it is not so rare, but in a strange way, we also developed a transactive memory. *Transactive memory* refers to shared knowledge about the distribution of knowledge in a group (in our case, a dyad). Rather than having all the information oneself, each group member knows who knows what and whom to ask for information about specific things (Wegner, 1986). Wegner, Guiliano, and Hertel (1985) identified this same phenomenon in married couples, who were shown to specialize in the recall of different types of events, becoming as mutually interdependent in this cognitive sense, just as they may be in more concrete task areas such as housecleaning, car maintenance, and looking after the baby.

So complete is this division of labor in our case that one of us even forgets which studies we have actually done! To the exasperation, followed by hilarity, of the other, he will sometimes suggest a neat 2 × 2 × 2 study that could provide "the perfect test" of some theoretical point. Once he has stopped laughing, the other will gently remind him that not only did we do this study but that we also published it some years ago. Nonetheless, there is a functionality to this division of memory. As Wegner pointed out, transactive memory makes it possible for groups to operate efficiently and adequately because it helps locate information and "the right person for the job." In our case, if we want to know something specific about pilot studies and experimental materials, we know which one of us can tell us; and if we want to know about where and when the study in question was carried out, we know to ask the other one.

Social Impact Theory

Social impact theory (e.g., Latané & Wolf, 1981) suggests that when an individual stands with others as the target of social influence, the source's impact will be divided among the target members. Each target will experience less impact than when he or she is alone, and as the size of the target group increases, the source's impact on each target will decrease. This perspective suggests that minority members would feel that they have to work harder than majority members to defend their position. We believe that, from this perspective, our collaboration provided significant benefits to our overall research goal.

We felt that we had to work harder to have any impact on a literature where we were proposing a novel, minority position. Like a few others before us, we had sought to use theory and methodology derived from the persuasion literature, such as the Elaboration Likelihood Model of Petty and Cacioppo (1986) to understand majority and minority influence. The idea of this new wave of studies was to manipulate source status (majority vs. minority) and argument quality (strong vs. weak arguments). This design allows the researcher to investigate which source is associated with more systematic processing. If processing is systematic, there should be greater persuasion by the strong than the weak message, as well as more message-congruent thoughts, and these thoughts should mediate attitude change.

There was, however, disagreement among researchers concerning which source condition, minority or majority, should elicit the most cognitive scrutiny of the message, with some advocating superior message processing associated with a minority, others advocating this for the majority, and others finding it for both. Unfortunately for us, Baker and Petty (1994) had just published a two-study paper in the *Journal of Personality & Social Psychology* arguing that systematic processing occurred in "imbalanced" conditions (e.g., with a counterattitudinal majority or proattitudinal minority). We say "unfortunately" because initially, we consistently found greater systematic processing for only the minority source. We thus found ourselves, like lawyers in an English court of law, faced with the challenge of overturning precedent (in legal systems based on English common law, a *precedent* is a principle or rule established in a previous legal case that is binding on or determines the outcome for decision about subsequent similar cases in other courts).

We initially cursed the Baker and Petty (1994) study, reread the paper systematically to try (unsuccessfully) to find fault with it, and bemoaned our bad luck that they had published before we had. We even contemplated giving up on this line of research, but then we did exactly what scientists should do—we questioned our theories, methods, and results. We literally went back to the drawing board, redesigned new studies, and introduced new variables to show when Baker and Petty's result could be found, and when not, and why. The road to getting our work published was not only long; it was also rocky. Reviewers consistently remarked, "Interesting findings, but how do you explain the Baker and Petty findings?" (Meanwhile, we wonder if anyone now gets reviewers saying, "How do your results fit in with Martin and Hewstone's?" If so, please let us know.)

The journey was made easier when one of us presented our research findings at a conference attended by the open-minded and collegial (not to mention utterly scholarly) Rich Petty, who welcomed our results and could see how our work and his own created a bigger picture to help understand about majority and minority influence. We are both convinced that our mutual support system helped to buffer us against the "slings and arrows of outrageous reviewing/editing," which we sometimes found to be rather unfair (a case in point being the editor who declined to publish our work, reviews notwithstanding, because he "didn't like" the way that we manipulated source status, a method widely used in the literature). We were similarly buffered by the support of close friends and established scholars in the area, including Charlan Nemeth, John Levine, and Bill Crano, who told us not to give up. The renowned Italian football manager Carlo Ancelotti has said, "The coach has the best job in the world, with the exception of the matches" (quoted in Kuper, 2013, para. 22). We think many academics (especially those having to submit to social psychology journals) might say the same thing, replacing "matches" with "journals."

We (Martin & Hewstone, 2008) developed a theoretical framework that accounts for these inconsistent results; our "source context elaboration model" now has extensive empirical support, but it was a long and rough ride. Essentially, this approach makes two broad sets of predictions concerning (1) the types of processes underlying majority and minority influence and when they occur and (2) the consequences for attitudes following majority and minority influence.

The first set of predictions states that the effects of source status (majority vs. minority) vary along an elaboration continuum (the extent to which the situation allows or encourages elaboration of the source's message). When the elaboration demands are low (e.g., the topic is low in personal relevance), message recipients do not process the source's arguments and attitudes can be guided through simple heuristics (such as the consensus heuristic, "the majority is more likely to be right than the minority"). When elaboration demands are high (e.g., the topic is high in personal relevance), then people will attend to and process arguments from both the majority and the minority source, and attitude change should occur in each case. However, most influence situations to which people are exposed are not characterized by either very low or high processing demands; rather, they are located at an intermediate level. In this situation, we proposed that Moscovici's (1980) conversion theory should apply (i.e., a minority should trigger "validation" of its message, whereas a majority should trigger "comparison" with this source)—that is, systematic processing of only the minority arguments takes place.

The second set of predictions concerns the nature of the attitudes that are formed following majority and minority influence. According to the persuasion literature, attitudes formed through systematic processing are "strong" (Krosnick, Boninger, Chuang, Berent, & Carnot, 1993) in terms of being more resistant to counterpersuasion, more persistent over time, and more predictive of behavior than attitudes formed via nonsystematic processing. We have published consistent evidence showing that minority influence leads to "strong" attitudes, in that attitudes following minority influence are more resistant to counterpersuasion, more persistent over time, and better predictors of behavior (for a review, see Martin & Hewstone, 2008) compared to attitudes formed following majority influence.

We submitted many papers to many journals before we made our breakthrough with a paper in the *European Journal of Social Psychology* (Martin & Hewstone, 2003), whose title says it all: "Majority Versus Minority Influence: When, not Whether, Source Status Instigates Heuristic or Systematic Processing." During these long years of publication famine, the fact that there were two of us "in this together" helped us not to give up, and to patiently build our case, both theoretically and empirically. Perhaps, too, as a "minority of two" against both precedent and the dominant view in the field (that majority sources had greater impact), we had to argue more persuasively and be more creative with our argumentation and our study designs.

We believe that the turning point for us came with a paper reporting three studies that take a different, and novel, approach to examining the hypothesis (based on the conversion theory expressed in Moscovici, 1980) that minority influence leads to greater message processing than does majority influence (Martin, Hewstone, & Martin, 2003). We describe briefly one study here, recalling the way the study design emerged as a reflection of our collaboration. We both agreed on the initial study design, the purpose of which was to see if minority influence leads to systematic message processing. One of us sent the other the study materials to check. The other did so sitting in his garden in Cardiff (while listening to sport on the radio, the other one claims) and had a eureka moment…if people process a minority message in detail, then their attitude should be strong and so should resist a countermessage. The one of us in the garden rang the other one, telling him to hold the presses and add another stage to the study (the countermessage stage). The other one was not impressed, claiming that materials were already designed and that it was not a good idea, but he was ultimately convinced to do so. Sometimes spur of the moment ideas are the most captivating.

In this study, the participants were exposed to two sequential messages. The first message (initial message) from either the majority or the minority source argued a counterattitudinal position, while the second (from the opposite source, either the minority or the majority) argued the proattitudinal position (countermessage). Only if attitudes following the initial message had been formed from processing the message in detail should these attitudes then resist the second countermessage. If attitudes formed following the first message were *not* based upon detailed message processing, then these attitudes should be influenced by (or yield to) the second message. We predicted that if minority influence leads to greater message processing, then attitudes formed following exposure to a minority should be more resistant to a second countermessage than would attitudes formed following majority influence. On the other hand, attitudes following majority influence would result from compliance, without considering the message arguments in detail; therefore, these attitudes should yield to a countermessage. This is what happened in the majority condition. In contrast, as predicted, attitudes following minority influence allowed participants to resist the countermessage.[6]

We believe that this study was the turning point because it was our first major publication on this topic in a leading North American outlet, the *Journal of Experimental Social Psychology*. Having published this paper, we went on to release several further studies, including a second paper in the *Journal of Experimental Social Psychology* and two papers in *Personality and Social Psychology Bulletin*. Together, this corpus was sufficient to encourage us to integrate

[6] There was, in fact, a certain serendipity about this paper. One of us was working at home over the weekend, typing up experimental materials and measures for a new study, as demanded by the other author (who happened to be at a Newport County football game). The planned study had a very different design. But then the computer crashed, and there was no backup of the draft. It was during the laborious business of retyping the various messages, manipulations, and measures that one of us realized that reading two opposed messages (e.g., one pro- and the other anti-euthanasia, one from a majority source and the other from a minority source) in close proximity appeared to have profound psychological consequences. And so the new manipulation was born, where we compared the impact of two sequential messages (one pro, the other anti; one majority, the other minority). Admittedly, this story is not quite as touching as the tale of Sir Isaac Newton's favorite dog, Diamond, who reputedly knocked over a candle, setting fire to and destroying Newton's notes on 20 years' worth of experiments. Newton is reputed to have said merely,"O Diamond, Diamond, thou little knowest the mischief thou has done,"but for the record, one of us was severely upbraided by the other (the publisher will not allow us to record the actual words used) for failing to back up the original file.

our new theoretical position and the cumulative empirical support for it, which we published as part of *Advances in Experimental Social Psychology* (Martin & Hewstone, 2008). An anecdote about this contribution perhaps serves to underline a further advantage of collaboration. One of us wrote and submitted an outline to Mark Zanna, then editor of this tome, without consulting the other. Had he done so, the other would have urged caution and the need to build a yet stronger empirical base before applying to such a prestigious outlet. Collaborations, when they do not involve two perhaps overly cautious, conservative scholars, may reach some unexpected goals unexpectedly faster.

Conclusions

It has been said that "history is written by the victors"[7]—and, we would add, by the first authors as well. Nonetheless, this chapter represents a more or less accurate report on our collaboration.

We have sought to analyze some of the key social-psychological processes that underlie our collaboration. We may not quite be Castor and Pollux,[8] but our collaboration has been sustained by a deep and trusting friendship, which owes much to a common, if warped, sense of humor, and the understanding that such things as practical jokes can promote rather than interfere with work (although, as we have both learned, serious collaboration is best not pursued on April Fool's Day). This friendship galvanizes us at the best of times (celebrating a new grant or article with an all-day-breakfast or curry), and sustains us at the worst of times (after grant or article rejections).

We have concentrated thus far on the positive aspects of our collaboration, but we acknowledge that collaboration may also have negative aspects. Different parties might work at different speeds, with different focuses and different ambitions. While each of us feels able to supply a separate volume, let alone a chapter, on the other's negative characteristics, we could also do that for ourselves. This has made us uncritical and accepting of each other's shortcomings as well as strengths.

Samuel Johnson once wrote that "marriage has many pains, but celibacy has no pleasures."[9] In short, we feel that the same could be said for collaboration versus solo scholarship. We believe that the evolution of this collaboration has made our work far better than it would ever have been had either of us worked alone. Our history of collaboration has included a long period in which we found it very difficult to publish our work. Perhaps, alone, one of us might have

[7] Attributed to Winston Churchill (1874–1965), but the saying is really of unknown origin.

[8] There are many stories in Greek and Roman mythology about the brothers Castor and Pollux, who personify mutual devotion. A prominent one concerns the death of Castor, whose spirit went to Hades, the place of the dead, because he was a human. Pollux, who was a god, was so bereft at this separation from his brother that he offered to share his own immortality with Castor or even to give it up so that he could join his brother in Hades. (The first author wishes to make clear that if any offer of immortality should be forthcoming, he is very willing to accept it, and he does not feel obliged to share it with the second author.)

[9] Samuel Johnson, *Rasselas* (1759), Chapter 26.

given up the fight. Instead, we encouraged each other to do that new study and, eventually, we hope, made a worthwhile and lasting contribution to the study of social influence.

We have been collaborating so long now that it has never really occurred to us to stop. To some extent it has become a "bromance" (except, being British, we feel uncomfortable with overt expressions of affection). It is a collaboration that goes much deeper than research, and we have each, at different times, provided much needed support to the other over significant life events. Perhaps we are like the famous pair of British burglars, the late George "Taters" Chatcham and Peter "Gentleman Thief" Scott, who worked together ("successfully," in their terms) for many years; apparently their secret was that each of them knew that the other would never inform on the other (no matter what they were offered to do so; Campbell, 2013). We like to think, however, that it is the shared passion for what we do, the mutuality of our contributions, and the social support network that we provide each other that offer the key to our (continued, we hope) collaboration.

We started this chapter by speaking of the surface differences between us and conclude that these have little to do with successful collaborations. It is the deeper-level similarities that matter: a common set of goals, complementarity of skills needed for task completion, and support through difficult times (namely, paper rejections) and also, greatly enjoying the journey. Finally, it is also the comfort of working with a long-term collaborator that makes collaboration easier. Collaboration is a process, of course, and it gets—or should get—easier with time. We almost instinctively know what the other will do or say, where our individual inputs are most needed, and how we can complement each other (we never compliment each other). Of Wolf Shenk's (2014) three archetypal duos, we suspect that we are closest to "the dreamer and the doer." Whether we more closely resemble Mozart and Da Ponte, Gaugin and Renoir, or, perhaps, Laurel and Hardy we leave to our colleagues and friends to decide. For ourselves, we model our relationship on the two incomparable half-backs of the legendary Wales rugby team of the 1970s: Gareth Edwards (scrum-half) and Barry John (fly-half). For readers not acquainted with rugby, the former must deliver a fast, accurate pass to the latter, who must first catch it and then decide whether to run, kick, or pass. When they were picked together for the first time for the national team, the pair went to practice on a beach. Edwards is reputed to have asked John how far away and how deep he liked to stand, and what sort of pass he wanted. John replied, "Just pass it, Gar. I'll catch it" (Kitson, 2013).

■ REFERENCES ■

Baker, S., & Petty, R. (1994). Majority and minority influence: Source-position imbalance as a determinant of message scrutiny. *Journal of Personality and Social Psychology, 67*, 5–19.

Campbell, D., (2013, January 20). Partners in crime who stuck together. *The Guardian.*

Hackman, J. R., & Morris, C. G. (1975). Group tasks, group interaction process, and group performance effectiveness: A review and proposed integration. In L. Berkowitz

(Ed.), *Advances in experimental social psychology* (Vol. 8, pp. 45–99). New York, NY: Academic Press.

Kitson, R., (2013, June 6). 50 greatest Lions: How *The Guardian*'s experts chose the top 10. *The Guardian*.

Krosnick, J. A., Boninger, D. S., Chuang, Y. C., Berent, M. K., Carnot, C. (1993). Attitude strength: One construct or many related constructs? *Journal of Personality and Social Psychology, 65,* 1132–1151.

Kuper, S., (2014, January 18/19). How to handle Ronaldo and other secrets. Interview with Carlo Ancelotti. *Financial Times Magazine.* Retrieved from http://www.ft.com/cms/s/2/7e89c58e-7e45-11e3-b409-00144feabdc0.html

Latané, B., & Wolf, S. (1981). The social impact of majorities and minorities. *Psychological Review, 88,* 438–453.

Martin, R., & Hewstone, M. (2003). Majority versus minority influence: When, not whether, source status instigates heuristic or systematic processing. *European Journal of Social Psychology, 33,* 313–330.

Martin, R., & Hewstone, M. (2008). Majority versus minority influence, message processing and attitude change: The source-context-elaboration model. In M. Zanna (Ed.), *Advances in experimental social psychology* (Vol. 40, pp. 237–326). San Diego, CA: Academic Press.

Martin, R., Hewstone, M., & Martin, P. Y. (2003). Resistance to persuasive messages as a function of majority and minority source status. *Journal of Experimental Social Psychology, 39,* 585–593.

Merton, R. K. (1968). The Matthew effect in science. *Science, 159,* 53–63.

Moscovici, S. (1980). Toward a theory of conversion behavior. In L. Berkowitz (Ed.), *Advances in experimental social psychology* (Vol. 13, pp. 209–239). New York, NY: Academic Press.

Moscovici, S. (1985). Social influence and conformity. In G. Lindsey & E. Aronson (Eds.), *The handbook of social psychology* (Vol. 2, 3rd ed., pp. 347–412). New York, NY: Random House.

Mullen, B., Johnson, C., & Salas, E. (1991). Productivity loss in brainstorming groups: A meta-analytic integration. *Basic and Applied Social Psychology, 12,* 3–23.

Petty, R. E., & Cacioppo, J. T. (1986). *Communication and persuasion: Central and peripheral routes to attitude change.* New York, NY: Springer-Verlag.

Schulz-Hardt, S., & Brodbeck, F. (2015). Group performance and leadership. In M. Hewstone, W. Stroebe, & K. Jonas (Eds.), *Introduction to social psychology* (6th ed., pp. 407–438). Chichester, England: Wiley–British Psychological Society.

Simmel, G. (1902). The number of members as determining the sociological form of the group. *American Journal of Sociology, 8,* 1–46.

Steiner, I. D. (1972). *Group processes and group productivity.* New York, NY: Academic Press.

Wegner, D. M. (1986). Transactive memory: A contemporary analysis of the group mind. In B. Mullen & C. R. Goethals (Eds.), *Theories of group behaviour* (pp. 185–208). New York, NY: Springer.

Wegner, D. M., Guiliano, T., & Hertel, P. (1985). Cognitive interdependence in close relationships. In W. J. Ickes (Ed.), *Compatible and incompatible relationships* (pp. 253–276). New York, NY: Springer.

Winch, R. F., Ktsanes, T., & Ktsanes, V. (1955). Empirical elaboration of the theory of complementary needs in mate-selection. *Journal of Abnormal and Social Psychology, 51,* 508–513.

Wolf Shenk, J. (2014). *Powers of two: Finding the essence of innovation in creative pairs.* London, England: John Murray.

Chapter 7: Social Cognition About a Collaboration in Social Cognition[1]

Charles M. Judd

Professor of Distinction
Department of Psychology and Neuroscience
University of Colorado Boulder

Bernadette Park

Professor of Psychology
Department of Psychology and Neuroscience
University of Colorado Boulder

This is a rare and most welcome opportunity for us to reflect on a collaboration that has defined, for each of us, major portions of our academic careers. Although we have each established lines of work independent of the other, there is no doubt that this collaboration has resulted in some of the work in which we take greatest pride. Our goal in these pages, like the intentions of all the contributors to this volume, is to reflect on this collaboration, to outline its substantive themes, and to share our thoughts about those factors that have made this collaboration so productive and enjoyable.

Origins of Our Collaboration

We published our first paper together in the *Journal of Personality and Social Psychology* (*JPSP*) in 1988. Since then, 33 articles with both of us as authors have appeared in refereed journals (including 11 in *JPSP*) and seven chapters in edited volumes. Not only that, but the rate of our publications has also remained fairly steady over the intervening 25 years, with only 3 years during that period passing without a jointly authored research publication.

[1] We would like to thank our many graduate students, postdoctoral fellows, and other collaborators and colleagues. Beyond each other, we are incredibly indebted to them for all they have given us over the years.

We take pride not only in the productivity of this collaboration, but also in the emerging substantive themes that have defined it. Accordingly, in the first section of this chapter, we outline what those themes are and how our ideas have progressed over the years. Having done this, we turn in the second section to lessons we have learned from our collaboration that we think might be useful to others, much younger than ourselves, who are launching careers that may very well also include scientific collaboration. Good collaborations are immensely rewarding for science and for scientists. We are fortunate to have benefited from one.

Themes of Our Collaboration

Broadly speaking, all our work can be located in what might be called the *social cognition approach* to stereotyping and prejudice. This approach, harkening back to Gordon Allport (1954), Henri Tajfel (1969), and other seminal thinkers, suggests that social perceivers spontaneously categorize others into useful social groups, just as we categorize individual pieces of furniture into categories (e.g., chairs or tables) or days of the year into month categories (e.g., May or June). Unlike pieces or furniture or days of the year, however, we are members of some of those social groups and not others. Therefore, social categories are strongly defined by the contrast between ingroups, of which we are members, and outgroups, of which we are not. And it is this distinction, and our need to find value in our own lives and the lives of significant others, that gives rise to an affinity for the ingroup, often with the by-product of outgroup derogation and prejudice. This was and is the theoretical orientation that has guided our work from the beginning and to which we hope to have contributed.

Finding ourselves in the same department, we recognized this shared theoretical orientation and began discussing possible projects of mutual interest. Our collaborative work started by focusing on a relatively well-documented difference between ingroup and outgroup stereotypes: the tendency to see ingroups as more variable than outgroups (often labeled the *outgroup homogeneity effect;* Park & Rothbart, 1982; Quattrone & Jones, 1980). That is, in addition to derogating outgroups relative to ingroups, research had shown that outgroup stereotypes are also more potent than ingroup stereotypes, in the sense that "they" tend to be seen as all alike, while "we" are seen as a rather diverse group. While this ingroup-outgroup difference in variability was judged by all to be theoretically important, work on what factors contributed to it and how various cognitive models of group representation might account for it was only beginning. On the one hand, Linville, Fischer, and Salovey (1989) argued that variability differences between ingroups and outgroups originated from differences in familiarity with ingroup and outgroup members, based on what was called an exemplar-based representation, where the groups were represented in memory only by particular instances or exemplars of the groups that had been encountered. On the other hand, Park and Rothbart (1982; see also Park & Hastie, 1987) argued for a more abstraction-based representational model in which differential familiarity with ingroups and outgroups mattered less. In an effort to examine more directly whether outgroup homogeneity would exist in the absence of differential familiarity, we reported data from a modified minimal-group study (Judd & Park, 1988), in which group membership was randomly assigned, with equal numbers of ingroup and outgroup members and equivalent information available about each (with the exception of the self, of course). Consistent with the argument that differential familiarity was not a sufficient explanation for outgroup homogeneity, we continued to find it even in this context.

This initial work gave rise to two different lines of work that we pursued over the years in various ways. One of these areas focused on refining how one measures perceived group variability, and group stereotypes more generally. A second continued to explore the nature of group representation in memory and the implications for stereotype change when confronted with new and potentially discrepant information about groups for which one already possesses stereotypes.

The measurement research was initially prompted by the realization that various researchers had used very different measurement approaches to assess perceived group variability and that these diverse approaches yielded very different results, particularly when examining gender stereotypes. On the one hand, for instance, Park and Rothbart (1982) had asked participants to report the percentage of men and women who possessed stereotypic and counterstereotypic attributes, with the assumption that the greater the difference in those reported percentages (stereotypic minus counterstereotypic), the more homogeneous the group is perceived to be. On the other hand, Linville and colleagues (Linville et al., 1989; Linville, Salovey, & Fischer, 1986) had used something closer to a histogram task, asking perceivers to indicate the relative percentages of group members who they thought possessed different levels of stereotypic attributes (e.g., *very warm, somewhat warm, neither warm nor cold, somewhat cold, very cold*). From these, they computed a standard deviation (or a related measure) for each perceived histogram. With their measure, Park and Rothbart (1982) showed a significant outgroup homogeneity effect using gender to define the groups, whereas Linville et al. (1989) failed to find the effect with their measure of perceived variability.

We suspected that the different measurement approaches might be responsible for the difference in the obtained results. Accordingly, we conducted a large study (Park & Judd, 1990), again using gender to define ingroups and outgroups and using a wide variety of different approaches to assess perceived group variability. Using latent variable modeling to examine the structure of these measures, we uncovered two latent factors, one of which we labeled *dispersion* and the other *stereotypicality*. The former was defined by measures similar to those used by Linville et al. (1989), assessing variability around the perceived mean of the group on both stereotypic and counterstereotypic attributes. The latter, stereotypicality, was defined by measures similar to those used by Park and Rothbart (1982), assessing the extent to which the group was perceived relatively extremely on both stereotypic and counterstereotypic attributes (high on the former and low on the latter). We found significant outgroup homogeneity with both latent constructs, although the findings were stronger for stereotypicality than dispersion, with the difference in part due to the difference in the reliability of the two constructs.

A further refinement to this model, taking into account the valence or evaluative connotations of attribute dimensions, led to the realization that stereotypes vary along three theoretically important dimensions: *dispersion,* defined as the variability around the perceived group mean on both stereotypic and counter-stereotypic dimensions of both positive and negative valence; *stereotypicality,* defined as the perceived difference between the group means on stereotypic minus counterstereotypic attributes of both valences; and *ingroup evaluative bias,* defined as the perceived difference between ingroup versus outgroup mean ratings on positively valenced minus negatively valenced attributes (across both stereotypic and counterstereotypic dimensions). And this thinking in turn led to what we regard as an important theoretical contribution (Judd & Park, 1993) that defined stereotypes using these three dimensions and considered how stereotypes may be accurate or inaccurate (i.e., exaggerations of actual group differences) along all three dimensions.

In the course of developing the ideas that eventually formed the basis for our 1993 *Psychological Review* paper (Judd & Park, 1993), we conducted empirical research examining the various components of accuracy (Judd, Ryan, & Park, 1991), and later, work showing that group evaluations and perceived variability are affected by intergroup contact in distinctly different ways (Wolsko, Park, Judd, & Bachelor, 2003). Two events occurred at about this time that profoundly affected the scope and duration of our collaborative efforts. First, we were fortunate to receive the first award of what eventually would span 15 years of funding from the National Institute of Mental Health. This funding greatly facilitated our ability to conduct the research. Second, the funding enabled us over the years to support many stellar postdoctoral and graduate students, and so our collaborative efforts expanded to include not just each other, but these students as well. Carey Ryan had just finished her PhD in sociocultural psychology at Colorado, and we hired her as a postdoctoral fellow to work on the grant. That experience made us understand just how much more we could accomplish through broader collaborations.

The second thrust of our work continued to focus on models of group representation in memory and their implications for stereotype change in light of subsequently learned information that disconfirmed existing stereotypic beliefs to some extent. From our earlier work, we came to the view that group representation was necessarily complex, with abstract information stored in memory as well as specific exemplars. For the ingroup, of course, the self was one very important such exemplar. Additional exemplars for both the ingroup and the outgroup might include specific subgroups. From there, we made the strong argument that perceived variability differences between ingroups and outgroups could be largely accounted for by both the importance of the self-representation to the ingroup (and the need to differentiate the self at least somewhat from other group members; see Brewer, 1991) and by the presence of many more subgroups stored in conjunction with the ingroup representation than with the outgroup one (Park, Ryan, & Judd, 1992).

As a result of this tendency to incorporate more different subgroups in the overall representation of the superordinate ingroup than the outgroup, when a new group exemplar is encountered who disconfirms the existing group stereotype to some extent, that exemplar is likely to be handled very differently in the case of the ingroup than the outgroup. With the ingroup, a new subgroup could well be constructed, still under the superordinate ingroup representation, thus allowing some modification of that overall representation. With the outgroup, on the other hand, since other subgroups are not as likely, the disconfirming exemplar is likely to be "subtyped" rather than "subgrouped," meaning that it is simply disregarded and judged as atypical and therefore irrelevant to the superordinate outgroup representation as a whole. It follows from this argument that disconfirming group exemplars are much less likely to lead to stereotype change and revision in the case of outgroup stereotypes than in the case of ingroup stereotypes (Maurer, Park, & Rothbart, 1995; Park, Wolsko, & Judd, 2001).

Both of these lines of work had been conducted largely in laboratory settings with target groups that were only of interest for theoretical reasons. We wanted to use the tools of stereotype assessment that we had developed to examine consequential ethnic stereotypes among large samples of American youth. Accordingly, we examined ingroup and outgroup stereotypes in diverse samples of Whites and Black Americans, assessing our components of stereotypes: dispersion, stereotypicality, and ingroup evaluative bias (Judd, Park, Ryan, Brauer, & Kraus, 1995). Given our earlier work, what we found came as a surprise to us (although upon further thought, it should not have); in fact, our initial surprise gave way to subsequent lines of work that were theoretically important. Our African-American respondents showed outgroup homogeneity and considerable ingroup evaluative bias, as we expected. On the other hand, our White American respondents did not. Instead, they seemed to espouse a sort of postethnic ideology, explicitly saying that ethnic divisions in our society were no longer useful and that we needed to treat individuals as individuals, not as members of particular ethnic categories. Our African-American respondents strongly disagreed with this point of view.

Given earlier work that was beginning to look at what came to be known as *implicit prejudice* (e.g., Devine, 1989), it seemed entirely possible that our White respondents were simply denying their ethnic prejudices and stereotypes in the interest of appearing egalitarian and nonracist. We suspected that the story, however, was more complicated than this—that our White students were not simply deceiving us and themselves but, rather, that they truly believed their explicit nonprejudiced espousals. This then led us to two further lines of work.

Following up on Devine's earlier research, Fazio, Jackson, Dunton, and Williams (1995) reported work on implicit racial attitudes, using an affective priming task that Fazio had earlier developed (Fazio, Sanbonmatsu, Powell, & Kardes, 1986). In this task, participants judge the valence of words (e.g., *wonderful, disgusting*) that are preceded by pictures of African-American or

White males as primes. White participants were faster to judge the valence of negative words following Black primes and positive words following White primes (evaluatively congruent pairings) than for the other two (evaluatively incongruent) pairings. Fazio et al. (1995) further reported that this automatic evaluative bias effect was largely uncorrelated with responses to explicit questions about racial prejudice. These results were thus at least somewhat congruent with the explanation that our White participants in the Judd et al. (1995) study were simply deceiving themselves (and us) in their failure to report ethnic ingroup bias.

Accordingly, led by Bernd Wittenbrink, who at the time was our superb postdoctoral associate, we developed our own task to examine the content of stereotypes (not just prejudice) measured at the implicit level (Wittenbrink, Judd, & Park, 1997). To look at the content of the stereotypes that were automatically activated by ethnic target groups, we had participants complete a primed lexical decision task, in which they saw letter strings and were asked to decide if these were words or not-words. Of the targets that were words, half were positively valenced traits and half were negatively valenced traits. Furthermore, of these, half were stereotypic of Whites and half were stereotypic of African Americans. Preceding each letter string to be lexically identified, subliminally presented prime words occurred. These primes were the word *Black*, the word *White*, or some other neutral word (e.g., *Table*).

If stereotypic associations are automatically activated, then we would expect that the stereotypic words would be identified as words more quickly when preceded by the group prime for which the words are stereotypic than when preceded by the neutral prime. In addition, if those stereotypic associations were largely negative for African Americans but largely positive for Whites, then the stereotypic pattern of facilitation should be especially true for Black-negative stereotypic words following the Black prime and White-positive stereotypic words following the White prime. The results of this experiment revealed exactly that, demonstrating automatically activated negatively valenced stereotypes of African Americans and positively valenced stereotypes of Whites by our White participants. Additionally and importantly, we found that individual differences in these automatically activated stereotypes were remarkably highly correlated with explicit questionnaire measures of prejudice and stereotyping, suggesting that participants' automatic responses were at least somewhat consistent with their overt and explicit responses. These results suggested to us that there need not be a dissociation between explicit and implicit racial stereotypes. Further, this work suggested that there were meaningful individual differences in implicit responses, contrary to earlier findings (Devine, 1989) that had argued that racial prejudice at the implicit level was more or less unavoidable in our culture and that there was an inevitable dissociation between implicit prejudicial responses and overt or explicit racial attitudes.

Building on this work, we subsequently showed that our implicit assessment of stereotypes, using a lexical decision task that necessarily involves processing the semantic content of target stimuli, yielded very different results from Fazio's evaluative priming approach (Wittenbrink, Judd, & Park, 2001a). In addition, we showed that automatically activated stereotypes were malleable and context dependent, rather than universal and rigid (Wittenbrink, Judd, & Park, 2001b).

The second line of work stimulated by the unexpected lack of ethnocentrism and outgroup homogeneity by White participants found by Judd et al. (1995) was with Chris Wolsko. It concerned alternative ideologies about interethnic conflict and how it might be resolved. Specifically, we realized that our White undergraduates had been socialized to adopt a colorblind perspective to interethnic relations, explicitly denying the importance of ethnicity and seeking to treat others as individuals rather than classifying them by their ethnicity. This perspective seemed quite different from that espoused by many of our African-American participants who, unsurprisingly, said that ethnicity did matter in American society and that only by valuing diverse ethnic groups and their traditions was ethnic harmony possible. We undertook to experimentally manipulate the espousal of these two different ideologies, which we labeled *colorblind* and *multicultural,* respectively. This confirmed that while both produced more positive evaluations of ethnic minority groups (relative to a control), the multicultural ideology resulted in stronger stereotypes, greater accuracy in these stereotypes, and greater use of category information when forming judgments of individuals (Wolsko, Park, Judd, & Wittenbrink, 2000). That multiculturalism could simultaneously lead to both stronger between-group differentiation and (at least on some tasks) more positive outgroup evaluations made us question an underlying assumption of most approaches to prejudice reduction. The majority of social psychological work on prejudice reduction assumed that social categorization inevitably leads to prejudice, and that in order to reduce prejudice, boundaries that separate categories must necessarily be weakened (Deffenbacher, Park, Judd, & Correll, 2009; Park & Judd, 2005). Our work suggested that the strength of category boundaries need not be related to the degree of outgroup derogation.

In subsequent work, we recognized that these two positive interethnic ideologies have a more negative counterpart. A colorblind perspective can easily morph into a demand for ethnic-minority individuals to assimilate to the dominant White culture, and taken to the extreme, the multicultural perspective can suggest that groups are so different that they should live and work separately—a sort of two-state solution (Hahn, Judd, & Park, 2010; Wolsko, Park, & Judd, 2006). In recent work, we have developed scales for measuring individual differences in endorsement of the interethnic ideologies resulting from this fourfold typology, and parallel versions of these as they pertain to perceptions of gender (Hahn, Banchefsky, Park, & Judd, 2015).

Finally, out of the work on implicit stereotypes, from the initiative of Josh Correll, we began a program of research examining whether automatic stereotypes might affect behavioral decisions to "shoot" Black and White targets who are potentially armed. Across a large number of studies, participants demonstrated a consistent race bias, shooting armed Black targets more quickly than armed Whites and mistakenly shooting unarmed Black targets more frequently than unarmed Whites (Correll, Park, Judd, & Wittenbrink, 2002). In addition to the robust bias across numerous White samples, bias was present among African-American participants. Police officers, although better overall at performing the shooter task, show the same race bias in response times as community members, but importantly, they do not show bias in their actual decisions—whether or not to shoot (Correll, Park, Judd, Wittenbrink, Sadler, et al., 2007). Stereotype accessibility—manipulated either through news stories of Blacks versus Whites as criminals, or through the frequency of pairings of Blacks versus Whites with guns in video games—plays a prominent role in producing this race bias effect (Correll, Park, Judd, & Wittenbrink, 2007). Finally, the effect seems to be a reaction to monitoring danger in the environment. When a secondary cue signaled danger (targets appeared in a threatening background such as a graffiti-covered wall or run-down city block), race bias was eliminated, primarily due to an increased tendency to shoot Whites (i.e., now all targets appeared to be dangerous; Correll, Wittenbrink, Park, Judd, & Goyle, 2011).

Lessons in Collaboration

We consider ourselves fortunate to have been partners in what has been a productive, enjoyable, and rewarding collaborative relationship. In reflecting on what worked and what didn't, we've tried to derive a set of lessons learned from the collaboration. Some of these we suspect are universal, while others are likely unique to our own specific dynamics. First and foremost, collaborations are synergistic. They create more energy than the sum of their individual contributions. In our experience, we were much more likely to push forward and develop projects by talking through ideas together than when thinking about them alone, and this was true both of projects involving just the two of us, as well as those involving our graduate students and postdoctoral fellows. Working in meetings, often with graduate or postdoctoral students, one of us might express a half-considered thought only to have the other take it up, elaborate on it and run with it, pass it back for further development, and so on, until before we knew it, there was a study to run.

Likewise, in working with results, one of us would puzzle over some facet of the data that was easy for the other to make sense of. Instead of getting stuck on some aspect in a project, the other person could nearly always provide the nudge to move forward. Put simply, the work seemed to move along more efficiently and with less effort than solo projects we each were doing. Collaborating is also conducive to making progress on a project, especially when you regularly encounter the person you are working with. When someone else is waiting for the introduction to a paper to be written, there are only so many times that you can pass him or her in the hall before being overcome with guilt. The project gets moved to the top of the to-do list, and before long, a finished product is ready for submission. Meanwhile, those projects that belong solely to you get pushed farther and farther to the back of the desk.

In our case, part of the efficiency created by the collaboration came from a shared perspective on how to do science and what questions seem interesting to pursue, something that came easily to us and that wasn't necessarily always shared by others with whom we were collaborating (including other faculty, students, and postdocs). And when we did disagree, we were not timid about expressing our viewpoints. For both of us, the discussions were about the science—they weren't personal attacks or condemnations. We would argue through things until we could agree, or at times, the meeting would simply end with "Well, it's an empirical question—we'll see." Part of what made working together enjoyable was that we shared similar procedural approaches to research. By and large, we have similar sensibilities about how best to approach a research question, how to design studies, and how to conceptualize the presentation of such. We track the research process similarly. At the same time, our collaboration has benefited from our having somewhat different strengths. One of us (CMJ) had particular interests and strengths in methodological issues and data analytic approaches. Although we both held our own in thinking about analytic issues, one of us was always thinking about new and informative ways of analyzing data sets and worrying about the assumptions underlying those analyses. On the other hand, the other of us (BP) brought extremely strong organizational skills that helped ensure that we tracked things properly and designed and executed the studies as intended. Those organizational skills also extended to tracking past literature so that as we designed research, we were able to situate it properly in the context of existing work. That helped us avoid reinventing the wheel. It was also a useful skill for understanding unexpected findings. In sum, then, for a collaboration to be successful, it is important to find someone who speaks and thinks about science in a manner that resonates with you. But at the same time, ideally, you would have somewhat different strengths that consequently stretch each other.

Some people are very successful at collaborating long distance. In our case, much of the success came from sitting in the same room and hashing out ideas. We share a particularly clear memory of sitting in the airport after a meeting of the Society of Experimental Social Psychology, mapping out our *Psychological Review* paper (Judd & Park, 1993) on a legal notepad as we waited for our flight back to Colorado. This wasn't a "scheduled" meeting. Of course, we had been thinking about many of the issues for some time, but the codification happened spontaneously. It is just much harder to have the opportunity for such experiences at a distance.

Relatedly, many of our most productive collaborative projects emerged from work inspired by graduate students and postdoctoral fellows. There, too, we would all sit in a room and begin with either an idea or puzzle (often brought by the student/postdoc) and mull it over for comments, observations, thoughts, questions, and if it was a good day, we would leave the meeting with a research project. The chance to mentor some truly exceptional graduate students and postdocs is one of the aspects of our collaboration for which we are most grateful. They undoubtedly pushed us to do better and more interesting work than had we been left with just our own ideas. And importantly, we believe that these interactions helped model successful collaborations for many of these students. At the same time, it became clear over the years that students had to be "strong" for the collaboration to work—otherwise, we would talk right over them and they wouldn't get a word in edgewise.

Maybe because of the pride we have taken in our collaboration, we believe that to some extent, it set a model for the social psychology program as it developed at the University of Colorado. Two characteristics of the program seem particularly unique as we look at other such training programs across the country. First, the program as a whole is highly collaborative, with faculty more frequently working together than alone on research projects, and graduate students working under multiple collaborating advisors. Second, the program over the years has emphasized the importance of strong quantitative and empirical training, reflective to some extent of our own interests and proclivities.

Perhaps one of the trickiest issues to navigate in collaborative work is the division of credit. We know that when asked about the proportion that they contributed to the completion of a given task, the pooled estimates of collaborators (be they spouses or colleagues) typically sum to greater than 1 (Ross & Sicoly, 1979). As individuals, we are privy to the amount of time and energy we spent working on some task, and are less likely to have that same information available when considering others' work. It seems important to simply understand this aspect of human nature. In our case, we both typically erred on the side of being generous with credit (as with this chapter, where so far we both keep insisting that the other be first author). So long as both parties adopt a generous approach (think the Prisoner's Dilemma here), this frees up energy to focus on the ideas and the data—to be excited about the product. It leads to feelings of goodwill and productivity rather than a defensive need to protect. But this is a delicate balance and probably works best over an extended period of collaboration.

Also, it is crucial to treat each other as equals, even if one member of the team has more seniority. It is critical to find the strengths that each person brings to the table, to value and respect them, and to let go of any sort of status-based hierarchy in the collaboration. Otherwise, it will be a short-lived enterprise. This sounds strikingly like the formula for successful intergroup contact, which probably makes a lot of sense (Cook, 1985; Pettigrew, 1998). And if you struggle to find things to value in the other person's contributions, that's probably a good sign that you should end the collaboration.

At the same time, it remains important for promotion and tenure to identify the magnitude of each individual's contributions to the field. To this end, we see it as critical to maintain other lines of work independent of the collaboration. Such work could either be solo or in conjunction with different collaborators. Both would demonstrate a distinct and different dimension of contributions to the field.

On a personal level, good collaborations can help you stay engaged with your work when other aspects of life threaten your ability to do so. Because we are human, pretty much all of us will struggle with "life" issues—a sick parent or child, a divorce, our own health, a car accident, or a flood. It can be difficult to continue to exert the energy that it takes to do research when these external forces are at work. For us, specifically, BP remembers clearly how hard it was to continue the pace of academic life with two young children. There was a time when leaving academia was becoming a very attractive option. Had it not been for the energizing support and ease of our collaborative work, that would very likely have been the decision. Twenty years later, BP is certainly grateful to have stayed, but she remains acutely aware of the importance that the collaborative relationship played in making that decision possible. For CMJ, the collaboration simply made doing work so very enjoyable that it was an easy thing to commit time and energy to. The research enterprise became all the more valuable simply because of the collaboration. Academic life can certainly be stressful and daunting, particularly for young scholars, and having a solid, productive, and enjoyable collaborative relationship can no doubt buffer one through difficult times. Indeed, looking over our careers, the good friendships and collaborations that we have been fortunate to have over the years with each other, with our students, with our other colleagues at Colorado, and with our colleagues at many universities across the world have formed our most rewarding and lasting memories.

Conclusions

We feel very lucky to have had the chance to work together on so many projects over the years. For young people looking to forge successful collaborative relationships, look for interactions where the working relationship flows naturally and the other person shares your approach, values, and priorities in research. These are not easy things to find, and in many ways, they cannot be forced: they either are there or they aren't. Don't be discouraged if your first attempts are not successful. Keep exploring possible collaborators. You never know which one will work or what wealth of experiences you might be lucky enough to take away from the relationship.

▨ REFERENCES ▨

Allport, G. W. (1954). *The nature of prejudice*. Garden City, NY: Doubleday.

Brewer, M. B. (1991). The social self: On being the same and different at the same time. *Personality and Social Psychology Bulletin, 17*, 475–482.

Cook, S. W. (1985). Experimenting on social issues: The case of school desegregation. *American Psychologist, 40*, 452–460.

Correll, J., Park, B., Judd, C. M., & Wittenbrink, B. (2002). The police officer's dilemma: Using ethnicity to disambiguate potentially threatening individuals. *Journal of Personality and Social Psychology, 83*, 1314–1329.

Correll, J., Park, B., Judd, C. M., & Wittenbrink, B. (2007). The influence of stereotypes in the decision to shoot. *European Journal of Social Psychology, 37*, 1102–1117.

Correll, J., Park, B., Judd, C. M., Wittenbrink, B., Sadler, M. S., & Keesee, T. (2007). Across the thin blue line: Police officers and racial bias in the decision to shoot. *Journal of Personality and Social Psychology, 92*, 1006–1023.

Correll, J., Wittenbrink, B., Park, B., Judd, C. M., & Goyle, A. (2011). Dangerous enough: Moderating racial bias with secondary threat cues. *Journal of Experimental Social Psychology, 47*, 184–189.

Deffenbacher, D. M., Park, B., Judd, C. M., & Correll, J. (2009). Category boundaries can be accentuated without increasing intergroup bias. *Group Processes and Intergroup Relations, 12*, 175–193.

Devine, P. G. (1989). Stereotypes and prejudice: Their automatic and controlled components. *Journal of Personality and Social Psychology, 56*, 5–18.

Fazio, R. H., Jackson, J. R., Dunton, B. C., & Williams, C. J. (1995). Variability in automatic activation as an unobtrusive measure of racial attitudes: A bona fide pipeline? *Journal of Personality and Social Psychology, 69*, 1013–1027.

Fazio, R. H., Sanbonmatsu, D. M., Powell, M. C., & Kardes, F. R. (1986). On the automatic activation of attitudes. *Journal of Personality and Social Psychology, 50*, 229–238.

Hahn, A., Banchefsky, S., Park, B., & Judd, C. M. (2015). Measuring intergroup ideologies: Positive and negative aspects of emphasizing versus looking beyond group differences. *Personality and Social Psychology Bulletin, 41*(12), 1646–1664.

Hahn, A., Judd, C. M., & Park, B. (2010). Thinking about group differences: Ideologies and national identities. *Psychological Inquiry, 21*, 120–126.

Judd, C. M., & Park, B. (1988). Out-group homogeneity: Judgments of variability at the individual and group levels. *Journal of Personality and Social Psychology, 54*, 778–788.

Judd, C. M, & Park, B. (1993). Definition and assessment of accuracy in social stereotypes. *Psychological Review, 100*, 109–128.

Judd, C. M., Park, B., Ryan, C. S., Brauer, M., & Kraus, S. (1995). Stereotypes and ethnocentrism: Diverging interethnic perceptions of African American and White American youth. *Journal of Personality and Social Psychology, 69*, 460–481.

Judd, C. M., Ryan, C. S., & Park, B. (1991). Accuracy in the judgment of in-group and out-group variability. *Journal of Personality and Social Psychology, 61*, 366–379.

Linville, P. W., Fischer, G. W., & Salovey, P. (1989). Perceived distributions of the characteristics of in-group and out-group members: Empirical evidence and a computer simulation. *Journal of Personality and Social Psychology, 57*(2), 165–188.

Linville, P. W., Salovey, P., & Fischer, G. W. (1986). Stereotyping and perceived distributions of social characteristics: An application to ingroup-outgroup perception. In J. F. Dovidio & S. L. Gaertner (Eds.), *Prejudice, discrimination, and racism* (pp. 165–208). Sand Diego, CA: Academic Press.

Maurer, K. L., Park, B., & Rothbart, M. (1995). Subtyping versus subgrouping processes in stereotype representation. *Journal of Personality and Social Psychology, 69*, 812–824.

Park, B., & Hastie, R. (1987). Perception of variability in category development: Instance- versus abstraction-based stereotypes. *Journal of Personality and Social Psychology, 53*, 621–636.

Park, B., & Judd, C. M. (1990). Measures and models of perceived group variability. *Journal of Personality and Social Psychology, 59*, 173–191.

Park, B., & Judd, C. M. (2005). Rethinking the link between categorization and prejudice within the social cognition perspective. *Personality and Social Psychology Review, 9*, 108–130.

Park, B., & Rothbart, M. (1982). Perception of out-group homogeneity and levels of social categorization: Memory for the subordinate attributes of in-group and out-group members. *Journal of Personality and Social Psychology, 42*, 1051–1068.

Park, B., Ryan, C. S., & Judd, C. M. (1992). The role of meaningful subgroups in explaining differences in perceived variability for in-groups and out-groups. *Journal of Personality and Social Psychology, 63*, 553–567.

Park, B., Wolsko, C., & Judd, C. M. (2001). Measurement of subtyping in stereotype change. *Journal of Experimental Social Psychology, 37*, 325–332.

Pettigrew, T. F. (1998). Intergroup contact theory. *Annual Review of Psychology, 49*, 65–85.

Quattrone, G. A., & Jones, E. E. (1980). The perception of variability within in-groups and out-groups: Implications for the law of small numbers. *Journal of Personality and Social Psychology, 38*(1), 141–152.

Ross, M., & Sicoly, F. (1979). Egocentric biases in availability and attribution. *Journal of Personality and Social Psychology, 37*, 322–336.

Tajfel, H. (1969). Cognitive aspects of prejudice. *Journal of Social Issues, 25*, 79–98.

Wittenbrink, B., Judd, C. M., & Park, B. (1997). Evidence for racial prejudice at the implicit level and its relationship with questionnaire measures. *Journal of Personality and Social Psychology, 72*, 262–274.

Wittenbrink, B., Judd, C. M., & Park, B. (2001a). Evaluative versus conceptual judgments in automatic stereotyping and prejudice. *Journal of Experimental Social Psychology, 37*, 244–252.

Wittenbrink, B., Judd, C. M., & Park, B. (2001b). Spontaneous prejudice in context: Variability in automatically activated attitudes. *Journal of Personality and Social Psychology, 81*, 815–827.

Wolsko, C., Park, B., & Judd, C.M. (2006). Considering the tower of Babel: Correlates of assimilation and multiculturalism among ethnic minority and majority groups in the United States. *Social Justice Research, 19*, 277–306.

Wolsko, C., Park, B., Judd. C. M., & Bachelor, J. (2003). Intergroup contact: Effects on evaluative responses and stereotype change. *Group Processes and Intergroup Relations, 6*, 93–110.

Wolsko, C., Park, B., Judd, C.M., & Wittenbrink, B. (2000). Framing interethnic ideology: Effects of multicultural and colorblind perspectives of judgments of groups and individuals. *Journal of Personality and Social Psychology, 78*, 635–654.

Chapter 8: Dialogues Across Difference: The Two-Self Solution

Hazel Rose Markus

David-Brack Professor in the Behavioral Sciences
Stanford University

Shinobu Kitayama

Robert B. Zajonc Collegiate Professor of Psychology
Director, Center for Culture, Mind, and the Brain
University of Michigan

Our East–West, male–female collaboration across three decades has given rise to a theory of the mutual constitution of cultures and selves (i.e., how cultures make selves and selves make cultures). Our shared social psychological perspective, combined with our many differences in experience and interpretive frameworks, led us to theorize the wide-ranging behavioral consequences of two ways of being a self. One way of being derives from an atomistic, individualistic understanding of the person and the world and the other from a more holistic, collectivist understanding of the person. Tacking back and forth between these perspectives makes the invisible visible and continually generates ideas about the sources and consequences of having one perspective or the other. In retrospect, we used our two selves to develop a theory of two selves and to forge a strong collaboration.

In the course of our work together, we have found that both an independent and an interdependent self are necessary for collaboration and, we hypothesize, for effective functioning and well-being more generally. Our long-term collaboration has been a lot of fun and has led to the willingness to take intellectual risks that we might not have otherwise taken. Our diversity in experience and perspective has been joined by two shared attractions—social psychology and good food—and both continue to fuel our research. As fresh ingredients blended in the right proportion are the secret to a successful stew or sukiyaki, so it is with collaboration. For us, some of the most important ingredients are

(1) shared irritation and purpose; (2) speculation, questioning, and appreciative listening; (3) trust and solidarity; and (4) patience and adjustment.

Origin of Our Collaboration: Shared Irritation and Purpose

Our collaboration begins with a shared theoretical interest in interdependence. Each of us was (and still is) irritated with two binaries that structure theorizing and research in psychology—the individuality/sociality divide and the thought/feeling divide. Why is the self defined as separate from others? Why is sociality always in tension with individuality? Why is thought defined as separate from feeling? And why are both separate from the thoughts, feelings, and motives attributed to others? These questions gave rise to our collaboration— to our interdependence and to our study of interdependence. The role of these foundational divides and the fact that we found them troubling derives in some part from our identities and ourselves. For Hazel, it was being a woman in the then-male-dominated field of psychology. For Shinobu, it was being Japanese in the U.S.-dominated field of psychology. For some time, each of us didn't quite fit with the field. In retrospect, this sense of not fitting the normative categories was instrumental in helping us to shine a light on those very categories. Furthermore, by staying away from the mainstream of the field, we could raise questions more easily about the social construction of reality and of psychology in particular.

Our theories about cultural variation in ways of being a person and about the mutual constitution of culture and selves (e.g., Fiske, Kitayama, Markus, & Nisbett, 1998; Kitayama, Markus, Matsumoto, & Norasakkunkit, 1997; Markus & Kitayama, 1991) have their roots in our experiences in the hallways of the Research Center for Group Dynamics (RCGD) in the Institute for Social Research (ISR) at the University of Michigan. As part of a long-standing scholars exchange program between the RCGD and the University of Osaka, Hazel had visited and lectured in Japan a number of times in the 1980s. Japan was an unbelievably fascinating site for a student of social behavior, but the more she knew of Japan, the less she understood. Around that time, Shinobu had just finished his MA in Kyoto and subsequently found himself in Ann Arbor negotiating a land of smiling, friendly, but sometimes distant people. For each of us, our travels brought us into contact with worlds that, however agreeable, just did not feel right. The ISR was a safe space for our initial conversations and theoretical speculation. All topics were on the table and ripe for deconstruction and reconstruction.

Shinobu first became acutely aware of the interdependent self when he drew on his independent self and moved from Kyoto to Ann Arbor. Hazel had been in Japan as part of an exchange between the University of Michigan and Osaka University and, like many American social psychologists, was amazed and confused and wanted to talk about Japan. Meanwhile, Shinobu wanted to practice his English. Our conversations began just as psychology's social cognition movement was beginning to flourish. Shinobu was struck by how *asocial* American social psychology was, focusing on individual attitudes and schemas and much less on relationships and groups. He also noticed that Americans seemed to think that agency, or the energy for action, came from inside the person rather than from relations with others. He began to see that a schema of self as separate from others was related to the Western view that feeling is separate from thought and perception—another Cartesian divide. From his perspective, affect influences perception and attention; it is part and parcel of perception and attention—they were interdependent processes. This early questioning culminated in a conference on culture and emotion in 1991—the first of its kind. Furthermore, it was to bear fruit some years later, when both of us began raising questions about how emotion might be conditioned to play central roles in cultural variations in cognition and behavior (Kitayama & Markus, 1994).

As we began to talk, our converging irritation was with the mainstream assumption that there was one right way to be a self—an independent, self-interested, rational actor (meaning that the actor is separating his feelings from attention and cognition). Together, we shared the view that some people are clearly more independent, but some others are more obviously interdependent. At the same time, though, we also recognized that these two selves often coexist within the same person. Thus, one may use her independent self at work, but use her interdependent self at home. Our many different cultural contexts—those defined by region, race, gender, social class, religion, and type of workplace, among others—foster one self or another (see Markus & Conner, 2014, for recent discussions of this idea).

At this point, the field of social psychology was deeply (and, we should add, uncritically) wedded to the Western assumption that independence is better, more ethical, more active, and more potent than interdependence, which represents a secondary, weaker, and often compromised way of being. The resulting irritation fueled our conversations and the start of our collaboration. We discussed how in some social contexts, the self could be defined in relation to others and as part of a larger, encompassing social whole. In these contexts, the self was not a free agent but an agent that is committed to significant relationships. We both believed that there was more than one right answer to the questions of what is a person and what is the nature of agency. We saw no reason to believe that one self is better or more necessary than the other. Yet, the status quo of the field privileged one self over the other. We heeded Bob Zajonc's claim that good work often begins with irritation.

Some support for our thinking was grounded in gender studies. Before beginning to think about U.S.–Japan comparisons, Hazel had recognized that men often made the "me"/"not me" divide in a somewhat different way than women. Specifically, given the requirements and conditions of their social existence, women tended to include more people in the "me" and to elaborate a self that is rooted in relationships—a more interdependent self. Furthermore, the resulting model of social relations as more connected (versus separate) seemed to provide a model for more nonsocial objects, events, and situations. In this way, gender differences in self-schemas could give rise to somewhat different patterns of perception, thought, and feeling (Markus & Oyserman, 1989). Moreover, it seemed that having a connected, interdependent self instead of the more valued, separate, independent one need not comprise a difficulty or a conflict for women. The interdependent self was not a deficient self, just a different one.

Notably, Hazel's dissertation advisors (who were men) counseled against pursuing this topic in her research. They said that she would be marginalized and have difficulty finding a job. Moreover, identifying differences at a time when women were marching to show that they were equal to men was awkward because no matter the theoretical setup, a different self was invariably cast as a lesser self. So instead of comparing the selves of men and women, Hazel first worked on "the self."

At this point, there was not yet much outside interest in this cross-cultural project, but we thought that one way to raise important questions about the hegemonic social psychological paradigm might be to run a series of careful American/Japanese comparisons within standard social psychological experiments. Whatever is basic in basic social psychological processes, it is defined by a set of phenomena that are dear to the field, such as the fundamental attribution error, self-serving bias, and cognitive dissonance. There was a strong belief that these phenomena are universal and somehow reveal the very basic components of basic social psychological processes.

After a while, it became very clear that the Japanese do not always show effects that are taken for granted in the social psychological literature. As we revealed these differences in our research, people did not immediately assume as they did with gender, that the typical, the normative pattern for the United States was the *superior* pattern. This was because the 1980s had been the decade of "Japan is number one," and the idea was that Americans should be worried about Japanese success, just as Americans now worry about Chinese success. In many ways, Japan seemed superior to the United States—its cars were problem-free, its workers productive, and its children high-scoring. As a consequence, people became interested in learning about the Japanese way of doing business, work, school, and many other things. Some became open to the possibility that people in Japanese contexts might have different modes of being as well.

Our concern then, as now, was not with differences per se. Indeed, the world is rife with fascinating differences among groups of people, but cataloging them was not our agenda. Instead, our focus was on interdependence and the difference that the assumption that a person was not separate, but was in fact connected to others, made for thought, feeling, and action. We saw that so-called basic psychology was hardly context neutral but, instead, was a psychology of people engaged in particular cultures with specific ideas, patterns of interactions, and institutionalized policies and practices. More specifically, the notion of the independent self was not an empirically derived fact, but rather a philosophical and historical construction rooted in the idea of the authority of the individual—a product of Western enlightenment thinking, Christianity and the Protestant ethic, the Declaration of Independence, the frontier, the American dream, and all the institutions and interactions that carry and animate these ideas. Other contexts, other histories, other philosophies, other institutions, and other daily practices would foster other formulations of self.

Speculation, Questioning, and Appreciative Listening

Our shared irritation with mainstream psychology led to numerous conversations, and then to the realization that it was safe for us to talk about differences in behavior and their cultural sources. Neither of us would charge the other with insensitivity, with essentializing or stereotyping. We began to speculate in this safe environment. We looked for metaphors that might highlight the key cultural differences that we observed. Food, as always, was relevant. Perhaps the American self was like a jelly doughnut—the good stuff was in the middle—whereas the Japanese self was more like a bagel—it was not the middle, but the outside that mattered most? Or might Americans be more like dry rice and Japanese more like sticky rice? Are social relations really different in "stickiness," and if so, why?

As we developed a sense that the other would not take offense, we began to tell stories about our experiences. There were endless recountings of odd tendencies and weird patterns of behavior. One of our conversations began with Hazel's statement that the Japanese were "just weird." Some weeks later, Shinobu, in obvious frustration with this observation, countered, "If you want to know who is weird—it's Americans." Recently, Joe Henrich, Steve Heine, and Ara Norenzayan (2010) came to the same conclusion about many Westerners, and noted that *weird* is a perfect word because it is an acronym—W for Western, E for educated, I for industrialized, R for rich, and D for democratic. Moreover, they observed that that our current psychology knows everything about the weirdest people in the world, but much less about the 85% of the world who are the nonweirds.

As we speculated and traded observations, we began to ask questions. Why was it, Hazel wondered, that after weeks of lecturing in Japan to students with a good command of English, no one said anything—nothing—no questions, no comments. Even after assuring students that she was interested in their ideas, and especially in ideas that were different from hers, why was there still no response? What was wrong with these Japanese students? Where were the arguments, the debates, the signs of critical thinking? And, moreover, if you asked somebody a completely straightforward question, such as "Where is the best noodle shop?" why was the answer invariably an audible intake of air followed by the response, "It depends." Didn't Japanese students have their own preferences, ideas, opinions, and attitudes? What is inside a person's head if it isn't these kinds of things? How could you know someone if she did not tell you what she was thinking?

Shinobu listened and then asked his own questions. He was curious about why students shouldn't just listen to a lecture, and why American students in particular felt the need to be constantly active, to talk all the time, often interrupting each other and talking over each other and the professor? And why did the comments and questions of his fellow students reveal such strong emotions and have such a competitive edge? What was the point of this arguing? Why did intelligence seem to be associated with getting the best of another person, even within a group such as a class, where people knew each other well?

Sure, it was true, Hazel responded, that some Americans were on the extroverted side. However, wasn't that better than the reticence and low self-esteem of Japanese professors and students? Why, for example, did Japanese visiting scholars begin their talks with an apology? "I'm sorry, but I am not the best qualified person to give this presentation, and I hope that you will forgive the fact that I may waste your time." How could you learn something from someone who had this type of self-presentation? And on the topic of presentations, why is it when you gave a talk as a visitor in Japan, people were completely impassive and said almost nothing when you were finished?

Shinobu asked why American psychologists began their talks with a joke, even in important settings. And why do friends of the speaker gather around after the talk and give hugs and say the talk was "great" and "fantastic" and "the best ever," sometimes even in spite of the quality of the talk? Why the constant evaluation? Why the superlatives and the extreme reactions? Why the need to distinguish a particular talk from all others? And why the effort to make the speaker and the audience feel good?

And, he continued, why at the party after a talk, do hosts bombard their guests with questions and choices? Do you want wine or beer or soft drinks or juice or water, or would you rather have something hot, coffee or tea? Wine? Do you want red or white? What was the point of burdening the guest with these trivial decisions? Surely the host knew what would be good refreshment to serve on this occasion? (See Markus & Kitayama, 2003, for more on these initial speculations and answers.)

These questions about the peculiarities of everyday life in different cultural contexts led to all types of larger questions, and finally to questions that were tractable and that became the basis of our research programs. Speculative conversations and the questions they generated (like the ones discussed here) will never appear in journal publications, but such exchanges are critical in developing new ideas in uncharted terrain. To make such exchanges both meaningful and productive, however, one needs collaborators one trusts and can confide in. Collaboration, we discovered, requires a great deal of the very phenomenon we began to examine—interdependence. Many small practices encourage it; many small practices can subtly discourage it. Shinobu had a habit that Hazel found particularly valuable. He would often ask, "*How* are you thinking?" Very often, it was easier to describe the process even if the outcome wasn't clear yet. "*What* are you thinking?" is a more challenging question.

Trust and Solidarity

As we became committed to the idea of a cultural psychology project, we discovered fellow travelers who had cleared some of the brush. Rick Shweder and Bob Levine's (1984) book, *Culture Theory*, was important. The book included a paper that Shweder and Edmund Bourne (1992) written, titled "Does the Concept of the Person Vary Cross-Culturally?" The same year, Carol Gilligan (1982) wrote *In a Different Voice*, in which she argued that men's way of being moral was not the model for everyone and, in contrast to Lawrence Kohlberg's theory of moral development, claimed that women's ethic of caring and relationships was not an inferior or secondary way of being, but instead a different and equally viable ethic. Around the same time, Harry Triandis presented an empirical analysis of the concept of *sympatia*—an emphasis on creating and maintaining warm, agreeable feelings toward others that is common among Mexicans and in Latino-American contexts but not in European-American ones (Triandis, Marin, Lisansky, & Bettancourt, 1984). Another significant paper was by Joan Miller (1984), who revealed that both children and adults in India are much less likely than children and adults in North America to make the fundamental attribution error and are more likely to explain behavior in terms of the situation. This latter work marked the beginning of intensive research efforts to figure out the cultural basis of daily social cognitions, emotions, and motivations and to document it with multiple methods.

Despite our view that cultural psychology was in many ways a straightforward extension of the social psychological perspective that the situation matters, our research programs produced a wide variety of detractors. Especially numerous were people who insisted that calling attention to differences based on ethnicity or region of origin was stereotyping and potentially racist. We argued that noting difference is not the problem—discovering patterns in behavior is the goal of psychology. The problem comes with what is believed to be the source of the difference and then what is done about that difference. Difference need not be essentialized, and noticing a difference need not lead to creating, maintaining, and justifying some groups as more equal than others.

The mainstream of social psychology until relatively recently has been almost completely color-blind (read culture-blind, gender-blind, ethnicity- and race-blind, class-blind, religion-blind, etc.)—and proudly so because the original notion of color-blindness was a progressive ideal from the civil rights era tied to the view that everyone could claim rights and equal protection before the law and that no one should be devalued or limited by one's social category affiliations. From our point of view, however, it was quite problematic to authenticate only one "color"—the "Western color"—and use it as a single, one-size-fits-all kind of model for the rest of humanity. Much more desirable, we felt, was to identify some different "colors," with a clear recognition that each of these colors may have its own logic and standards of truth, goodness, and beauty grounded in the commitments and practices of everyday lives. Yet, the vast majority in the field, or so it seemed to us, was so deeply committed to the idea of psychic unity or a "single color" view of humanity. Given this situation, it was a risky proposition to argue that there might in fact be different "colors," or multiple psychologies. Much needed to be explicated before we could show that this "multicolor" view would eventually be more justifiable, fairer, and closer to the truth. The rest of the field was quite impatient with our argument.

In these circumstances, a collaborator who understands the roll of your eyes and with whom you can share your rant is invaluable. So is a collaborator who tells you to calm down, who can take the critic's point of view and explain how what you have written or just said is really not very clear or persuasive. Intellectual risks are easier to take if at least one person has your back. There is strength and confidence in collaboration. Collaborators can say your words back to you in ways that give them new meanings and take them in new directions. They can challenge you and tell you that things make no sense, or construct the sentence that says exactly what you mean. They can buffer you from stress and expand your consciousness. One and one equals much more than two.

At the aforementioned conference on culture and emotion in 1991, we found other collaborators. Along with these new partners, we made an implicit pact to create and maintain a cultural perspective in psychology. We didn't work together on every project, but we shared a framework and a commitment to that framework that we honed through stories and anecdotes about our experiences and data that reflected our efforts to make sense of them. Nothing beats a partner who listens and who tries to connect with your notion or who says "yes, and" rather than "no" to an idea or a hypothesis.

The meaning and psycho-logic of the small acts and minor social encounters that were the stuff of our first conversations and anecdotes were obvious to the native, yet surprisingly difficult to articulate to the outsider. Comprehending these situations required layer upon layer of culture-specific knowledge and understanding and then a series of studies to draw out the differences. Although accused of practicing anthropology without a license, we insisted on drawing out how the differences we observed were the result of a distinct culture cycle of ideas, institutions, interactions, and individuals. A classroom was not just a classroom, a party was not a party, and a talk was not a talk. Each was a site of social significance, but the significance varied by cultural context. We studied and analyzed interactions, everyday practices, institutional policies, and cultural products—ads, websites, songs, books, newspapers. Themes began to emerge.

In recounting her experiences, Hazel often found that Japanese hosts and colleagues were taking too much control and undermining her independence while simultaneously refraining from expressing themselves. For Shinobu, such "control" was "taking care" and maintaining a relationship. And just as Hazel did not experience a comfortable feeling of being taken care of when she did not get to choose her own dinner in Japan, Shinobu felt irritated when given what seemed to him to be an excessive amount of choice to make in, say, an American restaurant. Just as Hazel was completely comfortable and in fact enjoyed making the choice at the American restaurant (isn't the choice an additional spice to enhance the taste of the food?), Shinobu's "autonomy" was not undermined at all just because the Japanese dinner afforded him no choice about what to consume and enjoy. To him, keeping one's preferences and opinions to oneself was not a result of low self-esteem or false modesty but was most often an act of consideration and an effort not to burden others. And the answer "It depends" reflected a sense that one should not impose one's preferences on others and that there is no absolute best taste. What tastes good will depend on the context and the preferences of the diner at that moment. Subtle distinctions were drawn out in hours of conversation that were often very murky in the beginning. Our frustration with the field and our mutual trust fueled our faith that mapping and explaining our psychologies to each other was worth the effort.

We took turns making the strange familiar and the familiar strange. Japanese students, Shinobu explained, typically do not question or challenge or interrupt because, as a student, one's role is to take in information from the professor, who is presumably an expert on the topic. If a question has not been answered, one should pay closer attention. Before asking a question, a student should ask, "Does this question need to be asked, and, if so, am I the right one to ask it?" If, for example, there is a senior student in the room, a student with more knowledge and experience, and the question has not been asked, then there is probably not a need for the question to be asked. For American students, this attention to one's place in the social order is replaced with a concern for self-expression. You cannot wait for someone to read your mind; you have to reveal your own thoughts and feelings. And having attitudes and opinions and being able to articulate them is a sign of intelligence. We are what we think. And debating with others is a way to sharpen and clarify one's thoughts. To get ahead, to be a successful person, it is important to be a squeaky wheel—isn't it?

For Shinobu, the idea of purposely drawing attention to oneself was not immediately sensible. Being the tall poppy or the nail that stands out sets one apart and makes one vulnerable. There is comfort in fitting in with others, in being part of a larger social whole, and in being sure of the sympathy of others. Apologizing before a presentation is not a sign of low self-esteem; it is an effort not to set oneself apart from others and to engender their sympathy. Deferring to others works to maintain a sense of interdependence with the audience. Not only that, but the way that most people do things is also a good way.

For an American social psychologist, marching to the beat of the other guy's drum is potentially problematic. After all, much of social psychology is devoted to the perils of conformity and obedience, and "others" are often cast as exerting unwanted pressure. Sociality and individuality do not often hold hands; they are usually conceptualized as antagonistic. Going one's own way and choosing for oneself are acts of self-definition and self-affirmation. Similarly, one's products and one's achievements are self-defining, and for that reason, praise and positive feedback after giving a talk, for example, are ubiquitous. It is not enough to feel part of things and connected; it is necessary to feel good about oneself, and positive evaluations all around accomplish this task. In Japan, such praise is less necessary because the honor is in being invited in the first place. The invitation communicates what matters most, which is one's valued place in the social network.

When you are trying to make the case for something that is counterintuitive from the mainstream social psychological perspective—for example, the idea that choice is not always that pleasant and can in fact be a burden, that talking doesn't equal thinking, or that a sense of sameness can be a good or desirable feeling—it is invaluable to have a collaborator who shares your view and bolsters your view. It is easy to lose confidence when many people simultaneously stare at you blankly.

Patience and Adjustment

Trust and solidarity are critical to collaboration because they foster patience. Very often, given the pressures of academic life, we dismiss or give up on ideas, concepts, or people we don't understand. Once you trust that a colleague has good ideas, you are likely to try harder to understand and to be patient with that person. Often, real insight ensues. We found this to be the key to our own collaboration, and we have tried to convey this to our own students. Benefiting from dialogues across difference requires patience. In the case of an East–West divide, language and terms are often an issue, but even when language is not an issue and the divide is gender, class, or workplace within one region of the world, understanding contexts other than one's own requires the communication of a great deal of historically and culturally specific knowledge that we are not used to unpacking.

As an example, our own two-person collaboration now has expanded to include a team of researchers from four locations within the United States and two in Japan. The project we are all working on focuses on physical, mental, and social well-being in middle adulthood and involves a comparison of multiple types of data from two large representative samples of Japanese and Americans participating in the Midlife in the United States (MIDUS) and Midlife in Japan (MIDJA) survey studies. In-person meetings of this group take place twice a year, but we also meet once a week by Skype. First of all, this means that several members of the team are meeting at less than optimal times, (e.g., 3 p.m. in Palo Alto means 7 a.m. in Kyoto). And this is only the first of many adjustments required for this collaboration. The Americans need to be patient and to adjust to the idea that silence does not mean that the other people on the call have nothing to say or that they agree with what has just been said. Rather, it often means disagreement or that people are taking their time to present their views in a way that does not seem contentious or competitive.

Among the Americans, disagreement or confusion often takes a combative form ("That doesn't make sense!"). Among the Japanese, it is much more indirect and is often expressed as a question rather than a statement ("Is that a new type of analysis?"). Furthermore, the Japanese collaborators need to be patient with and adjust to the fact that many Americans use talking as a way of discovering what they are thinking or clarifying their thinking. Americans need to adjust to the fact that the silence does not always have to be immediately filled with the sound of their voices. Given these sharp cultural differences in how people communicate and in what they feel is proper to say directly, our team has found that asking everybody to track comments on a paper before a Skype meeting works best to ensure that everyone (or almost everyone, anyway) participates and has a say.

Our Japanese collaborators have learned to adjust to the Americans' strong displays of emotion—for example, anger with reviewers who fail to see the world their way—and effusive displays of happiness when they do. And the Americans on the team have now come to appreciate the calmer emotions of the Japanese members. Somehow the Japanese collaborators don't seem to have the same sharp dip in well-being when things don't go their way. Instead, they are relatively more attuned to hardship and to finding a way to *gamberu* (i.e., keep working hard).

Our weekly efforts at patience and adjustment to cultural practices different from our own strengthen our interdependence and also our theorizing about interdependence. Through our discussions and our repeated efforts to explain ourselves to each other, we have begun to understand the ways in which our emotions are culturally shaped. What is really fascinating is that casual observations in collaborative efforts themselves constitute the source of ideas and questions, which may then be further discussed and even tested by the collaborative team itself. In this way, our collaborative work as a social institution has become a self-reflecting mirror to learn the larger cultural world in which the team is embedded and of which it is part.

For example, although everyone seems to experience negative emotions, they seem more consequential for the well-being of the Americans. Our Japanese collaborators appear annoyed by negative feelings (e.g., such as those instigated by the rejection of a grant proposal), and they tend to see them as a step toward a better state of affairs, or, failing that, at least as a necessary part of life that carries no particular evaluative connotations for the self. In sharp contrast, our American team members seem to take their negative feelings very seriously because they are experienced as an indication of a threat or a self-deficit of some sort. For our Japanese members, it is strained relationships, not negative feelings, that are a major threat to well-being. Our work has documented that these observations are valid when tested against the large-scale survey data we have at hand (Curhan et al., 2014; Miyamoto et al., 2013).

We also see that when our American team members cannot realize their goals, they are frustrated and express anger. This is not the same for the Japanese, for whom expression of anger is much less common. It does occur, but primarily by those at the top of the social hierarchy who are afforded the privilege of anger. This curious cultural mark on the apparently basic emotion of anger has consequences. For example, in the United States, people with lower social status express anger more than those with higher status because they are frustrated, whereas in Japan, people in higher social status express anger more than those with lower status because they have more authority to display this anger (Park et al., 2013).

In these and many other cases, the cultural psycho-logic that gives rise to divergent subjective and intersubjective experiences among the colleagues on our collaborative team is illuminated through, as well as tested in, our close, highly rewarding, and collaborative effort. These experiences on the collaborative team are local in the sense that they take place only among the limited number of people involved in this project. What is increasingly apparent, however, is the fact that they have been years in the making, and they contain foundational components that give rise to larger, collective cultural patterns that we as a team seek to understand and analyze, first in a series of academic publications, and then in publications prepared for a more general audience.

Conclusions

In sum, it seems to us that four ingredients have been identified here as the basis of our collaboration: (1) shared irritation and purpose; (2) speculation, questioning, and appreciative listening; (3) trust and solidarity; and (4) patience and adjustment. Shared irritation and purpose and speculation and questioning are easy, but listening, patience, and adjustment are harder, especially for academics in North American settings that constantly afford the opportunity to express one's self and seldom require holding one's tongue or thinking from another's point of view. Quieting one's own internal chatter in order to listen appreciatively to someone else making a point is difficult—and all the more so when you are sure you have already heard and rejected the point in question. Yet it is a skill that we have come to see is worth cultivating.

The cultivation of independence in our own relationship has been a guide to understanding and exploring the phenomenon of interdependence more generally. To understand it, we needed to model it ourselves. Collaborative dyads or larger groups will typically have to figure out ways to do this on their own because there is not yet much cultural support for interdependence. While there is a growing discourse about the importance of team science and the virtues of a quick spread of innovation among minds, few schools, workplaces, or communities explicitly foster the development of interdependent practices.

Successful collaboration, then, requires the judicious use of both the independent and interdependent selves. The independent self sees differences, expresses one's preferences and goals, tries to influence others and remain free from control by others, doubts, and criticizes. The interdependent self sees commonalities, listens, makes connections, is committed to relationships, and tries to adjust to others and to fit in with them. Both ways of being are necessary, and neither is sufficient by itself. The independent way of being is familiar and well practiced. In the West, the interdependent way of being is less valued and therefore less practiced. The secret is to develop both of these selves and to know which self to use when. Our collaboration is an important source of ideas and inspirations, as well as social support and a sense of direction for the future. It is a mirror of the two very different cultural worlds that we are studying. In the mirror, the worlds are writ small, manageable, and safe to analyze, dissect, and then eventually reconstruct. The resulting view of the worlds that we developed is the mutual constitution of culture and the self—a view that we are extending beyond the original focus on psychological differences between the United States and Japan. Hazel has extended the basic framework not only to gender (as mentioned earlier) but also to social class, achievement gaps in the United States, and many clashes of subcultures and groups (Markus & Conner, 2014), while Shinobu has recently ventured into neuroscience, asking questions on how culture might be interdependent with the brain and genes that underpin it (Kitayama & Huff, 2014). In the MIDUS-MIDJA collaborative effort, the focus is gradually shifting to another kind of interdependence—namely, interdependence between culture, biological health, and morbidity and mortality.

In retrospect, then, we were very lucky to have met in Ann Arbor. The interdependence that we initially analyzed between culture and self has remained the basic framework for studying all other kinds of interdependencies that are abundantly present in society. If we are successful in some aspects of this endeavor, it is because of the very interdependence that we ourselves have developed. And the nature of this interdependence seems to provide a key to any successful collaborative effort.

▪ REFERENCES ▪

Curhan, K., Sims, T., Markus, H., Kitayama, S., Karasawa, M., Kawakami, N., … Ryff, C. (Eds). (2014). Just how bad negative affect is for your health depends on culture. *Psychological Science, 25*(12), 2277–2280.

Fiske, A., Kitayama, S., Markus, H. R., & Nisbett, R. E. (1998). The cultural matrix of social psychology. In D. Gilbert, S. Fiske, & G. Lindzey (Eds.), *The handbook of social psychology* (Vol. 2, 4th ed., pp. 915–981). San Francisco, CA: McGraw-Hill.

Gilligan, C. (1982). *In a Different Voice*. Cambridge, MA: Harvard University Press.

Henrich, J., Heine, S. J., & Norenzayan, A. (2010). Most people are not WEIRD. *Nature, 466*, 29.

Kitayama, S., & Huff, S. (2014). Cultural neuroscience: Connecting culture, brain, and genes. In R. Scott & S. Kosslyn (Eds.), *Emerging trends in the social and behavioral sciences*, pp. 1–16. Hoboken, NJ: John Wiley & Sons.

Kitayama, S., & Markus, H. R. (1994). Culture and self: How cultures influence the way we view ourselves. In D. Matsumoto (Ed.), *People: Psychology from a cultural perspective* (pp. 17–37). Pacific Grove, CA: Brooks/Cole Publishing Company.

Kitayama, S., Markus, H. R., Matsumoto, H., & Norasakkunkit, V. (1997). Individual and collective processes in the construction of the self: Self-enhancement in the United States and self-criticism in Japan. *Journal of Personality and Social Psychology, 72*(6), 1245–1267.

Markus, H. R., & Conner, A. C. (2014). *Clash! How to thrive in a multicultural world.* New York, NY: Penguin (Hudson Street Press).

Markus, H., & Kitayama, S. (1991). Culture and the self: Implications for cognition, emotion, and motivation. *Psychological Review, 98*, 224–253.

Markus, H. R., & Kitayama, S. (2003). Culture, self, and the reality of the social. *Psychological Inquiry, 14*(3–4), 277–283.

Markus, H. R., & Kitayama, S. (2010). Cultures and selves: A cycle of mutual constitution. *Perspectives on Psychological Science, 5*(4), 420–430.

Markus, H., & Oyserman, D. (1989). Gender and thought: The role of the self-concept. In M. Crawford & M. Gentry (Eds.), *Gender and thought* (pp. 100–127). New York, NY: Springer-Verlag.

Miller, J. G. (1984). Culture and the development of everyday social explanation. *Journal of Personality and Social Psychology, 46*(5), 961–978.

Miyamoto, Y., Boylan, J. M., Coe, C. L., Curhan, K. B., Levine, C. S., Markus, H. R., … Ryff, C. D. (2013). Negative emotions predict elevated interleukin-6 in the United States but not in Japan. *Brain Behavior and Immunity, 34*, 79–85. doi:10.1016/j.bbi.2013.07.173

Park, J., Kitayama, S., Markus, H. R., Coe, C. L., Miyamoto, Y., Karasawa, M., ... Ryff, C. D. (2013). Social status and anger expression: The cultural moderation hypothesis. *Emotion*, *13*(6), 1122–1131. doi:10.1037/a0034273

Shweder, R., & Levine, B. (Eds.), (1984). *Culture theory: Essays on mind, self, and emotion*. Cambridge, England: Cambridge University Press.

Shweder, R. A., & Bourne, E. J. (1982). Does the concept of the person vary cross-culturally? In A. J. Marsella & G. M. White (Eds.), *Cultural conceptions of mental health and therapy* (pp. 97–137). Dordrecht, the Netherlands: D. Reidel Publishing Company.

Triandis, H. C., Marin, G., Lisansky, J., & Betancourt, H. (1984). Simpatia as a cultural script of Hispanics. *Journal of Personality and Social Psychology*, *47*, 1363–1375.

Chapter 9: A 50-Year Conversation

Richard E. Nisbett

Theodore M. Newcomb Distinguished University Professor
Department of Psychology
University of Michigan

Lee Ross

Stanford Federal Credit Union Professor of Humanities and Sciences
Department of Psychology
Stanford University

Origins of Our Collaboration

In 1965, Dick was in his fourth year as a graduate student at Columbia University, working with Stanley Schachter, when Lee arrived as a new student. Our first contact involved discussions about each other's work—especially Dick's dissertation work on obesity—but we soon began to discuss psychology in general, to gossip about fellow students and senior figures in the field, and ultimately to talk about each other's lives. That conversation has gone on ever since, always mixing the personal and the intellectual, sometimes talking about the relevance of psychology to a better understanding of real-world issues and events, and sometimes focusing on specific phenomena and working backward in an effort to discern the role of psychological processes, as well as political, social, and economic ones.

Over the next two decades, we continued to talk to each other frequently. But it was only a dozen years after the beginning of our relationship that we actually began to collaborate. The joint project produced the book *Human Inference: Strategies and Shortcomings of Social Judgment* (Nisbett & Ross, 1980). A decade later, we collaborated on a second book, *The Person and the Situation: Perspectives of Social Psychology* (Ross & Nisbett, 1991). We have never formally collaborated on a journal article or research project. Yet we have scarcely published anything that we thought might be of value without seeking each other's feedback. And we lean on each other heavily in the earliest stages of any project, when we are considering whether an idea is worth pursuing and how it can be pursued most effectively and interestingly.

We could scarcely have come from more different backgrounds. Dick was raised Protestant in a conservative middle-class family in El Paso, Texas, but early on, he recognized that his views and aspirations differed from those of his peers. Lee was raised in a Jewish working-class family in a primarily Jewish neighborhood in Toronto, with parents who were Communists and thoroughly (even aggressively) antireligious. He too recognized early on that he did not share his parents' politics, and he came to be skeptical about political radicalism in general. Interestingly, both mined their backgrounds in later research. In Dick's case, that was studying the culture of honor; in Lee's case, it was research into belief perseverance and rationalization in the face of disconfirmation of belief.

Our conversations have always included heavy doses of politics. Despite the difference in our backgrounds, our politics converged very quickly in the direction of pragmatic liberalism—with a respect for the human values of classical liberalism, but a shared skepticism about conventional leftist diagnoses and proposed remedies. The adjective that best describes Dick and Lee is *reformist* rather than *liberal* or *leftist*. We are not entirely unsympathetic to some elements of classic conservative and libertarian critiques (especially those involving the need to promote personal responsibility and sense of agency, and the pitfalls of big government bureaucracies). But we are decidedly unsympathetic to the remedies typically proposed by classic conservatives (to say nothing of the views of the loony, extreme right wing of the current Republican Party in the United States). Much of our discussion focuses on the characteristics of wise intervention and the need to test ideas rather than argue from fixed political positions.

Dick has always wanted to be up on everything political, but he has never been willing to devote the time and energy necessary to become as knowledgeable as he would want in order to have well-grounded opinions. He feels that Lee has always been more politically attuned. Dick generally has enjoyed the luxury of simply borrowing Lee's opinions about any matter about which he is ignorant. Lee in turn notes that any ideas Dick "borrows" get returned in a somewhat revised form. Beyond engaging in armchair commentary, we occasionally have enjoyed the opportunity to provide input to Democratic candidates, including both John Kerry and Barack Obama. Usually, our reward has been the ability to say that our advice has been ignored at the very highest levels, but on occasion (notably, working with other social scientists to craft "Get out the Vote" telephone calls), we actually saw our suggestions adopted.

Whether discussing politics or policy, our conversation is peppered with references to psychological and other social science concepts. Some of the most commonly discussed concepts include causal attribution, dissonance, assimilation biases, naive realism, prospect theory, framing effects, priming effects, and applications of statistical and methodological reasoning to everyday thought. Discussions frequently center on class, gender, and cultural factors.

Just as there is little daylight between them politically, Dick's and Lee's views on psychology and intellectual matters more generally have been, if not always identical, at least highly compatible. This is more remarkable than it might seem, given their backgrounds. As a Canadian rather than an American, as Jewish rather than Protestant, and as someone with an early distrust of laissez-faire economic policies, Lee was well prepared to adopt the situational field theory of Kurt Lewin and his intellectual grandson, Stanley Schachter. For Dick, encountering the Lewin/Schachter view of psychology was a pronounced shock. His independent subculture had led him to view the world in highly individualistic and dispositional terms. The Dustbowl learning theory and the psychoanalytic theory that he absorbed at Tufts as an undergraduate reinforced those predilections. The Lewinian tradition gave Lee and Dick a common framework, which Lee accepted implicitly but which was always a struggle for Dick. Lee benefited from his cultural preparation for situationism in picking up the Lewin/Schachter orientation, but Dick actually also benefited from having to radically revise his views and prejudices into that framework.

When Dick joined the faculty at Yale in 1966, he continued to travel frequently to New York to visit with Lee and other friends. The fact that Lee had a spouse who created a real home, as well as room for a guest in his apartment, was a situational factor that promoted their post-1966 contact. We continued to educate one another and to jointly develop views that became the basis of our careers. Our conversations never felt like work, even when we both were highly focused on advancing our research.

Schachter had taught us, by example, that not only is it the case that when people are doing their most important work, they can be having great fun; but when they are having the most fun talking and gossiping, they may be doing the spadework for work that they value greatly. Indeed, we share the view that the great thing about being a social psychologist is that it's never clear when you're *not* working. Our discussions move seamlessly from psychological topics to politics to literature and gossip in a way that seems to add depth to theoretical ideas and empirical contributions. The benefit of this loose-lipped conversational style is more of a boon for the Protestant, nose-to-the-grindstone Dick than for the more laid-back Lee, who needs much less in the way of excuses to assuage his guilt about not working.

Despite their common theoretical orientation, Lee and Dick have very different skills and interests. Lee is a classic social psychologist with a cognitive bent, whereas Dick is more of a cognitive psychologist who cares about the social implications of the way people reason and the errors and biases they succumb to. This difference seems to both of them to be a source of synergy as they go back and forth from the social to the cognitive.

Dick feels that he has always made far more use of Lee intellectually than Lee has of him. (The way he pictures this is that he is able to attach an extra brain to his own at will.) Dick regards Lee as having impeccable taste in psychological ideas (and, for that matter, in ideas generally). Whenever he has a new idea, he takes it to Lee for appraisal. If Lee is not thrilled, Dick generally drops it. If Lee is interested, it's full speed ahead—always checking back with Lee for criticism and reframing.

Dick's contribution to Lee's career began with his encouraging him to begin working with Stan Schachter in 1966, as well as his insistence that Stan take on Lee as a student. Dick literally told Stan that he *had* to work with Lee. Lee feels that Dick has always been his professional guru, spurring him to work harder and to do the necessary things to improve and showcase his work, as well as advance his career. Dick also introduces Lee to new issues that merit more consideration than they are currently receiving. Over the years, this has included introducing Lee to the problem of awareness of the causes of one's behavior (stemming from Dick's work with Tim Wilson when Tim was in graduate school at Michigan), the role of culture both in violent behavior and in modes of thinking, and, most recently, the nature of intelligence and the inseparability of genetic and environmental influences.

The earliest big payoff of our continuing conversation came when Dick was beginning to write a paper called "The Actor and the Observer" with Ned Jones. The thrust of this analysis (Jones & Nisbett, 1972) was that the actor tends to attribute his behavior to the situation, whereas the observer of the action tends to attribute the behavior to dispositions—traits, attitudes, abilities, etc. Without any hesitation at all, Lee said that that hypothesis was undoubtedly correct, but it missed the larger point that attribution in general is far too dispositional. This, of course, was an early source of Lee's later work describing lay dispositionism and the Fundamental Attribution Error (FAE). The episode illustrates a common occurrence: One of us has an idea that the other thinks is provocative, but that could be even better and deeper with a little tweaking. Most recently, Dick has been encouraging Lee to hone his account of naive realism, as well as its relevance both to everyday misunderstandings and to intergroup and intercultural conflict.

One of the most important aspects of the FAE idea, which figured so heavily in our second book, *The Person and the Situation*, is that beyond reviewing evidence supporting an empirical proposition, it contains a critique of human behavior on normative grounds. It's hard to overemphasize the extent to which that was unusual in the 1970s. Social scientists of the time had all been raised on the injunction that it was inappropriate for social scientists to prescribe—their job was strictly to describe.

The normative stance, which both of us recognized as one of the great strengths of the Kahneman and Tversky work on judgmental heuristics (Tversky & Kahneman, 1974), soon became important in Dick's research at Michigan with Gene Borgida on base-rate neglect and in Lee's research with Mark Lepper on belief perseverance. The tremendously influential work of Ned Jones and Hal Kelley on attribution theory was largely descriptive, focusing on the principles that people use in assessing the causes of actions and outcomes and the inferences that can reasonably be made about actors on the basis of their responses to particular situations. One such principle involved behavioral consensus (whether all, most, or only a few actors respond in a particular manner to a particular object or situation). What Nisbett and Borgida showed was that consensus information has oddly little impact on behavior. People were almost as likely to attribute behavior to the stimulus if most people behaved toward it as the actor did as they were if only a few behaved that way.

When Dick told Lee about this finding, Lee told Dick about the work of Kahneman and Tversky, showing that people tend to ignore base rate information in general and to focus on individuating information about the target. The Kahneman and Tversky interpretation was, of course, profoundly normative at its base: subjects' behavior was being compared to statistical standards and found wanting. It's hard for people today to realize how radical that move was at that time and how bitterly it was attacked by scandalized psychologists and philosophers. The attack had two prongs: (1) it was wrong to ascribe to people intellectual failings (or any other kind of failing), and (2) in fact, people weren't wrong—it was Kahneman and Tversky (and fellow travelers like Nisbett and Ross) who were wrong.

Critics tried to establish that the research was badly done, subjects' behavior was perfectly correct, and the investigators' reasoning about how to think about their problems was mistaken, or preferably both. This line of criticism continued through Gerd Gigerenzer's unending efforts to prove that the biases and errors were on the investigators' part, not the subjects' (Gigrenzer & Brighton, 2009; Gigerenzer & Goldstein, 1996). It continues today, though it is pretty clear that the normative tradition, including both its prescriptive and descriptive aspects, won the argument within psychology. Moreover, Kahneman and Tversky's investigation of departures from normativeness has literally transformed the field of behavioral economics (which Lee insists is social psychology with "a name change for business reasons").

The normative stance was integral to *Human Inference* (Nisbett & Ross, 1980), a major expansion of Dick's work with Gene Borgida and Lee's 1977 Advances Chapter on attributional biases. That chapter was titled "The intuitive psychologist and his shortcomings: Distortions in the attribution process" (Ross, 1977), but it basically was restricted to a discussion of attributional biases, including the fundamental attribution error and belief perseverance. The *Human Inference* book took on a broad range of intuitive psychology tasks, from the interpretation of events using cognitive schemas to the accommodation of theories to empirical evidence. It included prediction and induction, as well as covariation assessment—a task that is implicit in the attribution process described by both Jones and Kelley. In short, we attempted to provide a framework for the type of inferences that people make about the social actors, behavior, and contexts that they encounter.

The book made normative proposals throughout: (1) Schemas are sometimes relied upon too heavily, (2) the vividness of information is given too much weight, (3) generalizations from population data to case data are too weak and from case data to population assumptions too strong, (4) assessment of covariation is poor and far too driven by preconceptions, (5) causal analysis makes too much use of the representativeness heuristic and too little use of base rate information, (6) prediction is often nonregressive, and (7) theories are often impervious to change in the face of data that ought to compel alteration of beliefs. Not all of this work, including the normative assertions, was entirely original, of course. What made the book distinctive was its comprehensive approach to such a broad range of reasoning about human behavior.

The original impetus, and most of the content of *Human Inference*, was provided by Dick—especially the idea of going beyond social psychology to consider inductive and deductive processes more generally. He presented the basic outline of the book to Lee more or less in its entirety. Lee had ideas about every chapter, and it quickly became clear: A book could be produced by teamwork that would be far better than anything Dick could produce by himself.

Endless conversations followed, with Dick (who was childless at the time) spending weeks at a time in Palo Alto, alternately talking with Lee and working on the book when Lee was occupied with work or family. Most chapters were first-drafted by Dick (Lee did the first draft of only three of the nine chapters), with Lee weighing in most heavily in second drafts and Dick doing most of the prose polishing. We are not sure now why we did it that way—Dick's stronger work ethic no doubt played a role, and Lee found it very satisfying to critique Dick's drafts—but it proved to be a very comfortable and productive way to work.

Interestingly, neither Lee nor Dick ever felt the need to go back and examine the prior drafts of his coauthor. Remember that this was in the days of handwritten manuscripts being typed by secretaries and sent back and forth via snail mail—with no computers to track changes. Neither were there any significant disagreements about what should or should not be in the book. (However, there were several times when Dick talked through an outline of a chapter to Lee, and Lee had serious doubts. Invariably, when Lee saw the written product, he endorsed the thrust and general content and then went on to revise it in a way that erased those doubts.)

In retrospect, given our shared reputation for being strongly opinionated, it seems odd to us that ego played so little role in that book—or, for that matter, in any other aspect of our relationship. Neither of us ever dug in on a position to a degree that the other felt was unreasonable. Moreover, we can recall only a very few occasions when there was a dispute about who had a particular idea first—and on those occasions, it always was an insistence that the original idea was the *other* guy's!

It also seems odd to us that though we talked theory and research all the time, we never were particularly motivated to collaborate on research. Lee had his set of ideas that he was pursuing, and Dick had his. We admired and made use of each other's research but were never inclined to take part in it. We also seem to have recognized, without discussing the issue, that collaboration with each other would likely have diminished the role of our students in the various steps from conception of an idea to completion of a project, robbing them of the experience that we found so valuable in working with our mentor.

Our second book, *The Person and the Situation: Perspectives of Social Psychology* (Ross & Nisbett, 1991) was prompted by Lee's continuing focus on issues of attributional processes and biases, and also by the graduate course he had been teaching for many years (and still teaches, with his colleague Mark Lepper). Lee felt that there were a few core messages of social psychology that could get lost in standard textbooks, and that the forest was much more important than the sum of the trees that appear in textbooks. The book was in one sense a huge expansion of the FAE: People fail to see situational factors as clearly as they could, and they overemphasize the role of dispositions. It also dealt heavily with the importance of construing situational factors and the role of dynamic tension systems, and sought to highlight Walter Mischel's critique of the then-contemporary trait-based focus of personality theory and at the same time, to point out ways in which individual differences, though often outweighed by situational factors (and sometimes confounded or reinforced by such factors), matter a great deal over the long haul. The book was intended partly as an olive branch to personality psychologists—many of whom treated it as if it were a cat-o'-nine-tails instead.

We're not quite sure why we never collaborated on research. The following are our best guesses:

1. Except for 1 year, we always lived 2,500 miles or more apart. We both believe that research collaboration involves very close and continuing hands-on attention to detail.

2. We never happened to be doing work in the exact same domain at the same time.

3. We realized that if we did collaborate, it would have been at the expense of our student collaborators. They would have been excluded from too much of the fleshing out of ideas and thrashing out details of what to do, what data mean, and other issues.

Nor are we sure what we have to offer in the way of advice for others. Each collaboration is unique (as the readers of the present volume will soon recognize), so general prescriptions are unlikely to be useful. You don't choose longtime collaborators—you just recognize again and again that you want the collaboration to continue because it is proving to be satisfying (again, no doubt in different ways and for different reasons for different partnerships). However, we do believe that nourishing a collaboration with discussion of more than just the joint work is important. Having the freedom and using the opportunity to continue to explore ideas that you are *not* working on are keys to enjoying and fully appreciating the greatest privilege of an academic life. And such dialogue no doubt also strengthens the specific joint projects.

We have supported one another through many a personal crisis and have become deeply involved with each other's families. In addition to thinking that Lee is his extra brain, Dick feels that Lee is his therapist. Lee is capable of transforming what seems to be a serious problem into a relatively minor one. Only recently did Dick think to ask Lee why he was so gifted at helping people with their problems. Lee was not sure the compliment was fully warranted, but he suggested that the principle was fundamental to his applied work in conflict resolution. In contrast to the typical input of a sympathetic friend, he tries to take not his or her perspective but, rather, the perspective of whomever he or she is dealing with.

Conclusions

Our history of conversations will soon celebrate its golden anniversary. We update each other about family news, and we still talk about some of the issues that we first began discussing as graduate students through the turbulent times (particularly at Columbia) of the 1960s. We talk about politics in general and what we think the Left gets right and what it gets wrong. We also talk about issues that we think will weigh on our children and grandchildren—growing economic inequality and the need to transition from a product-oriented to a service-oriented society in a way that provides people with reasonable life-styles and security. And we continue to talk endlessly about class, race, gender, culture (and the recurrent themes of Jews and Gentiles, of interdependent and independent societies, of California vs. New England and the Midwest, and of Stanford vs. Michigan).

But that capsule account doesn't quite capture the flavor of our conversations—an average of perhaps one phone conversation every few weeks and two meetings a year. All academics, of course, talk about family, and politics, and their schools, and the challenges that lie ahead for our society. So is there something special about our ongoing colloquy? Rather than trying to answer this question directly, we decided to end this account of our collaboration with a more or less stream-of-consciousness recollection of (some of) the things we talked about during one recent 24-hour period when Dick was visiting Lee.

We offer it in part to provide a more intimate peek at our collaboration, but in part because we believe that one of the great things about being a social psychologist is that it's never clear when you're not working. For younger colleagues pursuing their academic careers with a single-minded focus on the data they are collecting and the papers they are writing, the implication should be both welcome and liberating. What feels at the time like having fun reminiscing, gossiping, or just chatting informally about the news of the day can later turn out to be the impetus for some of a person's most important and satisfying work.

In our particular case, the conversation over the years has served another function. As we have reflected on what is going on in our lives, in our field, and in our society, we have practiced bringing to bear and sharpening the ideas and insights about human psychology that we are incubating and developing or learning about from the work of our colleagues.

The snippets of conversation that follow came during a particularly stressful time in the Ross household, as Lee's brother–in-law, who lived with him and Lee's wife, Judy, was in the very final stages of his struggle with neck cancer (and actually succumbed early in Dick's visit). As a result, existential issues about mortality and aging played a larger than typical role in our dialogue, but the mix of philosophizing, contemplation of current events, nostalgia, and gossip—all with an undergirding of psychology—is typical:

■ *Easing the discomfort of loved ones in their dying days.* Lee's Protestant brother-in-law Tim saying that he "didn't want to impose more than absolutely necessary," a sentiment Dick said he would share, and Lee's responding, "Tim, your death will be a difficult and devastating experience for the people who love you and they wouldn't want it to be otherwise. They want to maximize the sense that they did for you all that could be done." Dick recognized the wisdom and generosity of Lee's more interdependent approach to the problem.

- *Reflections about students and colleagues who died much too young, including two of Dick's most treasured students—Ziva Kunda and Andy Reaves.*

- *The cultural evolution of "hipsterdom" from the 1950s (On the Road hipsters) to the 1960s (hippies), and the role of both types as transitional figures: pro-Black, anticapitalist, pro-drugs, and antiestablishment.* The wry and financially well-off denizens of Portland, Brooklyn, and the Berkeley Hills whose politics mix libertarianism, social liberalism, and distrust of government.

- *The literary and intellectual "canon" one could once assume "everyone" knew and the changes in it that occur over time.* Lee's surprise at Dick's indifference to two parts of that canon: *The Tempest* and *King Lear*. Lee's observation that both plays, being about old men of declining power (and also the movie *The Graduate*), have completely different meanings when we reprise them at 70 than when we first encountered them in our early 20s.

- *Solomon Asch's complaint to Lee that "there's no moral dimension to Festinger's work: he looks down at people as if they were flies or puppets on a string".* Lee's reflection that while Leon emphasized dissonance reduction as an individual phenomenon, the most consequential forms of it involve not mere resolution of cognitive inconsistency, but rationalization of genocide, slavery, extreme exploitation, and other evils through processes and institutions that are *collective*, and profoundly social, not intrapersonal.

- *The debates going on in the field today about embodiment and priming work: outright fraud and deception versus "p-hacking."* How Festinger and Schachter and Co. did a lot of post hoc internal analysis to strengthen their findings but were perfectly transparent when they did so, essentially saying "Not only is the prediction confirmed but the predicted effect becomes stronger when the assumptions underlying that prediction are best met—that is, when we do some post hoc analysis to focus on the specific individuals and circumstances explicitly or implicitly assumed in the theory." Would that be seen today as p-hacking? The relevance of the distinction between simple replicability (which in the truest sense of the term is never what is being tested) and robustness, or the extent to which findings hold up when factors not specified in the theory are allowed to vary.

- *Stanley, Stanley, Stanley: What he would say—or at least convey nonverbally— when we presented ideas.* "I'm listening to you while you tell me something obvious (or shallow, or uninteresting) only because you have accumulated a reserve of idiosyncratic credit. The idea itself is too boring for me to listen to much longer." But he took us to his summer home in Amagansett to work, schmooze, and play for days at a time.

- *Changes in the field: Decline in the prominence of laboratory experiments in favor of applied work that looks at more dynamic processes that unfold over time and reflect cumulative consequences.* The disappearance of regular tenure-line jobs in nonelite universities, the lure of high business school salaries for mainstream social psychologists, and what will be the effects of distance learning featuring master lectures, further reducing opportunities for many but giving "stars" the chance to earn more than we had ever imagined possible.

■ *Gender, race, social class, and ethnicity: The increasing dispensability of men as they become less needed for the things that evolution prepared them for, namely "protection, provisioning, and impregnation."* To what extent are women so underrepresented in so many STEM (science, technology, engineering, mathematics) fields because they are pushed out by norms and practices of those fields or by simple sexism and to what extent are women experiencing difficulties in those fields pulled into other fields (including psychology) by their interests and capabilities more than men experiencing those same difficulties? The fact that the gap between Blacks and Whites in academic achievement and financial outcomes is being reduced just as the gap between the middle class and the lower class is becoming greater.

■ *The different face of nepotism—and what versions of it are permissible or nonpermissible in Western versus non-Western cultures.* Jewish domination of certain areas of American intellectual life, their role in the film industry and in creating the genre of the Broadway musical, and the popular music from the 1920s until the Beatles.

■ *People we admire because they retain their intellectual vigor in old age, including Walter Mischel, Donald Kennedy (former president of Stanford), George Schulz (former U.S. secretary of the treasury), and the great Stanford economist Ken Arrow.* What do they have in common?

■ *Our surprise at how little we lament the loss of our physical and mental powers.* And, unspoken, our sense that the loss is partly compensated for by the Conversation.

■ REFERENCES ■

Gigerenzer, G., & Brighton, H. (2009). Homo heuristicus: Why biased minds make better inferences. *Topics in Cognitive Science, 1,* 107–143.

Gigerenzer, G., & Goldstein, D. G. (1996). Reasoning the fast and frugal way: Models of bounded rationality. *Psychological Review, 103,* 650–669.

Jones, E. E., & Nisbett, R. E. (1972). The actor and the observer: Divergent perceptions of the causes of behavior. In E. E. Jones et al. (Eds.), *Attribution: Perceiving the causes of behavior* (pp. 79–94). Morristown, NJ: General Learning Press.

Nisbett, R. E., & Ross, L. (1980). *Human inference: Strategies and shortcomings of social judgment.* Englewood Cliffs, NJ: Prentice Hall.

Ross, L. (1977). The intuitive psychologist and his shortcomings: Distortions in the attribution process. In L. Berkowitz (Ed.), *Advances in experimental social psychology,* Vol. 10 (pp. 173–220). New York, NY: Academic Press.

Ross, L., & Nisbett, R. E. (1991). *The person and the situation: Perspectives of social psychology.* London, England: Pinter & Martin.

Tversky, A., & Kahneman, D. (1974). Judgment under uncertainty: Heuristics and biases. *Science, 185,* 1124–1131.

Chapter 10: An International Collaboration Based on Similarity and Complementarity

Phillip R. Shaver

Distinguished Professor of Psychology, Emeritus
University of California, Davis

Mario Mikulincer

Professor of Psychology
Provost, Interdisciplinary Center
Herzliya, Israel

A few years ago, one of our colleagues in the relationship research field said in an e-mail: "In relationship research circles, you two set the bar for what it means to collaborate. Your collaborative efforts are legendary: People say that at conferences you get together and, using a laptop, generate an article or two." What those people said is true, and in this chapter, we provide some of the behind-the-scenes details.

Similarities and Complementarities: A Brief Overview

Like many productive relationships, ours is based on a combination of similarity and complementarity. With respect to similarity, both of us are unusual social psychologists in having been interested since college in a psychodynamic model of the mind, an interest that was not encouraged by most of our undergraduate and graduate mentors. Both of us love research and enjoy being innovative in ways that encourage others to continue the lines of work that we initiate. (In other words, we enjoy starting new lines of research and hoping that other scholars will elaborate on them, which—fortunately—has happened repeatedly.) Both of us value applied as well as basic research and have worked more than most social psychologists with clinically oriented graduate students, who usually want their work to be clinically useful. This has helped us to conduct studies that are already affecting clinical practice, especially in the realm of couples therapy. Both of us have

117

held administrative positions—for example, as psychology department chairs and, in Mikulincer's case, as a dean. We are both more frustrated than most people by bureaucracy, but we have had to deal with it continually. Therefore, we readily sympathize with each other's ordeals.

Both of us are ambitious workaholics but are also (we hope) good-humored, playful, and collegial. We take each other's opinions, needs, and personal preferences seriously. We both love modern art and have shared many gallery visits while attending conferences around the world. We have enjoyed finding just the right artworks for our book jackets and have appreciated our publishers' willingness to follow our suggestions. Both of us have maintained long marriages and enjoyed being parents of two children—girls in Phil's case, boys in Mario's. Some of our conference-supplementing shopping expeditions in various countries have been initiated by our sons' and daughters' wishes for special presents from those countries. All of our similarities were discovered gradually, as we worked on one project after another together. They weren't all known in advance, and their gradual discovery kept the relationship interesting and more rewarding than our collaborative work would have been without our deepening friendship.

Our differences, which offer opportunities for complementarity, include ethnicity and religious background, age, and different preferences for methods and statistics versus speculative interpretations and literary narratives. Living in different countries, with different primary languages (English in Shaver's case, Spanish and Hebrew in Mikulincer's case), allows us to replicate findings in different cultural contexts. It also gives us a broader range of political, philosophical, and economic issues to discuss and, at times, finds a voice in our books and articles.

Overall, however, knowing how little of the variance in social phenomena we researchers are able to account for, there is probably a great deal that we don't know about our successful collaboration. The mysteries are probably as important as the things we think we can explain, because the mysteries keep the relationship interesting.

How We Met

Our relationship can best be understood if we begin by explaining how we came, individually, to attachment theory, began to influence each other indirectly, and then eventually decided to work together. As mentioned, both of us had been interested in psychoanalytic theory as undergraduate and graduate students, despite the hard knocks that it has always received from critics. We had both spent hours in our respective psychology libraries reading psychoanalytic writings and personality theories influenced by psychoanalysis. Anyone who is curious about what goes on in real people's diverse lives and minds—who reads novels or poems or watches artful films—realizes that the issues raised by psychoanalysts, beginning with Freud, are extremely important, like sexual attraction and desire; romantic love; artistic creativity and expression; the development of personality, beginning in infant–caregiver relationships; painful, corrosive emotions such as fear, anger, death anxiety, jealousy, hatred, guilt, and shame; intrapsychic conflicts, defenses, and psychopathology; individual and intergroup hostility; and the brutality of war.

When we first encountered academic social/personality psychology, much of it seemed disappointingly superficial compared with psychoanalysis (a characterization that is much less apt today than it was decades ago). But its strong point—the weakest point of psychoanalysis—was academic social/ personality psychology's powerful empirical research methods. Psychoanalytic theorists seemed capable of endlessly inventing and debating hypothetical constructs and processes without worrying about operational definitions, psychometrics, or replicable empirical studies.

Both of us began our careers as experimental researchers pursuing existing topics in the social-personality field (stress and learned helplessness in Mikulincer's case; self-awareness and fear of success in Shaver's case), but our interest in deeper psychodynamic processes never abated. When John Bowlby's (1969/1982, 1973, 1980) books began to appear, we both independently realized that a psychoanalytic thinker could incorporate the full range of scientific perspectives on human behavior, seek empirical evidence for psychoanalytic propositions, and reformulate psychoanalytic theory based on empirical research. Bowlby was openly influenced by evolutionary biology, ethology, cognitive developmental psychology, community psychiatry, cybernetics, and many other fields and topic areas.

Bowlby's collaborator, Mary Ainsworth, developed a laboratory "Strange Situation" assessment procedure (Ainsworth, Blehar, Waters, & Wall, 1978), which allowed her to classify infants' attachment patterns and relate them to home observations of parent–child interactions. This greatly added to our confidence that an extension of attachment theory to adults and adult relationships would be productive.

In the mid-1980s, Shaver and his students were investigating adolescent and adult loneliness (a consequence of Shaver's experience of grief following the death of his 28-year-old brother). They noticed both that attachment theory is useful in conceptualizing loneliness (as explained by Robert Weiss in a 1973 book and at a 1979 conference organized by Anne Peplau and Daniel Perlman, which Weiss and Shaver attended), and that patterns of chronic loneliness are similar in certain respects to the insecure infant attachment patterns identified by Ainsworth and her colleagues. Building on this insight, one of Shaver's doctoral students, Cindy Hazan (now a professor at Cornell University), wrote a seminar paper suggesting that attachment theory could be used as a framework for studying romantic love—or "romantic attachment," as Hazan and Shaver (1987) called it in their first article on the topic.

That article caught the eye of Mikulincer, an Israeli professor and researcher who had become interested in attachment theory while studying affect-regulation processes related to learned helplessness, depression, combat stress reactions, and posttraumatic stress disorder (another example of the influence of personal experience—personal loss, in Shaver's case, and living in a society under duress and repeatedly at war, in Mikulincer's case—on research interests). Mikulincer noticed similarities between (1) certain forms of helplessness in adulthood and the effects of parental unavailability in infancy, (2) intrusive images and emotions in the case of posttraumatic stress disorder and the anxious attachment pattern described by Ainsworth et al. (1978) and adapted for adults by Hazan and Shaver (1987), and (3) avoidant strategies for coping with stress and the avoidant attachment pattern described by these same authors. A few years later, Mikulincer, Florian, and Tolmacz (1990) examined attachment patterns and conscious and unconscious death anxiety, in one of the first studies to use the preliminary self-report measure of adult attachment devised by Hazan and Shaver (1987), and the first to show its connections with unconscious mental processes (measured with the psychodynamically inspired Thematic Apperception Test).

Shaver served as an enthusiastic reviewer of that paper, about which the then editor of the relationships and groups section of the *Journal of Personality and Social Psychology* (*JPSP*) said, "People keep saying that a lot of what we publish isn't very novel or interesting. *This* is novel and interesting!" That article was the first in a long line of fascinating work at the intersection of terror management theory (TMT) and attachment theory (Florian & Mikulincer, 1998; Mikulincer, Florian, & Hirschberger, 2003).

Beginnings of the Collaboration

From 1990 on, both of us (turning now to a first-person voice) continued to pursue the application of attachment theory to the study of adults' emotions, emotion-regulation strategies, close interpersonal relationships, and the accomplishment of various life tasks, noticing that we were both interested in the experimental study of attachment-related psychodynamics—the kinds of mental processes, including intense needs, powerful emotions and conflicts, and defensive strategies, that had captivated the attention of psychoanalysts from Freud to Bowlby. After exchanging e-mail messages and conversing face-to-face at conferences, Mikulincer offered Shaver an opportunity to work together on studies of security-enhancement (via conscious and unconscious priming) as a method of reducing intergroup hostility in the Middle East. This work (Mukulincer & Shaver, 2001) revealed the advantages of collaboration. These advantages include the vitality that arises when two engaged minds grapple with common issues and take advantage of each other's special skills—in this case, Mikulincer's exceptional talent for experimental design and Shaver's for writing in professional English. (Mikulincer was trained originally as an experimental psychologist, not specifically as a social or personality psychologist; Shaver has always been interested in teaching writing, and he enjoys editing.)

Once we began working together, as already mentioned, we found additional areas of similarity and complementarity, as always happens in good relationships. (The idea that it should be *either* similarity *or* complementarity, as has sometimes been debated in social psychology, is misguided.) Among similarities, we found a deep appreciation of 20th-century art, modern fiction, films, and football (although the word *football* means soccer in Mikulincer's case and

American football in Shaver's)—and, of course, as already explained, interest in psychodynamic theories. Other, more complicated, similarities include intense achievement motivation combined with distaste for egotism, a deep and perhaps neurotic bipolar tension between ambition and sloth, and extended experiences with psychotherapy. (Regarding ambition and sloth, Shaver once asked Mikulincer what he thought would happen if Mikulincer slowed down a bit instead of working so hard, and he replied that he would "lie down and do nothing"—a false but unalterable belief that Shaver also possesses about himself.)

Among complementarities, we found that Mikulincer likes the Methods and Results sections of articles, whereas Shaver likes Introductions and Discussions—a great combination when writing articles together. Another, perhaps more mysterious, complementarity is that Shaver was raised as an Irish Catholic who later dated almost only Jewish women (and happily married one, Gail Goodman, a fellow professor at the University of California, Davis), while Mikulincer was raised as a Jew living in a Catholic neighborhood in a Catholic country, Argentina, where he was curious about what was going on inside the local church. He went to Israel as a teenager, planning to return to Argentina as a Zionist youth leader, and met his wife-to-be, Debi Engel, now a school psychologist but at the time a Zionist youth leader from Brazil. They decided to marry and make Israel their permanent home.

Another complementarity—this time residing within a similarity—is that Shaver's experience with psychotherapy was at the neo-Freudian Columbia Psychoanalytic Institute in New York, whereas Mikulincer's experience was with a Jungian analyst in Israel. Our different experiences in psychotherapy make it easier for us to adopt a broad, eclectic approach to studying psychodynamic processes without the results having to fit within a single theoretical tradition. Attachment theory itself is a broad, eclectic approach to psychodynamic processes that includes concepts similar to ones in both neo-Freudian and Jungian theories. Neo-Freudian theories emphasized mother-infant relationships and psychological defenses. Jungian theory emphasized an evolutionary-based set of expectations and motives. Both kinds of theories included "complexes," which are similar in some ways to Bowlby's concept of "internal working models."

Without these similarities and complementarities, our relationship would not have blossomed or deepened to the extent it has, and we probably would not have studied attachment-related aspects of religion (e.g., Granqvist, Mikulincer, & Shaver, 2010) or attachment-related themes in dreams (e.g., Mikulincer, Shaver, & Avihou-Kanza, 2011).

Some Details of the Collaboration

So, what about our reputation for writing articles in hotel rooms at conferences (something we definitely do)? Of course, we exchange messages and manuscript components constantly by e-mail as well, but it's easier to make rapid progress in person, and because of family commitments (as mentioned, each of us has a wife, and we also each have two still partially dependent offspring) and little leisure time, it's practical to meet at professional conferences that we would attend whether we were working together or not. Because we are both somewhat introverted, although in different ways, neither of us is a conference gadabout or schmoozer, so we attend crucial sessions of conferences but otherwise spend most of our time in hotel rooms, coffee shops, and gourmet restaurants (another shared passion) working on grant proposals, research plans, and manuscripts. For some reason, we can both sit in front of a shared laptop for hours, taking breaks only for stretching or walking to a nearby coffee shop. (Mikulincer is an espresso addict, and the trips to coffee shops have turned lactose-intolerant Shaver into a soy latte addict.) We often add 2 or 3 extra days to a conference trip in order to work on collaborative writing projects. During those days, our work sessions are not interrupted by needing to participate in conference sessions.

When writing together at a laptop, we are very relaxed and compatible, in comparison with experiences we have had with other coauthors. We respect each other's opinions and knowledge bases, and we do not strongly insist on only one way of viewing or stating issues. We acknowledge each other's strengths and easily take each other's suggestions. As one of us types, the other comments, offering relevant references, small wording problems, and additional ideas. It is usually easy to work both people's ideas into a coherent, smoothly flowing narrative. This is partly because of compatible preexisting views about ideas, theories, logical arguments, other people's work, and so on. We also enjoy humor and poking fun at each other, which reduces tension and fatigue.

It is advantageous that we live in different time zones, 10 hours apart. One of us can send the other part of a draft or comments on a draft, and the other can work on it while the sender sleeps. One of us is always awake, and this allows us to accomplish more than if we both slept at the same time. When one of us is eating breakfast and checking e-mail, the other is checking e-mail before going to sleep for the night. Almost nothing gets put off for more than a day. As in a relay race, one of us hands the baton to the other and rests.

Over a period of 12 years, with the help of many energetic colleagues and students, we have produced one coauthored book and nine edited books. (In addition, Mikulincer coauthored a book with Shaver's wife in celebration of Shaver's 60th birthday.) We have also coauthored several grant proposals and over 100 articles and book chapters. This body of work has fueled the imaginations of researchers all over the world, many of whom we have corresponded with and met at international conferences. At times, we have been able to work together for extended periods. We received two 3-year research grants from the Fetzer Institute in Michigan for research on compassionate love and were able to work at their lovely conference facility. We have visited each other's homes and universities, sometimes for weeks at a time, which has allowed us to work on longer projects. (We both know each other's family members fairly well, and all of us have dined together and celebrated holidays together in Israel.)

When Mikulincer became dean of the School of Psychology at the Interdisciplinary Center in Herzliya, Israel, he obtained funding for five annual social/personality miniconferences, each of which formed the basis of an edited volume (Mikulincer & Shaver, 2009, 2012, 2013; Shaver & Mikulincer, 2011, 2012). This allowed us to explore such diverse topics as prosocial behavior, aggression and violence, moral psychology, existential psychology, and social neuroscience. Each year, we were honored to work with some of the world's top researchers and theorists in fields of our choice. We also, as is our general wont, took side trips with the conference participants to major cultural sites and restaurants in Israel. Before and after each of the conferences, we were able to take long walks along the Mediterranean and talk about both work and life. We have occasionally had special opportunities to travel together, in one case to visit the Dalai Lama in India and in other cases to enjoy castles in the Netherlands while speaking at marital therapy conferences. These trips have benefited both our friendship and some of our research projects (which now include therapeutic relationship interventions and the ironic connections between attachment theory's concept of secure attachment and the Buddhist concept of "nonattachment").

Our collaboration on these five conference-based books, published by the American Psychological Association (APA), led to our being invited to coedit four volumes of the organization's monster series of handbooks. Our four volumes cover the different subfields of social/personality psychology. (Fortunately, each volume has one or two excellent volume editors, making our roles fairly easy to manage.)

Another extremely important part of our collaboration is that both of us have had a stream of creative graduate students and postdocs. Some of them have studied in both of our labs. Many of them have gone on to expand our line of research in creative directions and now have very successful independent careers. What the two of us have accomplished would have been impossible without our collaborators. Anyone looking at the "References" section of our 2007 book, *Attachment in Adulthood: Structure, Dynamics, and Change*, will see how many collaborators and intellectual offspring have contributed to what we have learned so far. We are currently working on a revised version of that book, and have seen—with amazement and trepidation—that there are at least 1,500 new references since 2007 to consider adding.

Remaining Mysteries of Collaboration

At a deep psychological level, there are probably aspects of our successful collaboration that we do not recognize or understand. Both of us are conscientious by nature (a positive term from contemporary personality research, which is easier for us to self-ascribe than related traits such as obsessive-compulsiveness and guilt-proneness). Once we commit ourselves to projects, organizational roles, or relationships (with students, colleagues, granting agencies, universities, and publishers), we do our damnedest to deliver on time rather than feel embarrassed or guilty. (Guilt is a Jewish–Catholic similarity, fueled by our surprisingly similar Jewish and Irish-Catholic mothers.) Outsiders, like the colleague who said we "set the bar for what it means to collaborate" (which probably refers to both the bar for collaboration and the bar for productivity), may imagine that we experience ourselves as choosing to work so hard. But in fact, we typically perceive ourselves as overburdened and harassed by demands, deadlines, and e-mail messages. We have to be reminded, sometimes by our wives, that we voluntarily agreed to a particular project, deadline, or role as department chair, editor, or dean. In other words, although there are numerous pleasures and rewards associated with our collaborative workaholism, it has its downside, like any other obsession or addiction. Neither Freudian nor Jungian therapy has eliminated that downside, partly because of our persistent if irrational conviction that if we slowed down, we might do nothing at all.

One of us (Shaver), having reached age 71 and decided to retire, is finishing up two books while taking exercise, golf, and painting classes. Mikulincer is only 57, is provost of his university, and has no hope of relaxing any time soon. Our age difference is another source of complementarity, and because Mikulincer and his wife had children early and Shaver and his wife had them late, each of us has "seniority" in some senses and domains, and we can each offer guidance of various kinds to the other.

The kinds of similarity and complementarity enjoyed by successful collaborators probably differ across dyads, but in all such collaborations we have witnessed or participated in, there is mutual respect, generosity, gratitude, and care, along with a delicate balance between individual ambition (i.e., ego) and sharing the limelight. Younger professionals might worry that being closely associated with a collaborator will hinder both people's chances of winning recognition and awards, but in our case, this has certainly not been so. We have both received awards and countless opportunities to present work at conferences and at major universities. Our impression is that the large amount of work that a person can accomplish with a good collaborator outweighs the possibility of diminished individual credit, but anyone worrying about this issue, as pretenure researchers might, could do independent as well as collaborative work. The balancing of collaborative rewards and costs is probably an important part of any high-functioning relationship, whether academic or not, which is—come to think of it—a great topic for future research and another grant proposal.

■ REFERENCES ■

Ainsworth, M. D. S., Blehar, M. C., Waters, E., & Wall, S. (1978). *Patterns of attachment: Assessed in the Strange Situation and at home.* Hillsdale, NJ: Erlbaum.

Bowlby, J. (1973). *Attachment and Loss: Vol. 2. Separation: Anxiety and anger.* New York, NY: Basic Books.

Bowlby, J. (1980). *Attachment and Loss: Vol. 3. Sadness and depression.* New York, NY: Basic Books.

Bowlby, J. (1982). *Attachment and Loss: Vol. 1. Attachment* (2nd ed.). New York, NY: Basic Books. (Original work published 1969)

Florian, V., & Mikulincer, M. (1998). Symbolic immortality and the management of the terror of death: The moderating role of attachment style. *Journal of Personality and Social Psychology, 74,* 725–734.

Granqvist, P., Mikulincer, M., & Shaver, P. R. (2010). Religion as attachment: Normative processes and individual differences. *Personality and Social Psychology Review, 14,* 49–59.

Hazan, C., & Shaver, P. R. (1987). Romantic love conceptualized as an attachment process. *Journal of Personality and Social Psychology, 52,* 511–524.

Mikulincer, M., Florian, V., & Hirschberger, G. (2003). The existential function of close relationships: Introducing death into the science of love. *Personality and Social Psychology Review, 7,* 20–40.

Mikulincer, M., Florian, V., & Tolmacz, R. (1990). Attachment styles and fear of personal death: A case study of affect regulation. *Journal of Personality and Social Psychology, 58,* 273–280.

Mikulincer, M., & Shaver, P. R. (2001). Attachment theory and intergroup bias: Evidence that priming the secure base schema attenuates negative reactions to outgroups. *Journal of Personality and Social Psychology, 81,* 97–115.

Mikulincer, M., & Shaver, P. R. (Eds.). (2009). *Prosocial motives, emotions, and behavior: The better angels of our nature.* Washington, DC: American Psychological Association.

Mikulincer, M., and Shaver, P. (2012). An attachment perspective on psychopathology. *World Psychiatry, 11*(1), 11–15.

Mikulincer, M., & Shaver, P. R. (Eds.). (2013). *Mechanisms of social connection: From brain to group.* Washington, DC: American Psychological Association.

Mikulincer, M., Shaver, P. R., & Avihou-Kanza, N. (2011). Individual differences in adult attachment are systematically related to dream narratives. *Attachment and Human Development, 13,* 105–123.

Shaver, P. R., & Mikulincer, M. (Eds.). (2011). *Human aggression and violence: Causes, manifestations, and consequences.* Washington, DC: American Psychological Association.

Shaver, P. R., & Mikulincer, M. (Eds.). (2012). *Meaning, mortality, and choice: The social psychology of existential concerns.* Washington, DC: American Psychological Association.

Weiss, R. S. (1973). *Loneliness: The experience of emotional and social isolation.* Cambridge, MA: MIT Press.

PART III

Collaboration and Interdisciplinarity

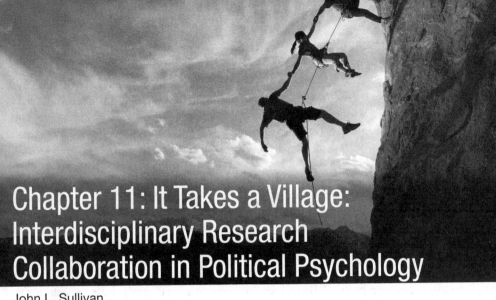

Chapter 11: It Takes a Village: Interdisciplinary Research Collaboration in Political Psychology

John L. Sullivan

Emeritus Regents Professor of Political Science
University of Minnesota

Eugene Borgida

Professor of Psychology and Law
Morse-Alumni Distinguished Professor of Psychology
University of Minnesota

The Origin Story

Our collaboration began where it is ending: with a laserlike focus on graduate student education. Not training, but education. The concept of "training" graduate students conjures notions of shaping the behavior of pets, whereas the concept of "educating" them invokes what we think more accurately describes the process we have aspired to practice. We have tried to create and sustain a set of formal and informal norms intended to guide students' comprehension of the existing state of knowledge in political psychology, to enhance their understanding of cutting-edge methodologies and the limitations of each one, to participate in the students' process of discovering their own nascent talents and abilities, and finally to join with the students as team members in creating new knowledge. As a result, our joint work has not been a narrow collaboration focused on a particular stream of joint scholarship and publications. Instead, it has been more broadly centered on the educational experiences of our graduate students as they strove to advance scientific understanding of matters of political psychology. Along the way, we believe, we have discovered a couple of things about what can best serve to create and recreate fertile incubators of "scholars who make a difference."

That has been the central aspiration of the collaboration that we have engaged in over the last 35-plus years. This aspiration has not always been the result of a fully mindful process. Our collaboration evolved quite serendipitously in the latter part of the 1970s. Sullivan had recently returned to the University of Minnesota's political science department, from which he had received his undergraduate degree in 1967, and Borgida had just joined Minnesota's faculty in the psychology department upon completion of his PhD at Michigan.[1] Sullivan had done postdoctoral research in the Psychology and Politics Program at Yale University in 1970[2] and was teaching a graduate seminar in political psychology for the political science program. Borgida had a core interest in psychology and law that was rapidly broadening to incorporate psychology and politics, and he was regularly teaching his graduate seminar in social cognition, as well as a course on attitudes and persuasion for the psychology program.

Although political psychology at the University of Minnesota had a long and storied history by this time, there had been little direct collaboration and only modest cross-training in recent decades. The first political psychology class at Minnesota was offered in the psychology department by Professor Charles Bird in the 1920s, and by the 1940s, Bird was joined in his interdisciplinary interest in political psychology by psychology professor Paul Meehl and political science professor Herbert McClosky. McClosky completed his PhD in Minnesota's political science department in 1946, followed by a 2-year postdoctoral training fellowship in the Minnesota psychology department. McClosky accepted a joint appointment in the political science and psychology departments' Social Relations Lab (its social psychology group, run at that time by Leon Festinger). Together with Paul Meehl, McClosky worked with a graduate student, Harrison Gough, to develop measures of "social responsibility" and "dominance" as personality characteristics. McClosky developed and taught courses at Minnesota in psychological approaches to political behavior until his departure for Berkeley in 1960. There was little or no direct collaboration involving faculty and students from both departments in the 1960s or 1970s. Political science turned more fully to graduate courses on public opinion and political behavior that relied largely on political science research, and although the department left a graduate seminar in political psychology on the books, it was offered sparingly.

---

[1] At Michigan, Borgida's mentor and primary research collaborator was Richard Nisbett, who arrived at Michigan from Yale the year before Borgida started his graduate program in social psychology. We were ensconced within the Research Center for Group Dynamics (RCGD) at the Institute for Social Research (ISR), which was a wonderful scholarly environment. In RCGD, Bob Zajonc kept everyone on their toes 24/7. Borgida took classes and schmoozed with the Lewinian old guard (Dorwin Cartwright, Al Zander, Dan Katz, Robert Kahn, Ted Newcomb, and Jack French), and he learned survey research from Howard Schuman and sociological methods from Andre Modigliani and Bill Gamson. There was plenty of contact with the psychologically oriented political scientists at ISR (Phil Converse, Angus Campbell, M. Kent Jennings, and Warren Miller). The norms were collaboration and interdisciplinary thinking, and Borgida deeply internalized them.

[2] At Yale, Sullivan was exposed not only to the work of political scientists whose research was in the area of political psychology, such as Fred Greenstein, James David Barber, and Robert Lane (who presented their ongoing research to the postdocs), but also to psychologists such as Robert Abelson and Irving Janis, who also presented their new work on political psychology. This proved pivotal in encouraging political science graduate students to work directly with leading psychologists rather than merely digesting their work indirectly.

In the late 1970s, several of Sullivan's graduate students—Stanley Feldman, Pamela Conover, Michal Shamir, Jon Hurwitz, and Mark Peffley among them—took Borgida's graduate seminar in social cognition. This was somewhat unusual since most political scientists who did research in the area of political psychology during this era did so with little or no formal graduate training in psychology. They did their graduate work with an emphasis either on what political scientists called "political behavior" or on a psychoanalytically oriented form of psychology. Those with an emphasis on the former obtained almost all their training in political science departments, resulting in a lack of depth and nuance in the comprehension and use of modern psychological theory. Those with an emphasis on the latter focused on an approach that mainstream psychology had largely abandoned. A consequence was that much of the research in political psychology that was conducted by political scientists at this time was at the margins of the discipline both theoretically and methodologically. Most of this research did not address the central, core issues and concerns of the larger disciplines, and only a very few political psychology publications made it into major disciplinary journals in either field.

Connections: Forging the Link

The aforementioned graduate students, however, insisted on learning their psychological theory from expert psychologists rather than secondhand from political scientists, who were largely self-taught at that time, and it paid great dividends for them and for the two of us. Feldman and Conover asked Borgida to help mentor their dissertation research, and he and Sullivan began working closely with a subsequent stream of graduate students from both programs. In each and every case, we discovered that the students who had been educated in theory and research methods in both disciplines, and who were inclined to focus their research on the core, central concerns in both disciplines, emerged from graduate school prepared to help fashion new directions in the interdisciplinary field of political psychology.[3] To some extent, the "mainstreaming" of political psychology into the political science discipline was spearheaded by this group of graduate students from Minnesota. Theoretical work from rigorous, mainstream psychology provided new and exciting perspectives on enduring concerns and controversies in political science, such as the issues surrounding the concepts of ideological constraint and issue voting. Feldman, Conover, Peffley and Hurwitz, among others, helped create a theoretical and methodological set of alternatives to the extant "Michigan model" of ideological constraint and mass political competence (Conover and Feldman, 1984; Feldman & Conover, 1983; Peffley & Hurwitz, 1985).

---

[3] Although we focused our efforts on mainstream, central disciplinary questions, we were fully aware of and exposed our students to the full range of approaches and research questions in the field of political psychology. For example, Sullivan's graduate syllabi from this era, in addition to more mainstream theoretical and methodological approaches, included coverage of topics such as Gestalt theory, humanistic theory, psychoanalysis, and Q-methodology.

Around this time, econometricians were pushing the frontiers of parameter estimation in structural equation models but continued to be vexed by the significantly imperfect measurements that were available and that could vitiate gains made by the use of increasingly complex statistical estimation. At about the same time, psychometricians were enhancing their ability to identify and correct for problems of nonrandom measurement error. Connecting these two somewhat parallel streams of statistical analysis led to an aggressive marriage between measurement models and structural equation models (e.g., LISREL and related approaches). Our graduate students in political psychology along with the faculty were fortunate to have a social psychologist available, Geoff Maruyama, who taught a graduate seminar on the use of LISREL, and by the late 1970s, we and our graduate students were applying these models (e.g., Sullivan, Marcus, Feldman, & Piereson, 1981; Sullivan, Piereson, Marcus, & Feldman, 1979).[4] Applications of these more sophisticated methodologies, coupled with the application of mainstream social psychological theories to core issues in political science, helped to set the stage for the mainstreaming of political psychology, first in political science and somewhat later in social psychology.

The Research Village

Because of the students' rigorous training in both disciplines, we discovered that incorporating them into our own ongoing research projects helped push them intellectually and assisted us in our own efforts to remain abreast of cutting-edge developments in theory and methods in both political science and psychology. These early experiences shaped a pattern of interdisciplinary education and scholarship that persisted throughout our careers, and that helped direct our efforts to institutionalize what we were experiencing. These forces, more than any other, influenced our collaborative research agendas and guided our joint research projects. The research we did together was aimed at making important contributions to social science knowledge. In order to increase the likelihood that this work would succeed, it was equally aimed at providing opportunities for full collaboration with graduate students from our two programs. They made all of the research we conducted so much better than if they had been merely research assistants (RAs) rather than coequals and coauthors.

One way to characterize the collaboration that evolved between the two of us and our predilection to incorporate multiple graduate students into our research teams is as a "village approach to research." It most certainly took a village to conduct the sometimes larger-scale projects we undertook, and almost all the contributions we made to the literature were the result of a synergy between and among the faculty and graduate students who were directly involved in the projects. We'll say more about this later in this chapter, but for now, we will simply note that this approach was unique in political science at the time (the late 1970s and early 1980s), and also represented something more

---

[4] To our knowledge, this was one of the very first, if not the first, applications of LISREL in a political science journal.

than the usual mentor-centric experimental lab group common among social psychologists at the time.

These evolving experiences and their subsequent norms led us eventually to institutionalize our collaborative style and goals. In the mid-1990s, we created and obtained intramural and extramural funding streams to support infrastructure in the form of the Center for the Study of Political Psychology and a joint PhD minor in political psychology at the University of Minnesota. Through the center, we set up interdisciplinary research groups that included both faculty and graduate students from more than one discipline, usually drawn from the political science and psychology departments, as well as from the School of Journalism and Mass Communications. The graduate student participants were usually coauthors and often functioned as paid RAs as well. Graduate students provided an incredible mix of creativity and savvy, as they worked to conceptualize and design projects, collect and analyze data, and publish scholarly articles. We were able to provide seed money and support pilot projects that led to grants to support other projects. Eventually, students began to set up their own study groups and research projects that did not involve any faculty coauthorship.

Another of our major collaborations involved coediting, with Wendy Rahn and Jamie Druckman, *Political Psychology*, the flagship journal of the International Society of Political Psychology. We served two terms (for a total of 6 years) and ran the entire operation through the center. Consistent with our long-term modus operandi, we involved graduate students in all aspects of the editorship from the start to the finish of our editorial terms. Graduate students not only served as editorial assistants and interns, they read manuscripts for their study groups and evaluated them as reviewers when they had the appropriate expertise. It gave our students an opportunity to be at the cutting edge of scholarship in their chosen field and to learn editorial and management skills that served them well when they took their first academic position.

Another pylon in the infrastructure that our collaboration created is the PhD minor in political psychology. For the last 20 years, this formal program has allowed students in various PhD programs across the University of Minnesota to take courses and conduct research in political psychology. It has always included a proseminar, which meets weekly through the academic year and provides a forum for students from different programs to interact with each other and with faculty from the various academic disciplines. The bulk of the faculty comes from psychology, political science, and mass communications, but there has been participation from many other programs across the university. Students complete graduate coursework from outside their major program, with a focus on core theoretical approaches and recent research. It has institutionalized the desideratum we identified in the early 1980s—that students doing interdisciplinary work need to be strongly grounded in the theory and methods of each discipline. Our best efforts have been directed at providing political science graduate students with a deeper experience in experimental methods and evolving psychological theory, and providing psychology graduate students with a deeper experience in survey research methods and long-standing core theoretical issues in the political behavior field of political science, particularly the important role played by context and institutions in shaping behavior, over and above the usual individual-level focus at the core of most social psychological research. Over time, especially during the last decade and a half, the distinction between political psychology and political behavior among political scientists has broken down. Most research in political behavior is now heavily psychological in theoretical orientation, thanks in no small part to graduate programs such as ours and, among others, those at Ohio State and the University of California, Los Angeles.

The proseminar has long provided an ongoing forum and opportunity for both faculty and students to try out nascent ideas for research, as well as give formal presentations of completed or nearly completed projects. Perhaps one of the more important functions that it has performed over the years is to create a setting for beginning students to be "socialized" and mentored by senior students who are further along in their mastery of the research process. Indeed, to this day there has been a tradition for more senior students in the program to remain engaged with the proseminar even through their dissertation year.

As noted at the beginning of this essay, the two of us have worked closely together for over 35 years. There have been peaks and valleys during those three-plus decades, and our joint research efforts peaked in the 1980s and 1990s. Yet, as we noted previously, one of the central focuses of our joint research was always the education of our students and our desire to assist them in getting their careers off to a running start. This led us directly to the "Research Village" concept and approach mentioned earlier. Multiple coauthors characterize almost all of our work together. This is perhaps less unusual in psychology than it has been in political science, but we think that the depth of the interdisciplinary experience we tried to provide was unusual even for psychology.

The point here is to note that even at times when we were not directly engaged in joint research—during our very early years in the profession and more recently—our programmatic focus has been on educating our graduate students jointly. The infrastructure surrounding those efforts and that focus are now largely independent of our joint efforts, and they have and will evolve in different directions—all centered, however, on the same overarching goal.

Although our joint research projects initiated this concept, many other faculty and graduate students have participated wholeheartedly in various ways over the last 30 years, including John Aldrich, Barbara Allen, Patricia Avery, Jamie Druckman, Ron Faber, Chris Federico, Marti Gonzales, Paul Goren, Heather LaMarre, Howard Lavine, C. Daniel Myers, Joanne Miller, Wendy Rahn, Mark Snyder, Al Timms, and Daniel Wackman.

Collaboration: A New Perspective on an Old Problem

The focus in this chapter thus far has been on the larger infrastructure— formal and informal—that has characterized our collaboration. Although we have emphasized the central role of graduate education in creating and maintaining our collaborative research, of equal importance is the substance of the work itself. One of the first joint projects involved our work on presidential elections in the 1980s. Working with John Aldrich, who later departed for Duke but who was at that time in Minnesota's political science department, we received a National Science Foundation (NSF) grant to conduct a national opinion survey just after the fall election. In those days, conducting a nationwide, in-person opinion survey was a major task—major in a way contemporary scholars who use telephone and Internet surveys could barely comprehend. It was also incredibly expensive. We worked with graduate students Jason Young from psychology and Wendy Rahn from political science to examine the role of issues and issue salience on voting behavior and assessed a social cognitive model of vote choice (Aldrich, Sullivan, & Borgida, 1989; Rahn, Aldrich, Borgida, & Sullivan, 1990; Sullivan, Aldrich, Borgida, & Rahn, 1990; Young, Borgida, Sullivan, & Aldrich, 1987; Young, Thomsen, Borgida, Sullivan, & Aldrich, 1991).

The value of interdisciplinary collaboration became apparent almost immediately while carrying out this project. Political scientists had been studying issue voting, ideological constraint, and public opinion by conducting regular national opinion surveys for several decades. On the whole, they had concluded that voting choice was dominated by party identification with only a secondary role for ideology and issues, at least for most voters. They concluded that individual political attitudes and opinions tended to be incoherent and unstructured, and when they were structured, the cohesive factor seemed to be emotional group identification rather than anything more rational or cognitive (see, among others, Campbell, Converse, Miller, & Stokes, 1960; Converse, 1964). Although there have been controversies swirling around these conclusions (e.g., Achen, 1975; Nie, Verba, & Petrocik, 1976), there has been very little conceptual effort (and even less empirical work) that attempts to specify and evaluate any alternative underlying psychological models of how voters process political information and make political choices.

One fairly well accepted conclusion from extant research had been that there was very little (in fact, probably no) role for foreign policy issues in the voting behavior of citizens during presidential elections. While domestic issues may well have played some part, foreign policy attitudes really did not exist and did not play a measurable role in candidate evaluation and selection, according to the prevailing academic consensus in political science. In the early stages of our collaboration, Borgida educated Aldrich and Sullivan about some basic principles of information processing, including concepts of attitude availability, attitude accessibility, and priming. These concepts had not really found their way into the political behavior lexicon at that time, at least not in a way that influenced the debates raging in the literature.[5] Adopting the perspective of social cognition that had evolved in social psychology, however, led us to rely on an information processing model that provided

---

[5] The concepts of priming and attitude accessibility were first persuasively introduced somewhat later to the broader political science audience by Iyengar and Kinder (1987).

stronger theoretical grounding for assessing whether, when, and how foreign policy attitudes might affect vote choice.

Reframing the conventional wisdom of political science at that time in the language of the social psychology of attitudes and social cognition, political scientists had implicitly assumed that most citizens did not have attitudes on foreign policy available to them, and even among those with attitudes that were potentially relevant and might have been available, they were not accessed during presidential election campaigns; hence, they had no impact on the outcome of elections. Using data from several election cycles, we discovered that many citizens had reasonably well-developed foreign policy attitudes; that when elections and candidates primed foreign policy attitudes, many citizens were quite willing and able to vote based on these attitudes; and that most candidates have behaved, and conducted their election campaigns, in a way that recognized this reality. Imposing new conceptual tools from social psychology on existing controversies in political science allowed us to rethink how to test empirically a long-standing truism—that foreign policy attitudes did not and could not affect voting behavior.

When we conducted this first project, most political scientists who studied political behavior were firmly wedded to the use of surveys and opinion polls, and conducted large-N research projects. Very seldom could a study with a small sample make it through the review process at most major political science journals, and that included experimental studies that often relied on student samples. In the other world, social psychologists were wedded to the experimental method and didn't especially trust the lack of control, and the resulting emphasis on correlational data, that large-scale surveys entailed. Despite Campbell and Fiske's (1959) early call for multimethod research, the lion's share of publications in the political psychology and behavior field was unimethodological. In subsequent decades, this was turned on its head, and the prevailing desideratum became multimethod studies in both disciplines. Taking seriously the growing call for validating findings using methods that were different in important ways, our project morphed into a more experimental examination of the roles of issue salience, cognitive accessibility, and self-interest in political attitudes and vote choice. Working with psychology graduate students Jason Young, Howard Lavine, and Cynthia Thomsen, we followed up our large-scale survey work with controlled experiments to examine the roles of priming, attitude accessibility, and issue salience on political behavior and ideology (Lavine, Borgida, & Sullivan, 2000; Lavine, Sullivan, Borgida, & Thomsen, 1996; Young et al., 1987, 1991).

Social and Political Capital: Community Adoption of Information Technology

Later, in response to the growing concern about the consequences of social capital and its absence (Putnam, 2000), we created the Grand-Net Project to broaden the focus beyond social capital to incorporate political capital as well. We assessed how communities and individuals with varying levels of social and political capital were positioned to take advantage (or not) of the ongoing revolution in information technology. We obtained several NSF grants to study two communities that adopted totally different approaches to the Internet revolution during the 1990s. This project included seven graduate RAs, three from psychology and four from political science. All these projects spanned multiple years and coexisted with other large projects that incorporated multiple graduate students from the two departments. Using community surveys, focus groups, elite interviews, and archival analysis, we and our teams of graduate students identified some of the individual and community-level factors that led some communities to move aggressively into the Internet age while others left this largely to the market and individual action. Among other things, our analysis showed that in the town with a broad-based community electronic network, individuals' political and economic resources were linked to their knowledge and use of computer resources, whereas in the comparison community, economic stratification alone drove computer access (see Borgida et al., 2001; Oxendine et al., 2007; Oxendine, Jackson, Sullivan, & Borgida, 2003; Riedel et al., 2003; Riedel, Dresel, Wagoner, Sullivan, & Borgida, 1998; Sullivan, Borgida, Jackson, Riedel, & Oxendine, 2002; Sullivan, Borgida, Jackson, Riedel, Oxendine, & Gangl, 2002). Our analysis supported the central role of collective endeavors, rich in social capital, in promoting individual well-being and economic development.

Long-Term Glue and Its Consequences

Certainly the forces that brought us together in the first place are the same ones that sustained our collaboration over the longer term (with the sole exception of our fondness for rigorous lunchtime pick-up basketball games). Central to this has been our mutual love of and respect for our graduate students and our desire to provide them with the very best possible day-to-day experiences, as well as the very best possible academic training and broader education. Yet more has been required. Long-term collaborations are rare—and for good reason. Academics may not have the largest egos in the occupational world, but neither do they have the most modest ones. Not only that, but the kinds of projects with which we have been involved are also very intense, much is riding on them, and they are intellectually and emotionally challenging. Making things even more complicated is the documented tendency for us all to selectively remember our own contributions best; unsurprisingly, we are not very good at remembering those things that our collaborators did that we knew nothing about. We have had our share of disagreements, real and perceived slights, misunderstandings, and very real foibles that have caused significant discomfort and even pain. *Of course!*

What, then, explains the persistence of our collaborative efforts, beyond what we have already proffered, viz., focusing on graduate students and their needs? Although we are reasonably certain that our insights on this point are limited (and maybe even self-serving), we now offer a few keys to the longevity of our collaboration that may be useful guides to collaboration in a more general sense.

One factor that has helped us immeasurably, which we think others would be well advised to keep in mind, has been a single-minded focus on the precepts of social science research. We want to discover and validate knowledge. Most practicing social scientists do. The rub is that when strong egos seek knowledge together, at times they have strong disagreements about theory, method, analysis, and even the scientific meaning of their results. It is all too easy to stake out a position and try to defend it, and then try to make the results confirm one's previous assumptions. One knows this with clarity if one merely reads the research literature on hotly disputed topics, where one scholar's line of research directly contradicts another scholar's ongoing work. Each conducts research that seems to confirm his or her theory and contradicts the "opponent's" theory. Seldom does a scholar carry out a crucial test and publish a paper that disconfirms his or her theory and confirms the opponent's. "I surrender" does not appear in the literature very often ... in fact, we're not sure we have ever seen it. So, unless collaborators are very much in sync on the core aspects of their work, they will encounter episodes that challenge their commitment to science.

In our case, there were the usual differences in disciplinary norms and methods: Psychologists know/think x, and political scientists know/think y. How can we rely on student samples to study political behavior when the nature of political behavior likely differs so wildly depending on the context? Students are just beginning to participate in voting, whereas most adult voters have years of experience, which fundamentally alters their decision-making processes. How can we draw inferences about causality when we have not directly controlled and manipulated the independent variables? We can honestly say that when we have encountered such fundamental disagreements, we have always found a way to "go with the science" and abandon our prior commitments. That has been no small part of sustaining our collaboration, but, in our view, it is an essential feature to any successful interdisciplinary collaboration.

Both of us have always tried hard to create an open and democratic ethos with our students, and we shared a commitment to have our students play key roles from the start to finish of our projects. Most often, graduate students have helped us to conceptualize and design research projects, write grants, collect data, conduct analyses, and write up research papers for publication. With such an ethos and commitment, which were deeply ingrained in each of us, this greater purpose kept our focus off the smaller issues to a large extent. Status distinctions were minor (or if they weren't, we were unaware of them). We used a rotating order of authorship, and in some cases, even with five or six coauthors, everyone had the opportunity to be lead author, last author, and almost every order in between. The graduate students had strong views and were unafraid to express them, leading us to continuously assess and reassess the source and nature of our own intellectual commitments. At the end of the day, this collaborative process was fueled by open communication and a shared understanding that the science would be enhanced as a result of this way of working together.

Another factor that played a central role, we think, was the flexible (some might say loose) nature of the central focus of our research. We generally did not have a rigid design that dictated how we would proceed with the project from the start to the finish. It was a fluid experience, and often the focus and design would shift in response to twists and turns instigated by one of us or, equally likely, by one or more graduate students. Ideas and suggestions flowed continuously, and the nature of the process made digging in one's heels less likely. Each and every one of the researchers had pet ideas fall by the wayside, often without even noticing that it had happened. For some unknown reason, we were headed in a different direction. It was an organic process—one that we believe is critical to successful collaboration.

Finally, coming full circle, we believe that the fact that we had only open, permeable boundaries between teaching and research aided the collaborative process. Since our research was about teaching, how could we teach graduate students openly and honestly if we failed to model as best as possible the precepts of social science openness and commitment to go where the results lead us? If we modeled a closed-minded desire to prove ourselves right, regardless of the evidence, we would lose the synergy between teaching and research that we were striving first and foremost to attain, and in effect we would have been teaching our students the wrong things. While this dynamic certainly has worked well for our collaboration over time, we believe that it is exportable to other collaborative contexts as well, especially if the goal is to educate and train graduate students to become independent scholars in the field.

▓ REFERENCES ▓

Achen, C. (1975). Mass political attitudes and the survey response. *American Political Science Review, 69,* 1218–1231.

Aldrich, J., Sullivan, J., & Borgida, E. (1989). Foreign affairs and issue voting: Do presidential candidates "waltz before a blind audience'?" *American Political Science Review 83,* 123–142. Also reprinted in Niemi, R. & Weisberg, H. (1992). *Controversies in voting behavior* (3rd ed., pp. 167–186). Washington, DC: Congressional Quarterly Press.

Borgida, E., Sullivan, J., Riedel, E., Jackson, M., Oxendine, A., & Gangl, A. (2001). Community electronic networks: Will on-line access enhance off-line relationships? *Journal of Social Issues, 58,* 125–141.

Campbell, A., Converse, P., Miller, W., & Stokes, D. 1960. *The American voter.* Chicago: University of Chicago Press.

Campbell, D., & Fiske, D. (1959). Convergent and discriminant validation by the multitrait-multimethod matrix. *Psychological Bulletin, 56,* 81–105.

Conover, P., & Feldman, S. (1884). How people organize the political world: A schematic model. *American Journal of Political Science, 28,* 95–126.

Converse, P. (1964). The nature of belief systems in mass publics. In D. Apter (Ed.), *Ideology and discontent* (pp. 206–261). New York, NY: Free Press.

Feldman, S., & Conover, P. (1983). Candidates, issues, and voters: The role of inference in political perception. *Journal of Politics, 45,* 810–839.

Iyengar, S. & Kinder, D. (1987). *News that matters: Television and American opinion.* Chicago, IL: University of Chicago Press.

Lavine, H., Borgida, E., & Sullivan, J. (2000). On the relationship between attitude involvement and attitude accessibility: Toward a cognitive-motivational model of political information processing. *Political Psychology, 21,* 81–106.

Lavine, H., Sullivan, J., Borgida, E., & Thomsen, C. J. (1996). The relationship of national and personal issue salience to attitude accessibility on foreign and domestic policy issues. *Political Psychology, 17,* 293–316.

Nie, N., Verba, S., & Petrocik, J. (1976). *The changing American voter.* Cambridge, MA: Harvard University Press.

Oxendine, A., Borgida, E., Sullivan, J., & Jackson, M. (2003). The importance of trust and community in developing and maintaining a community electronic network. *International Journal of Human-Computer Studies, 58,* 671–697.

Oxendine, A, Sullivan, J., Borgida, E., Riedel, E., Jackson, M., & Dial, J. (2007). The importance of political context for understanding civic engagement: A longitudinal analysis. *Political Behavior, 29,* 31–67.

Peffley, M., & Hurwitz, J. (1985). A hierarchical model of attitude constraint. *American Journal of Political Science, 29,* 871–890.

Putnam, R. (2000). *Bowling alone: The collapse and revival of American community.* New York: Simon & Schuster.

Rahn, W., Aldrich, J., Borgida, E., & Sullivan, J. (1990). A social-cognitive model of candidate appraisal. In J. Ferejohn & J. Kuklinski (Eds.), *Information and democratic processes* (pp. 136–159). Urbana: University of Illinois Press. Reprinted in R. Niemi & H. Weisberg (Eds.), *Controversies in voting behavior* (3rd ed., pp. 187–206). Washington, DC: Congressional Quarterly Press, 1992).

Riedel, E., Dresel, L., Wagoner, M., Sullivan, J., & Borgida, E. (1998). Electronic communities: Assessing equality of access in a rural Minnesota community. *Social Science Computer Review, 16,* 370–390. Reprinted in G. Garson (Ed.). (2000), *Social dimensions of information technology: Issues for the new millennium* (pp. 86–108). Hershey, PA: Idea Group Publishers.

Riedel, E., Gangl, A., Oxendine, A., Jackson, M., Sullivan, J., & Borgida, E. (2003). The role of the Internet in national and local news media use. *Journal of Online Behavior, 1,* 1–17. Retrieved from http://behavior.net/JOB/v1n3/riedel.html.

Sullivan, J., Aldrich, J., Borgida, E., & Rahn, W. (1990). Candidate appraisal and human nature: Man and superman in the 1984 election. *Political Psychology, 11,* 459–484.

Sullivan, J., Borgida, E., Jackson, M.S., Riedel, E., & Oxendine, A. R. (2002). A tale of two towns: Assessing the role of political resources in a community electronic network. *Political Behavior, 24,* 53–82.

Sullivan, J., Borgida, E., Jackson, M. S., Riedel, E., Oxendine, A., & Gangl, A. (2002). Social capital and community electronic networks: For-profit vs. for-community approaches. *American Behavioral Scientist, 45,* 868–886.

Sullivan, J., Marcus, E., Feldman, S., & Piereson, J. (1981). The sources of political tolerance: A multivariate analysis. *American Political Science Review, 15,* 92–106. Reprinted in W. Shively (Ed.), *The research experience in political science* (pp. 9–35). Itaska, IL: Peacock Publishers.

Sullivan, J., Piereson, J., Marcus, G., & Feldman, S. (1979). The more things change, the more they remain the same: The stability of mass belief systems. *American Journal of Political Science, 23,* 176–186.

Young, J., Borgida, E., Sullivan, J. & Aldrich, J. (1987). Personal agendas and the relationship between self-interest and voting behavior. *Social Psychology Quarterly, 50,* 64–71.

Young, J., Thomsen, C., Borgida, E., Sullivan, J., & Aldrich, J. (1991). When self-interest makes a difference: The role of construct accessibility in political reasoning. *Journal of Experimental Social Psychology, 27,* 271–296.

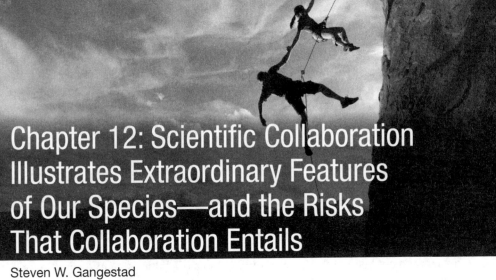

Chapter 12: Scientific Collaboration Illustrates Extraordinary Features of Our Species—and the Risks That Collaboration Entails

Steven W. Gangestad

Distinguished Professor of Psychology
University of New Mexico

Across my 30-plus years of doing research and publishing, virtually every project I've participated in has involved deep collaboration. Naturally, during graduate school I worked closely with my primary graduate advisor, Mark Snyder, and other faculty at Minnesota (notably, Ellen Berscheid and Eugene Borgida). In addition, I've worked with numerous graduate students in the psychology department at the University of New Mexico (UNM; most extensively to date, I have worked with Christine Garver-Apgar, Robert Thoma, Alita Cousins, Glenn Scheyd, Josh Tybur, and Nick Grebe). But most of my papers have resulted from collaboration with other faculty, both at UNM and elsewhere, as well. My first collaborative partner in this way was Jeffry Simpson. We became fast friends during our graduate school days together. Over a quarter-century span, we've worked together on numerous projects. Shortly after I arrived at UNM in the late 1980s, I began working on projects with Ron Yeo, a clinical neuropsychologist. And at about the same time, Randy Thornhill, an evolutionary biologist at New Mexico, and I performed our first joint research study, the beginning of a long-standing collaboration culminating in a coauthored book (Thornhill & Gangestad, 2008). I've also worked closely on research with other biologists (e.g., Paul Andrews, Anders Møller, and Stephan Van Dongen), anthropologists (e.g., Hillard Kaplan, Mark Flinn, and Melissa Emery Thompson), and, in new work, an MD (Joe Alcock), in addition to other psychologists (e.g., Martie Haselton, David Buss, and Marco Del Giduce). Just in the past year, I've initiated new collaborations with another half-dozen scholars.

I have worked with several of these collaborators over a many-year period, spanning multiple projects—again, notably with Jeff Simpson, Randy Thornhill, and Ron Yeo, but others too. Also, much of my work has clearly been interdisciplinary, crossing traditional boundaries of psychology into biology, anthropology, endocrinology, physiology, genetics, and neuroscience. I've been attracted to interdisciplinary collaboration.

These collaborations have benefited me tremendously careerwise. When compiling my history for this chapter, I was curious to find that, as of this writing, out of my 50 peer-reviewed papers that were most cited (according to the Web of Science), 20 had Thornhill as a coauthor, 12 had Simpson as a coauthor, four were written with Yeo, and I wrote six with Snyder (all but one when I was a graduate student, with Simpson a coauthor on two of them). Collectively, 80% (40/50) were written with at least one of those four partners. Most of the other 10 resulted from collaboration with a number of others (Haselton and Buss among them). Only one of them did I write by myself. While the majority of these papers also involved collaborators who were graduate students at the time, only one was coauthored with one of my own graduate students alone—and even that one was completed when he was a former student (Gangestad & Scheyd, 2005).

The greatest benefits that I've accrued as a result of these collaborations, however, have not been in the form of publications or citations, or even the financial consequences of those indicators of productivity (such as salary raises). They've taken the form of my personal satisfaction and intrinsic enjoyment derived from the research process—in short, the fun and excitement that I've experienced doing my job. These outcomes ultimately have maintained my engagement in research. (Extrinsic positive consequences, such as publication and citation, are nice, but far too distant in time from the behavior of performing research to effectively motivate that behavior, at least in my case.) Quite simply, I would not be very happy doing research in the absence of deep and broad collaboration.

What Makes Collaboration Fun? Sketch of a Scholarly Perspective

What elements make collaborative research fun and exciting that are lacking in noncollaborative research? My own reflections on that question come in a couple of different forms. One is, admittedly, scholarly in nature, and prior to sharing my personal reflections, I'll indulge in sketching out this viewpoint. It reflects my own understanding of the key role that collaborative efforts play in human endeavors, in general, and have for many generations, such as the fact that human nature has been shaped to seek and be sought out for collaborative efforts (very broadly speaking), which profoundly influences human motives. Increasingly, primatologists are coming to understand the breadth and depth of individuals' interdependence with nonkin ("friends" and allies) across a variety of species (e.g., in helping to negotiate and maintain status within groups; see Seyfarth & Cheney, 2012). In no species, however, is this interdependence more evident or important than in humans (e.g., Barclay, 2013; Nesse, 2007). Given heavy reliance on cooperation to make a living, nonkin matter in other ways: Individuals' success and fitness depend not only on their own skills and those of kin, but also on the skill sets of others with whom they cooperate—in broad terms, their collaborators. That is, individual success depends partly on the strength of their collaborative partners. Or, put otherwise, in human societies, others embody potential fitness-enhancing resources to be tapped. Over the long course of human evolution, this fact has had broad and deep implications for the nature of human sociality.

The reason can be stated quite simply: Members of human societies that could best choose and attract good associates (with collaborators key among them), as well as act in ways that maintain and foster effective collaborations, tended to succeed in those societies. One important outcome of this social selection was the "need to belong" (Baumeister & Leary, 1995), which now is stressed within social psychology. But I emphasize here that much more than a need to belong is involved. A *need* to belong does not, by itself, create belongingness. One must possess the features that lead others to be "belonged to." Not only that, but one should also be discriminative when we choose with whom to belong. We should want connections with others who have competencies that are both notable and work well with our own, such that we benefit from the association, as well as cooperation-enhancing features that lead us to feel that we indeed get a net gain from the association.

From this viewpoint, then, why are collaborative efforts in science both energizing and, potentially, very enjoyable? The reason is that they represent, within the microcosm of academia, a broader kind of effort that has fostered human success over millennia. In short, we come from a long lineage of ancestors, all of whom succeeded in surviving and reproducing. (Naturally, none of us is a direct descendent of anyone who failed to reproduce.) In addition, at least over the past 1,000 generations, I suspect that almost all were consummate collaborators as well. So, just as we enjoy the tastes of certain foods because those tastes served our ancestors well, we are drawn to and motivated to succeed within the context of collaborative efforts.

What Makes Interdisciplinary Collaboration Fun? Personal Reflections

My other reflections on this question come directly from my own experience. (Admittedly, however, reflections on my personal experience, at this time, are inextricably filtered through my thoughts about the key role of collaborative efforts in shaping human nature generally.) Because many of my collaborations have been interdisciplinary in nature, I specifically reflect on what makes interdisciplinary collaboration enjoyable.

Again, what I've found valuable in collaboration far exceeds the value of the scholarly outputs of that collaboration. Collaboration has been fun. What follows are reflections on a few reasons why that is.

My Collaborators Have Been My Teachers

Much of the joy of being a university researcher comes from the opportunity to pursue my own curiosities and interests—to continue to engage in what, in a child's world, constitutes play. Like most academics, I love to acquire new knowledge, especially as it relates to my attempts to address questions of interest that I see as being unanswered. That's much of why I have gravitated toward interdisciplinary work. As an undergraduate and as a graduate student, I confess, I never had formal coursework in evolutionary biology, reproductive biology, endocrinology, neuroscience, molecular genetics, but I've published writings on those topics. Very often, frankly, I've done research on matters that, at least at the outset of the research, I've known very little about.

Ultimately, I think I have come to understand something about what I hope are the meaningful contributions of my research. But to the extent I do, it's largely through my collaborations. Perhaps most of what I have learned is directly through reading. But in most cases, I could not possibly navigate the pertinent research studies without having collaborators to reveal my ignorance to, and to ask for advice on how to rectify it: what background literature to read, how to interpret and understand particular technical (even if very basic) language used in specific research, where the interesting controversies lie, what the big recent achievements have been, and who is doing the latest cutting-edge work.

Can I do independent work on these topics now? Typically not—which is one of the reasons why I continue doing interdisciplinary work. But again, preparing to be able to do independent work on the topics has not been the point of these collaborations. I've taken a great deal of satisfaction out of simply learning, and then having the opportunity to think about, new material. It's been by deliberate choice that I've gravitated toward research on matters that, at least at the outset of the research, I knew very little about—choices made possible through interdisciplinary collaboration.

Interdisciplinary Collaborative Work Has Permitted Me to Think About Bigger Questions

Interdisciplinary work is, of course, simply research on matters that lie at the intersection between two or more traditional disciplines. There's nothing intrinsic about such work that leads it to address big questions any more than research within a traditional discipline. (Charles Darwin's theory of evolution by natural selection, for instance, addresses not just one, but several, scientific issues of extraordinary breadth and depth, which not only lie within, but have come to define, the traditional subdiscipline of evolutionary biology.) De facto, however, interdisciplinary collaborative work has led me to be able to think about questions of much broader significance than I could reasonably fathom in its absence.

In the late 1990s and early 2000s, for instance, Randy Thornhill and I began research concerning how women's olfactory preferences (and later, other mating-related preferences) change across the menstrual cycle (specifically, based on fertility status). Coming from a background in psychology, I was focused on trying to understand the nature of the preference shifts themselves (albeit in the context of evolutionary psychology). Given his background in evolutionary biology, however, Randy became interested in trying to understand these shifts in a phylogenetic framework. What was the evolutionary history of these shifts? What patterns of shifts would have been characteristic of ancestors whom we share with close relatives? More distant primate ancestors? Ancestors shared with mammals or vertebrates in general? Once led to think of it in terms of this broader perspective, I came to see the centrality of certain issues that I hadn't thought deeply about before.

Perhaps most notably, from a phylogenetic perspective, what is perhaps remarkable about the human female reproductive cycle is the extent and nature of sexual receptivity and proceptivity outside the fertile phase, rather than within the fertile phase itself. (By contrast, most psychologically oriented research—including my own, until recently—has tended to focus theoretically on what occurs during the few days of the fertile phase.) I now cannot help but think about what I study from a phylogenetic perspective (see, e.g., Gangestad & Thornhill, 2008; Thornhill & Gangestad, 2008). Similarly, I've had the pleasure of being able to think about such issues as the evolutionary processes that have maintained genetic variation in propensity to developing neurodevelopmental disorders (with Ron Yeo) and the hormonal underpinnings of changes in women's sexual interests across the cycle and their phylogenetic origins (with Melissa Emery Thompson)—a breakthrough made possible only through interdisciplinary collaboration.

Thinking About Interdisciplinary Issues Is Fun—But Talking About Them Is Better

A lot of thinking, both generative and critical in nature, obviously goes into scientific research. Having the opportunity to converse with someone equally invested in a research agenda is both profitable and satisfying, particularly for me through interdisciplinary work, in which my collaborators have knowledge, insight, and technical expertise that I lack, and I may have background that they lack which is useful to the project as well. I've begun many conversations with collaborators over the years with an admission of my own ignorance, and I have asked to be given a brief overview of a topic (for example, signaling theory of intent within evolutionary biology, the basics of immunoreactive assaying of hormones, assumptions behind the idea of an extrinsic mortality rate within life history theory and their limitations, and how particular chemicals detected by magnetic imaging spectroscopy in neuroscience might be understood functionally). Occasionally, I've also learned enough to reflect on what I know and give back to collaborators something that they hadn't thought about in connection to the topic.

I've Been Able to Accomplish With Collaborators What I Could Not on My Own—But More Important, I Gain Much More Satisfaction From the Same Accomplishment

Naturally, interdisciplinary work calls for collaboration because each collaborator may not possess the knowledge or skills to accomplish the work alone or with individuals with the same background (e.g., graduate students).

Perhaps some scholars would prefer to do research in which they have the skill set to execute the work and interpret the results on their own or in collaboration with members of their lab. I too can derive a good deal of satisfaction from that kind of work. But I find that accomplishing work with collaborators, each of whom contributed something unique to the effort, brings a special kind of satisfaction. Work of that sort brings a feeling not only of accomplishment but also of interdependence and belongingness—and, importantly, mutual belongingness that led to accomplishment. As already emphasized, collaborative efforts to reach goals and accomplish feats have, to my mind, been extraordinarily important in human history. It's no surprise from this perspective, then, that fruitful participation in a collaboration that yielded an outcome judged worthy by a scientific community brings rich satisfaction—a satisfaction partly derived from the fact that one has, as collaborators, people who have considerable talents. In addition, it partly derives from recognition that one has been able to contribute to the success of the collaboration.

It's probably for this reason, more than any other, that I have maintained an interest in doing collaborative research.

The Pitfalls of Collaboration

While interdisciplinary collaborative research can be a lot of fun—and almost always has been such for me—I naturally recognize that collaboration entails dangers as well, and, in very real cases, can even be nightmarish. Collaborators have shared interests. They want to accomplish something together. They also may mutually want to learn from each other, experience the satisfaction of interdisciplinary conversations, and enjoy the outcomes of interdependent success. Pursuit of shared interests, again, is much of what makes collaboration fun.

But with collaboration also comes inevitable conflicts of interest. The interests of collaborators greatly overlap, but typically they do not perfectly align. One collaborator may benefit more from the success of the project than others. The relative benefits that collaborators earn may not match the efforts or levels of expertise that they contribute. Collaborators may have different opportunity costs to efforts that they put into a project, such that one collaborator may be less motivated to put in effort than another. Collaborators may differentially benefit from specific outcomes of a research project—for instance, this might be the case when one collaborator's ideas predict a particular outcome, with implications for the collaborator's reputation that may not be shared by the other collaborators.

Despite the many rewards associated with collaboration, it can become decidedly unpleasant should conflicts of interest undermine shared interests, of course. For example, one collaborator is not given the credit by others that he or she feels has been earned; collaborators do not feel that their returns match their efforts; one collaborator is not as motivated as others to put needed effort into a project (which is especially problematic when others have already exerted effort); collaborators disagree over interpretation of the results. I've seen collaborations falter due to each of these specific circumstances, and in some cases, the experiences of one or more collaborators have been hellish (thankfully for my sake, I have only seen this from the sidelines). Clearly, then, the key to engaging in intellectually and personally satisfying collaboration is to do all one can to avoid these conflicts.

Partner Choice

Perhaps the most important choice that anyone makes during a collaboration is the first one: whom to get involved with as collaborators. Although I've collaborated with many people during my career, I have by no means collaborated indiscriminately. The paths that I deliberately did not choose might have worked out as well as any I took. But in almost all cases where I became involved in a collaboration, I knew enough to feel confident that the collaboration would not be deeply undermined by conflicts of interest. To the extent that I had much to do with the personal satisfaction that I've derived from collaboration, it might simply have had to do with these choices made at the very outset. That's not to say that there haven't been potential conflicts of interest. (Indeed, not long ago, I joined what I call an "adversarial collaboration"—a joint effort to write a conceptual paper by multiple collaborators with different published points of view on the topic at hand.) Interdisciplinary collaboration can be especially risky. Precisely because collaborators have their own expertise, not shared by all the others, it sometimes can be difficult for collaborators to judge the potential benefits of a collaboration prior to a good deal of investment in that collaboration: That is, how others' knowledge will contribute to one's own interests in the subject matter and how one's own knowledge will benefit the collaboration.

To work together on a project, collaborators must share some basic assumptions about the nature of the phenomena that they are investigating. Scholars from different fields, however, often come from very different backgrounds, with implicit assumptions that are unshared. Communication can at times seem inefficient, as collaborators must sometimes explain very basic facts and approaches within their field. In addition, collaborators within a given field can often agree on what is a timely question to be addressed, one begged by the existing state of affairs, or just what kind of contribution offers a big statement. Scholars may have a much more difficult time appreciating the value of questions that drive the interests and passions of someone in a different, unfamiliar field. Relatedly, one can often feel as though one really doesn't know much about that which they're trying to make a seminal contribution (albeit through working with others who have some knowledge about that which one doesn't). Hence, decisions to initiate such a collaboration (at least provisionally) are not uncommonly made with a good deal of uncertainty.

Naturally, however, conflicts of interest do not by themselves doom collaborative efforts. They only do so when they undermine shared interests. When shared interests are potent, conflicts of interest are less likely to undermine them. So when are they potent? For starters, when collaborators all seek the beneficial outcomes of interdisciplinary collaboration, when all collaborators are motivated to learn from others' expertise, when all parties seek to examine questions that they could not address without extensive collaboration, when all enjoy what comes from talking about research ideas (both learning from others and sharing their knowledge with others), and when all are especially attracted to the rich satisfactions that come from accomplishment that can be acquired only through collaboration. In short, and not surprisingly, when the collaborators distinctly desire outcomes that are possible only with the success of the collaboration—including deliverables, but also, importantly, experiences achieved through the process of collaboration—a partnership is unlikely to be derailed by individual interests.

It's also no surprise that because certain personalities tend to be attracted to the outcomes achievable through the process of interdisciplinary collaboration, people with certain personalities tend to foster their success. These would include people who want to learn from others; people especially attracted to thinking, both generatively and critically, with others; people who value the special personal rewards that come from joint accomplishment; and those who have the capacities to ensure that other collaborators are rewarded too (e.g., a sense of fairness than can satisfy others as well as self). More generally, I am talking about those who "play well with others."

In addition to these features, which almost anyone would find valuable in a collaborator, good collaborators complement each other. They must possess some shared interests and perspectives. At the same time, it is important that my collaborators know much that I do not—and, hopefully, I know things that they do not. Again, as noted previously, that's a reason I find interdisciplinary collaborations especially attractive: I am sure to lack key knowledge on the project that others possess (and, again, to some extent, vice versa).

It also doesn't hurt if collaborators are also friends (or become friends). Two close friends, in essence, have come to be valuable to each other because of how they can support each other (and demonstrated such support in the past), such that they are personally motivated to protect and enhance the interests of the other. A loss of well-being to one's friend is, in effect, a loss of well-being to oneself (e.g., Tooby & Cosmides, 1996). Because friends value outcomes for each other much as they value outcomes for themselves, friendship naturally suppresses conflicts of interest and enhances shared interests. Not coincidentally, then, most of my long-standing collaborators have also either been good friends of mine before we began collaborative projects, or they became good friends through the process of collaboration. (Indeed, yet another benefit of scientific collaboration is that it provides a wonderful context in which to develop and cement friendships.)

Embracing Your Ignorance—While Also Seeking to Rectify It

Scholars tend to pride themselves on their knowledge, not their ignorance. Yet, as researchers well know, a key to doing meaningful research is to identify interesting questions for which they—and the field in general—have no good answers, as well as to identify and redress one's own ignorance on matters that might be useful to address. Interdisciplinary research involves much the same pursuits, but to a degree much exaggerated. Again, I've spent a good deal of my career studying topics that, at the outset, I had very little understanding of. To be able to contribute effectively to the kind of collaborative work I've done, however, I've needed to understand something about those topics. And, with my collaborators as guides, I've rectified some of my ignorance (even if I have not yet become an expert). To do so, however, I've had to confess my own ignorance and try to overcome it. As already noted, I like acquiring new knowledge, so I've enjoyed working on interdisciplinary topics very new to me at the outset.

Ensuring That Collaborators Derive Satisfaction From the Collaboration Too

Although I've been fortunate enough never to have had a collaboration go badly, I have enjoyed some projects more than others. The ones that I have found least satisfying are those to which I felt I contributed the least. Those also happen to be projects from which, in some sense, I reaped the greatest (extrinsically generated) benefits—for example, publication—for the least cost (in terms of my own time and effort). One might wonder, then, why wouldn't these be opportunities I cherish the most? From the perspective that I sketched out earlier, the answer is pretty clear: People not only want to belong to collaborations; they are also typically even more motivated to be *desired* as collaborators and, hence, meaningfully contribute to the success of a collaboration, even though it requires considerable time and effort from them. I suspect that when people garner the benefits of collaboration without having put in a good deal of effort, they may wonder (even if only implicitly) whether, in fact, their lack of effort may diminish their reputation as a valuable collaborator, at least in the eyes of their current collaborators.

That's primarily why I personally would rather put a good deal of effort into each and every collaboration I am involved with. I presume that many others feel the same way that I do. And, hence, I presume that many others would just as soon be given the opportunity to contribute meaningfully to a collaboration. Perhaps the one thing that can make the biggest difference when it comes to collaborators' satisfaction is their perception that they came to be valued as collaborators, and they earned it.

It goes without saying, then, that someone who takes more credit for a collaborative accomplishment than what others consider deserved lessens his or her value as a collaborator, and for a similar reason: By taking more credit than is deserved, this person implies that others did less to earn a reputation as a valued collaborator than was the case. Everyone wants a competent collaborator, and lack of perceived competence by one collaborator can certainly cause the collaboration to dissolve. And everyone wants a hardworking and responsible collaborator—one willing to do his or her fair share.

But, in fact, most scholars are quite competent and hardworking. In what I've observed, then, what killed off collaborations—either ones that fall apart or, perhaps more often, rendered them dead-end efforts, with no future beyond a current project—has often been a perceived lack of modesty in one of the collaborators.

Conclusions

Collaboration is part of what has made science fun for me. There are multiple reasons. One is that it permits scientific outcomes that are much more interesting than I, at least, could produce on my own. That's partly why, again, I've been drawn to interdisciplinary research. But other reasons have probably played even more important parts, and perhaps the overarching theme of all this is that collaboration brings rewards that extend well beyond successfully completing a scientific project itself.

I began this discussion by placing scientific collaboration in a broader context of human activity—the idea that scientific collaboration represents, within the microcosm of academia, a broader kind of effort that has fostered human success over many millennia, specifically, the idea that our human ancestors succeeded partly because they have been consummate collaborators. Collaborative activity, then, not only helps us accomplish the tasks at hand. Broadly speaking, it also is a fundamental means through which we develop meaningful social relationships, enhance our own value and connection to others, and thereby ground a sense of life's purpose and meaning. I try to remind myself, then, that when I begin a collaboration, there's much, much more at stake for me in its success than simply doing what the collaboration set out to do—completing the project at hand. For precisely that reason, in fact, the success of the collaboration is not defined narrowly in terms of the success of completing the project at hand. For that very reason, when the collaboration does succeed, in broader terms, much more than the project at hand is accomplished. And for that reason, fundamentally, is why I'm drawn, over and over again, to collaborative work.

▓ REFERENCES ▓

Barclay, P. (2013). Strategies for cooperation in biological markets, especially for humans. *Evolution and Human Behavior, 34,* 164–175.

Baumeister, R. F., & Leary, M. R. (1995). The need to belong: A desire for interpersonal attachments as a fundamental human motivation. *Psychological Bulletin, 117,* 497–529.

Gangestad, S. W., & Scheyd, G. J. (2005). The evolution of human physical attractiveness. *Annual Review of Anthropology, 34,* 523–548.

Gangestad, S. W., & Thornhill, R. (2008). *The evolutionary biology of human female sexuality.* New York, NY: Oxford University Press.

Nesse, R. (2007). Runaway social selection for displays of partner value and altruism. *Biological Theory, 2,* 143–155.

Seyfarth, R. M., & Cheney, D. L. (2012). The evolutionary origins of friendship. *Annual Review of Psychology, 63,* 153–177.

Thornhill, R., & Gangestad, S. W. (2008). Human oestrus. *Proceedings of the Royal Society B, 275,* 991–1000.

Tooby, J., & Cosmides, L. (1996). Friendship and the Banker's Paradox: Other pathways to the evolution of adaptations for altruism. In W. G. Runciman, J. Maynard Smith, & R. I. M. Dunbar (Eds.), *Evolution of Social Behaviour Patterns in Primates and Man. Proceedings of the British Academy, 88,* 119–143.

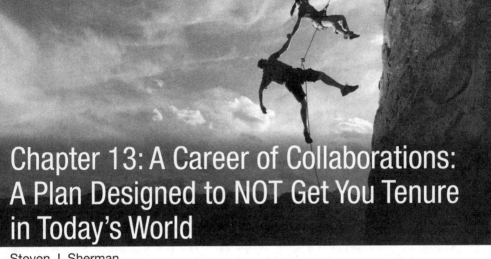

Chapter 13: A Career of Collaborations: A Plan Designed to NOT Get You Tenure in Today's World

Steven J. Sherman

Emeritus Chancellor's Professor of Psychological and Brain Sciences
Indiana University

It is, perhaps, the ultimate irony that I am writing this chapter concerning collaboration by myself, with no collaborators. Over all my years of publishing empirical articles and chapters, I have exactly one single-authored publication (before this one). Perhaps the fact that it is one of my most cited articles should have taught me something.

Let me begin this chapter with an important disclaimer. What I am about to say here is *not* meant to tell you that any particular way of developing and pursuing a research career in psychological science is better than any other way. The ideas are meant to motivate readers to think about what they might do in order to develop and pursue a program of work that will make them happy, and possibly successful. The chapter is especially relevant for graduate students and for young faculty. For full professors, what I have to say might cause them to think about how they evaluate job candidates and tenure/promotion cases.

If an untenured assistant professor asks administrators at her university what she ought to do in order to enhance her likelihood of achieving tenure and promotion, she is likely to hear that (in addition to productivity, grants, good teaching, etc.) there are two very important principles to follow:

1. Make sure that you have a coherent, programmatic line (or perhaps two lines) of research. Your past work, present work, and planned future work should fit into a structured whole that is guided by theory and supported by empirical work. You need to be able to articulate clearly what you will be doing five years from now and how that work will expand on what you are doing now.

2. Don't collaborate! In particular, be sure that you have publications that do not continue work with advisors or other graduate school

coauthors. Be wary of collaborating with other faculty members at your university, especially senior faculty members. Show your ability to do independent work and to establish an independent line of research.

I want to discuss both of these principles while reflecting on my own career in light of them. With regard to the first principle, I have never understood why one has to be identified with one particular line of work so that one might be referred to as a "leader" in this field. (As an aside, within the area of stereotypes and prejudice, we probably have a few hundred researchers who are known as leaders in this field.) I have always been proud to be an eclectic. Whether this predilection is due to attention deficit disorder, boredom, or curiosity about all aspects of behavior, I don't know. I do know that this is not a particularly good choice if one is looking for fame, fortune, or recognition.

Because most researchers are involved in somewhat narrow areas of work, an eclectic's publications in some areas will be completely unknown to most people. For example, researchers in the area of social cognition may be aware of my work on illusory correlation or individual and group social perception or counterfactual thinking, but they are unlikely to have any clue that I have done rather significant work in the areas of cigarette smoking, anagram solving, or metaphors in the law. Thus, developing a name for oneself is much more difficult when one chooses to be an eclectic. Of course, this fact makes it all the more difficult to earn tenure and promotion. That was true when I was young, and it is true a hundredfold today.

Why is this principle considered to be so important? I believe that this is, in part, due to the metaphors that we use to think about research. When one is eclectic, there is the belief that he is broad but shallow—a jack of all trades and a master of none. But why does *broad* necessarily imply *shallow*? Perhaps this is based on the metaphor of water in a container. If the water is in a narrow container, it will be rather deep. If it is then poured into a broad container, it becomes much more shallow. So, naturally, being broad in anything implies being shallow. However, what if we look at a different metaphor, involving water? Water in Lake Erie is broader than the water in any local pond, and water in the Pacific Ocean is broader than the water in Lake Erie. But which of these bodies of water is deeper?

I have never believed that being eclectic rendered one a dabbler. One can achieve expertise in many areas of psychology and conduct important research in these many areas. Why is it difficult to believe that one must be broad only at the expense of depth? Why can't we achieve levels of expertise in several areas?

And what about the part of this principle that requires young researchers to know what they are likely to be doing 5 years from now? What a crock. I have never known a prominent researcher in psychology who could predict what they would be doing 5 years in the future. In fact, I would worry about someone who had a clear plan for her research program that extended very far into the future. Look back at any prominent psychologist's career and judge whether what that person was doing at any point in time could have been predicted with any assurance 5 years earlier.

I have a rather sad story that is related to the belief that we all ought to have a 5-year plan. A graduate student with whom I worked was on the job market. This student was (and is) terrific. Like me, this student was a bit of an eclectic and did wonderful work in several areas. In my letter of support for jobs, I concluded: "I don't know exactly what—will be doing five years from now; but, whatever it is, it will be creative, important, and elegant." I was surprised when the student did not get an offer after an important interview. When I asked why, I was told that it was because the student had no clear vision of a research plan for the next 5 years. I regret that my letter may have had a negative effect, but I don't regret saying what I did, and I firmly believe that what I said should have been taken as a strongly positive statement.

Now, I will admit that I carry my eclecticism much further than most. A quick tally identifies 44 different topics in psychology in which I have published research, theory, or both. These publications have appeared in outlets from many different areas, including social psychology, cognitive psychology, developmental psychology, clinical psychology, personality psychology, organizational behavior, judgment and decision making, language, law, medicine, addiction, perception, and memory. The fact of working in so many diverse areas has brought many challenges, but it has also brought some great benefits. It has certainly kept me from ever getting bored. It has allowed me to see connections between very different areas of work that I would never have otherwise seen. And I believe that this has had the effect of enriching ideas in these different areas. But most of all, the greatest benefit of such eclecticism has been the opportunity to do what the second principle for getting tenure tells us *not* to do—that is, the opportunity to collaborate. With an eclectic approach and a deep interest in so many areas of work, I have had the great fortune to collaborate with fantastic colleagues who do wonderful work in these different areas. The fact that some of these colleagues happen to live in great places such as Italy, Portugal, New Zealand, Australia, and Israel has not hurt either.

So let me now turn to this second principle, focusing on collaboration in psychological science. Over the years, I have collaborated with more than 50 different colleagues (in addition to the many graduate students with whom I have worked)—some only once or twice, and some for a very long period of time.

People often ask me, "How did you get to collaborate with so many people?" or "How can I get opportunities to collaborate with the kinds of people who do such good work?" I think that providing my own answers to these questions can be instructive and perhaps tell us something about the dynamics of collaboration. One thing that I know for sure—my large number of collaborations is not because I am an extravert with marvelous social skills, or that I make friends easily and am socially popular. On the contrary, I am pretty much your basic introvert. I hate small talk at conferences and avoid talking to people whom I don't know. So what are the bases of my collaborations?

Proximity. One of the first pieces of research to which I was exposed as a graduate student was early work by Festinger and colleagues, as they investigated how friendships formed in a housing complex. They found that a major determinant of friendship ties in the complex was simply the proximity between families. Just seeing people and having some contact with them greatly increased the likelihood of further interaction and growing friendships. I have found that proximity is also an important determinant of collaboration. One of the aspects of the psychology department at Indiana University that motivates cross-area collaborations is the way in which offices are assigned—more or less randomly. In many other departments, each area has its own little corner, niche, or floor in a building. This greatly reduces the likelihood of interacting with people in different areas of work. For many of my years here, I had Eliot Hearst (animal behavior) as an across-the-hall neighbor, Linda Smith (developmental) as a neighbor on one side, and Rich Shiffrin (cognitive) as a neighbor on the other side. I am convinced that this led to interactions with them that, in each case, helped to promote productive collaborations. With Eliot, we worked together on the feature-positive effect in both animals and humans. The idea of being relatively insensitive to the absence of features led to some interesting further research on how people make inferences about others and how people go about detecting change involving additions or deletions. For example, we quickly notice when a friend grows a beard, but we have a very difficult time identifying exactly what has changed when the friend shaves his beard. With Linda, I was introduced to principles of cognitive development in children. This led to some very interesting ideas about emotion inferences and about the development of assimilation and contrast. I recently wrote a chapter that included a substantial section on the development of stereotypes in children. Many of my ideas came from interactions with Linda. With Rich, I learned much about memory and cognitive representations. We were able to apply some of his ideas to work that I had done as a graduate student on the cognitive representation of social structures. Although only one published manuscript emerged from this collaboration, what I learned became part of a great deal of my later work.

It's in the genes (or perhaps in the shared environment). Sometimes blood matters more than proximity. Being liberal parents during the early 1970s, my wife and I were quite laissez-faire. With regard to our kids' decisions about date choices, hairstyles, and college majors, we were pretty much hands off. I don't think that either child had any clue about what I did in my work. And yet both ended up with PhDs in social psychology—my daughter, Bonnie, with John Darley as her advisor at Princeton, and my son, Jeff, with Dave Hamilton as his advisor at the University of California at Santa Barbara. Bonnie chose not to go into academia, but Jeff did. Although we did not collaborate for the first part of his career, we have been doing quite a bit of collaboration lately, and it has been a joy. Finding someone genetically close with whom to work has special meaning.

My collaboration with Jeff has an unusual history. John Kruschke is a colleague of mine at Indiana University. I was generally aware of the research that John did with regard to category learning, but I didn't really know the nuts and bolts or the implications. Jeff met John at a conference, and he noticed how John's model could easily be applied to issues of stereotype development. He and John developed some of these possibilities, and because the implications involved illusory correlation (a topic that I knew something about), they brought me into the conversation. But without the family connection between Jeff and me, this collaboration would never have started.

John's theory is that, in learning the features of category, the most frequent category is learned first. Then attention is shifted to a rarer category, and the features that can best discriminate the rare category from the frequent category are given special attention. Importantly, the strength of connection between the rare category and its features will be greater than the strength of connection between the frequent category and its features. Thus, if a headache is a perfect predictor of a frequent disease and a rash is a perfect predictor of a rare disease, a patient with both a headache and a rash will be, surprisingly, perceived as suffering from the rare disease. This judgment, of course, violates base rate considerations and is referred to as the *inverse base rate effect.*

Jeff, John, and I used this model to further our understanding of category accentuation and of illusory correlation in the perceptions of majority and minority groups. The model also explains why minority stereotypes (concerning both physical and personality features) are stronger than stereotypes of majority groups. In addition, along with Jamin Halberstadt, we used this model to understand the phenomenon of hypodescent—that is, why people of mixed race are perceived as belonging to the minority race.

Recently, Jeff and I have been discussing the use of this category learning model for impressions of a single individual (e.g., Harry at work versus Harry at home). The application to individual cases has allowed us to see the possibilities for reducing stereotypes and for increasing the likelihood of the cessation of habitual or addictive behaviors such as cigarette smoking.

Go to small conferences. The format of small conferences (such as Bibb Latane's Nags Head Conference and the social cognition conference that has been held at Duck, North Carolina), where a limited number of people live together for 5 or 6 days, is an ideal setting for the development of collaborations, even for introverted and socially unskilled people like me. One of my most important, enjoyable, and productive collaborations began at a Nags Head Conference. Dave Hamilton presented his most recent work on distinctiveness-based illusory correlations, showing how stereotypes of groups might develop on the basis of cognitive mechanisms alone, without the necessity of motivation (or even awareness). His ideas and data fit nicely with thoughts that I had been having about similarities and differences between the perceptions of individuals in terms of person perception and the perception of groups in terms of stereotypes. We talked at length during that conference, and we agreed to meet again later that summer, at which point we developed a grant proposal. Happily, the proposal was funded, and we have worked together productively since then. The growth and development of our work over the years clearly demonstrate the great benefits of collaborative efforts. Because my collaboration with Dave represents the most significant of my collaborations, this is an appropriate place to talk about the tremendous advantages of working with others.

Quite honestly, at the beginning of our collaboration, the kinds of issues that Dave and I dealt with were somewhat circumscribed and specific in nature. I would not describe them as simply dotting *i*'s and crossing *t*'s, but neither was the research of major conceptual and theoretical importance. We dealt with questions such as

- What if one of the groups was an ingroup?
- What if the most distinctive group became distinctive only after some initial learning period where both groups were equivalent in frequency?
- Was the process primarily an encoding phenomenon or a retrieval phenomenon?
- What about memory for target information, and how was memory related to judgments?
- What would result in terms of illusory correlation if there were three rather than two target groups?
- Did illusory correlation effects apply when the targets were individuals as opposed to groups?

As we proceeded to answer these questions and expand some of our ideas, other researchers (e.g., Smith, Rothbart, Fiedler, and McGarty) provided accounts of the illusory correlation phenomenon that differed from what had been our distinctiveness-based account. Thus, some of our research turned toward trying to distinguish the various accounts and to provide process-related evidence to identify the underlying mechanism.

But the biggest breakthrough came as we asked the last of the questions listed here. Did illusory correlation effects apply when the targets were individuals as opposed to groups? Results indicated that at times, the data looked similar regardless of target type, but at other times, the data were very different. In trying to figure out why, we arrived at the importance of a long-forgotten psychological construct—*entitativity* (the property of being a real thing). The extent to which group targets were entitative predicted very well whether an illusory correlation would form and what impressions of those groups were likely to look like. But more than this, we came to understand the importance of target entitativity. This allowed us to explore certain processes that were involved in stereotyping and to finally get a handle on important similarities and differences between the impression formation process for individuals and the stereotyping process for groups. Clearly, the collaboration took us far beyond what either of us could have accomplished alone.

Working together, Dave and I were able to develop "big-picture" ideas that went far beyond our initial ideas and conceptions. The truth is that neither of us could have achieved these things alone. It was only through collaborative efforts that ideas were crystallized and developed into theories and research plans. We were far better as a team than the sum of what we could have achieved alone. We made each other better. And this has been true of all my collaborations. It may be the case that some individuals work better alone rather than putting their heads together with others. But I think that this represents a significant minority. If collaborations make psychologists better thinkers and better researchers, why would we do anything to discourage collaborative efforts? I will return to this question toward the end of this chapter.

There was one other significant collaboration that emerged from one of these small Nags Head Conferences. And there is an interesting story behind it. I came to the conference very excited to talk about some recent work that I was doing involving hypothesis testing, confirmation bias, and the role of diagnosticity. The talk was written and ready to go. About a week before the conference, I came across a brilliant article about these issues written by Klayman and Ha. This was clearly the best treatment of these issues that I had ever seen—lovely work. I rewrote part of my talk to reflect many of the ideas that Klayman and Ha had presented with the intent to give them all the credit that they deserved. The night that I arrived at Nags Head, I met the other conference attendees. One of the people whom I had not met previously was a social developmental psychologist named Jackie Gnepp. She introduced herself, and then she introduced her husband, who was there simply to watch and enjoy the beach. His name was Josh Klayman. Needless to say, this made me both very positively excited and very nervous at the same time. Would I do his work justice? Thankfully, Josh is a very kind and open person. We spent many hours talking about our mutual interests during the week. We then initiated collaborative efforts to pursue some novel ideas about hypothesis confirmation biases, and some good and productive work developed.

Choose sabbaticals well. One of the truly great benefits of an academic lifestyle is the ability to have a sabbatical every seven years. What a wonderful opportunity. I have always been bewildered that so many faculty spend their sabbaticals at their home university, holed up in their home or office writing books or papers. I know that this choice is often made because there are children at home—but actually, young children do fine on sabbaticals. If the sabbatical is in a foreign country, the opportunity for children to experience a different culture and possibly learn a new language is invaluable. Even high school teenagers can survive a sabbatical. I took one sabbatical when our kids were a junior and a freshman. If your experience is anything like mine, it was an ordeal to get them to agree to go. They refused to leave their school, their friends, and their activities. We pretty much had to kidnap them. Then, at the end of the sabbatical, they hated to leave and go back to Bloomington. They loved where they were and didn't want to return to such a boring city.

In any case, sabbaticals provide a great opportunity for beginning or continuing collaborative work. From a professional standpoint, the proper way to choose a sabbatical location would be to focus on a person or a set of people from whom one could learn new ideas, new techniques, new approaches, etc., and to contact them in advance to arrange for things that will make the sabbatical easy, fun, and productive (e.g., an office, good housing, setting up some colloquia). I must admit with some embarrassment, however, that this has *not* been my approach to choosing sabbatical locations. Instead, my wife and I decide where we would like to live, and then I look for potential colleagues.

This strategy has led to sabbaticals in Italy, Portugal, Amsterdam, New Zealand, and Australia. Maybe I have been lucky in my less than professionally rational decision making, but these sabbaticals have culminated in wonderful and lasting collaborations, learning, and interactions, in addition to being able to spend quality time in these wonderful places. The list of people with whom I have collaborated while on these sabbaticals is extensive, including Anne Maass, Luciano Arcuri, Mara Cadinu, Luigi Castelli, Gun Semin, Leonel Garcia-Marques, Tammy Garcia-Marques, Mario Ferreira, Andre Mata, Marc Scholten, Bob Cialdini, Yoshi Kashima, Nick Haslam, Jamin Halberstadt, Chick Judd, Bernadette Park, Reid Hastie, and Yaacov Trope.

During one sabbatical, Tammy and Leonel Garcia-Marques and I generated some very interesting ideas about language and thought. The ideas lay dormant for many years until a graduate student, Elise Percy, showed excitement about these ideas. We resurrected them, and Elise improved them. She began the program with a consideration of the mental effects of noun–adjective word order in native language speaking. In addition, a graduate student from Portugal, Andre Mata, had come to Indiana University to work with me. Tammy and Leonel were brought back into the conversation, and the work went forward. We have now explained and demonstrated some extremely interesting effects of noun–adjective word order on judgments of frequency, judgments of similarity, memory, perception, impressions, and stereotypes. Current work is exploring other native language differences as they affect such things as causal attributions and counterfactual thinking. All this stemmed from a late afternoon on sabbatical in Italy.

Do what you love. Sometimes just doing in your professional life things that you love in other aspects of life is rewarding and affords the opportunity for meaningful collaborations. I have been part of two such collaborations.

First, I have always loved wordplay—British cryptic crossword puzzles, palindromes, anagrams, double meanings. And I'm good at it. We pay people very well if they can shoot a ball through a hoop or hit a ball that is thrown at 95 miles per hour. We pay lots of money to people who sing well or play an instrument well. I have always thought that if there were a worldwide competition for anagram solving, I might be among the finalists (or even win). Why don't we pay for this skill? Every year, I enter a contest that combines trivia, wordplay, and flexible and creative ways of thinking. There are 50 items in the contest to solve within a month. It is a mind-numbing experience. Here is one of the simplest items: "The first name of the singer and the last name of the actor are anagrams of each other. The last name of the singer and the first name of the actor are the two first names of a pair of famous Hollywood relatives. Name the singer, the actor, and the Hollywood relatives."

Some years ago, Laura Novick came to Indiana University to talk about her research on anagram solving. Naturally, I was greatly stimulated by the talk. We met and discussed possible factors that might distinguish expert anagram solving from the ways in which nonexperts go about trying to solve anagrams. We continued our conversations after she left, and we proceeded to research our ideas. If I can brag a bit, I believe that this work is the clearest and most definitive in identifying the processes and approaches that determine expertise in solving anagrams. (We promised to turn next to cryptograms, but that has yet to happen.)

My second area of love is sports, especially baseball, as well as decision making in sports. After I gave a colloquium at the University of Chicago, I went to dinner with Dick Thaler and Reid Hastie, and we talked about our mutual interest in decision making in sports. We decided to pursue this further by setting up a small sports decision-making conference. Naturally, it would have to be held in Phoenix during spring training. There were about 20 invitees, including psychologists, statisticians, and behavioral economists. In addition, we were somehow able to induce Bill James (the guru of sabermetrics) to come. Billy Beane (the general manager of the Oakland A's and the focus of the theory illustrated in the recent movie *Moneyball*) also came, as did one of ESPN's news guys.

I learned a lot at this conference, which was clearly a collaborative effort. The meeting got some news coverage, and I was asked to come to Chicago to be interviewed along with Dick Thaler for a segment of the *NewsHour with Jim Lehrer*. Much of the interview was done on the field before a game between the White Sox and Yankees. I got the opportunity to do a 20-minute taped interview with Joe Torre, the Yankee manager at the time (while I was wearing my Boston Red Sox hat). So collaborative work in psychology can help you cross items off your bucket list.

Serendipity. Sometimes productive collaborations emerge simply because of fortuitous circumstances and coincidences. But one must be alert to these and take advantage of them—or else they might be gone forever. Three of my most important collaborations began in this way.

Some years ago, I was asked by Tory Higgins and Dick Sorrentino to write a chapter for their *Handbook of Motivation and Cognition*. The chapter was to focus on thinking about the future. I had done research on (inaccurate) predictions of the future and on the effects of imagining and explaining hypothetical future events, so I could easily write such a chapter. But it would have been boring to simply write about things that I already knew. I looked at what other chapters were being written for this volume. One in particular caught my attention. Marcia Johnson was going to write a chapter on thinking about the past. I didn't know Marcia well, but I loved her work on reality monitoring. I decided to call and ask her if she would be interested in doing a chapter together that combined our interests (i.e., thinking across time). She agreed that it would be a good idea. The result was a lovely synthesis of thinking backward and thinking forward—the origami of time. It is my single favorite piece of work. When someone asks me what writing of mine they should read that would be fun and informative, I always recommend this chapter. Marcia and I agreed to collaborate on a second chapter that would focus on feelings across time (e.g., nostalgia for the past and fear for the future), but that has not yet happened.

One day in 1978, I was having lunch with two postdocs at Indiana University, Laurie Chassin and Clark Presson. This in itself was an odd circumstance because I almost never eat lunch. Laurie was trained as a clinical psychologist, and Clark as a developmental psychologist. We were talking about a news story. Joe Califano, then secretary of the Department of Health, Education, and Welfare (HEW), had earmarked lots of money for the study of adolescent cigarette smoking. Among the three of us, we knew next to nothing about any kind of substance use, including cigarette smoking. But we started joking and fantasizing that we could probably do this kind of research as well as anyone else. After all, we had expertise in clinical psychology, developmental psychology, and social psychology. We knew how to do good research. And wouldn't it be nice to have some federal funding?

Although the conversation began as a joke, we soon got more serious. Maybe we actually could do it. We decided to spend two weeks reading the current literature on adolescent cigarette smoking. If the work was competent, and if there was really good theory and research going on already, it would be silly to think that people with no record in this area could hope to get funding.

After 2 weeks, we met again. We agreed that the research in this area was pretty woeful. It was primarily descriptive and correlational, and there were no good theories and no understanding about the kinds of psychological processes that underlie smoking behavior. So we forged ahead and prepared a grant proposal, not really expecting much. To our surprise and delight, the grant was fully funded in the first round. Now, more than 30 years later, this project is still federally funded and is still ongoing; it is the longest longitudinal study of smoking. And our work has been good. We have investigated the social psychological factors involved in smoking initiation and cessation, the natural history of smoking in terms of various transitions, and the impact of stress and socialization on smoking behavior. The project also has recently included children of the original participants, so we have been able to investigate the intergenerational transmission of smoking attitudes and behavior.

A combination of expertise in the three areas of psychology has made this research unique, and the opportunity for me to work closely with others with different areas of expertise has been a fantastic experience. Because the work appears primarily in health and addiction outlets (although much has also appeared in developmental and social psychological outlets), few of my experimental social psychology colleagues have ever known about this part of my life. But this is what happens when one chooses to be an eclectic.

The third collaboration that is the product of serendipity is the one that is currently the most important to me professionally. During the 1990s, I served two terms on the Bloomington City Council. It was a great experience, and in the realm of local politics, some really good things can be achieved. One city council member also had to serve on the Bloomington Planning Commission, the body that decides about land use, zoning, and development. That member was usually me.

During the Planning Commission meetings, I was seated next to Joe Hoffmann. Joe is a professor in the law school who specializes in criminal law. Now, these meetings were often very long and very boring. The planning director was extremely long-winded, and the slide shows went on interminably. To reduce the boredom, Joe and I often talked during the presentations. One night, our topic of conversation was a recent automobile accident in Bloomington. A truck driver had run a yellow light and killed two pedestrians who were crossing. The prosecutor decided that the penalty was to be the same as for anyone who ran a light—a monetary fine, with no charge of manslaughter. The argument was that many drivers run that particular light, and this one happened to be unlucky. The public was outraged. I told Joe that psychology theory and research could help us understand people's reactions and could also help us understand the basis for any legal principle involving accidental deaths, as well as other issues of causality. There was much literature on blame, causation, perception as well as intent, and punishment.

Suddenly, it became clear to us. We really needed to develop a course involving psychology and law that focused on how psychology theory and research can inform the law. This was to be a course on social analytic jurisprudence rather than the more usual psychology and law course on evidentiary matters (e.g., eyewitness testimony) or the psychology of the criminal (e.g., what constitutes mental illness). It was a unique course.

Working with Joe has been marvelous. Of course, I prefer the law part of the course, and Joe prefers the psychology part. In addition to teaching this course (which both law students and graduate students in psychology have taken), we have written articles in both psychology and law publications. For example, along with Elise Percy, we have developed the concept of sticky metaphors and how such metaphors can help us understand the voluntary manslaughter doctrine and how this doctrine has developed and evolved.

In a nutshell, a *sticky metaphor* is one that is constrained and culturally universal. For example, there are thousands of metaphors for love, but the only metaphors for anger involve heat, pressure, and explosion. Metaphors for emotions are often sticky. This is because the physiological reactions to the emotion are very similar to the physiological reactions brought about by something else. The body's reaction to anger is very similar to the body's reaction to heat—increased blood pressure, increased heart rate, increased skin temperature, a reddening of the face, and so on.

Because of this similarity, the metaphors develop. But metaphors become more than words or linguistic devices. Anger is not only spoken about as heat and pressure—it is actually conceptualized as a boiling pot. A lay theory, then, develops about the time course of anger. When the heat is applied (whether an actual flame or the sight of an adulterous spouse), the anger rises quickly, up to and beyond the boiling point. But once the flame is removed, there is a quick cooling off. This is exactly the lay theory that underlies the voluntary manslaughter doctrine, often called the "heat of passion doctrine."

Of course, these ideas about anger are quite wrong. Anger does not necessarily diminish quickly once a wife and her lover are out of sight. However, if the husband waits for more than an hour before killing them, he cannot benefit from the voluntary manslaughter doctrine (which would reduce his punishment by half) because he is assumed to have cooled off. Similarly, the voluntary manslaughter doctrine assumes that anger rises very quickly once the "flame" is applied. However, work in psychology tells us that anger can rise very slowly as one ruminates and thinks about events.

In addition, the sticky metaphor for fear involves cold—icy chills. Fear is cold; anger is hot. Thus, the metaphors for fear lead to a misfit for the necessary conditions for applying the voluntary manslaughter doctrine. Husbands who kill their wives out of anger when their wives have been unfaithful often benefit from the voluntary manslaughter doctrine, but wives who have been battered and beaten and then kill their husbands out of fear do not often benefit from this doctrine. Fear simply does not fit into the metaphorically driven heat of passion murder. Of course, psychology tells us that fear can be just as powerful an emotion as anger and that fear can drive people to acts of aggression and violence. This is only one of the topics that we cover in our course and have written about. We are currently pursuing empirical work to understand better what makes metaphors sticky and how such metaphors operate. We are also currently writing a book that reflects all of the psychology/law topics covered in our course.

Conclusions

In this discussion, I have talked about my career as a social psychologist and about the fact that I have violated the two principles that are likely to reduce the likelihood of earning tenure (according to current theory). That is, I am an eclectic without one single area of work with which I am heavily and uniquely identified, and I have collaborated with many, many colleagues. These two things, of course, go hand in hand. In part, it is my eclectic and generally curious and inquisitive nature that has led me to seek out many collaborative efforts; and it is my desire for collaborative work that has led me to lots of different areas of research. Of course, one does not need to be eclectic in order to collaborate extensively. Petty and Cacioppo collaborated for many years on research in a rather specific and circumscribed area, and Kahneman and Tversky collaborated for many years on research and theory involving only heuristic principles.

What are the costs and benefits of extensive collaboration? On the cost side, one is likely to receive somewhat less credit for collaborative work than for single-authored publications. This strikes me as very strange. This way of assigning credit employs a zero-sum view. There is a fixed amount of credit to go around, and this ensures that authors of multiauthored papers get less credit than authors of single-authored publications. But why should the amount of total credit be fixed? I have always believed that the product of good collaboration is usually better than the product of what the coauthors could have achieved alone. If the product is of greater value, shouldn't the total amount of credit actually be greater? Instead of believing that collaboration enhances research and makes each collaborator better, the current general viewpoint implies that more collaboration equals less input, less responsibility for the outcome, and thus less credit. Single-authored papers receive, in my opinion, more value than they deserve.

Also on the cost side, by discouraging collaboration, researchers may not be as knowledgeable about all approaches, methodologies, and analytic tools as they might otherwise be. And, by brainstorming, each collaborator can be better than either one alone. This is a Gestalt-like view of collaboration, but I have always found it to be true. The whole of collaboration is greater than the sum of the individual parts. I have never found that the outcome of a collaboration was worth less than what I could have achieved alone.

Therefore, one benefit of collaborative research is the improvement of the research itself. At least, this has been true in my own case. The other major benefit of collaboration is more ancillary. It is simply more fun and more invigorating to be involved in a collaborative effort. I enjoy nothing more than to kick around ideas with colleagues and see these ideas develop into a productive program of research. The best theories, principles, and research approaches that have been adopted in my work never would have come about without some collaborative effort. Just a few of these include the development of a model of detection of change, a feature-matching model of choice, the role of entitativity in group perception, the ideas behind the self-erasing nature of errors of prediction, and a better understanding of what causes potency in counterfactual thoughts.

Why, then, are departments and administrators so concerned about research collaborations? Such concerns have increased dramatically in recent years. Right now, at Indiana University, when an assistant professor is being considered for tenure and promotion, all collaborations with other faculty (especially already tenured faculty) are scrutinized. A letter from each collaborator from every collaboration is required to go into the tenure dossier. The letter must spell out the precise role the tenure candidate played, and it must ensure that this person made a substantial and independent contribution. But why do we doubt the contribution of a young researcher who collaborates a lot with a very renowned full professor? Why would a renowned and productive researcher care to continue collaborating with someone who does not contribute heavily to research projects? The fact that a well-established scientist continues to work with a young researcher should be taken as an indication of the meaningful contribution that that young faculty member has made to the project.

I believe that one reason for such scrutiny is found in the current approach to viewing and evaluating all behaviors. I liken the scrutiny of collaboration in research to the scrutiny adopted in recent years under the heading of "welfare reform." We are so afraid that some welfare recipients might not deserve their benefits—afraid that they might be cheating the system. Thus, we carefully scrutinize all applicants and, in addition to all the time and effort that this takes, we greatly reduce the number of welfare recipients. We may congratulate ourselves on catching some cheaters, but we are also likely to be refusing welfare to many who are deserving and should receive it. There will always be cheaters—in the welfare system, on income tax returns, and in research collaborations. Are the costs of such scrutiny in terms of money, effort, and human resources worth the scrutiny that we have given to young faculty who collaborate?

By scrutinizing and devaluing collaborations, we may refuse tenure to some candidates who don't deserve it, which would be fine. But we may also be denying tenure to many who do deserve it and would develop into stars in the future. Which is worse? In addition, and more important, because collaboration is so carefully scrutinized and devalued, research collaboration will certainly be discouraged. Assistant professors will be careful to minimize collaborations with their former advisors and with higher-ranking faculty in their departments. This may lead us to miss the next Kahneman and Tversky. But, of course, we can never know what possible outcomes we have missed, and we can take pride in developing a generation of independent researchers.

To those young researchers who, despite the urging to limit collaborations and to be more independent, to those who still want to seek out collaborations, I offer the following advice:

1. Interact with your colleagues. Find out what they're up to and let them know what you do.

2. Expose yourself especially to colleagues who work in areas that are different from yours. Go to colloquia and weekly brown bags in different areas in your department or even different schools. If the topics interest you, go hear about them.

3. Go to small conferences where a relatively small number of people interact together over a period of time.

4. Take advantage of sabbaticals. These are great opportunities to establish and develop productive and lasting collaborations.

5. Look for connections. One of the most important elements of successful collaboration is the ability to see links between your own ideas and research program and the ideas of other folks—even though, at first blush, there would seem to be little in the way of connection. You will be surprised at the extent to which there is common ground in very seemingly different lines of work.

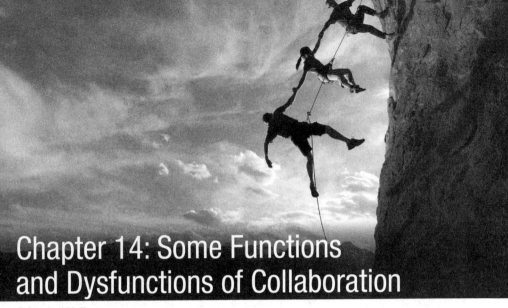

Chapter 14: Some Functions and Dysfunctions of Collaboration

Gary L. Wells

Distinguished Professor of Psychology
The Wendy and Mark Stavish Chair in Social Sciences
Iowa State University

Collaboration in research and publishing is something to which I had never given much systemic thought until I was asked to write this chapter. Gene Borgida told me that I had collaborated with a lot of people over the years, and I suppose the implication was that I would have useful observations to share. But I had not necessarily thought of myself as someone who had collaborated with large numbers of people, so one of the first things I did was sit down with a copy of my résumé and count the number of individuals with whom I had collaborated on work that resulted in publications. It turns out that I have had 74 unique coauthors over the years. That seems like a lot of people—but that might just speak to my somewhat advanced age. I do not know how it compares to other psychologists who are my age (35 years post-PhD). Among the 74 coauthors, 32 have been students (mostly my own graduate students but sometimes the graduate student of a colleague or an occasional under-graduate). The other 42 collaborators have been colleagues, the vast majority of whom have been at institutions other than where I was employed. Over-all, only 25% of my publications have been solo-authored. Among the 75% on which I collaborated, the mean number of coauthors has been 2.5. Again, I do not know how these numbers compare to other psychologists.

There are, of course, many different angles to take on research collabora-tion. There are potential issues of authorship order, the problem of slackers in the collaboration, potential for disagreement about interpretation of the results, and other somewhat problems that can arise in any multiperson enterprise. I will reflect on some of these issues here. But first, I want to explore the question of motivations. Why do we collaborate? There is considerable evidence that collaboration in psychology has been steadily increasing over the last two to three decades. And yet, as I examined my own résumé, I was surprised to find that I saw no trend over time; I was just as likely to collaborate early in my career as I have been late in my career. This was surprising because collaboration was so much more difficult prior to the advent of personal computers, free long-distance calling, Skype-like electronic meetings, and the Internet. In the early years of my career, collaboration was definitely not convenient, especially with colleagues at other universities. This leads me to the main theme of this chapter, which is that we collaborate not because it is convenient, but because it is functional.

Functions of Collaboration

The Better-Product Function

I taught a graduate course in research methods for many years and I designed it around my thesis that research success requires five abilities or skills. These are (1) the ability to generate testable and justifiable hypotheses, (2) the ability to operationalize the variables and create a design set of procedures that can test the hypotheses, (3) the ability to carry out the protocol and produce data, (4) the ability to analyze and interpret the data, and (5) the ability to effectively write the manuscript that summarizes the work. I always taught my students that they must master all five skills or abilities and that being weak on any one of these five was a recipe for failure. How can you be a successful research psychologist if you are an outstanding writer but are testing a silly hypothesis? How can you be successful if you have outstanding statistical skills but you are analyzing data with a flawed design?

My goal was to motivate students to be excellent at all five of these skills. Over time, however, people tend to excel at some of these five skills more than they do at the others. Most people know which skills are their best and which ones are a bit more of a struggle for them. Hence, one of the primary functions of collaboration is to capitalize on this dispersion of skills. A well-selected collaboration team can help ensure that there is excellence with each of the five components. By selecting a collaboration team that has complementary skills, it might be possible to produce a better final product than could have been achieved by any individual on the collaborating team. Moreover, when reviewers critique the manuscript on a particular point (which almost always happens), the team member with specific expertise on that point can take the lead in responding to (and perhaps rebutting) that criticism.

The Learning Function

Getting a better final product, however, is not the only result of the dispersion collaboration skill set. In my experience, collaborators learn from each other. The collaborator who struggles with design is able to watch and learn how the collaborator who excels at design produces his or her ideas. The collaborator who has great hypotheses but lacks vision for operationalizing manipulations and measures to test the hypotheses is able to observe the creative process of someone who has mastered that process. One of my early collaborations was writing a chapter with Elizabeth Loftus (Wells & Loftus, 1984). I considered myself to be a decent writer, but I learned a great deal from her about how to engage the reader. Being a successful research psychologist is a constant learning process, and you can pick up a great deal by collaborating with people who might be better than you on one or more of the five basic skills.

There are, of course, different kinds of collaboration. About 40% of my coauthors have been students. The mentor–student collaboration is understood as being part of the process of a graduate education. The default presumption is that the mentor (e.g., major professor) is bringing the student into the process, and that the student is not contributing unique skills or teaching the mentor something that the mentor did not already know. But in reality, this is often not the case. Sometimes the major professor has a partially developed idea and shares it with the student, and then the student develops it in ways that would not have occurred to the professor. In my case, I frequently find that advanced graduate students are more familiar than I am with the latest statistical techniques and I end up learning from them. Hence, every collaborator—even the more senior collaborator—has the potential to emerge from the project with better research skills as a result of collaboration. Of course, this reciprocal learning does not always occur in collaborations. Student collaborators, especially in their initial collaborations, are likely to be almost solely on the learning end of the relationship—and there is nothing wrong with that. I suspect that almost every senior researcher (myself included) was primarily on the learning end in their initial collaborations with a more experienced researcher.

The Efficiency Function

In my experience, most collaborations involve assigning primary responsibility for components of the project to different individuals. There are many different models, but it is often the case that the person who initiated the research idea (proposed the hypothesis and convinced the collaborators of its value) is the same one who takes primary responsibility for writing at least the initial draft of the manuscript. The operationalization of the variables, design, and procedure is often broadly shared among the collaborators, but the actual running of the study and collecting of the data is usually coordinated by one of them. In many cases, responsibility for data analysis is linked with the collaborator who is responsible for data collection. Whatever the agreement, a well-planned collaboration tends to be efficient. The person with primary responsibility for data collection is the one with the most suitable lab facilities and equipment, the best supply of research subjects, and most available lab time. Likewise, the most effective and experienced writer, or the one who best knows the relevant literature, is the one who is poised and ready to quickly generate a manuscript draft once the results are known. Of course, everyone should be involved in every phase of the project, but primary responsibilities tend to be assigned to individuals in the group.

This division of responsibility tends to be efficient for two reasons. First, primary responsibilities tend to be assigned to those who are especially skilled at the task and are well prepared to do it. For example, the highly skilled writer tends to produce good initial drafts in less time than a less skilled writer would. Likewise, the statistically sophisticated collaborator knows right away what the appropriate analysis should be and can generate the statistics quickly. A second reason why collaboration can be highly efficient is that each individual experiences a fair amount of time in which the "ball is in someone else's court." In theory, therefore, one can successfully juggle three or four collaborative projects in the same total time that might be involved on one solo project.

The Demographic Function

The research operations of an individual researcher sometimes involve questions that require collaborations with individuals in distant settings. It is not surprising, then, that the important and interesting questions that cultural social psychologists have been asking in recent years almost always involve looking at collaborators from the perspective of their culture. In some cases, this type of collaboration is the only way to secure an appropriate subject sample for the cross-cultural comparisons. Of course, these cross-cultural collaborations are also driven by the fact that the collaborators in the other cultures can have important insights about any differences that emerge between the cultures.

I have a longstanding research interest in the reliability of eyewitness identification. One factor that affects the reliability of eyewitness identification is whether the eyewitness and the target person are of the same race or different races. For example, my labs and subject pool are in Iowa, which has a very small African-American population. If I want to study cross-racial identification using an African-American population, it is more efficient if I collaborate with people at other places across the country.

Sometimes it is important to move completely outside the lab to test populations in settings that cannot be fully created in the lab. In my work on eyewitness identification, for example, the findings have important applications in the real world. Some skeptics within the legal system, however, have suggested that the college sophomore who witnesses a simulated crime is not at all representative of actual eyewitnesses to serious crimes, many of whom are also victims. Accordingly, my colleagues and I have studied actual eyewitnesses to serious crimes, including victims.

This kind of research clearly requires collaboration. In this case, however, the collaboration is not with other scientists, but rather with practitioners and professionals. In a recent project examining eyewitness identification errors in actual cases, our collaborators were police detectives, prosecutors, the Innocence Project, and the Police Foundation (Wells, Steblay, & Dysart, 2015). In this case, collaboration was not an option; it was the only way this work could be done. And, although it was highly rewarding, and our findings largely corroborated the lab findings, the study was also fraught with difficulties that do not typically arise when collaborating with other scientists.

When the Functional Malfunctions

Anything that is functional has the capability of malfunctioning as well. Collaboration is no exception. In fact, each of the functions that I described in the previous section has a malfunction counterpart. Consider, for example, the better-product function. The idea is that the collaborative team is composed of people who excel in certain skills, and those individuals then take primary responsibility for one or more of the components that have to be completed in order to produce a final product. Each partner is chosen for a reason, and that makes each partner critical to the production of the product. But that also means that each person must do his or her part and do so in a timely fashion. People being people, however, it is not always the case that partners follow through with their commitments. Some projects are simply slowed by the fact that the whole cannot move faster than its slowest part. But in other cases, projects are actually scuttled by the failure of just one person. In theory, it would seem to be simple to replace the lagging partner. In practice, replacement is not so simple. In part, this is because we tend to collaborate with people with whom we have some type of relationship. Cutting someone out of a collaborative partnership is a last resort. Hence, efforts are made to move the slacking partner along. E-mails to the effect of "Can you ask XX if he has collected those pilot data yet? It has been six months!" are exchanged.

The reasons for a nonperforming partner are as varied as they are in any other aspect of life. The reasons might include illness, divorce, or other personal tragedies. More often than not, though, it is the result of overcommitment. The partner knows that she or he is not working at top capacity, but that is because she or he is also collaborating on three other projects that also need to be completed in the same time frame. Overcommitment happens at some level at some time to all of us (although it seems to happen to some people repeatedly). Overcommitments are related to the planning fallacy—the tendency to think that it will take less time to complete a task than it actually does. As a result, many people tend to accept too many invitations to collaborate.

I would never identify by name someone who has caused this type of dysfunction in one of my collaborative projects. But as I write this, I can think of five such instances. All were somewhat painful. Four of the five resulted in a complete abandonment of the respective research projects. In two of these four projects, the delay was so significant that other researchers thoroughly beat us to the finish line by publishing their work before we could get our slacker to do his part. In the other two cases of project abandonment resulting from a slacker, the nonresponsiveness of the slackers was so prolonged (more than a year) that we all somehow lost interest in the projects. I recall one of these very well, and yet I still cannot understand why we did not simply move forward without that partner. But it seems that a bad collaborative experience that unfolded over a long period of time somehow tainted the very idea that was driving us toward the project in the first place. The fifth (and most recent) collaborative project of mine that involved a dysfunctional collaborator only slowed the project rather than killing it. I estimate that the delay was nearly 18 months. The solution in this case was replacement of the slacker. We all dreaded the moment at which we had to tell the slacker that he was off the project. We did so in a conference call. It turns out that he was relieved to have the pressure off him. That made us wonder why we did not cut him out sooner, but it also raised the question of why he did not pull himself off the project.

There are lessons in these collaboration–slacker malfunction examples. One lesson, of course, is not to be the slacker and to make sure that you in fact have the time and other resources to carry out your part. But another lesson is to carefully question your potential collaborators before you invite them in as partners. Make sure that they understand the timeline and exactly what their obligations would be. Moreover, ask them what other projects they have going and what other commitments they have that might compete with this project.

In a collaborative project, all authors need to be involved in the writing of the manuscript. In practice, there is usually a lead author who prepares the initial drafts, which is then circulated to the partners for their input, corrections, and ideas. Sometimes different partners will write different sections, with the idea of blending the sections into a coherent whole. When a manuscript is accepted for publication, the authors sign various forms that are kept by the publisher. One of these is a stipulation that the authors agree on the content of the article. But what if they do not agree?

I have only experienced this problem once, but it was relatively recent (about three years ago). My primary roles in the project were contributing to the theory and to the experimental design. I found both of those roles to be relatively easy, so I indicated that my order in the authorship should be fourth or fifth because others had a larger role. I wrote a draft of the introduction and circulated it to the team prior to any of the data being collected. I often write a draft introduction before finalizing a design and procedure because it helps clarify the conceptual problem being addressed and helps a team maintain focus on what the important questions are as the design and procedures are finalized. The entire team then worked to finalize the design, and we made sure that critical control conditions were in place to be able to answer the questions that we were asking. But I chose to be uninvolved at the level of procedural details (e.g., materials, instructions) in the experiments. That turns out to have been a mistake on my part, but it was a long time before I discovered that.

The experiments were completed in a timely manner, the data were analyzed using appropriate methods, and we were soon examining a full draft of a manuscript. It had all the appearances of a successful and smooth collaboration—but as it turned out, it was neither successful nor smooth. Two of us began asking questions about the way the "Method" section was written, with suggestions for more explicit information such as "Readers are going to want to know the verbatim instructions that were given to the research participants immediately prior to Phase 2 in all three experiments" and "We need to tell readers how we managed to keep the experimenters blind to the participants' experimental condition when the experimenters were asking critical questions of the participants face to face." It turned out that the verbatim instructions were very problematic, and a reader could not know that from the gist description in the "Method" section. Moreover, the experimenters were never blind to the experimental conditions of the participants. A debate ensued about whether these were critical flaws. Two team members took the position that we should simply let reviewers decide. One person was silent. The other two of us took the position that we needed to redo the experiments, and we threatened to withdraw our names if it were submitted. A compromise was reached to rerun the critical third experiment with the change to the instructions and in a double-blind procedure and see what happened. The new data turned out to be—for lack of a better term— garbage. As far as I can tell, none of us have spoken about this project since.

So the collaborative project mentioned in the previous paragraph was not a success. To be more blunt (and more honest), it was a failure. But somehow I think that failing as a group is less stinging to the ego than failing alone. There is something about being wrong collectively that cushions the blow in ways that failing alone cannot.

In a previous section, I mentioned the idea of collaborating with nonscientists (practitioners or other professionals). Sometimes, as with my earlier example, there is simply no choice but to engage in such collaborations. Such was the case when we decided to examine eyewitness identification with actual eyewitnesses in ongoing criminal investigations. Typically, eyewitness identification researchers have steered clear of studying actual eyewitness identification cases because, unlike lab experiments for which the identity of the culprit is known, it is not possible to definitively establish with total certainty as to whether the identification of a suspect is an accurate identification in actual cases. However, so long as a police department would agree to a rule for constructing lineups in a particular way, we knew that we could study how commonly one particular type of error occurred. Specifically, we required police departments to guarantee that when they constructed a lineup that there was only one person in the lineup who was a possible suspect, and the remaining lineup members were known-innocent fillers. Hence, if the witness identified the possible suspect, we would not know definitively if it was an accurate identification or an error. However, if the witness identified a filler, we could clearly classify it as an identification error. Laboratory experiments showed this type of error to be fairly common. How often would actual eyewitnesses make such an error?

It might seem straightforward, but the project was over four years in the making and one of the most frustrating experiences in my research career. The entities collaborating to pull off this project included psychological scientists, the Innocence Project (New York), the Police Foundation (Washington, DC), and four metropolitan police departments (the cities of San Diego, CA; Tucson, AZ; Austin, TX; and Charlotte, NC). Moreover, each police department required the cooperation of their respective district attorney's offices. Consider as well the fact that each detective in these police departments was, in effect, an experimenter who had to follow a very specific protocol. Part of that protocol required that the case detective could not be the one who administered the lineup. In other words, we required that the lineups be conducted using a double-blind procedure. We required that they use specially designed software that, among other things, randomly assigned the position of the suspect among the fillers in the lineup; that the procedure specify a priori which lineup member was the suspect; and so on. In the end, the project was very successful and informative. Among witnesses who made an identification, over one third identified a filler. On the whole, the results corroborated lab studies.

I am glad we did this project. But collaborating with nonscientists in the field is an endeavor that presents unique challenges. Indeed, some things that scientists take for granted, like the importance of protocol compliance, are simply not as clearly appreciated in the nonscientific world. Hence, we had to continually constrain the ability of the lineup administrators to deviate from protocol by actually having the procedure (instructions, presentation, recording of witness responses, etc.) controlled by a computer program. And we learned that the concept of double-blind testing can evoke controversy and resistance. Specifically, our procedure would not permit the case detective to administer his or her own lineups; lineups had to be administered by someone who was uninvolved in the case and did not know which person was the suspect and which were fillers. But many detectives were resistant to this and seemed insulted because they thought that we did not trust them.

As scientists, we learned a lot from this. We learned, for example, that nonscientists tend to believe that the purpose of double-blind testing is solely to prevent cheating or fraud. So we learned to approach this topic by first describing the experimenter expectancy effect, noting how testers can *unintentionally* influence the people they test, and that this can happen without awareness that they are having this influence. We learned to not introduce the double-blind idea to police detectives until we had fully talked about the fact that double-blind testing is required in science for reasons that have nothing to do with the idea of cheating or fraud.

My point here is that some very worthwhile collaborations are not with other scientists, but instead are with practitioners or other types of professionals. But such collaborations can have their own unique difficulties.

Conclusions

This chapter on collaboration had two parts. The first part described the good functions that collaboration serves: Collaboration can create better final products, collaborators learn from each other, and collaboration can increase efficiency and enhance productivity. The second part was an attempt to articulate some difficulties that can arise in collaboration. But this second part was a bit of a stretch for me. I could think of only one example in my collaborations where it turned out rather poorly, and one example of where the collaboration was extremely difficult and time consuming. And in the latter case (the field study), I would do it again because it was the only way it could be done. Moreover, in both of these problematic cases, I learned a great deal. Therefore, I think the ratio of enjoyable, productive collaborations to problem-ridden collaborations is perhaps 100 to 1 (or even better) in my experience.

Of course, not every collaboration that I have had on a research project has resulted in successful publication of the results. Two, three, or four heads can generate a poor hypothesis or design a weak research study, just as one head can. I have participated in many collaborative projects that proved to be wrongheaded ideas that ended up in a file drawer. But that leads me to one final observation: It seems to me that failing as a group hurts less than failing alone, whereas succeeding as a group is perhaps even sweeter than succeeding alone.

▨ REFERENCES ▨

Wells, G. L., & Loftus, E. F. (1984). Eyewitness research: Then and now. In G. L. Wells & E. F. Loftus (Eds.), *Eyewitness testimony: Psychological perspectives* (pp. 1–11). New York, NY: Cambridge University Press.

Wells, G. L., Steblay, N. K., & Dysart, J. E. (2015). Double-bind photo-lineups using actual eyewitnesses: An experimental test of a sequential versus simultaneous lineup procedure. *Law and Human Behavior, 39,* 1–14.

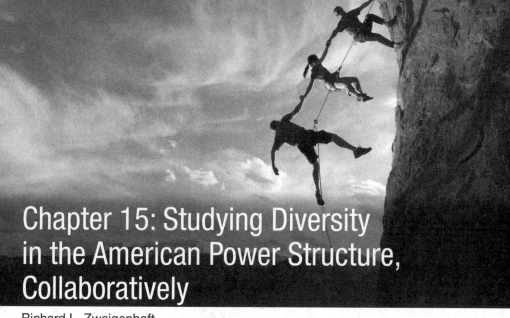

Chapter 15: Studying Diversity in the American Power Structure, Collaboratively

Richard L. Zweigenhaft

Charles A. Dana Professor of Psychology
Guilford College

In the Beginning: Ralph Nader, Bill Domhoff, and Me

In the summer of 1974, when I left Santa Cruz, California, to drive across country with my partner, Lisa (now my wife), and my dog (the late, great Throckmorton), on the way from graduate school to a teaching job in North Carolina, I had little sense that I would be an active researcher. My dissertation work at the University of California, Santa Cruz (UCSC), had been, to put it mildly, less than enjoyable, and I had chosen to teach at Guilford College, a small Quaker-affiliated undergraduate institution, in part because I assumed that I would not be under the same kinds of pressure to publish that was the case at most large universities and elite liberal arts colleges. In fact, during my job interview, the chair of the psychology department told me that at Guilford College, many excellent teachers had received tenure even though they had not published at all and, he stressed, they were both valued and respected at the college.

That sounded good to me. It also turned out to be liberating, for, even with a fairly heavy teaching load, from the time I arrived until now, I have been engaged in research projects, and I have published far more than I imagined I would—some on my own, some in collaboration with both students and colleagues.

During my first year at UCSC, I had gotten to know Bill Domhoff, a young faculty member, because we both played on psychology department intramural teams (our basketball team, Rage Reduction, was named after a primal-scream-type therapy that was popular at the time in San Jose). In the spring of 1972, Ralph Nader wrote to Bill to ask him to bring a team of graduate students to Washington, D.C., that summer to work on the Congress Project, a large-scale study that was to include detailed profiles of every member of Congress and reports on key congressional committees. Bill, married with four young children, could not do it but, aware of my political interests and that I had grown up in the D.C. area, encouraged me to participate. I spent the summer, along with 350 other undergraduates, graduate students, and law students, working on the project.

Bill was editing a special issue on "New Directions in Power Structure Research" for a journal now called *Critical Sociology*, and he asked if he could include a revised version of one of the things that I wrote while working for Nader (Zweigenhaft, 1975). So, during the summer of 1972, I worked as a Nader's Raider, I met my future wife, I wrote my first power structure article, and (not realizing it at the time) I planted the seeds for what was to become a decades-long collaborative relationship.

Prior to driving back east to work for Nader, I had arranged to write my dissertation under the guidance of my advisor, David Marlowe, though I didn't quite have a topic. David was well known for a scale that he and Douglas Crowne had developed ten years earlier to assess social desirability (the Marlowe-Crowne Social Desirability Scale; Crowne and Marlowe, 1960), but, although he had coedited a 1970 book (Gergen & Marlowe, 1970), he had not done any original research in at least 5 years. I remember a meeting of the psychology faculty that I attended as the graduate student representative at which one faculty member, angry with David for not being sufficiently involved in departmental work, or research, or both, yelled at David, "Come out of retirement, David!" (I was shocked—I didn't know faculty yelled at each other in meetings.)

In my first year at UCSC, David and I had coauthored an article (Zweigenhaft & Marlowe, 1973) that extended some research linking signature size and status that I had done in my senior year of college (Zweigenhaft, 1970), but it did not seem to me that this topic was dissertation material. Although I had become very interested in Domhoff's work on the American power structure and had agreed to be a teaching assistant in one of his classes ("The Social Psychology of the Upper Class"), I knew that it would be tricky and potentially awkward to tell Marlowe that I wanted Domhoff to supervise my dissertation. After a series of conversations with David about some of the prevailing beliefs held by many in the counterculture, I came up with a plan for an attitude study about those we called "modern transcendentalists."

A month or two later, after I had run the experiment with about half of the participants, David, his wife, Cynthia, and their infant daughter were in a terrible, freak automobile accident—a boulder rolled down one of those southern California mountains and crushed their car. Cynthia was killed. David and the baby survived, but this was obviously a devastating blow. It was clear that I was on my own. I carried out the study I had designed, analyzed the data, wrote it up, submitted it, and defended it in front of my dissertation committee. They accepted it, and I got my PhD. I set the dissertation aside and have never looked at it again. I headed off to my new teaching job in Greensboro, North Carolina, thankful that I would not be under pressure to publish.

A Secular Jewish Agnostic Arrives in the South

Before I got there, I held many stereotypes about the South, one of which was that it probably wasn't such a great place for Jews (even secular Jewish agnostics like myself who rarely set foot in a synagogue). Therefore, I was surprised to discover that the Jews of Greensboro had been, and continue to be, quite prominent and influential in the local community. I began to study the local power structure systematically in order to learn if, in fact, Jews were as much a part of the local power structure as it appeared, and, if so, how that happened. This led to a number of articles—first, one about the Jews of Greensboro (Zweigenhaft, 1978b), then one comparing the Jewish community in Greensboro with the (very different) Jewish community in nearby Winston-Salem (Zweigenhaft, 1979), and then looking at Jews throughout the South in terms of the extent to which they had become part of various local power structures (Zweigenhaft, 1978a). Bill read and critiqued each of these articles in manuscript form before I submitted them for publication. After I had published four or five articles, including some that began to look at whether Jews had become part of the national power elite (Zweigenhaft, 1980, 1982), he encouraged me to draw and expand upon this work to write a book. I told him that I doubted that I could write a book, and that even if I could, it would be a better one if he were not merely to critique what I wrote but were to be a part of it—that is, to be a coauthor.

He agreed to do so, but only with the stipulation that I would do all the work—the interviewing, the empirical studies we had in mind, any more studies that we thought of along the way, and the initial writing. His role, he made clear at the outset, would be to provide ongoing guidance and encouragement, to critique every word I wrote, and to suggest additions to the text that I had written. If, by the time we finished, he had not done enough work to warrant being a coauthor, I would be the sole author, and I would simply thank him in the preface for his help. Over the next few years, I traveled to New York, Boston, Chicago, and Cleveland to interview Jewish directors of *Fortune* 500 companies, and I had the tapes of these interviews transcribed. In the spring of 1980, I received tenure and was granted a sabbatical leave for the following spring. In January 1981, I set up a small desk in our living room in front of our wood stove and began to write on my trusty typewriter (I was a year or two away from my first home computer).

As I completed each chapter, I mailed it to Bill and began work on the next chapter. When he received my draft, 4 or 5 days later, he read it—always quickly and always thoroughly—and mailed it back to me with suggested revisions. Sometimes he proposed changes in my prose or in the analyses I put forth, sometimes he encouraged me to look at sources that I had not considered, and sometimes he wrote sentences, paragraphs, or entire sections to insert into the text. As the working manuscript went back and forth, we each carved up some passages so extensively that now it is impossible for either of us to know who wrote them. By the end of my sabbatical, we had a working draft of much of the manuscript.

That summer, my wife and I drove cross-country, stopping for me to do some additional interviews in Minneapolis, Seattle, and San Francisco (our dog, Throckmorton, then age 12, stayed in Greensboro). We settled in the guest room of some good friends in Santa Cruz, and Bill and I worked intensively on the manuscript every morning. I also traveled to Los Angeles to interview a few more corporate directors. By the time we drove back east, the working manuscript was much further along, and, by sending drafts back and forth through the mail over the next few months, we completed it. In terms of the depth of understanding of the power structure that Bill brought to the project, the intensity of his work during the concentrated period in the summer of 1981, the ongoing careful feedback that he provided, and the passages that he wrote, he had certainly earned his role as coauthor, although there was no doubt that I had done the bulk of the work. We joked then, and still joke, that because I had done about two thirds of the work, the authorship should have been Zweigenhaft, Zweigenhaft, and Domhoff.

We were working in a sociological tradition, one that grew out of C. Wright Mills's (1956) classic book, *The Power Elite*, but we also drew heavily on the work of other sociologists like E. Digby Baltzell (1958, 1964), Michael Useem (1978), and Domhoff himself (four of Bill's books are on the list of 50 top-selling books in sociology for 1950–1995, including *Who Rules America?* [1967] at #12 and *The Higher Circles* [1970] at #39; see Gans, 1997). We also brought social psychological issues and methods to bear on our analyses. I'll give one example in some detail, designed to show how we sought to combine a social psychological perspective with the sociological work that we were doing.

Among other things, we were interested in the extent to which Jewish identity might decrease as Jews became a part of the predominantly gentile corporate elite. That is, we wondered if class came to trump ethnicity for those Jews who were successful enough to be accepted into the highest levels of the corporate world. One way to assess Jewish identity was through the interviews I conducted. I asked those I interviewed various questions designed to understand the nature and the extent of their Jewish identity, including if they had married Jews or gentiles, if their children had been bat or bar mitzvahed, if they attended temples or synagogues (and, if so, how often), if they had visited Israel (and, if so, how often), and, most directly, what being Jewish meant to them.

I also used an unobtrusive measure based on a 1933 study that I had first learned about when I read Webb, Campbell, Schwartz, and Sechrest's (1966) classic book *Unobtrusive Measures: Nonreactive Research in the Social Sciences*. In that 1933 study, C. Luther Fry compiled all the names of Jews who were listed in *Who's Who in American Jewry* and the *American Jewish Yearbook* and then looked them up in *Who's Who in America*. He wanted to see if those Jews who were in *Who's Who in America* included or omitted the fact that they were Jewish in their listing information. He found that 650 Jews from the two books he looked at were also in *Who's Who in America*, but only 218 indicated that they were Jewish—in fact, a much lower percentage revealed their religion than was the case for the gentiles in *Who's Who*. Fry (1933, p. 246) concluded, "Certain individuals may hesitate to classify themselves as Jews because such an admission would be considered a liability."

We had the names of more than 3,000 members of three Jewish clubs: the Harmonie Club in New York, the Standard Club in Chicago, and the Hillcrest Country Club in Los Angeles (Bill had the lists for the Harmonie Club and the Hillcrest Country Club from previous research that he had done; I had scored a copy of the list of Standard Club members during one of my interviews in Chicago). We found that 351 of them were in *Who's Who in America*, and we looked to see not merely if they listed "Jewish" as their religion but also if they included memberships in any organizations that were obviously Jewish (such as the American Jewish Committee, or B'nai B'rith), if they listed memberships in clubs that were known to be primarily Jewish (like the Harmonie, Standard, and Hillcrest clubs), or, alternatively, if they gave no indication at all that they were Jewish. Our key finding was that those Jews who were corporate directors of *Fortune* 500 companies—those who were the focus of our book—were significantly less likely to reveal their Jewish identity than other club members (Zweigenhaft & Domhoff, 1982, pp. 94–97).

From Jews to Blacks, and Then to White Women, Latinos, Asian Americans, Gay Men, and Lesbians

Jews in the Protestant Establishment (Zweigenhaft and Domhoff, 1982) turned out to be the first of four books that we now have written together over more than 30 years (we also have written substantially revised second editions of two of these books, and we have coauthored articles together as well). Although we've come to rely on computers, not typewriters, and e-mail, not snail mail, and I've managed to persuade Bill to write the first drafts of a few chapters here and there, for the most part we have adhered to the pattern we established when we wrote *Jews in the Protestant Establishment*.

For our second book, *Blacks in the White Establishment? A Study of Race and Class in America* (Zweigenhaft & Domhoff, 1991), I again traveled to cities around the country to conduct in-depth interviews. This time, the interviews were with African American men and women who had grown up in economic poverty but, through a scholarship program called A Better Chance (ABC), had attended elite boarding schools (some attended upscale public high schools in college towns). I again had a sabbatical leave (second sabbatical, second book— these two things are not unrelated), this one spent in the friendly confines of my undergraduate alma mater, Wesleyan University in Middletown, Connecticut. I wrote the first draft of each chapter, but, when I found myself struggling with the final chapter, I persuaded Bill to write a draft of it. He did, and we revised his version, and revised it some more, sent it out to some colleagues to look at, and revised it yet more based on their feedback. Finally, we concluded that it said what we wanted to say in the way that we wanted to say it.

At this point, we added another metaphor to our ongoing conversation about our collaborative work. I'm the starting pitcher, and I put most of my academic energy into the project, while Bill continues to focus primarily on other work he is doing. Late in the game—maybe the seventh inning, but maybe not until the ninth—I bring Bill in from the bullpen, and his full attention is required. He throws smoke. We combine to get the victory; in baseball lingo, I receive the win for pitching at least five innings, and Bill gets the save.

By the time we published our third book (yes, written during my third sabbatical leave), titled *Diversity in the Power Elite: Have Women and Minorities Reached the Top?* (Zweigenhaft & Domhoff, 1998), we were aware that sociologists had shown much more interest in our work than psychologists. Perhaps this is why, in the preface, we wrote the following explanation of the interdisciplinary nature of our work (it is, perhaps, a tad defensive): "In this book, as in the previous two, we have tried to blend our appreciation of the two disciplines of sociology and psychology. We have explored both structural processes (often considered part of stratification) and more personal processes related to identify formation (often considered part of personality and social psychology). We think of our work as 'social psychological' in the broadest, and we believe, best, sense of the term" (pp. vii–viii).

Although in some ways the power elite has not changed all that much over time, in terms of the issues we have focused on—its increasing diversification since Mills (1956) introduced the concept—the changes have been real, dramatic, and sometimes rapid. It has helped us to have two sets of eyes scanning the world and trying to understand it. For example, as we were working on our most recent book, about chief executive officers (CEOs; Zweigenhaft & Domhoff, 2011/2014), both of us were reading the *New York Times* almost every day, so we were much less likely to miss the announcement of another African-American CEO of a *Fortune* 500 corporation, of another White woman becoming a CEO, or of the first Indian CEO. It was of particular interest to us that the *New York Times* article about Ajay Banga, the newly appointed CEO of MasterCard in April 2010, was accompanied by a photo in which he was wearing a turban (Martin & Dash, 2010). Why? In a book we had worked on 12 years earlier, we had stressed that it was important not to appear too different from the White males who made up the large majority of the power elite. Writing about corporate directors, we had claimed that one could be African-American, but one probably should not wear a dashiki to work, and one could be Jewish, but one probably should not wear a yarmulke to work.

Clearly, in 2010 we needed to think more carefully about what a CEO with a turban meant (and we did; see Zweigenhaft & Domhoff, 2011/2014, pp. 69–70). Correspondingly, it has enhanced our work, I believe, that we teach different courses, we read different articles and books, and we bring different sources and insights to the projects that we have done together. Moreover, with two of us reading and rereading our emerging manuscripts and galley proofs, we are more likely to spot errors and confusing or misleading passages.

Social Capital

We also have more social capital to cash in as a duo than either of us would have on his own. Many sociologists draw on the work of Pierre Bourdieu (1977) to emphasize that what once were called "connections" are important in getting ahead and maintaining the advantages that come from privileged class status. I believe that whatever one's class background, having two sets of connections (and thus what might be twice as much social capital) can improve the quality and visibility of one's academic work (it is possible that larger collaborations, in which one has three or more coauthors, might yield even more social capital). Consider the following two examples (only two of many that I could provide), the first having to do with visibility, and the second having to do with quality.

Shortly after the publication of *Jews in the Protestant Establishment* (Zweigenhaft & Domhoff, 1982), Bill recalled that one of his Duke undergraduate friends worked for the *New York Times*. He called this friend and proposed that we write an article based on some of the key findings in our book. The friend encouraged him to send him something; we did, and it was published in the Business section of the paper (Domhoff & Zweigenhaft, 1983).

The second example is from our most recent book about those we call the "new CEOs"—that is, women, African Americans, Latinos and Asian-Americans who have become the CEOs of *Fortune* 500 companies, as opposed to the "old CEOs," by which we mean White men (Zweigenhaft & Domhoff, 2011/2014). We sought to assess the class background of what then had been 74 of these "new CEOs" (as of December 2015, it was up to 121). This entailed a lot of digging to determine, among other things, their parents' level of education and occupations. I was unable to get a handle on the class background of William Perez, who at different times had been the CEO of both Nike and Wrigley, two *Fortune* 500 companies. I learned that he was born in 1947 in Colombia and that he had attended the Western Reserve Academy in Cleveland. I contacted the public relations departments at Nike and Wrigley, but neither would provide information about him or help me contact him. I recalled that one of my undergraduate buddies at Wesleyan University had gone to Western Reserve and was about the same age as Perez. I e-mailed this friend, he contacted the alumni office at Western Reserve, they gave him an e-mail address for Perez, he sent it to me, I wrote Perez, and, within an hour, I heard back from Perez. He and I exchanged a few e-mails, and I was able to learn that even though his father had little formal education, he had been so successful in his career that at one point, he ran all the Goodyear plants in Latin America. It was just what I needed in order to conclude that Perez had indeed grown up in relative economic privilege (simply the fact that he had attended Western Reserve was not enough because some students attend boarding schools on scholarship).

So, two upper-middle-class White guys, one of whom did undergraduate work at Duke and the other at Wesleyan, brought more social capital to the projects that we worked on over the years than if either of us had been working solo. Periodically, this social capital paid dividends.[1]

What Works, What Doesn't? Collaboration Can Be Tricky Business

This collaborative writing relationship would not have become a long-term one if it didn't work for each of us, both academically and interpersonally. It is probably not irrelevant that by the time we began to write together, I was no longer Bill's student, nor were we departmental colleagues, or even colleagues at the same school. We did not have to deal with the power dynamic of student and teacher, and we did not have to deal with what can be competitive elements in even the friendliest of departmental or collegial relationships. Each of us brought different strengths to these projects, and we came to trust one another enough so that either could tell the other when something he had written was confusing, contradictory, insensitive, or, for whatever reason, just didn't work.

We continue to provide frank and honest feedback to one another, not only on collaborative work, but when we are writing on our own. In the summer of 2010, I was working on an article for *Academe*, the magazine published by the American Association of University Professors (AAUP), about the deeply flawed way that my college accepted a $500,000 grant from the BB&T Foundation. This grant included a commitment in which over a 10-year period, some students were going to be required to read *Atlas Shrugged*, Ayn Rand's lengthy, polemical novel that endorses individualism, justifies selfishness, and idealizes capitalism. I knew that many administrators and some faculty at my school were not going to like what I wrote about the way the college agreed to the conditions of this grant and the faculty's unwillingness to challenge the decision, and I knew some were not going to like my decision to go public with this embarrassing but revealing institutional episode.

I asked Bill to read the draft before I sent it to the editor. He not only gave me valuable feedback about some passages he thought I should omit and suggested some things he thought I might add, but he sent me information on other grants that the BB&T Foundation had given that he drew from a data

---

[1] The book that you are reading provides yet another example of the benefits of combining social capital, although in this case, the bulk of it came from my coeditor, Gene Borgida. When I encouraged Gene to work with me on this project, I knew I had a good idea for a collection of essays on collaboration, and I suspected that he would not only have many good ideas about how we might do this (he did) but that he would know many social psychologists who we might encourage to contribute. Indeed, he did know them, and many agreed to write essays for us, partly because they, too, liked the idea but also because of their relationship with Gene. In some cases, they agreed to contribute only because it was Gene who was asking. As one put it, "Although I did not have the stamina for a handbook chapter, I will do this for you." So, if the general principle is that two collaborators bring more social capital to a project than does a solo author or editor, an accompanying guideline is choose a collaborator whose social capital will help get you where you want to go.

set he was using for a project he was working on. He therefore helped me to put what had happened at Guilford in a broader context in a way that very much improved the article (Zweigenhaft, 2010). Correspondingly, in the summer of 2012, when Bill was soon to submit a book manuscript to a publisher, he asked me to read it and give him honest, critical feedback, especially about what he might cut (he and his editor feared it was too long). I was glad to do so. The fact that we had been longtime collaborators made these editorial responses natural and valuable, even when the feedback was critical.[2]

In addition to writing with Bill, and the work I have done on my own, I have collaborated with many others over the years, including undergraduates at Guilford College (the college has no graduate programs), some departmental colleagues, colleagues at other institutions throughout the country, and, in a few cases, colleagues in other countries. Most of these have gone well, others not so well, and, especially in contrast to my ongoing work with Bill, they provide some clear warnings about what can go wrong in collaborations.

For example, some of my collaborations have been with students or colleagues who have very different working styles than I do, especially in terms of the amount of time that they take to get work done or to respond to letters, phone calls, or e-mails. Some collaborations have been with students or colleagues who don't write very well or, perhaps more problematic, have written in a style or voice that doesn't work for me (my name is going to be on *that?*). Of course, one can call for editorial changes in the text, but, depending on the extent and the nature of these changes, this can create hurt feelings in some collaborators. In contrast, Bill and I still joke about words or phrases that one of us put pressure on the other to include or take out. I still tease him about wanting to refer to Sweden as "nicey-nice," and he periodically teases me for once having used the cliché "halcyon days."

In a few cases, I have gotten myself into collaborations in which I discovered that my coauthors had political axes to grind or theoretical views they much wanted to endorse, and I realized belatedly that these were not my political axes or theories that I endorsed with the same fervor that they did. Perhaps I could have seen these things coming if I had been more vigilant. In contrast, because I know his theoretical perspectives well and I am familiar (and comfortable) with most of the axes he wants to grind, when I write with Bill, I am unlikely to be surprised.

In one case, in the 1990s, it got back to me in a roundabout way that a student who helped me gather data for a study that I had designed (one that subsequently became the first of a series of studies in an article that I wrote as the sole author) thought that he should have been a coauthor of the article

---

[2] When I sent Bill an early draft of this chapter, asking him if he wanted to read it or instead wait to read the final draft, he sent the following reply:"I will take the nonreading option. In fact, I was going to talk to you about not reading it ever to give you more freedom to write your thoughts. Who knows what reading it, discussing might bring? Never spoil a good thing."Although he is pleased that I have edited this volume, and he knows this chapter is in part about him, I think it is highly unlikely that he will ever read these words. And, of course, my memories about our collaborative relationship might be quite different than his.

rather than merely thanked, along with a few other research assistants, in a footnote. Even though I think I was justified in not including him as a coauthor, this affected our relationship, and I still feel uncomfortable about the way it played out. I regret that I was not clearer at the outset about whether he would be a coauthor if the study we were working on ultimately was published.

At a small undergraduate liberal arts school like the one at which I teach, coauthoring with one's students does not occur nearly as frequently as coauthoring with graduate students at larger schools. I supervise independent studies almost every semester, but only rarely do these turn into collaborations that are submitted for publication. Because of what apparently disappointed that student, ever since that time, when I have worked with students on projects (mine or theirs), I have tried to establish a clear understanding early on about who will be coauthors and the order of authorship in the event of publication. Given the increased emphasis on undergraduate research and publication of work by undergraduates, small liberal arts schools like Guilford would be wise to have written guidelines in effect to address these matters.

I am the only contributor to this volume who teaches at an undergraduate liberal arts college with no graduate programs.[3] Those of us at small undergraduate institutions, especially those with heavy teaching loads, face somewhat different decisions when it comes to collaboration. In some cases, researchers with projects that require the subject pool, equipment, or grant money more likely to be found at large schools need to maintain collaborative relationships with colleagues at bigger schools in order to continue to do the kind of research they have been trained to do and want to do. At times, faculty members at small liberal arts schools collaborate with other faculty on smaller-scale projects, and at times, they do research with their advanced undergraduates.

At teaching-intensive colleges, finding time for, and support for, research is an ongoing challenge, and many of my Guilford College colleagues over the years, both in psychology and other disciplines, have been frustrated by the lack of institutional support for research. Interestingly, in a recent national search that my department conducted, a number of the more prolific applicants mentioned in their cover letters that they would be interested in collaborating with me and certain of my departmental colleagues, and they identified us by name and noted the areas of overlapping research interests. As an application strategy, I thought this was clever, though if not done carefully, it could come across as sucking up too much. It not only indicated that they had taken the time to look into the research that we had done, but it signaled that, if they were to be hired, they were amenable to the possibility of collaboration.

Some of the other applicants, aware that those of us at liberal arts schools collaborate with our advanced students, wisely stated in their cover letters that they are interested in collaborating with undergraduates. Here is an example from one of those who applied: "My research program has the

---

[3] Sheldon Solomon, a coauthor of Chapter 5, teaches at Skidmore College—but Skidmore does have a graduate program, a master of arts in liberal studies program.

virtues of being flexible, inexpensive, portable, and above all, engaging to undergraduate collaborators."

The volume that you are reading runs the risk of overemphasizing the benefits and pleasures of collaboration. The challenges of working with others may lead to unpleasantness and the loss of friendships, and these are probably much harder to write about than collaborations that have gone well. As one colleague wrote in an e-mail to me, "What you learn from a collaboration is fascinating, and never to be anticipated—but I sure wouldn't want to write about it for a book." As I think more about my (long-term but not monogamous) collaboration with Bill Domhoff, which has worked, and has in fact deepened what was already a good friendship, and as I think about certain of the other (shorter term, "one-night-stand") collaborations that have not worked so well, I am increasingly aware that collaboration can be tricky business.

Conclusions

What are the lessons I might offer based on my idiosyncratic collaborative journey? First, I would emphasize that those who choose to teach at smaller liberal arts schools can still stay engaged in research, and that collaborating may enhance the range of possible topics, as well as the quality of the finished work. As I have indicated, I have worked extensively in a long-term, cross-country collaborative relationship with Bill Domhoff. Some of my colleagues, especially those in the sciences, who need big grants and costly equipment to do their research, collaborate with colleagues at nearby universities like Wake Forest or Duke.

Second, and related to the first, if you are considering positions at smaller schools, pay close attention to the school's sabbatical policies. As I have noted, my school has a generous policy that has allowed me to take on larger projects every seven years or so.

Third, I encourage those considering collaboration to think carefully about whom to collaborate with, and to try, if possible, to look for skill complementarity and style similarity. By that, I mean that collaborators can, and should, bring different skills to the project, but they are likely to work effectively together if they share some behaviors, like responding to one another and meeting deadlines. As I have suggested, and as others in this volume make quite clear, collaborations that don't work can be quite frustrating, and projects can go down the tubes as a result of bad collaborative mixes.

Fourth, and finally, keep in mind that collaboration allows for the combining of resources, and this not only includes sets of skills (e.g., a person who writes well with a person who does sophisticated statistical analyses) but also social capital. Two people have more contacts they can draw on than one person, and if one takes this observation further to include consideration of Stanley Milgram's small-world research, the connections of two people are likely to lead to many more connections to others who are just one step away than the connections of one person. Others in this volume have made this same general point, though not focused on social capital—in Chapter 8, Markus and Kitayama assert, "One and one equals much more than two," and in Chapter 1, Hatfield and Berscheid write that "in a good collaboration 1 + 1 can equal 4 or more."

▦ REFERENCES ▦

Baltzell, E. D. (1958). *Philadelphia gentlemen: The making of a national upper class.* Glencoe, IL: Free Press.

Baltzell, E. D. (1964). *The Protestant establishment: Aristocracy and caste in America.* New York, NY: Vintage Books.

Bourdieu, P. (1977). Cultural reproduction and social reproduction. In J. Karabel & J. Halsey (Eds.), *Power and ideology in education* (pp. 487–511). New York, NY: Oxford University Press.

Crowne, D. P., & Marlowe, D. (1960). A new scale of social desirability independent of psychopathology. *Journal of Consulting Psychology, 24*(4), 349–354.

Domhoff, G. W. (1967). *Who Rules America?* Englewood Cliffs, NJ: Prentice Hall.

Domhoff, G. W. (1970). *The Higher Circles: The Governing Class in America.* New York, NY: Random House.

Domhoff, G. W., & Zweigenhaft, R. L. (1983, April 24). Jews in the corporate establishment. *The New York Times.* Retrieved from http://www.nytimes.com/1983/04/24/business/jews-in-the-corporate-establishment-board-rooms-clubs-and-identity.html?pagewanted=all

Fry, C. L. (1933). The religious affiliations of American leaders. *Scientific Monthly, 36,* 241–249.

Gans, H. J. (1997). Best-sellers by sociologists: An exploratory study. *Contemporary Sociology, 26,* 131–135.

Gergen, K. J., & Marlowe, D. (Eds.). (1970). *Personality and Social Behavior.* Reading, MA: Addison Wesley.

Martin, A., & Dash, E. (2010, April 24). Naming a new chief, MasterCard signals it is open to changes. *The New York Times,* p. B4.

Mills, C. W. (1956). *The power elite.* New York, NY: Oxford University Press.

Useem, M. (1978). The inner group of the American capitalist class. *Social Problems, 25,* 225–240.

Webb, E. J., Campbell, D. T., Schwartz, R. D., & Sechrest, L. (1966). *Unobtrusive measures: Nonreactive research in the social sciences.* Chicago, IL: Rand McNally. Subsequently published in 1981 as Webb, E. J., Campbell, D. T., Schwartz, R. D., Sechrest, L. & Grove, J. B. *Nonreactive measures in the social sciences.* Dallas: Houghton Mifflin.

Zweigenhaft, R. L. (1970). Signature size: A key to status awareness. *Journal of Social Psychology, 81,* 49–54.

Zweigenhaft, R. L. (1975). Who represents America? *The Insurgent Sociologist, 5*(3), 119–130.

Zweigenhaft, R. L. (1978a). Jews in the American South. *New Society, 46*(839), 263–265.

Zweigenhaft, R. L. (1978b). The Jews of Greensboro: In or out of the upper class? *Contemporary Jewry, 4*(2), 60–76.

Zweigenhaft, R. L. (1979). Two cities in Carolina: A comparative study of Jews in the upper class. *Jewish Social Studies, 41*, 291–300.

Zweigenhaft, R. L. (1980). American Jews: In or out of the upper class? In G. W. Domhoff (Ed.), *Power structure research* (pp. 47–52). Beverly Hills, CA: Sage Publications.

Zweigenhaft, R. L. (1982). Recent patterns of Jewish representation in the corporate and social elites, *Contemporary Jewry, 6*(1), 36–46.

Zweigenhaft, R. L. (2010). Is this curriculum for sale? *Academe, 96*(4), 38–39. Retrieved from http://www.aaup.org/AAUP/pubsres/academe/2010/JA/feat/zwei.htm

Zweigenhaft, R. L., & Domhoff, G. W. (1982). *Jews in the Protestant establishment.* New York, NY: Praeger.

Zweigenhaft, R. L., & Domhoff, G. W. (1991). *Blacks in the White establishment? A study of race and class in America.* New Haven, CT: Yale University Press.

Zweigenhaft, R. L., & Domhoff, G. W. (1998). *Diversity in the power elite: Have women and minorities reached the top?* New Haven, CT: Yale University Press.

Zweigenhaft, R. L., & Domhoff, G. W. (2011/2014). *The new CEOs: Women, African American, Latino, and Asian American leaders of Fortune 500 companies.* Lanham, MD: Rowman & Littlefield.

Zweigenhaft, R. L., & Marlowe, D. (1973). Signature size: Studies in expressive movement. *Journal of Consulting and Clinical Psychology, 40*(3), 469–473.

PART IV

Collaboration with Institutional and Community Partners

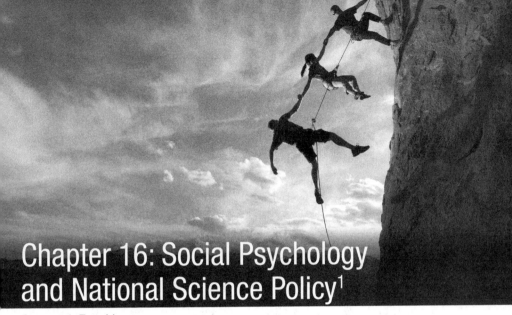

Chapter 16: Social Psychology and National Science Policy[1]

Steven J. Breckler

Former Executive Director for Science
American Psychological Association

I spent nearly 9 years as a Program Director at the National Science Foundation (NSF), and more than a decade after that as Executive Director for Science at the American Psychological Association (APA). During that time, I had a front-row seat, if not a (very small) part in shaping and influencing national science policy.

As a social psychologist, I was not surprised to learn that the development and application of science policy in the United States is an exquisitely social process. From the funding priorities of federal research agencies to the implementation and utilization of research to address societal challenges, it takes collaboration and compromise to succeed.

In this chapter, I review the common meanings of science policy—from the appropriation of research dollars to the enactment of laws, regulations, and government priorities. I also offer a brief tour of the agencies, organizations, and people who play a role in establishing and promoting science policy in the United States. Stakeholders pursue their goals with great passion, but rarely do they succeed in the absence of collaboration.

Next, I turn to social psychology and its role in national science policy. Our discipline is relevant to nearly every societal challenge and therefore is of great potential value in national policy-setting arenas. Yet, all too often, social psychology and social psychologists do not have a seat at the relevant tables. I consider why this might be so, and what social psychology might do to make itself a more regular participant in policy setting.

---

[1] The views expressed in this chapter are those of the author and do not represent the views of the National Science Foundation nor of the American Psychological Association.

The theme of this volume is collaboration in psychological science. The success of such collaboration clearly depends on how science policy evolves and where its priorities are placed. Yet, to anticipate the ultimate conclusion of this discussion, a switching of figure and ground is necessary. Rather than focusing on collaboration in social psychology, I will suggest an equally important and productive focus: social psychology in collaboration.

What Is National Science Policy?

The concept of *policy* generally refers to a set of principles or plans of action to achieve desired outcomes. We typically use the term in reference to governments or institutions, such as *energy policy* or *education policy*. Thus, *national science policy* refers to the principles and plans to promote, support, and utilize science (and research) on behalf of the nation and its citizens (Neal, Smith, & McCormick, 2008).

The government's goal in establishing and promulgating national science policy is to improve and advance the nation's interests in defense, industry, and human welfare. As a result, such policy can be quite far-reaching and diverse in the activities that it promotes. It can include, for example, efforts to improve and expand science education, financial and infrastructure support for basic and applied research, and translating the results of science to inform pressing societal needs and challenges.

Most contemporary national science policy of the United States can be traced to Vannevar Bush's 1945 report *Science: The Endless Frontier*. In the wake of World War II, an opportunity existed to celebrate and expand the nation's scientific enterprise. Bush, who had been director of the wartime Office of Scientific Research and Development, pointed out that although the support of science is clearly in the government's interest, no infrastructure existed within the federal government to establish, develop, and promote science policy.

Bush emphasized the need to support basic research conducted principally in the nation's university laboratories. He also placed a very high priority on supporting and nurturing the pipeline of scientific talent. *Science: The Endless Frontier* concluded with the proposal to establish a National Research Foundation, a variation of which became the NSF.

Now, 70 years later, U.S. science policy is supported and advanced by a vast and complex array of executive and legislative branch committees, agencies, advisory boards, and other stakeholders, including colleges and universities, scientific professional associations, and industry.

Perhaps the earliest and clearest example of focused national science policy developed during the Sputnik era. Throughout the early 1950s, both the United States and the Soviet Union were in a race to launch an orbiting scientific satellite. Significant federal resources were devoted to this effort, but everything changed in 1957, when the Soviets succeeded in launching Sputnik 1. Suddenly, it became an urgent national priority for the United States to catch up with, and even surpass, that accomplishment, and that became the foundation for national science policy. The resources and funding of intelligence and defense agencies was expanded, and ultimately led to the creation of the National Aeronautics and Space Administration (NASA). The National Defense Education Act (NDEA) provided an infusion of training dollars to fund graduate fellowships needed to feed the pipeline of scientists and engineers.

Within the last decade, two reports from the National Academy of Sciences (NAS) have had a strong influence on national science policy. A report called *Rising Above the Gathering Storm: Energizing and Employing America for a Brighter Economic Future* (Committee on Prospering in the Global Economy of the 21st Century and the Committee on Science, Engineering and Public Policy, 2007), and its sequel, *Rising Above the Gathering Storm, Revisited: Rapidly Approaching Category 5* (Members of the 2005 "Rising Above the Gathering Storm" Committee, 2010), provide the blueprints for U.S. science policy in the early part of the 21st century. Starting with the premise that the scientific infrastructure of the United States is eroding at a time when other nations are investing heavily, these reports call for an increase of funding for basic research, significant improvement in K–12 science education, increased incentives for students (both from the United States and internationally) to pursue graduate education in science and engineering, and encouraging innovation by modernizing U.S. tax laws and patent policies.

The *Rising Above the Gathering Storm* reports clearly provided the framing rationale for the America Competes Act of 2007, and its reauthorization in 2010. These laws provide myriad directives and authorizations to dozens of federal agencies to increase U.S. investments in science and technology innovation, and in science, technology, engineering, and mathematics (STEM) education. Together, these two pieces of legislation come the closest to articulating the current national science policy of the United States.

Social psychologists may be familiar with the 2007 America Competes legislation because during its debate, some members of Congress sought language that would remove the social and behavioral sciences from the portfolio of the NSF. Thanks to other members of Congress, however, the final bill actually emphasized the social sciences as a priority. Section 7018 of the NSF authorizing language stated:

> The Director shall give priority in the selection of awards and the allocation of Foundation resources to proposed research activities, and grants funded under the Foundation's Research and Related Activities Account, that can be expected to make contributions in physical or natural science, technology, engineering, *social sciences* [emphasis added], or mathematics, or that enhance competitiveness, innovation, or safety and security in the United States.

The presence of this kind of language in legislation is a prime example of how national science policy gets framed and then articulated as directives for federal funding priorities. It is equally important to understand that the fight over the inclusion of social and behavioral sciences in the priorities of U.S. national science policy has reemerged in almost every congressional debate since 2007. In the current era, we can never assume that the social and behavioral sciences (including social psychology) are considered a priority in national science policy.

Who Determines National Science Policy?

A U.S. president's administration (including all of the executive branch agencies that report to the president) plays a crucial role in establishing and promoting national science policy. An instructive example is policy surrounding federal support for stem-cell research.

Early in his first term, George W. Bush established a policy to limit the number of embryonic stem cell lines that could be used for research. Large segments of the scientific community voiced objections. The policy had major implications for the funding of important lines of research at the National Institutes of Health (NIH). Over several years, Congress passed bills to loosen the restrictions, but the president vetoed most of them. Clearly, national science policy relating to this particular issue reflected the moral and ethical prerogatives of the president, and it stayed that way for 8 years.

Early in his first term, Barack Obama signed an executive order lifting most of the restrictions that had been implemented by George W. Bush. The president's comments during the signing ceremony (White House, 2009) offer a good example of how the executive branch establishes and articulates national science policy:

> Today, with the Executive Order I am about to sign, we will bring the change that so many scientists and researchers, doctors and innovators, patients and loved ones have hoped for, and fought for, these past eight years: we will lift the ban on federal funding for promising embryonic stem cell research. We will vigorously support scientists who pursue this research. And we will aim for America to lead the world in the discoveries it one day may yield.

President Obama used the executive order relating to expansion of embryonic stem cell research to articulate some bigger issues relating to national science policy as well. In the order, he stated that promoting science "... is about ensuring that scientific data is never distorted or concealed to serve a political agenda—and that we make scientific decisions based on facts, not ideology." The president then directed the Office of Science and Technology Policy (OSTP) to "develop a strategy for restoring scientific integrity to government decision making." Here, in this one episode, we see the many social and political facets of national science policy.

On a more detailed level, the infrastructure of the executive branch includes many agencies, offices, and committees supporting the development of national science policy. The president's science advisor heads the OSTP, the mission of which is to (1) provide the president with scientific and technical advice, (2) ensure that policies are informed by good science, and (3) coordinate matters of science and technology across all executive branch agencies (About OSTP, 2015).

The National Science and Technology Council (NSTC) facilitates the work of OSTP. This group includes the secretaries of every department and the directors of every science agency in the executive branch. The NSTC is composed of five primary committees, one of which is the Committee on Science (COS). The COS is cochaired by a senior staff representative of the OSTP, the director of the NIH, and the director of the NSF. The COS, in turn, is composed of four subcommittees, one of which is Social, Behavioral, and Economic Science.

The policy agenda of the NSF is established by the National Science Board (NSB), one purpose of which is to "recommend and encourage the pursuit of national policies for the promotion of research and education in science and engineering" (About the NSB, 2015). The NSB is composed of 25 presidential appointees whose backgrounds and experience span the range of sciences supported by the NSF. It is not unusual for at least one member of the NSB to have a background in psychology.

The legislative branch represents the other significant government force behind national science policy in the United States. In the U.S. House of Representatives, the Committee on Science, Space, and Technology provides jurisdiction over substantive matters concerning science and engineering. Its counterpart in the U.S. Senate is the Committee on Commerce, Science, and Transportation. In both bodies, these committees typically provide oversight for matters pertaining to national science policy.

Of course, much of science policy is promulgated through funding. Thus, the House and Senate Committees on Appropriations play crucial roles in national science policy. Earlier in this chapter, I mentioned the debate surrounding the 2007 America Competes legislation, which included efforts to weaken, if not remove, the social and behavioral sciences from the NSF funding portfolio. Much of this effort came from ranking members of the Senate Appropriations Subcommittee on Commerce, Justice, Science, and Related Agencies.

Ultimately, that effort failed, and the final 2007 America Competes bill actually singled out the social sciences as being among the priorities of the NSF funding portfolio. This dramatic reversal of fate can be attributed to ranking members of the House Committee on Science and Technology. In particular, Congressman Brian Baird (D-WA) led the House's effort to remove the Senate's limiting language. Baird is a psychologist by training, and he was recognized in 2007 by the APA for his efforts in this regard. Very often, matters of national science policy come down to the actions and efforts of individuals.

Another important participant in national science policy is the NAS. I mentioned earlier the importance of the *Gathering Storm* reports in framing today's science policy agenda. Those reports were developed under the auspices of the NAS Committee on Science, Engineering, and Public Policy (COSEPUP).

The NAS Board on Behavioral, Cognitive, and Sensory Sciences provides the oversight for many of the academy's efforts relating to psychology. Just in the past few years, this board has played a role in reports on proposed revisions to the Common Rule (institutional review boards), social and behavioral factors bearing on military environments, applying principles of learning science to education, and emerging technologies in cognitive neuroscience.

One landmark project of this board was *How People Learn* (Bransford, Brown, & Cocking, 2000), which explored how basic research in social and behavioral science (especially psychology) can be applied to learning and educational settings. This report became very influential and provided much of the rationale for the NSF's development of its Science of Learning Centers program (described in more detail later in this chapter).

Abraham Lincoln established the NAS as a society of distinguished scholars in 1863. Woodrow Wilson significantly expanded its scope in 1916, to allow the academy to better provide scientific advice to the government (its principal mission). The NAS remains independent of the federal government, and its proceedings tend to be insulated from political influence. This often gives NAS reports and advice considerable prestige and authority.

Many psychologists have been inducted into the NAS, including social psychologists Leon Festinger, Stanley Schachter, Carl Hovland, Harold Kelley, Gardner Lindzey, Richard Nisbett, Lee Ross, Susan Fiske, Claude Steele, and Shelley Taylor. Academy members can be very influential in guiding and participating in NAS boards, committees, studies, and reports. Thus, they can be seen as important participants in the national science policy landscape.

Many other stakeholders and individuals play influential roles in the development, framing, and pursuit of national science policy goals. Among these, professional scientific societies and associations are especially important. For psychology, these include the APA and the Association for Psychological Science (APS). It also includes a number of specialized societies, such as the Society for Research in Child Development (SRCD), the Society for Industrial and Organizational Psychology (SIOP), and the Society for Personality and Social Psychology (SPSP), all of which maintain an advisory presence, if not an actual office, in Washington, D.C. Most of them also coordinate among themselves in the form of advocacy consortia, most notably the Consortium of Social Science Associations (COSSA) and the Federation of Associations in Behavioral and Brain Sciences (FABBS).

The psychology professional associations were a driving force behind the creation of the NSF's Directorate for Social, Behavioral, and Economic Sciences and the establishment of the Office of Behavioral and Social Sciences Research (OBSSR) at the NIH. Thus, they have played a very significant part in promoting research funding in support of psychological science.

The professional associations occupy a fascinating niche in the national science policy enterprise. When it comes to budgets, for example, the federal funding agencies all tend to fall within the executive branch. Their priorities are established or limited by the president's administration. This may or may not produce funding goals desired by disciplinary stakeholders.

The professional associations are not similarly constrained. At the APA, I provided the higher-level oversight for a staff of lobbyists and advocates who often communicated psychology's priorities vis-à-vis appropriation bills, even if those priorities were not the main focus of the president's budget or of funding agency leadership. Thus, every year, the professional associations (including the APA) submit formal written comments and deliver oral testimony on pending appropriation and authorization bills that bear on research funding.

As social psychologists are well aware, a common tactic for some members of Congress is to ridicule the funding of grants in social and behavioral science. These attacks are rarely about the specific projects, but they provide a sensational way for legislators to gain media attention and political leverage in their pursuit of other goals. The professional associations—especially the big ones like the APA—often become the lead defenders in such attacks.

A great illustration of how these events play out relates to congressional debate over the 2007 NSF reauthorization bill. Two members of Congress filed amendments to the bill that would take away the funding of nine specific NSF grants. Among these grants was one led by a social psychologist for research on cross-cultural expressions and understanding of emotion. The APA activated its grassroots advocacy machine to urge psychologists to contact their own members of Congress and encourage opposition to the amendments. This is the kind of advocacy for which professional associations are especially well suited. It is both ironic and frustrating that such attacks continue, especially in light of the relevance and importance of social psychological research in addressing critical national and societal challenges.

Where Is Social Psychology?

I think it is fair to assume that many of us pursued our passion for social psychology because of the discipline's relevance to society's greatest challenges. Our subject matter includes violence and aggression, love and close relationships, stereotypes and racism, attitudes and persuasion, group and organizational functioning, prosocial behavior and helping, and cross-cultural understanding of emotional expression.

The October 2014 inaugural issue of the journal *Policy Insights from the Behavioral and Brain Sciences* was devoted to social psychological contributions to national policy concerns. The articles covered education, work and organizations, justice, interrogation, inequality, negotiation, environment, health and well-being, and public reaction to policy. The authors were some of the best and brightest early- to mid-career social psychologists. The collection of articles leaves no doubt that social psychology is quite relevant to society's greatest challenges and should therefore feature prominently in the goals and priorities of national science policy.

It is not difficult to identify major social psychological contributions to matters of societal concern and public policy (Shafir, 2013). As just one specific example, social psychologists have produced groundbreaking research on eyewitness identification. This work has inspired many programs of research, influenced the research funding priorities of federal agencies, provided much of the focus of a report from the NAS (Committee on Scientific Approaches to Understanding and Maximizing the Validity and Reliability of Eyewitness Identification in Law Enforcement and the Courts, 2014), and informed the U.S. Department of Justice in developing its guidance to law enforcement across the country (Technical Working Group for Eyewitness Evidence, 1999).

More generally, social psychology offers a rich array of contributions to improving public health (Klein, Shepperd, Suls, Rothman, & Croyle, 2015). This has been clearly recognized in the funding priorities of the NIH. Not only do many of the NIH disease-related institutes incorporate significant behavioral science in their funding portfolios, the cross-cutting importance of social and behavioral research is also coordinated at a very high level by the OBSSR. Thus, it is fair to say that social and behavioral science (including social psychology) is a prominent part of national science policy relating to health research.

One of the earliest actions of U.K. Prime Minister David Cameron was the creation within the Cabinet Office of a Behavioural Insights Team. Composed mainly of psychologists and economists, it was a variation of the U.S. Council of Economic Advisors. It came to be known as the "Nudge Unit," in recognition of Thaler and Sunstein's (2008) best-selling book *Nudge*, on which many of the operating principles of the team are based. Social psychologists will recognize many of the successful implementations of research on social influence, decision making, and motivation applied to efforts to encourage participation in retirement savings, increase organ donor registrants, and improve compliance with tax laws.

The success of the U.K. Behavioural Insights Team drew so much attention that it evolved into a "social purpose" company, representing a unique and powerful public–private enterprise. Its work touches numerous areas of government policy in the United Kingdom and beyond. With social psychology being so central to the team's work, this effort provides a stunning example of how our field has come to figure prominently in the national public and science priorities of a nation.

Barack Obama drew from similar expertise to support his 2012 presidential campaign (Carey, 2012). And very early in 2014, the Obama administration announced the formation of its own Social and Behavioral Sciences Team (SBST) to help advise the U.S. government in much the same way as the U.K. Behavioural Insights team (Shankar, 2015). The hope is that utilization of such scientific expertise will continue to figure prominently in future administrations, including the insights offered by social psychology.

Social Psychology and Collaboration

With this policy landscape as background, I now turn to the topic of this volume—collaboration in social psychology. The chapters collected here provide a wealth of examples and inspiration for collaborations within our subdiscipline. Many of the greatest advances in social psychology are the result of collaborations among social psychologists.

When I started off as a program director at the NSF, my focus and responsibility was social psychology. This work clearly required collaboration, especially with the social psychologist panel reviewers, who helped prioritize the funding of grant proposals. Yet I soon learned that the best opportunity to advance social psychology required collaboration with those who represented other fields of science, including biology, computer science, engineering, and education. The NSF has always been the home of support for basic, discipline-based research. But the real growth in funding—and hence the new funding opportunities—is at the intersection of traditional disciplines. To do my job on behalf of social psychology required effective collaborations with many others outside of social psychology.

The latter half of my tenure at the NSF was focused on the development of the Science of Learning Centers program. The idea was inspired by the NAS *How People Learn* report I mentioned earlier. The premise was that significant advances in our understanding of learning could be made by supporting multidisciplinary teams of investigators—by bringing together psychologists, computer scientists, biologists, engineers, and education researchers who share common interests in learning and who each bring unique skills and insights to bear. Social psychology plays a role, and the Centers program was open to (and indeed, even encouraged) collaborations that included social psychologists.

A major thrust of science policy over the past two decades has been on the science of learning. The Science of Learning Centers program at the NSF was one instantiation of that policy. It was open to multidisciplinary teams of investigators from all relevant fields, including social psychology. Although some of the proposed and funded projects included social psychological components, in the end social psychology was not heavily represented. In part, this is because social psychology may play a relatively smaller role in the larger mosaic of relevant disciplines. But it may also reveal a failure of social psychologists to pursue the kinds of collaborations supported by such funding opportunities.

An interesting parallel is found in health-related research, which is central to national science policy. Indeed, when it comes to federal funding of research, one of the largest allocations of dollars is to the NIH. Psychology, including social psychology, has been the beneficiary of considerable funding from the NIH over a period of many decades. Yet, Klein et al (2015) show that a surprisingly small percentage of mainstream social psychology research (based on articles in the *Journal of Personality and Social Psychology* [*JPSP*] and the *Personality and Social Psychology Bulletin* [*PSPB*]) is concerned with health-related topics. In part, this may be because social psychology plays a relatively smaller role in the larger mosaic of health-related disciplines. But it may also reveal a failure of social psychologists to pursue the kinds of collaborations supported by the funding opportunities available at the NIH—collaborations that link social psychology with other relevant disciplines.

The strength of disciplinary-based science is that the priorities, topics, and research directions are determined within the field. As social psychologists, we can (and do) pursue avenues of research that hold the greatest promise and invite the greatest attention among ourselves. Thus, what may resonate most within the discipline (as reflected in *JPSP* or *PSPB* articles) may or may not connect to the funding priorities of federal agencies, or even the thrust of national science policy.

This is important to understand. If social psychologists are concerned about shrinking research dollars for the discipline, or about exclusion from important policy-related venues, they need to ask whether their work is relevant to national priorities. There is no requirement that work carries such relevance, nor is there any reason to expect support and inclusion when it does not.

One of my main responsibilities at the APA was to advocate on behalf of the discipline of psychology. This required interaction with many of the participants in national science policy, including members of Congress and their staff, federal agency staff, and the NAS infrastructure. What became quite evident was that our discipline *qua* discipline was far less relevant to these stakeholders than what our discipline offered toward the solution of societal and governmental priorities.

What are those priorities? Clearly, they include the economy, health, crime, environment, and education. And equally clearly, social psychology has something to contribute toward every one of these priorities. The catch is that none of these priorities is exclusively about social psychology, nor is social psychology exclusively about any of them. As a discipline, social psychology is one of many disciplinary stakeholders.

To participate in research relevant to these national societal and science priorities, social psychologists need to accept roles that make them a collaborative partner with researchers from other disciplines. And more often than not, those roles will not be controlling ones. The goal is to solve societal and scientific challenges, not to promote a single discipline. That often makes social psychology a minority partner.

Collaboration in social psychology allows new social psychological discoveries and advances that would not otherwise occur. Social psychology in collaboration allows new scientific discoveries that would not otherwise occur. When we celebrate the power and utility of collaboration, it is important to ask, "With whom does one colloborate?" When the collaborators are other social psychologists, the beneficiary tends to be the discipline itself. When they are other scientists, the beneficiary extends beyond the discipline to include all of science and society.

▪ REFERENCES ▪

About OSTP. (2015, February 17). Retrieved from http://www.whitehouse.gov/administration/eop/ostp/about.

About the NSB. (2015, February 17). Retrieved from http://www.nsf.gov/nsb/about/index.jsp.

Bransford, J. D., Brown, A. L., & Cocking, R. R. (Eds.) (2000). *How people learn: Brain, mind, experience, and school.* Washington, DC: National Academy Press.

Bush, V. (1945). *Science: The endless frontier.* Washington, DC: U.S. Government Printing Office.

Carey, B. (2012, November 12). Academic "dream team" helped Obama's effort. *The New York Times.*

Committee on Prospering in the Global Economy of the 21st Century and the Committee on Science, Engineering and Public Policy. (2007). *Rising above the gathering storm: Energizing and employing America for a brighter economic future.* Washington, DC: National Academies Press.

Committee on Scientific Approaches to Understanding and Maximizing the Validity and Reliability of Eyewitness Identification in Law Enforcement and the Courts. (2014). *Identifying the culprit: Assessing eyewitness identification.* Washington, DC: National Academies Press.

Fealing, K. H., Lane, J. I., Marburger III, J. H., & Shipp, S. S. (Eds.). (2011). *The science of science policy: A handbook.* Stanford, CA: Stanford University Press.

Klein, W. M. P., Shepperd, J. A., Suls, J., Rothman, A. J., & Croyle, R. T. (2015). Realizing the promise of social psychology in improving public health. *Personality and Social Psychology Review, 19*(1), 77–92.

Members of the 2005 "Rising Above the Gathering Storm" Committee. (2010). *Rising above the gathering storm, revisited: Rapidly approaching category 5.* Washington, DC: National Academies Press.

Neal, H. A., Smith, T. L., & McCormick, J. B. (2008). *Beyond Sputnik: U.S. science policy in the 21st century.* Ann Arbor University of Michigan Press.

Shafir, E. (Ed.). (2013). *The behavioral foundations of public policy.* Princeton, NJ: Princeton University Press.

Shankar, M. (2015, February 9). *Using behavioral science insights to make government more effective, simpler, and more people-friendly.* Retrieved from https://www.whitehouse. gov/blog/2015/02/09/using-behavioral-science-insights-make-government-more-effective-simpler-and-more-us

Technical Working Group for Eyewitness Evidence (1999). *Eyewitness evidence: A guide for law enforcement.* Washington, DC: U.S. Department of Justice.

Thaler, R. H., & Sunstein, C. R. (2008). *Nudge: Improving decisions about health, wealth, and happiness.* New York, NY: Penguin Books.

White House, Office of the Press Secretary. (2009). *Remarks of President Barack Obama—as prepared for delivery, signing of stem cell executive order and scientific integrity memorandum* [Press release]. Retrieved from http://www.whitehouse.gov/the_press_office/Remarks-of-the-President-As-Prepared-for-Delivery-Signing-of-Stem-Cell-Executive-Order-and-Scientific-Integrity-Presidential-Memorandum/

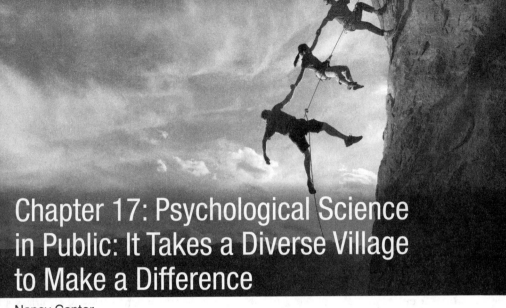

Chapter 17: Psychological Science in Public: It Takes a Diverse Village to Make a Difference

Nancy Cantor

Chancellor
Rutgers University—Newark

Peter Englot

Senior Vice Chancellor for Public Affairs and Chief of Staff to Chancellor
Rutgers University—Newark

Setting the Context for a Discussion of University-Community Collaboration

We face an ever-intensifying perfect storm of challenges in cities and towns across our country: failing schools, massive health disparities, and stalled economies collide with demographic growth in precisely those groups most often left behind and a social polity torn apart by zero-sum thinking and intergroup conflict. Psychological science, and social psychology in particular, has much to offer here—applying the lessons that we have learned about the ways in which diverse groups do better problem solving—to build the kinds of "communities of experts," including scientists and citizens, public and private, through partnerships that harken back to the best traditions of action research while moving us all forward through the storm. To be successful, however, we too must transform our practices and norms—everything from who is on our research teams to what constitutes scholarship and how we reward it—if we are to truly serve the public good.

In this chapter, we will consider some of the obstacles, rewards, and potential of publicly engaged scholarship in the context of lessons learned from nearly a decade of collaboration on the ground, engaging campus with community in one Rust Belt city: Syracuse, New York. For the most part, these collaborative efforts focused on challenges beyond the direct sphere of psychological science alone, drawing in architects, information technologists, journalists, public health practitioners, entrepreneurs, environmental scientists, education specialists, artists, and more. Yet the strategy of collaboration was distinctly influenced by the traditions of action research, an approach that gained currency in the latter half of the 20th century in many academic disciplines, especially in the social sciences and professional fields that embrace social science methodologies, such as social work and education.

A plurality of traditions have emerged, but broadly construed, they share a commitment to an expansive notion of expertise that can and should be brought to bear on research, engaging academic scholars as well as professionals and everyday citizens who might otherwise be considered mere subjects of traditional research. The inherent advantages of such an approach include the now well documented benefits of bringing diverse perspectives to bear on problem solving (e.g., Page, 2007), but more fundamentally, a democratization of the research process that is both more respectful of the agency of nonacademics and more likely to yield the kind of buy-in from stakeholders needed to significantly increase the impact of research results in practice in the world. Psychologist Kurt Lewin is often cited among the pioneering and most successful practitioners of this approach, credited with attracting a wide range of social scientists to employ it by emphasizing not only its efficacy and impact, but its liberating effects (Brydon-Miller, Greenwood, & Maguire, 2003).

We broadly labeled our work in Syracuse as "scholarship in action," as a nod to the action research tradition. The resonance with the Lewinian tradition lies in the specifics of the methodology of collective action and reflection in the service of improving intergroup dynamics and community well-being, as well as the intent to seamlessly intertwine the knowledge and tools of academics with the experiential expertise of "ordinary citizens" in situ, in schools, churches, and in numerous neighborhood settings and groups. Moreover, the multigenerational composition of the "community of experts" of which the collaborative action is composed makes this work as much about cultivating new, diverse talent and creating avenues of social mobility as about the public problem solving itself. In this sense, it harkens even further back in history to another moment when higher education engaged in collaboration beyond its boundaries—to the days of the early land-grant movement.

Looking Back to Go Forward

Interestingly, the resonance of this history is striking and very timely these days. Over 150 years ago, for example, Abraham Lincoln faced a fractured country and a stalled agrarian economy following the most divisive war in U.S. history, and he looked to higher education to heal the wounds of the Civil War through direct engagement in communities. Lincoln signed the Morrill Act in 1862 and created what came to be called "democracy's colleges" (Peters, 2011)—public universities throughout this country committed to innovation through collaboration and to social opportunity through education. Indeed, the iconic metaphor for the time—barn-raisings—says it all: the collective work of a community (including universities) to spur the economy through agricultural technology innovation, and simultaneously build avenues of social mobility by educating the sons and daughters of working farmers.

As historian Scott Peters says, the democratic purposes of higher education were fine-tuned in this period after the Civil War, when scholars and experts worked side by side with their community neighbors to spur innovation and solve problems in "work that taps and engages and develops the civic agency, talents, and capacities of everyone, inside and outside the academy." He goes on to describe this work as "grounded in the "daily life" of the people, where "the world's problems" play out in ways that women and men can do something about."

Appropriately for the recent 150th anniversary of the Morrill Act, there is a movement of such "civic science" occurring today as well. For example, psychologist John Spencer of the DeLTA Center at the University of Iowa, joined with community leaders, policymakers, and other psychological scientists to explore "the processes of learning and development by promoting interactions between basic and applied researchers, training the next generation of collaborative scientists, and actively engaging with community partners," in this case addressing ways to enhance the school readiness of Iowa's children in a statewide initiative they are calling "Get Ready Iowa."[1] This is a barn-raising in the true traditions of both action research and the land grant movement, with a very broad-ranging collective of expertise, from parents to policymakers to developmental scientists, coming together to plant the "seeds," as they called it, for action.

Planting Seeds for Action

As the civic science movement and our own work in Syracuse suggest, we, as institutions, disciplines, and scholar-educators, need to take on public problem solving in our metropolitan communities, using everything that we know about education and health and the environment and entrepreneurship to collaborate with citizens and scientists, government, and industry to get things moving again. We need to embrace the power of art and culture and dialogue to leverage diversity and build social cohesion. We need to keep our eye on the children, even as we tackle the burdens of aging. We need to create pathways of opportunity, especially through inclusive education. To do this, our own institutions and disciplinary habits must expand to reward and value publicly engaged scholarship, to reach, rather than weed out, the diverse talent in our midst who might not already look like professionals, even though they surely have the lived wisdom necessary to succeed. We need to embrace having a collective impact, and to work for as long as it takes (certainly longer than the typical grant cycle), and probably with less individual acclaim, and less of the "cult of the expert," as Harry Boyte (2009) calls it. As collaborative innovators, we can't always obsess over intellectual property; as interdisciplinary problem solvers, we can't keep guarding our disciplinary silos; as institutions with place-based identities, we can't just be content to

---

[1] For a complete description of the Get Ready, Iowa initiative, see http://deltacenter.uiowa.edu/.

remain neighbors living cheek by jowl but feeling no interdependence with our communities. All of this needs to change for us to be effective, trusted, sustained catalyzers of real social change, and good partners in it.

And this is where a framework on publicly engaged collaborative work informed by the theories and findings of psychological science can be very helpful. In light of the bundled nature of the challenges that many legacy cities and metropolitan regions face, addressing issues of educational attainment, economic growth, and civic and community well-being requires complex, interdisciplinary, cross-sector, and resident-driven engagement, and the psychology of negotiating this terrain is very tricky.[2] To reap the full benefits in this work of a richly diverse "community of experts," with and without pedigrees, and therefore successfully mount a 21st-century barn-raising, awareness of the lessons of group dynamics can be very helpful. Often coalitions and collaborative infrastructure have to be built across precisely the fault lines in American society that are so entrenched—race, class, power—and this is intensified by the norms and practices of different sectors—business, educational, government, and resident- and community-based organizations. There is tremendous intergroup and intersector suspicion to overcome, requiring skill and agility at confronting rather than avoiding difference and conflict, as one might do in a somewhat safer space in the confines of a structured curriculum on intergroup dialogue (Gurin, Nagda, & Zúñiga, 2013). Therefore, as a first step—but one that must constantly be repeated—there is a strong need in this work to create those "third spaces" of joint ownership, democratic practice, and collaborative interaction. Sometimes, as we found in Syracuse, it helps to make those spaces real fixtures as a more or less permanent stake in the ground that spurs the growth of social bonds that last.

Building Bonds That Last

In Syracuse, an older industrial city with an urban core full of grand history, richly diverse but long-abandoned talent, and plenty of potential for collaborative revival, for the "eds and meds" to fulfill our potential as anchor institutions and barn-raising partners, it was critical that we cross some substantial boundaries of geography, both physical and social. In good Lewinian tradition, Syracuse University (SU) came off its hill, renovating an abandoned furniture warehouse downtown—dubbed, aptly, "The Warehouse"—and creating not only space for faculty, staff, and students from the School of Architecture and the design programs in the College of Visual and Performing Arts to work 24/7 but also dedicating space for collaborative work with the community. That work is anchored by the Near West Side Initiative (NWSI)—a 501c3 nonprofit organization headquartered in The Warehouse, of which SU is a

---

[2] The Social Science Research Council has partnered with the group Opportunity Nation to create a multidimensional index for mapping opportunity county by county across the United States, accounting for a range of economic, educational, and community health indicators. For a complete description and interactive maps of the results of this work, see http://opportunityindex.org.

part along with numerous resident and community leaders, which raised over $70 million that was invested to build on the diverse assets of the neighborhood, which was the ninth-poorest census tract in the country.[3] In this shared third space, the hard interdisciplinary collaborative work draws in partners and participants of all kinds on a wide range of ever-evolving projects from sustainable, affordable housing to literacy and photography to intergroup dialogue. In every case, the work teams include partners of all generations and backgrounds—a third-generation grocer and SU public health faculty building a health center within the neighborhood store; psychologists and education faculty and students teaming with grandmothers and their grandchildren to build on a tradition of inclusive education; information school faculty and graduate students working with neighborhood leaders to build "little free libraries"; and artists and public scholars of all sorts working with residents to create La Casita—a Latino/a cultural center in another former warehouse.

The signifying definition of the NWSI is that it is on the ground and of the neighborhood, even as practically every discipline at SU finds its way into the community of experts that evolve for each project. And it is committed to using art and public narrative of all media to give voice to the residents of all ages. As Mary Alice Smothers, a leader on the NWSI board and a longtime resident of the neighborhood, proclaims—in what might be the motto of the group—"Ask us; we lay our heads down here at night." Or, as the banner on St. Lucy's Church, the iconic centerpiece of the neighborhood, announces, "Sinners Welcome." It is in this richly diverse context that dialogue serves as the centerpiece of action research, even as it is often messy, loud, and conflicted. Nonetheless, in seven long years of shouting, differences have been aired, trust cemented, and progress made again and again. At every turn, there are tests of commitment— such as when the neighborhood school was about to be closed, and SU faculty, students, and leaders stood side by side with residents to protest, and then to plan for new programs, as part of a districtwide school improvement collaborative called Say Yes to Education Syracuse, that is sending students from this neighborhood and others to college for free, among other things.[4] Likewise, when the Central New York Regional Economic Development Council (cochaired at the time by Nancy Cantor) funded what was viewed as a competitor grocery store, not far from Nojaims, the Near Westside's own grocery, the politics of collaboration got fierce. In this and many other examples, the trust built up by hours of engagement in shared spaces and with shared decision making won the day—at least until the next uproar.

This kind of collaborative work is a testimony to the insights of decades of action research on group dynamics—more gets done precisely because of the diversity of skills and perspectives and experiences brought to the

---

[3] It is worth noting that while the Near Westside neighborhood was the ninth-poorest census tract in the United States at the time of the 2000 census, it was no longer among the poorest in 2010, four years after the NWSI was founded.

[4] For complete information about Say Yes to Education Syracuse, see http://www.sayyessyracuse .org/.

problem-solving table. It is very hard work precisely because of that diversity of participants. There isn't a project in the Near Westside in which SU participated that some faculty or student hasn't stopped midway to say, "Couldn't we get this done faster if we just did it ourselves?" only to continue through the dynamics of the collaborative process to say at the end, "This is so much better than anything we could have done ourselves." Part of the complexity of the group dynamics of university-community collaboration is an insider–outsider phenomenon, with university participants finding themselves in the unusual position of being the outsiders, needing to listen more than to talk, to learn more than to instruct, to adapt more than to solidify their own expertise. Part of it is also the sheer diversity of expertise, language, methods, and even values that emerge in the collaborative partners and participants. For example, gone is the luxury of structuring the diversity of participants along a few dimensions (disciplinary, cultural, sector, age) with relatively equal representation across boundaries—the work groups tend to be much more varied—ranging from grandmothers to deans and embodying complex dynamics of social identity and power. The student who comes from a similar place may be better positioned to leverage the on-the-ground expertise of the residents, not to mention their allegiance, than is the senior faculty member. The nontenured professor of practice may have more credibility than the esteemed theoretician. The liberal politics of the faculty member with community-organizing experience may be less persuasive and effective than the professional staff member with economic development credentials and less preformed expectations about being a "hero" to or "doing good" in the neighborhood.

All of the role reversals and pressure to adapt and to listen can lead faculty members to feel a certain degree of angst and uncertainty, even as most of us feel exhilarated by the sense of doing something truly meaningful as part of a collective doing what Boyte calls "work by publics, for public purposes, in public" (Boyte, 2013, p. 2). Moreover, this angst can explode into a true existential identity crisis when the power of the work itself isn't recognized back on campus or in disciplinary circles because its form and output don't easily conform to the standard metrics and outcome measures. Many millions of dollars in external support have been raised by the NWSI, for example, with substantial contributions of time, expertise, and effort of SU faculty and staff, but none of those funds can be singularly claimed by either the individual SU faculty or the institution itself, precisely because this is intentionally a collaborative (501c3) enterprise, co-created and co-owned, in a third space beyond the direct bottom line of SU or the résumés of its participants (at least, it would be hard to claim Principal Investigator status on it). While this may seem insignificant as an obstacle to doing this kind of engaged, collaborative public scholarship, it has caused problems when either an individual faculty member or the institution's sponsored profile is evaluated.

Even more complicated, of course, is the tendency of academe to evaluate excellence and impact in rather reductionist, individualistic, and quantitative terms—as the national consortium Imagining America has noted in its study of "Scholarship in Public" (Cantor & Lavine, 2006; Ellison & Eatman, 2008). (At Syracuse, it took more than 4 years to get agreement from the university senate for a relatively small revision in the faculty manual to recognize collaborative and publicly engaged scholarship in tenure and promotion.)[5] This kind of collaborative work is protracted, marked by ups, downs, and small victories along the way, and whereas the output of any given project can be compelling (for instance, the photography and poetry of the children of the Near Westside is about as moving as one can find), the collective impact of the initiative is hard to separate into the kinds of compartments that we all typically measure. For example, how do you disentangle the contributions of specific projects to progress on aggregate indices such as the Opportunity Index of the Social Science Research Council (SSRC), measuring economic strength, educational attainment, and civic health in metro regions?[6] Increasingly, projects nationally are looking for "dashboard" measures of the impact of specific anchor institution work on these more communitywide indices of strength and opportunity,[7] and it will be important to consider how to use those collective impact measures to undergird rewards for individual faculty, students, and professional staff as they take part, with diverse communities of experts, in moving the dial forward in communities, near and far from their institutions.

A particularly significant piece of the collective impact of this anchor institution work is its firsthand immersion in the power of diverse groups to do good public problem solving, as Scott Page (2007) has demonstrated in many organizational settings. Not only does it raise one's appreciation for the power of diversity, but it provides a constant reminder that without "full participation," the legitimacy of the solutions will be undermined (Sturm, 2006). As social scientists, many of us espouse the importance of achieving critical mass and engaging in true intergroup dialogue in order to change stereotypes ("Not all blacks are poor, all Latinos speak Spanish, or all whites are rich," as Sherillyn Ifill, 2003, p. A27, notes), and to reduce stereotype threat (Steele, 2010) and fix power differentials (Gurin et al., 2013). But rarely are we on the front lines of the experiences that so embody these constructs, as occurs in this engaged public scholarship within diverse communities. When an autistic child in a Syracuse elementary school labeled as "nonverbal" uses digital

---

[5] See the section of the SU faculty manual where the definition of scholarship was revised to include explicitly "publicly engaged scholarship"; http://provost.syr.edu/faculty-support/faculty-manual/2-34-areas-of-expected-faculty-achievement-teaching-research-and-service/.

[6] This index encompasses 16 indicators across three major categories of opportunity (economic: jobs, wages, poverty, inequality, assets, affordable housing, and Internet access; education: preschool enrollment, on-time high school graduation, and postsecondary education; and community health and civic life: civic engagement, volunteerism, youth economic and academic inclusion, community safety, access to health care, and access to healthy food).

[7] For example, Ted Howard, executive director of the Democracy Collaborative at the University of Maryland and the Steven Minter Senior Fellow for Social Justice at the Cleveland Foundation, and his colleagues at the Democracy Collaborative have created a dashboard of indicators for the success of anchor institutions in meeting the needs of their communities. See http://community-wealth.org/indicators.

photography and types narratives to tell you that he understands what is going on around him,[8] or when middle school students work as collaborators on urban school reform in a project entitled "Smart Kids—Visual Stories" (Biklen & Nguyen, 2012), then truly do we turn on their head our preconceptions of talent, groups, and power, and the so-called experts become novice listeners while novices teach (Cantor, 2012).

Unearthing and Cultivating Talent

If this work is a testament to the intricacies of group dynamics as played out in collaborative public problem solving, then it is also a reminder of the wisdom of John Dewey (1916/1966), who characterized education as a *social* experience and talent as something to be cultivated, not taken for granted. Engaged scholarship and community development work—in the good Lewinian tradition—powerfully shifts one from an "exclusion" to an "inclusion" set, not only in the formation of communities of collaborators and the recognition of expertise but also in the identification of talent and the recognition of achievement among our current and future students. It is virtually impossible, for example, to work in the Near Westside neighborhood of Syracuse, or for that matter in any of the schools across the Syracuse City School District, and not be struck by the wealth of talent being left behind by our current system of selectivity in higher education, as it is aided and abetted by underresourced and inadequate urban schools and narrowly defined, test-driven definitions of merit and achievement.[9] Instead of focusing one's talent search at the high end of an SAT continuum known to disadvantage poor children and students of color all along the income continuum (e.g., Reardon, 2013; Steele, 2010), shouldn't we now finally turn to embracing more varied talents, not less, as the Posse Foundation does when selecting leaders who show perseverance, teamwork, and creative problem solving (ironically labeled in the testing field as "noncognitive" factors)?[10] Shouldn't

[8] This was the case with a boy named Tiran Robinson, a participant in the Photography and Literacy program conducted by Stephen Mahan at SU, Spring, 2012. To learn more about this project, see http://supalproject.wordpress.com/.

[9] For examples of how higher-education leaders are trying to move beyond the culture of defining merit narrowly, see the presentations and media coverage of the January 2014 conference of the University of Southern California Center for Enrollment, Research, Policy, and Practice, titled "Defining Merit: The Nexus of Mission, Excellence, and Diversity" at http://cerpp.usc.edu/conferences/2014con/.

[10] The Posse Foundation is a nonprofit organization that has established an impressive track record in identifying high-capacity students through intensive examination of their academic capabilities, employing a range of measures that reach well beyond traditional indicators such as test scores and grade-point average (GPA). Its model for placing cohorts of students in a nationwide network of colleges and universities and seeing them through to graduation is equally impressive. For a full description of their model, see http://www.possefoundation.org. For research by the College Board on "noncognitive factors," see, for example, http://research.collegeboard.org/sites/default/files/publications/2012/7/researchreport-2011-1-validation-measures-noncognitive-college-student-potential.pdf.

we (by analogy to the approach that Major League Baseball takes to talent cultivation) build "farm teams" in our major metropolitan regions, and then share that talent broadly across the diverse array of higher-education institutions (Cantor, 2013)?

In Syracuse, for example, boosting educational attainment is the main focus for the Central New York Regional Economic Development Strategic Plan,[11] and this involves not only SU becoming a much more diverse, vibrant, and inclusive campus, but also direct engagement with the front lines of opportunity making as represented by community colleges, where the vast majority of the nation's first-generation talent will first taste higher education.[12] Following this path, students, faculty, and institutions come much closer to embracing what Carol Dweck (2006) aptly called a "growth mind-set," obsessing less about cataloguing already demonstrated merit/ achievement and instead finding creative ways to uncover a broader array of potential and to focus attention on cultivating and sharing it widely.

Of course, this approach is not without controversy. As with the rewarding of publicly engaged scholarship and the sharing of sponsored research with cross-sector collaborators, those who guard "quality" and reputation in our institutions may well look askance at this broadening of the definition of merit and the aggressive cultivation of talent through collaborations all along the educational pathway from pre-K–16.

At Syracuse, this debate between engagement and inclusion on one hand and selectivity and ranking on the other came to the fore with a pair of articles in the *Chronicle of Higher Education*, one titled "Syracuse's Slide" (Wilson, 2011), and the other referring to an alternative plausible framing of "Syracuse's Surge" (Hoover, 2011). And while it may not always get as starkly or publicly drawn as that debate did, some tension between the "ivory tower" and the "anchor institution" models seems to us to be inevitable. The world is relentlessly urbanizing, and waves of migration are bringing new populations to join already ignored talent pools in our urban centers. With that will come a strong push for a renewed commitment to social mobility in this nation. As Ruth Bader Ginsburg (2013) noted in her dissent in the Supreme Court case *Fisher v. University of Texas*, which dealt with affirmative action, "only an ostrich could regard the supposedly neutral alternatives as race unconscious." By the same token, higher education can only continue to leave this much talent behind, and the country can only continue to underinvest in educational opportunity for this next diverse generation at our peril—it is time to take our ostrich heads out of the sand.

---

[11] See the Central New York Regional Economic Development Council plan in full at http:// regionalcouncils.ny.gov/themes/nyopenrc/rc-files/centralny/final%20CNY%20REDC%20 plan%20single%20pages.pdf.

[12] The Century Foundation has reported on the necessity of linking 2- and 4-year institutions of higher education more extensively and deeply. See Century Foundation (2013). *Bridging the Higher Education Divide: Strengthening Community Colleges and Restoring the American Dream.* New York, NY: Century Foundation Press.

Taking Our Ostrich Heads out of the Sand and Transforming Our Institutions

As we come more and more to terms with the interdependence between our institutions and the broader social polity, including the communities of which we are an increasingly important anchor in a knowledge economy and the next diverse generation of talent on whom we will depend, institutional transformations of many sorts will be the order of the day. Appropriately enough, that starts—in the finest tradition of action research—with the reflection that each of us can and should undertake about our roles in the broad ecosystem of research and our agency in affecting the kinds of change that will bring about transformation. We must be prepared for the likelihood that this often will translate into taking action that is countercultural. For example, talk of transformation in higher education today frequently focuses on distance learning and other technological innovations. These are certainly important in their own right, and yet the lessons learned from our collaborative work with diverse communities of experts as partners and participants suggests other kinds of transformation on the ground that academic leaders and faculty alike will also need to embrace going forward.

As academic leaders at SU, we learned quickly that faculty and professional staff and students all needed constant and vocal support from the institution's leadership to continue in this work. We needed to argue for those new tenure and promotion guidelines to support publicly engaged scholarship, and once we got them, we needed to reward and value this scholarly work publicly in seed grants for cross-campus–community interdisciplinary and engaged projects (which we called "Chancellor's Leadership Projects" and supported via an award from the Carnegie Corporation for Academic Leadership). We needed to acknowledge that the intensity and challenges of creating and sustaining those third spaces of campus–community collaboration on the ground required constant effort on the part of professional staff beyond the availability of involved faculty and students, so we supported those positions centrally and raised monies for them. We needed to make it possible for students who engaged in this work as undergraduates to remain in Syracuse when they graduated and continue their efforts, so we teamed up with the national consortium Imagining America to support "Engagement Fellows," who both worked with nonprofits in the community and took graduate courses at Syracuse with tuition scholarships provided by our deans.

Similarly, Imagining America's Publicly Active Graduate Education (PAGE) program served as a model for graduate education with a strong emphasis on community collaboration.[13] And perhaps most of all, it was up to us to implore our colleagues on campus to keep that two-way street open for

---

[13] For examples of the work of Imagining America's PAGE program, see http://imaginingamerica .org/consortium/student-networks/page/.

talented students from the community (and from other similar urban school districts in geographies of opportunity around the country) to come to SU, weathering criticism sometimes when concerns were expressed about selectivity and quality (based, of course, on quite narrow indicators). Moreover, the same expansive attitude toward recruitment needed to translate into a strong commitment to hiring a diverse cadre of tenured and tenure-track faculty, as well as professors of practice and professional staff, and it helped to show central support, as for example, in SU's National Science Foundation (NSF) Advance grant in science, technology, engineering, and mathematics (STEM), dedicated to an "inclusive connective corridor" between university and industry and community.

To both galvanize and benefit fully from this commitment to collaborative engagement, we found that it is ultimately critical to take a very deliberate stance toward institutional transformation so as to build a new and more welcoming environment for these new expressions of intellectual capital and the new human capital behind them. This involves what one of the Chancellor's Leadership Project groups called the creation of "just academic spaces."[14] These are spaces for intergroup dialogue, for listening to everyone, including members of heretofore often marginalized groups and members of both the campus and community.[15] These are spaces where identity is embraced, not hidden, where multiple modes and methods are adopted, and where power is negotiated on new terms that may well override legacies of title and position— not unlike the experiences we had in the neighborhoods of Syracuse. And these are contested spaces, where the oft-desired neutrality of the academy is eschewed for the much more realistic airing of conflict, diverse opinions and values, and passions, which are just as messy (and yet vibrant) as modern urban life turns out to be.[16] This is how we begin to build what Susan Sturm (2006) aptly called "the architecture of inclusion," mirroring on campus what we see in our collaborations beyond our gates. And in many respects, this is the best contribution that collaborative action research conducted in situ with many partners and many generations can bring back to the academy going forward.

---

[14] This particular, ongoing project, Democratizing Knowledge, draws scholars across the disciplines to focus, in their words, "on producing transformative knowledges and collectivities with the purpose of contributing to the growth of inclusive publics in higher education, in the workforce, and in the larger polity nationally and globally." See http://democratizingknowledge.org/.

[15] The multi-institution Intergroup Dialogue research project based at the University of Michigan cultivates and promulgates best practices in this area. For curricular examples from the Intergroup Dialogue project at SU, see http://intergroupdialogue.syr.edu/academic/.

[16] The Africa Initiative at SU promotes analysis and discussion of these dynamics, an example of which is their February 2013 conference titled "Dialogues on Deconstructing War Zones." For a specific example of the direction of such dialogue, see Cantor (2013).

■ REFERENCES ■

Biklen, S. K., & Nguyen, N. (April 2012). *The politics of talk about schools: Power relations in qualitative research with children.* Paper presented at the annual meeting of the American Educational Research Association in Vancouver, British Columbia, Canada.

Boyte, H. C. (2009). *Civic agency and the cult of the expert.* Dayton, OH: Kettering Foundation.

Boyte, H. C. (2013). *Reinventing citizenship as public work: Citizen-centered democracy and the empowerment gap.* Dayton, OH: Kettering Foundation.

Brydon-Miller, M., Greenwood, D., & Maguire, P. (2003). Why action research? *Action Research, 1*, 9–28.

Cantor, N. (April 2012). *Scholarship in action for a new generation.* Retrieved from http://www.syr.edu/chancellor/speeches/AERA_presidential_address_final.pdf

Cantor, N. (2013, August 2). Diversity and higher education: Our communities need more than "narrowly tailored" solutions. *Huffington Post.* Retrieved from http://www.huffingtonpost.com/nancy-cantor/diversity-higher-education_b_3695503.html

Cantor, N., & Lavine, S. (2006, June 9). Taking public scholarship seriously. *Chronicle of Higher Education,* p. B20.

Century Foundation (2013). *Bridging the higher education divide: Strengthening community colleges and restoring the American dream.* New York, NY: The Century Foundation Press.

Dewey, J. (1966). *Democracy and education.* New York, NY: Macmillan. (Original work published 1916)

Dweck, C. (2006). *Mindset: The new psychology of success.* New York, NY: Random House.

Ellison, J., & Eatman, T. K. (2008). *Scholarship in public: Knowledge creation and tenure policy in the engaged university.* Syracuse, NY: Imagining America.

Ginsburg, R. B. (2013). In *Fisher v. University of Texas at Austin,* 133 S. Ct. 2411.

Gurin, P., Nagda, B. A., & Zúñiga, X. (2013). *Dialogue across difference: Practice, theory, and research on intergroup dialogue.* New York, NY: Russell Sage Foundation.

Hoover, E. (2011). Syracuse, selectivity, and "old measures." *Chronicle of Higher Education,* Head Count blog, http://chronicle.com/blogs/headcount/syracuse-selectivity-and-%e2%80%98old-measures%e2%80%99/28973

Ifill, S. (2013, June 14). Race vs. class: The false dichotomy. *The New York Times,* p. A27.

Page, S. E. (2007). *The difference: How the power of diversity creates better groups, firms, schools, and societies.* Princeton, NJ: Princeton University Press.

Peters, S. (2011, December 7). Democracy's college [Blog entry]. Retrieved from http://DemocracyU.wordpress.com/

Reardon, S. (2013, April 28). No rich child left behind. *The New York Times,* p. SR1.

Steele, C. (2010). *Whistling Vivaldi: And other clues to how stereotypes affect us.* New York, NY: W. W. Norton.

Sturm, S. P. (2006). The architecture of inclusion: Interdiscplinary insights on pursuing institutional citizenship. *Harvard Journal of Law and Gender, 30,* 248–334.

Wilson, R. (2011, October 2). Syracuse's slide: As chancellor focuses on the "public good," Syracuse's reputation slides. *Chronicle of Higher Education,* p. A1.

Chapter 18: No Researcher Is an Island

Geoffrey L. Cohen

Professor of Psychology
James G. March Professor of Organizational Studies in Education and Business
Stanford University

Julio Garcia

Consulting Research Scientist
Graduate School of Education
Stanford University

There is a common conceit—more a myth, really—that we can entertain when thinking about what we do as researchers. The lone investigator who grapples with a problem in a solitary struggle is a near-heroic image. But most of us know this is far from the truth. Collaboration is a constant in the research process. It occurs while acquiring the resources to conduct the work in the back-and-forth exchanges between researchers and funders. At a more micro level, to conduct an experiment with human subjects requires collaboration with the human subjects review board, research assistants, study participants, and many others.

Of course, research has its solitary moments: those times spent plowing through the literature, the hours spent grinding away at data in order to test an idea or gain deeper understanding, the stolen moments tinkering with a study's design. But even in these periods of solitude, the collaborative process asserts itself. Its presence lies in the internalized voice of one's mentor; in the body of knowledge that permits us to formulate new ideas, apply a methodological practice, or use an analytical tool; and in the anticipated reaction of fellow scientists to our ideas. Although collaboration in research can be seen as one of many options, from a broader perspective it is not an option, but a necessity.

This chapter presents our understanding of collaboration in research based on our 15-year partnership conducting field experiments in public schools. We place our research in the collaborative contexts that created it.

These contexts include our collaboration with one another, our staff, the practitioners and administrators at the schools, and the student participants and their parents. The context also includes the powerful but invisible traditions that gave rise to the intellectual rationale and methodological approach of our research and the institutional ideologies and practices that shaped our work and presentation of it.

Two short scientific reports were the product of our collaboration (Cohen, Garcia, Apfel, & Master, 2006; Cohen, Garcia, Purdie-Vaughns, Apfel, & Brzustoski, 2009). They described field experiments in school testing if a self-affirmation exercise could boost minority student performance. Middle school children were randomly assigned to complete a values affirmation intervention both early in the school year and then before key stressors such as exams throughout the year. The intervention entailed a series of writing exercises in which students wrote about core values, such as religion or relationships with friends, and why they were important. By bringing to mind the "psychological big picture," the intervention was expected to broaden the self-concept and lessen the stress that minority students might feel about being negatively stereotyped in school. Consistent with expectations, we found that self-affirmed African Americans earned higher grades in their class than those students randomly assigned to complete a neutral writing exercise (Cohen et al., 2006). To our surprise, these effects rippled out to affect their grades in other courses and persisted for a long time—indeed, they remained evident two years later, at the end of the students' tenure at middle school (Cohen et al., 2009). Somehow, the affirmation process propagated itself through time. In retrospect, it seems strange that our two brief reports were actually the product of a long and serendipitous collaborative journey.

Research: A Collaborative Process From Beginning to End

On the Shoulders of Others: Our Collaborative Journey Begins

We, along with our collaborator Valerie Purdie-Vaughns, were trained in the experimental social psychology doctoral program at Stanford. Because we wanted to understand how social psychological processes play out in the real world, we conducted a series of field experiments in middle schools in the early 2000s. We began with a couple of well-supported theories, some initial findings, the methods of social psychology, and a desire to use social psychology to address social problems. Regardless of the originality of our research, it was, like all research, collaborative by necessity. The theories, findings, and know-how of social psychology were collaborative products. They had come from the efforts of many people building on one another's work over time, sometimes in concert and sometimes in conflict. We were a product of the zeitgeist, the social and intellectual fabric of the time. Of course, we wanted to add our contribution to the warp and woof of that fabric.

When we started our journey, research on stereotype threat and self-affirmation theory had undergone years of critical assessment by their originators and a host of critics and supporters (Steele, 1988; Steele, Spencer, & Aronson, 2002). Countless hours of cooperative effort had gone into designing the studies, and thousands of people gave their time to participate in them. Articles had been written and published, with theoretical battles waged over and within them. Obviously, the investigators were a necessary part of the process, but they were far from sufficient. Many others played a role as well. Among them were colleagues who provided critical feedback—reviewers and journal editors, and others who turned the electrical squiggles into the journal articles. These activities and many others make up the collaborative process of social psychology. Our work rested on the collectively constructed approach for systematically understanding social problems and other phenomena broadly known as experimental psychology.

The focus of our research was a social problem that our mentor, Claude Steele, had begun to explore in the early 1990s—the gap in academic achievement between many ethnic minority students and their peers. Members of such groups consistently perform below their European-American and Asian-American peers, even when prior indicators of success and socioeconomic status (SES) are taken into account. Our commitment to the problem was in large part driven by our social context. We were graduate students at a particular institution, working with a particular mentor at a particular time. To paraphrase the cliché, we stand, as does every researcher, on the ideas, discoveries, and tastes of those who have done or are doing what we do, past and present, unknown and renowned. Claude Steele and his colleagues had conducted laboratory studies demonstrating how a portion of the race gap arose from the stress that minority students felt about being seen in light of a negative stereotype in school, a phenomenon called *stereotype threat* (Steele et al., 2002).

We wanted to collaborate with inspirational figures in social psychology. We wanted to continue a tradition that married theory and application, a tradition begun by Kurt Lewin (1948/1997) and Solomon Asch (1952). Although application was not much in vogue in the 1980s and 1990s in mainstream experimental social psychology, we were also inspired by several originators of intervention studies: Elliot Aronson, who found that harmonious interracial relationships could be promoted in schools by creating a cooperative group structure (Aronson & Bridgeman, 1979); Milton Rokeach (1971), who found that confronting people with a hypocrisy in their value systems could motivate lasting behavior change; and Tim Wilson and Patricia Linville (1982), who found that brief interventions that provided students with a positive explanatory frame for academic difficulty could boost their grades. These researchers demonstrated that rigorous and appropriately timed intervention could help remedy a social problem. If targeted to a key social psychological process, even a brief intervention could have large and lasting effects.

We were steeped in the social psychological theories of stereotype threat and self-affirmation of Claude Steele and his colleagues (Steele, 1988; Steele et al., 2002; see also Cohen & Sherman, 2014; Sherman & Cohen, 2006). We were also trained in the science and art of the experimental method. Specifically, we were shaped by Kurt Lewin's approach to experimentation. He used the experimental method to mitigate big social problems—an act of folly to many. A subtle notion drove his method, summed up by a favorite maxim of both him and his developmental psychologist counterpart, Urie Bronfenbrenner (1977), namely, the best way to understand a system is to try to change it. The investigator introduced a new element into a system, such as boosting students' sense of personal adequacy in the classroom. The investigator then observed how the change in this element affected other parts of the system.

Our collaborators, in the form of our discipline, provided us a map for helping to remedy a major social problem—the gap in academic performance between minority and nonminority students. Their insistence on the importance of theory and the necessity of using the experimental method led us to a series of initial questions. First, did stereotype threat contribute to the gap in academic performance between minority and nonminority students in an actual school? Also, if it did, how could it be altered by other psychological processes?

Two psychological processes, we thought, could lessen the costs of stereotype threat: the self-affirmation process and the process of social belonging. The former allows people to assert an overall sense of adequacy by endorsing core values such as religion or relationships (Steele, 1988; see also Cohen & Sherman, 2014). The latter assures people that their struggles are not unique, but rather commonplace, and that they will be overcome in time (Walton & Cohen, 2007, 2011). We focus here on self-affirmation processes because they led to our first collaboration with a public school, its administrators, and teachers.

The Cast Multiplies and the Plot Thickens

Throughout our project, the vital role of collaboration was brought home to us. A story of our journey could emphasize our interests, goals, and grit, but that would omit two key and often related factors: collaboration and serendipity. Chance encounters with other people served as catalysts for better research. Because our earlier research spoke to the concerns of educators, unexpected opportunities began arising from outside academia.

Indeed, serendipitous social contacts provided the initial impetus for our field research. As an example, after reading a chapter that one of us had written about the effects of negative stereotypes on minority students, a senior staff member of a school district near our university began wondering if our work could be applied in her school to lift the performance of African-American students. She called us to discuss our work. This call led to a meeting with her and some of her colleagues from her school. At this meeting, it was suggested that we explore the possibility of working together. About the same time, one of us gave a talk to administrators and educators about stereotype threat at a nearby college. At this talk, a foundation representative who wanted to see this work applied to schools asked if we would be open to entering into a formal collaboration with the foundation.

After a year of discussion, the foundation wanted to formalize our collaboration, but because of its charter, the foundation wanted the work to be done in a school in the Northeast. Their stipulation naturally led us back to the people at the school with whom we had discussed the possibility of collaboration. We submitted a research proposal to the foundation, which it then funded, and we carried out the research at the school of the school staff member who had reached out to us. Years later, a similar course of events unfolded in another part of the country, leading us to replicate and expand our work to largely poor immigrant Latin-American students (Sherman et al., 2013).

These events did not happen because they were the planned steps of a research program. In fact, it could easily be said that they had no place in such a program. It is commonly assumed that the professional success of the academic social scientist depends on conducting programmatic research in a linear, planned-out fashion. By contrast, our journey was shaped in significant part by serendipity. We would not have taken the course we did had we not been open to collaboration when unexpected opportunities knocked at our door.

We became adept at recognizing new opportunities in the broader environment. Because we had said yes when opportunity knocked once, it was more likely to knock again. Clearly, this can sometimes prove a waste of time, but sometimes it can take one in surprising and productive directions.

Our broader view of collaboration had a pronounced influence on how we moved from the lab to the field. We recognized the interdisciplinary nature of our research problem, the achievement gap. We made ourselves aware of what other researchers were doing with respect to the achievement gap to an extent that we would not have thought necessary had we been working from a more individualistic perspective.

For example, we repeatedly called colleagues for advice. This was especially important because the problem was multifaceted. In contrast to the controlled confines of the lab, where extraneous variables can be controlled, a classroom contains multiple forces interacting in complex ways. We reached out to scholars in education (in particular Professors Ed Zigler and James Comer, both creators of impactful programs for at-risk youth). Coming from a social-developmental perspective, they both emphasized the wider context in which child development occurs. This collaboration helped put in check a careerlong danger for experimental social psychologists—the urge to simplify beyond the point of usefulness. It also led us back to the work of Kurt Lewin (1948/1997), which emphasized how the effect of any intervention will depend on the system of forces into which it is introduced. Although affirming a minority child in a racist environment would lead to little or no good for the child, a timely affirmation in an environment reinforcing positive development could nudge awake the forces already present to support and sustain the student's growth.

At the beginning of our journey, our understanding of the nature of the system of forces in a classroom was sadly lacking. This was brought home to us in our interactions with other scholars, as well as in negative feedback from people outside our discipline. For instance, a respected colleague suggested a possible funding source for our work. However, we were declined funding when we submitted our research proposal, even though the external reviews of our grant proposal were positive. We later learned that key members of the foundation's board, scholars with expertise in education, had refused to believe that our brief self-affirmation interventions could have much impact on student performance given the importance of larger structural forces. This occurred in spite of the fact that our proposal presented positive evidence of efficacy from two rigorous field experiments. In the final analysis, the board members preferred to rely on their own experience and theoretical view rather than on experimental evidence. Their theory emphasized the wider social context of child development. From this perspective, underperformance is a consequence of the structural, economic, and familial factors in a child's environment. Given this circumstance, how could a brief writing exercise close the achievement gap? Or, as one board member had reportedly commented, "We are funding projects that cost more and have far less impact than this one. So how could this project possibly work?"

These sorts of interactions had two effects on us. First, they gave us first-hand exposure to the perspectives that people in other disciplines had on the achievement gap. We had assumed that our project was a compelling and logical extension of robust laboratory findings. But it became apparent to us that outsiders sometimes saw it as a cavalier leap of faith based on conjecture. To our surprise, this was an assessment made by scholars with greater experience in studying actual schools than we had. From their vantage point, our results violated what they assumed to be possible, a denial of both common scholarly knowledge and common sense.

Having to confront this incredulity proved extremely helpful for our theory development. Incredulity points to where no theory or intuition offers understanding. We grappled with the implications of our data. Why did they provoke such incredulity? We became convinced that it was due to our cultural understanding of the nature of change, which rests on the idea that there is a direct relationship between the importance and complexity of a situation and the energy and resources necessary to change it. This implies that in order to change a multifaceted phenomenon, one must change many factors in it. From this viewpoint, simply changing one factor could not be sufficient—unless, of course, it is a big factor.

In contrast to this view of change, our data and our collaborations with other scholars led us to see how a targeted, well-timed change in one element of a system could trigger a chain reaction. The self-affirmation process occurred, but in the context of other institutional and psychological currents. We found, for instance, that an improvement in academic performance (even if only slight) could make it less likely that a minority student would be assigned to the remedial track by the school (Cohen et al., 2009). Because remedial education tends to sentence them to an institutional failure channel (Grubb, 2011; Steele, 2010), avoidance of this channel could change their academic trajectory for the better. To echo Bronfenbrenner (1977), our understanding of the relationship of the forces in a system is increased by observing how the forces in it react when one of them is nudged. A nudge in the psychology of the student illustrated how small initial differences in students' performance can have repercussions for their fate through the academic tracking system.

To paraphrase Douglas Adams (1998, para. 8), "[a]nything that happens happens; anything that in happening, causes something else to happen causes something else to happen; and anything that in happening, causes itself to happen again happens again." The feedback loop explains when and why an event triggers a cascade of consequences through time.

The second effect that interactions with people outside our field had on us was to increase our awareness of what was special about our discipline, social psychology. It asserts key ideas outside the perspective of much educational policy and research (Ross & Nisbett, 2011). Chief among these is the notion that it matters how people construe or perceive their social environment. Although a classroom may appear to be the same for all those in it to an outside observer, it may be seen very differently by different students. While a nonstereotyped student might see a classroom as a nurturing and secure location, a minority student, because of the potential to be negatively stereotyped, may experience it as a more stressful and evaluative place. Another key idea of social psychology is that because the processes in a social environment are interconnected, it is not necessary to change all (or even many) variables in order to alter the status quo. Changing one key or central factor, even if just a little, may be sufficient to set a chain reaction in motion. A third idea is the notion that rather than just measuring key educational variables, one can manipulate them. This includes not only visible incentives (the province of economists) but also subtler or even invisible social psychological factors.

When it came to building our team, the collaborative and interdependent nature of our research asserted itself in full force. It was not enough to recruit experienced researchers and trainable research assistants. The team members had to have other skill sets. Because our work took place in a school, they had to deal with educators and their support staff in a respectful way and to interact with middle school students in a professional but nonthreatening way. These are skills not normally taught in research environments. Our colleagues were more than willing collaborators in the search for qualified candidates, and so was the staff of the university employment office.

During this time, we also needed teachers at our middle school research site to be committed to our project. The experimental methodologies needed for a fair test of our hypotheses in classrooms required that teachers and staff members permit us to conduct our work with as little disclosure to them as possible about what we were doing. This is no small thing to ask of someone. We were asking educators to trust us in a way that could possibly make them professionally vulnerable, or at least waste their valuable time. We found that some of the demands of the experimental method, such as keeping teachers unaware of the hypotheses and the condition assignment of students, made trust all the more important and all the more challenging. Earning their trust (and subsequently their commitment) took about a year of meetings with them before we even ran any trials with participants. When it comes to cultivating relationships with institutions, the conclusion that we came to as consequence of our collaboration was "Don't rush it." Because of professional pressures, such as the push to publish, patience can be undervalued.

The educators' expertise provided the project with numerous benefits. One of our major concerns was to develop intervention materials so that middle school students found them understandable and engaging. The willingness of teachers to provide feedback during this process was invaluable. Teachers also proved helpful when we were puzzling over data from the sixth grade showing that girls, like African Americans in the seventh grade, benefited from affirmation. One of the teachers described how the transition to sixth grade from elementary school disrupted the social relationships of students. Moreover, the bonding experience of pretend play gave way to gossip. This was particularly stressful for girls, as relationships appeared to be more important to them. As this example demonstrates, even when practitioners do not know the theory behind a study, their understanding of social context can often improve the design of a study and inform the puzzle solving inherent in making sense of data.

Armed with a refined research strategy and materials, sufficient resources, and a research site, we moved on to the implementation phase of our research. This phase involved recruiting student participants, administering the intervention, developing a data processing system and analytical strategy, and managing our collaboration with personnel at the school. This stage produced some of the project's most challenging and rewarding moments.

One invaluable early step that we took was to hire a school liaison: a staff member at the school responsible for scheduling meetings with teachers and rooms for assessments and for requesting data. This meant that one institutional insider would handle such repeated requests. Ensuring that the required research permission slips went from classroom to students' homes, were signed by parents and got returned to the classroom, was one of the most time-consuming tasks. This proved a complex social psychological problem unto itself that benefited enormously from the input of teachers and staff, including the institutional insider who oversaw the process.

Administering the intervention during class required an intense collaboration between the research team and the school. The intervention needed to come when African-American students would be experiencing stereotype threat. Timeliness was critical. As arranged in meetings, on the key days, all teachers set aside 20 minutes to assign the intervention before an in-class exam. This occurred a few times throughout the year. Also arranged in this collaboration with teachers was a time to schedule our own survey of students in the school's auditorium—hard-to-obtain real estate at the busy beginning and end of the school year. As to data collection and entry, the school collaborated with us to provide official student records. They also provided these critical academic outcome data at the end of each school term so that we could discern in vivo the flow of students' experience through middle school.

The structures, routines, and schedule of institutions can be rigid. For this reason, collaboration is essential in the implementation stage. Events and timelines external to the research approach would have threatened experimental control if not for continual support from institutional allies. At one point, for example, after months of preparation, we drove an hour to school in order to administer the intervention prior to a big test, only to discover upon arrival that the school had declared a snow day. Thankfully, the school personnel, worked with us to reschedule the intervention on the new test day.

The Aftermath: Entering, Analyzing, and Presenting the Data

We underestimated the importance of many tasks in our planning, but none so much as data entry and consolidation. The entering, transferring, checking, and rechecking of each student's data took an inordinate amount of time and labor from our team and school collaborators. We repeatedly failed to request sufficient funding to do this task in a timely way. We got better at data consolidation over time. We came to see designing the longitudinal data file as a craft—even an art. The ideal was to make the data file self-explanatory to a future investigator who knew nothing of the project. In the conscientious and artful hands of our research assistants, these files became not data banks but quantitative biographies.

In addition, colleagues provided help in the initial analytic stage of the project. Were there additional factors that we needed to take into account in our analyses? It was self-evident that the impact of the teacher on a student's performance matters, as some teachers are more effective than others. In addition, it was evident that a student's previous performance contributes to their later academic performance, and there was also evidence that performance also can vary by gender. Later, in the data analytic stage, we became worried that our strategy might be lacking in necessary rigor, given the way that students were nested within classrooms. In response to our concern, we reached out to a national expert in field experimental methods, Professor Don Green, who provided helpful consultation with respect to our analytic strategy.

Naturally, we were pleased to show that an affirmation intervention could improve the academic performance of African-American students. However, we would have to replicate the effects. With the help of our now numerous collaborators throughout the school and beyond, we conducted the replication in the following year. During this time, we found ourselves in a curious situation. We wanted to be as sharing and transparent as possible when discussing the findings with the teachers, staff, and administration at the school, but we still could not disclose the details of the intervention because we wanted to maintain experimental control. We were very grateful that our school collaborators again displayed their commitment by having a great deal of trust and understanding when we gave a presentation conveying our key results, but few specifics about the intervention. We did this each year of the project, and despite the necessary ambiguity, it proved helpful to the school and to us.

Writing up our findings for publication marked the beginning of the next stage in our journey of taking knowledge first generated in a lab to a point where it could serve as a practice in schools. This initial phase of the dissemination stage of our journey entailed presenting the findings with our colleagues in both informal and formal settings, such as at lab groups and conferences.

It took about a year and a half of collaborative writing among everyone on our team before we finished our short report. Once published, our findings triggered a host of responses—some expected and others much less so.

Benefits of Social Psychologist–Practitioner Collaborations

Our collaboration with schools underscored how fruitful collaborating with people outside of one's specific discipline is. Whether it is with academics, scientists, or practitioners, collaboration not only deepens knowledge and understanding but also reinforces the distinctive lessons that one's own discipline offers to the goal of social and institutional reform.

During our collaboration with schools, it became obvious that few school practices are informed by robust experimental studies, or for that matter, by any data-driven analysis. This is particularly striking in light of the accountability movement in education circles. In carrying out initiatives like No Child Left Behind and Race to the Top, the federal government assumes that given enough incentive, it is up to the schools to figure out the best practices. But schools are complex social systems, with staffs that are often stretched to the breaking point. Most do not have the knowledge and methods to assess the impact of their practices on students accurately. As a consequence, it is not surprising that schools flit from one program to another, seldom able to discern what works and what does not. Indeed, research in social psychology on illusory correlation shows how badly people do at detecting real associations between events, and that they are even worse at discerning causation. Theories, intuitions, and politics often trump data. Indeed, in our experience, while an organization may collect data, it generally does not adequately analyze them. It is not hard to see how schools could come to be dominated by rampant subjectivity (even if well-meant) and self-interested analysis; see Wilson (2011) for a discussion of the many well-intended but costly practices used by schools throughout the United States. Clearly, a systematic method for determining best practices would prove truly helpful.

We were also struck by how foreign the idea of randomization—using chance to introduce a practice or treatment to some students and not others—was to gatekeepers at the school. In our work, we are still consistently confronted by this attitude in workplaces and schools. There is a risk that randomization will be undermined or rejected at every stage, often without our knowledge, by a well-meaning administrator. Chance is not what institutions cherish. It is seen as a violation of the cherished ethos of allocating reward and punishment based on merit, or as treating people like guinea pigs. Yet, to us, what seems worse is the perpetuation of the status quo, wherein reward and punishment are allocated in ways consistent with stereotypes and biases. Randomization breaks the normal and sometimes unjust relationship between input and output in a system.

Indeed, given that the practices used by teachers varied regularly, that a child's academic or even life trajectory could be changed as a function of the teacher they had, that the introduction of educational material (including textbooks) are staggered or done in a piecemeal manner, and that some schools receive more resources than others, this resistance to randomization seemed strange to us. It is difficult to maintain the belief that students' academic careers are determined by merit alone, rather than, in significant part, by chance. Worse, there is little likelihood that these events will be allocated in a way that could provide the opportunity to carry out a rigorous measure of their impact, like that provided when a practice is randomized.

Among the key benefits that social psychology can bring to collaboration is a systematic approach for gaining understanding of what is already happening in a school and why, and for programmatically introducing new practices. In collaboration with the practitioners and administrators on the front lines, who are well acquainted with many of the barriers in play, our methodologies and statistical tools can help to separate the signal from the noise, the wheat from the chaff—indeed, separate "common sense from common nonsense and make uncommon sense more common" (Stern, 1993, p. 1898).

By implementing rigorous methods, or simply instructing schools on how to evaluate the programs that they have implemented, this approach could help prevent the common practice of using untested or undertested interventions that are not only ineffective but counterproductive, such as Scared Straight and Dare (Wilson, 2011). One of the most troubling moments of our journey came when we analyzed whether programs that took place prior to our intervention had an impact on students. Among these was an intensive summer test-preparation program. After controlling for baseline variables, kids in the program performed better on the state achievement test than kids not in the program. Although not a controlled field experiment, the result provided compelling evidence of the program's efficacy. On informing a school official of this result, she told us that no one had known that the program was effective. We were told that after receiving a few complaints about the program from parents, the school board had eliminated it. The prevalence of untested, ineffective, and even counterproductive programs in schools is a problem (Wilson, 2011). But just as tragic is the termination of programs that change students' lives for the better, but whose impact goes unseen and unsung.

Another key contribution of social psychology is its insistence that methodological subtleties matter. The devil is in the details. Leon Festinger and Elliot Aronson were pioneers of this approach to experimental social psychology. They viewed method as an art, not just a science. It is not a process that simply requires defining conceptual variables in any which way and testing their relationship. Rather, good method requires attention to meaningful details in order to help ensure a compelling experience and impactful intervention. Small details can speak psychological volumes.

Consider, for example, how many lines children would have to write their responses on in the affirmation exercise's free response section. Too many, and children might be demoralized (Schwarz et al., 1991). Too few, however, and they might not have enough space to elaborate. Now consider how we discovered that low-income students did not understand what the word *values* meant. To avoid using alienating language that might undermine the affirmation exercise, we revised the instructions to refer to "things" that the child might find important. We were also careful to deliver and retrieve intervention materials after normal school hours, to avoid the possibility that any children would see a troop of adults dropping off boxes of packets at their school and link this strange event to the writing exercise they did in their class.

While field experiments are now conducted by other social sciences, they do not share the same degree of appreciation of the possibilities for subjective construal in a situation or the power that they can have in determining its impact. By contrast, social psychology pays attention to powerful but apparently irrelevant situational details that convey meaning. All of these unique aspects of our field came into sharp relief through our collaborations with outsiders.

Institutional Pressures Against Collaboration

Our experience has led us to see collaboration and, more generally, engagement in the wider social world as both ubiquitous and necessary for relevant and rigorous social science. By contrast, in much of the advice we have heard in the academy, the importance of collaboration is often unacknowledged. Although there have been many successful collaborations in our discipline, advice discouraging collaboration with colleagues is often given. This seems particularly true in the early careers of professors, when they need to demonstrate independence for tenure, or when collaborations with scholars in other disciplines seem to fall outside a predefined research agenda. The demands of having such an agenda block the influence of others not so invested in it. We lacked a commitment to a specific research agenda, which may have accounted for our openness to chance encounters, unexpected results, and serendipity. Whenever a senior colleague would ask, "Where do you see this work going?" we were tempted to answer, "To wherever the findings and our ongoing collaborations with our colleagues take us."

The academic profession also discourages collaboration in a subtler and often insidious way. It demands that a researcher's work be clearly distinct from that of others. Extensive collaboration, regardless of how successful and profound, is believed to put one at risk in the tenure process, as it is thought to obscure one's intellectual contribution. As one member of a university tenure committee put it to one of us, "[a]t some point, if the junior faculty member is serious, they have to stop all this collaboration and get down to work."

This injunction for independence has another cost. Applying the theories of others to a novel problem domain is discouraged. The individualistic criterion overrewards the generation of new explanatory constructs, novel reformulations, or repackaging of old explanatory constructs. There is a myopic concept of "novel theoretical contribution" that excludes expanding the explanatory reach of an existing theory. This is the case in spite of the fact that social psychologists of earlier eras did this very thing. Dissonance theory, for instance, was applied to topics ranging from rumor transmission to cult beliefs to abasement rituals.

Applying existing theories is currently a pervasive practice in other social sciences such as economics. As a result, this has a greater impact on social policy, as doing so shows the power of interventions and ideas that social psychologists pioneered in the 1940s and 1950s, such as the effects of decision defaults, reminders, and more generally, small situational channels that increase the ease of engaging in the desired behavior. Given the pressures of academic social psychology, attempting to set oneself apart is understandable. However, it can prove costly for both researchers and social psychology. No one gains when the chance of increasing our understanding of social psychological process and, more broadly, our understanding of the human condition is sacrificed to the drive for distinctiveness.

The insistence on such an individualistic criterion also discourages the multiple perspectives and interdisciplinary scholarship now known to be essential to progress in the sciences. For example, collaborations between social psychologists and biologists are advancing our understanding of how social environments affect health in lasting ways (Cacioppo & Patrick, 2008; Miller, Chen, & Cole, 2009; Taylor, 2010). Social psychology has distinguished itself as a hub social science, which the American Psychological Association (APA) defines as a science whose ideas sprocket outward to advance other sciences.

Ironically, in our own case, applying self-affirmation theory and stereotype threat research to actual classrooms took our journey to a new theoretical terrain, at the center of which was the question "How do social processes propagate their impact over time?" To answer this question, new constructs such as feedback loops, recursion, and sensitive periods assert their importance in social psychology (Cohen et al., 2009; Cohen & Sherman, 2014; Yeager & Walton, 2011).

Still other theoretical questions arose from our intervention study. For instance, what happens when teachers, students, and other stakeholders taking part in a study know the experimental hypothesis, as well as the theory and purpose of the intervention? We later explored this question in a series of studies with our collaborators David Sherman and Arielle Silverman, along with several other colleagues (Sherman et al., 2013). What dosage is sufficient to maximize a treatment's effects? One dose might not suffice, and too many exposures may dilute its impact. The pattern, frequency, and timing of a treatment over time may prove as important as the content of the treatment itself. In addition, how do we deal with the requirement that the assignment of any child to the treatment should not affect the outcome of another child (the stable unit treatment value assumption)? This may be unrealistic in a classroom, where children are constantly interacting with one another, so treatment effects can bleed over from one child to another. In fact, in certain cases, this would be a desirable outcome.

Still more new questions arise when the experimental method is applied in actual classroom settings, such as "How may the effects on individual psychology of a treatment affect the social climate of the classroom?" Using the same data set years later, we found that more treated minorities in a classroom improved the grades of the class as a whole (Powers, Cook, Purdie-Vaughns,

Garcia, Apfel, & Cohen, 2016). One need not start with a novel theory to arrive at novel theoretical contributions.

Conclusions

The journey that we have described here was always a collaborative effort involving those who worked directly with us, those whom we reached out to, and those who laid the groundwork for our research by providing not only a map for our journey, but also the inspiration and tools for embarking on it. To move the work forward in a chaotic school environment, we also had to find new collaborators at almost every stage.

This narrative relates only a part of this journey, which we are still taking. A cyclical process of administering the intervention, collecting and entering data, analyzing them, and then writing up findings still continues. Moreover, at this moment, we are still dealing with data produced by these studies and their implications in collaboration with new colleagues. This is possible because from the beginning, we took a long view of the work. It is a perspective that demands that we acknowledge the necessity for collaboration in order to accomplish any research.

■ REFERENCES ■

Adams, D. (1998). " Is there an artificial God? Retrieved from http://www.biota.org/people/douglasadams/

Aronson, E., & Bridgeman, D. (1979). Jigsaw groups and the desegregated classroom: In pursuit of common goals. *Personality and Social Psychology Bulletin, 5,* 438–446.

Asch, S. (1952). *Social psychology.* Englewood Cliffs, NJ: Prentice Hall Inc.

Bronfenbrenner, U. (1977). Toward an experimental ecology of human development. *American Psychologist, 31,* 513–531.

Cacioppo, J. T., & Patrick, W. (2008). *Loneliness: Human nature and the need for social connection.* New York, NY: W. W. Norton & Company.

Cohen, G. L., Garcia, J., Apfel, N., & Master, A. (2006). Reducing the racial achievement gap: A social-psychological intervention. *Science, 313,* 1307–1310.

Cohen, G. L., Garcia, J., Purdie-Vaughns, V., Apfel, N., & Brzustoski, P. (2009). Recursive processes in self-affirmation: Intervening to close the minority achievement gap. *Science, 324,* 400–403.

Cohen, G. L., & Sherman, D. K. (2014). The psychology of change: Self-affirmation and social psychological intervention. *Annual Review of Psychology, 65,* 333–371.

Grubb, W. N. (2009). *The money myth: School resources, outcomes, and equity.* New York, NY: Russell Sage Foundation.

Lewin, K. (1997). *Resolving social conflicts and field theory in social science.* Washington, DC: American Psychological Association. (Originally published in 1948)

Miller, G., Chen, E., & Cole, S. W. (2009). Health psychology: Developing biologically plausible models linking the social world and physical health. *Annual Review of Psychology, 60,* 501–524.

Powers, J. T., Cook, J. E., Purdie-Vaughns, V., Garcia, J., Apfel, N., & Cohen, G. L. (2016). Changing environments by changing individuals: The emergent effects of psychological interventions [Abstract]. *Psychological Science* Advanced online publication. Retrieved from http://pss.sagepub.com/content/early/2015/12/15/0956797615614591.abstract

Rokeach, M. (1973). *The nature of human values.* New York, NY: Free Press.

Ross, L. D., & Nisbett, R. E. (2011). *The person and the situation: Perspectives of social psychology.* London, England: Pinter & Martin Ltd.

Schwarz, N., Bless, H., Strack, F., Klumpp, G., Rittenauer-Schatka, H., & Simons, A. (1991). Ease of retrieval as information: Another look at the availability heuristic. *Journal of Personality and Social Psychology, 61*, 195–202.

Sherman, D. K., & Cohen, G. L. (2006). The psychology of self-defense: Self-affirmation theory. In M. P. Zanna (Eds.), *Advances in experimental social psychology,* Vol. 38, pp. 183–242. San Diego, CA: Academic Press.

Sherman, D. K., Hartson, K. A., Binning, K. R., Purdie-Vaughns, V., Garcia, J., Taborsky-Barba, S., . . . Cohen, G. L. (2013). Deflecting the trajectory and changing the narrative: How self-affirmation affects academic performance and motivation under identity threat. *Journal of Personality and Social Psychology, 104*, 591–618.

Steele, C. M. (1988). The psychology of self-affirmation: Sustaining the integrity of the self. In L. Berkowitz (Ed.), *Advances in experimental social psychology* (Vol. 21, pp. 261–302). New York, NY: Academic.

Steele, C. M. (2010). *Whistling Vivaldi and other clues to how stereotypes affect us.* New York, NY: Norton.

Steele, C. M., Spencer, S. J., & Aronson, J. (2002). Contending with group image: The psychology of stereotype and social identity threat. In M. P. Zanna (Ed.), *Advances in experimental social psychology* (Vol. 34, pp. 379–440). New York, NY: Academic.

Stern, P. (1993). A second environmental science: Human-environment interactions. *Science, 260*, 1897–1899.

Taylor, S. E. (2010). Mechanisms linking early life stress to adult health outcomes. *Proceedings of the National Academy of Sciences, 107*, 8507–8512.

Walton, G. M., & Cohen, G. L. (2007). A question of belonging: Race, social fit, and achievement. *Journal of Personality and Social Psychology, 92*, 82–96.

Walton, G. M., & Cohen, G. L. (2011). A brief social-belonging intervention improves academic and health outcomes of minority students. *Science, 331*, 1447–1451.

Wilson, T. D. (2011). *Redirect: The surprising new science of psychological change.* New York, NY: Little, Brown, and Company.

Wilson, T. D., & Linville, P. W. (1982). Improving the academic performance of college freshmen: Attribution therapy revisited. *Journal of Personality and Social Psychology, 42*, 367–376.

Yeager, D. S., & Walton, G. M. (2011). Social-psychological interventions in education: They're not magic. *Review of Educational Research, 81*(2), 267–301.

Chapter 19: The Program for Research on Black Americans: Team Science in the Study of Ethnic and Racial Influences

James S. Jackson[1]

Former Director, and Research Professor
Institute for Social Research
Daniel Katz Distinguished University Professor of Psychology
University of Michigan

This chapter is an opportunity for me to reflect on an interesting career spanning almost five decades, as a graduate student at the University of Toledo and Wayne State University, and later as a faculty member at the University of Michigan. The experiences in my training and professional career resulted in a long-term experiment within a largely White research university context in conducting team science research on race and ethnicity. Team science or collaborative science in social psychology, as in other areas of the social, biological, and physical sciences (e.g., Cooke & Hilton, 2015; Stokols, Shalini, Moser, Hall, & Taylor, 2008), is becoming the most prevalent form of research in all fields of science (Boyack, Klavens, & Borner, 2005; Cacioppo, 2007).

As discussed in this chapter, in the early 1970s (and perhaps it is even truer today), there were no alternatives except to embark upon a team science approach to studying the social, psychological, and material dimensions of

[1] The work reported in this chapter was supported by research grants from the National Institute of Mental Health, National Institute on Aging, National Institute on Drug Abuse, National Institute of Minority Health Disparities, National Science Foundation (NSF), MacArthur Foundation, Ford Foundation, Rockefeller Foundation, and Carnegie Corporation. Additional support was provided in the form of institutional and individual postdoctoral grants from the National Institute of Mental Health, National Institute on Aging, and the Rockefeller and MacArthur Foundations. I would also like to acknowledge the contribution of the numerous social scientists and students who have participated in this program of research. This list includes, but is not limited to, my colleagues and friends, Phillip J. Bowman, Gerard Lemaine, Ronald Brown, Letha Chadiha, Linda M. Chatters, Rose Gibson, Ishtar Govia, Gerald Gurin, Shirley J. Hatchett, Harold W. Neighbors, Robert J. Taylor, and Belinda M. Tucker.

life for Black Americans. The type of interdisciplinary perspective required to study the complexity of life for a discriminated-against race or ethnic group in the United States demanded cooperation among scholars bridging the broad range of the social and behavioral sciences. Knowledge and research from economics, psychology, sociology, anthropology, political science, history, medicine, and public health were needed for understanding the circumstances and lived experiences of African Americans. Our modest goal was to highlight the nature and meaning of these lived experiences by "giving voice to Black Americans." We did not know then that 30 years later, team science would be "all the rage." But in the 1970s, psychology was not the most hospitable place for large-scale team science projects, especially those focused on race and ethnicity. On the other hand, the Institute for Social Research (ISR) was founded 65 years ago based upon multidisciplinary, collaborative team science principles. Thus, ISR became a more viable and welcoming home for this research project than the psychology department at the University of Michigan.

Even so, the challenges posed in terms of student, faculty, institutional, disciplinary, external funding sponsors, and related factors to conducting team science on race and ethnicity at ISR have been notable over this nearly four-decade period. During this time, many things have changed. Research on culture (including race and ethnicity) has become more acceptable within psychology. The larger academic community, however, remains largely a White, ethnocentric environment.

I feel fortunate that I have been able to do so many interesting scientific and educational projects. However, one always laments what one could have done, absent structural and individual barriers to success. And in many ways, that is the conundrum faced by most Black academics, whether five decades ago or today. In environments fraught with institutional barriers, how does an individual Black academic obtain a firm grasp on his or her strengths, liabilities, and contributions? One is always facing the attributional ambiguity of what are personal failings or limitations and what are actual environmental impediments to success (J. L. Jackson, 2015).

For example, over the last few years, I have had occasion to speak with many of my faculty colleagues at Michigan upon the occasion of their retirement. One of the most interesting conversations included an apology from one person about what happened in 1971 when I was hired as the first full-time Black faculty member (at the time, the late Dr. Floyd Wiley was a part-time faculty member and Dr. Ewart Thomas was part-time in the psychology department and full-time in the Residential College) in a very large, all-White department. This person admitted that he opposed my appointment not on any individual basis, but solely because he did not believe that any Black person deserved to be a full faculty member in his outstanding department. This, of course, was not a revelation since I had known about this person and many others soon after I chose to come to Michigan. But it was interesting that after 40 years, there came a confession. I guess it is good for the soul.

Of course, the department has changed much over the years—it even recently had a Black chair. I don't claim any singular credit for this transformation, but it does lead one to lament: "When do I stop feeling like Jackie Robinson?" And it is this "the first one" phenomenon that is maddening. So to be explicit at the outset, the creation of a team science approach to the study of race and ethnicity within psychology was necessary both because of the broad array of social and behavioral science approaches needed to study the phenomena, *and* the social and psychological support and encouragement that a community of scholars and students could afford.

In addition to my training in physiological psychology and as an experimental social psychologist in graduate school, early on in my career, I had cause to participate in many activities with the fledgling Association of Black Psychologists (ABPsi) and the Black Student Psychological Association (BSPA), becoming national president of both organizations. Out of these roles, as well as the work of pioneers like Reginald Jones and Robert Williams, grew a perspective on what constituted "Black Psychology." To summarize, in the growth of Black Psychology, three major themes were consistently emphasized: (1) the development of research strategies that proceed from real-life needs rather than from theoretical imperatives, (2) the development of collaborative relationships with Black communities, and (3) the development of new research competencies and roles that will facilitate the advancement of collective Black interests (e.g., R. Jones, 1980). These same principles also guided the development of community psychology (J. S. Jackson, 1991), an area that has strong ties to Black Psychology.

To summarize what occurred at the University of Michigan, a number of historically important events, including an active BSPA and state chapters of the ABPsi, and, most important, a critical mass of bright, energetic Black graduate students and a receptive environment (largely contributed to by the unwavering intellectual and material assistance of Patricia and Gerald Gurin), culminated in 1975 in the formation of the Program for Research on Black Americans (PRBA) at the University of Michigan's Institute for Social Research. For many reasons, including a less supportive intellectual environment in the Department of Psychology, the need for true interdisciplinary perspectives on conducting social science research on the Black population, and the Black experience in the United States, as well as the support of ISR researchers like Robert Kahn, Steven Whitey, and Robert Zajonc, the ISR (an early pioneer and adopter of team science) was a much more receptive environment for developing the PRBA.

The purpose of this organized effort was to provide a scholarly, interdisciplinary, and basic social science research group that was sensitive to cultural and system factors in the social, psychological, economic, and political behaviors of Black Americans. The sample survey was selected as the primary empirical research vehicle. This was not necessarily because of its social scientific preeminence or hegemony over any other empirical research method, but instead because of its potential power in generating large quantities of representative data (Schuman & Kalton, 1985), links to public policy formulation, and the experience and background of the program founders at the ISR (J. S. Jackson, Caldwell, & Sellers, 2012; J. S. Jackson, Tucker, & Bowman, 1982).

Giving Voice to Black People

This chapter provides a brief description of the activities of the PRBA, its evolution, and the development of basic principles undergirding empirical social science research relevant to the study of Black Americans. Although not solely encompassing all my interests as a Black academician at the University of Michigan, it played a very significant role. The PRBA was and is an effort to develop a programmatic embodiment of the philosophical and conceptual foundations of these principles. The empirical research conducted within PRBA is driven by theory and the research literature. Attempts, however, have always been made to develop research strategies that proceed from real life rather than from theoretical imperatives in order to create collaborative arrangements and sensitive relationships with local communities (Bowman, 1983) and provide an enduring research training base with adequate physical and human resources and the potential for the continuing production of new scholars from Black and other ethnic groups (J. S. Jackson, Tucker, et al., 1982; J. S. Jackson et al., 2012 et al., 1982, 2012).

The basis of the initial development of PRBA lay in several major assumptions: (1) that there has been a long history of poorly conceptualized, poorly conducted, and poorly interpreted research on Blacks (J. Jones, 1983); (2) much of what is unique to Black Americans has been subjugated to deficit and "culture of poverty" theorizing (Jenkins, 1984; J. Jones, 1983); and (3) the lack of Black empirically trained social scientists has contributed to the first two points (J. Jones, 1983). Unfortunately, while the PRBA has worked on progressing in all these areas, the field itself still lags.

At the time of the creation of the PRBA, previous and ongoing studies of Black American adults, adolescents, and children were typically restricted to limited and special populations. National data on Blacks were usually gathered in the course of surveys of the general population. This procedure potentially introduces serious biases in the representation of Blacks since they are distributed geographically in a different way from the total U.S. population. This "oversampling" approach to data collection in national samples of Blacks also meant that concepts, measures, and methods developed in the study of the White majority were used without reflection in the study of Black Americans. There was little theoretical or empirical concern about the appropriateness of this simplistic, comparative approach (J. S. Jackson, 1991; J. S. Jackson et al., 2012). For the most part, prior national studies were not informed by an awareness of and appreciation for the unique cultural experiences of Blacks in the United States; and concepts, measures, and research procedures that reflect this uniqueness had not been developed or employed (J. S. Jackson, Tucker, et al., 1982; J. S. Jackson et al., 2012).

Partly because of the small, nonrepresentative samples of Blacks, national surveys were not able to go beyond superficial analyses of gross Black–White comparisons. This cursory treatment of and lack of attention to the cultural context of Black life in the United States in survey instruments and procedures served to perpetuate a simplistic scientific and policy view of the Black experience. Thus, poor science (J. Jones, 1983) and poor application dictated the need for data from large, well-designed national probability sample surveys that address major areas of the life experiences of Black Americans in a culturally sensitive manner (J. S. Jackson, Tucker, et al., 1982).

Over the past 40 years, members of the PRBA at the ISR have been involved in the development, execution, and analyses of data from numerous major studies. This research has attempted to address the major limitations in the existing literature (J. S. Jackson, Tucker, et al., 1981; J. S. Jackson et al., 2012).

NSBA

During the course of the first major project (i.e., the National Survey of Black Americans [NSBA]), three new questionnaires and related materials were completed. Recruitment and training procedures were developed, and a national team of Black interviewers was located and trained. It is important to note that the establishment of this well-trained team of Black interviewers facilitated subsequent PRBA research efforts and was important in pioneering methods and approaches that have been subsequently applied in data collection efforts (J. S. Jackson, Tucker, et al., 2012).

New sampling methods and related materials were developed that had an important influence on subsequent procedures used for sampling low-density population groups. Both the Wide Area Screening Procedure (WASP) and Standard Listing and Screening Procedure (SLASP) provided new methods for scientifically locating and selecting Blacks in rigorous multistage, geographical area sampling methods—methods that can be readily applied to different racial ethnic groups, as well as more traditional sampling problems (J. S. Jackson et al., 2012). In addition, inclusion rules, field procedures, and an efficient and novel sampling process to obtain random samples of families called the *Three-Generation Family Study* were developed by the staff so probability selections could be made based upon information from the original NSBA cross-section respondents. Notably, section B of the Re-interview in the 1979–1980 NSBA study provided family structure information for the multiplicity sampling process that we developed. This process permitted appropriate probability weights to be applied to the members of the resulting three-generation and elderly samples in the family study (Jackson & Hatchett, 1986).

In many ways, the scope of the NSBA data is represented by the summary of the questions asked in the interviews. The questionnaires cover multiple dimensions of the lives of Black Americans, many that had gone either underexplored or unexplored in earlier studies (e.g., the distribution and nature of experiences of racism and discrimination). The questionnaires took over two years to develop, and conceptually and empirically were based upon the multimethod, multitrait framework of Campbell and Fiske (1959), including focus groups, in-depth personal interviews, systematic observations, Q-Sort techniques, and a host of regional and national empirical pretests in varied Black communities.

It was discussed earlier in this chapter that many unique possibilities derive from the fact that these initial NSBA data were based on a large and nationally representative sample of Black Americans. Scientific knowledge, as well as public policies based on this knowledge, has been limited by a lack of appreciation of the heterogeneity of Black American life. The need to examine this heterogeneity is also relevant for subgroups within the Black population, particularly those that are likely to experience special problems. For example, much has been written about the unique challenges facing Black elderly (e.g., Taylor & Taylor, 1982). Because of the Three-Generation Family Study, a very large national probability sample of the elderly existed, which permitted complex multivariate analyses of their problems, strengths, and coping strategies (e.g., J. S. Jackson, Chatters, & Neighbors, 1982).

The scope and breadth of the NSBA interviews provided the opportunity to trace the interrelationships of events and reactions in different significant areas of Black people's lives. In the employment area, for example, the broader life implications of a history of dead-end jobs, a breakdown in the nuclear family, or a disabling illness can be very different for Blacks in the rural South than for those in the inner cities of the North, or for younger versus older cohorts (Bowman, Jackson, Hatchett, & Gurin, 1982). There are only a few other studies in the literature that have had a comprehensiveness of coverage that even to this day is comparable to that of the NSBA, but these other studies have been done on very limited and narrow segments of the Black population (usually poor Blacks in northern cities). It is often difficult in these latter studies to estimate to what extent the findings are generalizable beyond the particular settings and groups studied.

A major theme that served to integrate the different parts of the NSBA interviews is that of "social support" (Taylor, Jackson, & Quick, 1982). This is a concept particularly relevant to a study of Black Americans. Some writers have pointed to the breakdown of the Black family and social networks; others have commented on the strength of the Black extended family and pointed to family and friendship networks as providing major supports to Black Americans facing the difficult conditions in their lives (Taylor, 1990). There was an extensive focus on social support in the original NSBA study. It is not only the subject of the section of the interview specifically devoted to family and friendships, but it also appears as an aspect of other sections as well: the support provided by people in one's church (Taylor & Chatters, 1986), the availability of informal support when one is ill (Chatters, Taylor, & Jackson, 1985), the people one depends upon when dealing with the stresses of everyday life, and the use of informal resources when facing major personal problems in one's life (Neighbors & Jackson, 1984).

Analysis of these data provided invaluable input into the ongoing debate on the Black family and the functions that family and social networks perform in Black life in the United States (Hatchett & Jackson, 1993). In addition to their general interest, these findings have been particularly significant because of their policy relevance. For example, existing data suggest that Black Americans use formal psychological resources less than do White Americans. It has been hypothesized that one reason for this is that Black Americans rely more on family and friends for help with their personal problems. Others suggest, in fact, that those who use less formal resources turn less often to friends and family, not more often. Any assessment of what constitutes an unmet need would obviously depend on whether people who do not use formal resources have and use available alternative informal resources (Neighbors & Jackson, 1984).

The capability to test assumptions about the Black family, as well as the socialization and transmission processes within it, was facilitated by the Three-Generation Family data (J. S. Jackson & Hatchett, 1986). There are only a few data sets available, and certainly none on a large-scale national sample of Black families, which would have allowed the exploration of whether the transmission of life conditions is fostered by socialization processes within the family, as well as the nature of some of these processes (Bowman & Howard, 1985; J. S. Jackson, Chatters, et al., 1982).

The most recent of the PRBA national studies (2001–2005), the National Survey of American Life (NSAL), was designed to be a two-decade follow-up to the NSBA; field work ended in the United States in late 2002 (Jackson et al., 2004). Several aspects of the NSAL were different from earlier, national epidemiologic studies, as well as extending the prior NSBA and other PRBA studies.

First, the survey included a large, nationally representative sample of African Americans (about 4,000), something neither the Epidemiological Catchment Area (ECA) study nor the National Comorbidity Study (NCS) was able to do. Moreover, the NSAL contains a sample that also represents Caribbean Blacks (about 1,600) and important demographic subgroups within both the African-American and Afro-Caribbean populations (e.g., 1,500 African-American and Afro-Caribbean adolescents 13–17 years of age) and smaller samples of adult non-Hispanic Whites, (about 1,000), Hispanics (about 500), and Asian Americans (about 500). As a result, this project permits the exploration of similarities and differences among various subgroups within the Black American population, as well as comparisons with non-Hispanic Whites, and limited but important comparisons with other major groups of color. For example, these types of analyses are critical, due to the major changes that have occurred in family structure and function over the last 40 years (e.g., Farley, 1996; Frey, 2015; Jackson, 2000).

Second, the use of multiple, theoretically driven measures of socioeconomic status (SES; e.g., Krieger, Williams, & Moss, 1997) resulted in better assessment of this status being available for data analyses. Even when racial differences are explained by statistical adjustment for SES, the nature of status differences across groups makes the interpretation of such findings difficult.

Third, this NSAL study successfully employed the novel geographical screening procedures developed in the NSBA. Once again, these methods ensured that every Black American household in the continental United States had a known probability of selection (Hess, 1985; J. S. Jackson et al., 2012; J. S. Jackson, Chatters, et al., 1982).

Fourth, this study addressed the *heterogeneity of experiences* across ethnic groups within the Black population. Most prior research on African Americans has lacked adequate sample sizes to systematically address this ethnic variation. For example, the NSAL's incorporation of Blacks of Caribbean descent has permitted empirical analyses of issues never before addressed.

Fifth, this study not only assesses the presence of physical health and mental disorders, but also examines levels of impairment, improving on a major limitation of the data gathered in previous national mental health surveys.

Sixth, all respondents were selected from segments selected in proportion to the African-American and Afro-Caribbean populations, making this the first national sample of peoples of different race and ethnic groups who live in the same contexts and geographical areas as Blacks.

Continuing Inequality Linked to Race and Ethnicity

Survey research focusing on racial and ethnic disparities in health and psychopathology, as well as on within-group differences among Black Americans, is important because of the precarious economic and social situations of many Americans of color. In addition, there are differences across race/ethnic groups over and above considerations of SES. Explorations of these additional differences (e.g., acculturation, values, unequal treatment, health behaviors, etc.) can underscore just how much race and ethnicity matter in terms of explaining differences in outcomes at every level of SES (e.g., Williams & Jackson, 2000). As noted earlier, not all disparities reflect disadvantages for ethnic groups of color. These patterns are not well understood. Despite the impressive advances in knowledge concerning the assessment of national distributions of health and mental health disparities, the prevalence of psychological distress, and help-seeking behavior, our knowledge of the mental and physical health of African Americans and other Black subgroup populations remains meager. The NSAL survey addressed many of these limitations.

This brief summary of the research and data collections of the PRBA does not do justice to the major underlying dynamics of attempting to focus on noncomparative race research. In the early days of the formation of the PRBA, a great deal of criticism (and, frankly, skepticism) emanated from the ISR and around the country. Many of my then–more senior colleagues openly questioned the value of conducting research on an ethnic racial population without making explicit comparisons to the non-Hispanic White population. The PRBA team had persisted for many years in the belief that a nonrace comparative focus was valuable and even essential for many research questions, including being able to convince a skeptical funding agency (NIMH, in this case) of the value of the project.

All of this culminated early in the project, with a plenary research session at the ISR in 1977 where I was asked to speak to the assembled social scientists to argue why this approach was scientifically defensible. Even the strong assistance of Gerald Gurin did not diminish the importance of this meeting, and since the PRBA is now 40 years old, the defense must have succeeded. Of course, the argument addressed the nature of the research questions and why many of these questions have little to nothing to do with comparisons to Whites. In fact, we argued that trying to frame all social scientific research questions in race-comparative terms actually did a disservice to the questions.

While we were able to argue forcefully enough to conduct the first national survey, NSBA and the NSAL (although it had an ethnic/race comparative design), this question has never really gone away. Over the years, this issue has returned in different forms to dissuade young scientists from embarking on nonrace-comparative research in their attempts to understand the cultural, economic and social dimensions of life in the United States for Americans of African descent.

Research Training and Mentoring

In addition to the research objectives of the PRBA, it has always been a major goal to provide rigorous and systematic social science training at all levels. In fact, we believe strongly that mentorship and training is at the heart of any team science project. This is especially true for a project like the PRBA that has attempted to build effective teams of underrepresented groups. Early on, because of the lack of racial and ethnic minority researchers in the social and behavioral sciences, we attempted to provide a training vehicle for the production of social scientists. To this end, training activities are included as an integral part of the PRBA research projects.

In the beginning, there was no question that training had to be fundamental to the work of the research team. In fact, the majority of the researchers were graduate students and during the course of the first 10 years or so of the project, it was these graduate students who formed the largest and most important infrastructure for research. Research teams consisting of the meager number of PhD level staff (e.g., Gurin, Jackson, Tucker and Bowman), augmented by a national advisory panel from around the country who participated as full partners in the research and writing, made the process work; but there was nothing easy about it.

The PRBA was a naturally formed multidisciplinary group. Students were drawn from a broad array of departments and colleges. The formation of preliminary examination and doctoral committees was always a contested affair. It wasn't until well into the 1990s, as more students from the project were hired as junior faculty across the university (in the Medical School, Social Work, Public Health, Psychology, and other departments), that many of these problems eased. That is not to say that they ever fully disappeared, but the growth in numbers of junior and later tenured faculty in social work, psychology, sociology, public health, and other areas resulted in a cadre of faculty that were both tightly and loosely bound to the PRBA, who provided assistance in both its training and research goals. Support for these training activities was obtained from the research itself, individual postdoctoral fellowships, and postdoctoral institutional grants from the National Institutes of Health (NIH). Without this external validation from the federal research infrastructure, I am not sure we would have been successful.

Since the beginning of the program, over 250 graduate students, 150 postdoctoral scholars, and numerous undergraduates have participated in PRBA research projects. As indicated earlier, many of the postdoctoral scholars and graduate students trained in the program now form the core of the primary research team. Others have assumed positions in industry, research, and academic institutions throughout the country. One highlight has been the Summer Training Program, designed to bring research scholars to the ISR for up to 2 months to work on the data sets and produce completed analytic papers. These have had a thematic format over the years.

Early on, the focus was on issues of coping with stress in Black Americans. In subsequent years, a substantive topic has been the roles and resources of Black elderly. And, in many of these years, psychiatric epidemiology, mental health and disorders, and help-seeking behavior among Black Americans formed core areas of interest. Historically, one set of criticisms directed toward PRBA was the large number of edited books. One reason for this approach was to make sure that the large number of graduate students and postdoctoral scholars received credit for their input into the program.

Conclusions

The PRBA is the oldest currently operating social science research team devoted to the collection, analysis, and interpretation of data based upon national and regional probability samples of Black Americans. Based upon the nature of available mentors, role models, and a prevailing hostile environment to the work, without the effective development of a team science approach, the PRBA would not have been possible in the mid-1970s. The work completed thus far suggests that findings from analyses and writings on the NSBA and NSAL data sets will be of major scientific value and relevance to social policy issues (J. S. Jackson & Williams, 2003). Both the quality and the precision of the national cross section and three-generational samples make the results immensely important to social scientists and policymakers. The adult cross-section data permit, for the first time, national estimates to be made on the status and life situation of Black Americans across the entire range of socioeconomic and other demographic groupings in the population.

Complementing the types of analyses possible in the cross-section data set, the three-generation data provide an opportunity to analyze more fully two important at-risk subpopulations—Black elderly and Black youth. The three-generation study produced national samples of both groups that have permitted important analyses on their social, psychological, and structural statuses. An added opportunity is presented by the analyses potentially provided by a within-family lineage, three-generation sample. Analyses of this sample permit an assessment of family socialization patterns, economic and social transmission across generations, generational similarity and change, and for the first time in a data set of national scope on Blacks, the opportunity to causally assess parental and family social and economic contributions to the growth and development of children and grandchildren (J. S. Jackson & Hatchett, 1986).

In addition to the substantive contribution of the studies, as described earlier, we have had to develop novel and unique survey sampling and questionnaire methods. These methods are of general utility and make an important contribution to future surveys, particularly sampling of minorities and other high-visibility, low-density geographical groups. The development of these procedures permitted Blacks to be sampled for the first time in a cost-effective way that assured each and every Black household in the continental United States an equal probability of selection. In addition, the application of multiplicity sampling procedures contributed to, for the first time in any population group, a three-generation national probability sample. These large national probability samples, coupled with detailed, culturally relevant, and extensive questionnaires, make this research project unique in the social and behavioral science study of Black Americans.

As discussed earlier in this chapter, the PRBA staff also utilized the research described here and employed in subsequent studies as a fertile training ground and locus of intellectual interchange and development. Over its 40-year history, as also was noted earlier, the program has employed or been involved intensively with hundreds of graduate students and Black scholars from a wide array of disciplines.

Thus, these studies have attracted and focused the attention of a large number of Black professionals, from a large number of social science disciplines, on scientific and public policy concerns of the Black American population. Moreover, the research and related activities have involved training large numbers of postdoctoral scholars, doctoral students, and support staff in the methods and techniques of survey research; PRBA has significantly contributed to the developing (but still small) pool of Black social scientists in the United States. It is hard to imagine a better example of the virtues and potential of a long-term team social science project (Stokols et al., 2008).

For example, the breadth of areas and issues addressed allows more definitive scientific scrutiny of hypotheses regarding Blacks that have been advanced but never adequately tested. Issues of coping and adaptation (Bowman, 1984; Neighbors, Jackson, Bowman, & Gurin, 1983), family structure (Hatchett & Jackson, 1993; Hunter, 1997; Taylor, 1986), educational experiences (Hatchett & Nacoste, 1984), race attitudes and identity development (Allen & Hatchett, 1986; Jackson et al., 1981; Bowman & Howard, 1985), social support (Chatters, Taylor, & Jackson, 1985), and nontraditional economic networks (Jackson & Gibson, 1985) are only some of the areas that have been addressed in analyses of the NSBA and related PRBA data sets. PRBA research on physical health, mental health, employment, family life, individual and group identification, and political behavior provided the first in-depth investigation of these issues in large, representative samples of the entire Black population (J. S. Jackson, 1991; J. S. Jackson & Williams, 2003; J. S. Jackson et al., 2012). Scientifically, the results of these studies are having a significant influence on current theorizing about Blacks, as well as the content and direction of future research. The inclusion of many policy-relevant questions provides, for the first time, individual and group opinions and feelings that fully represent the breadth and diversity of Black people located in all walks of life across the entire United States.

Complementing the types of analyses possible in the cross-section NSBA data set, as noted earlier, the three-generation data have provided an opportunity to more fully analyze two important at risk subpopulations—the Black elderly and Black youth. Analyses of this sample have permitted an assessment of family socialization patterns, economic and social transmission across generations, generational similarity and change, and for the first time in a data set of national scope, the opportunity to assess parental and family social and economic contributions to the growth and development of children and grandchildren (J. S. Jackson, & Hatchett, 1986).

Although the National Black Young Adults (NBYA) study (Bowman, Gurin, & Howard, 1984), the National Black Election Studies (NBES) (Gurin, Hatchett, &

Jackson, 1989; J. S. Jackson, Gurin, & Hatchett, 1984), the National Studies of Race and Ethnic Pluralism (J. S. Jackson, Hutchings, Wong, Brown, & Elms, 2008), the Americans Changing Lives Study (ACL), the Detroit Area Studies, the Prevalence of Mental Disorders in Michigan Prisons, the NCAA Study of Social and Group Experiences (J. S. Jackson, et. al., 2002), and the new NSAL were not detailed fully in this chapter, their development and execution share the values, assumptions, and procedures as described here for the NSBA and other studies. For example, in examining how cultural, racial, and ethnic factors influence the nature and expression of productive activities and their antecedents and consequences over the life course (J. S. Jackson, 2001), we have ongoing collaborations with many other programs of research at ISR (and, in fact, around the country and world).

PRBA research continues to make major contributions to the general investigation of how social, cultural, and other contextual factors relate to the ways in which racial status and racialized treatment affect the behavior, physical and mental health, attitudes, and values of Blacks in the United States. This research has focused particularly on the role of ethnicity, race, and sociocultural factors in shaping theoretical and empirical developments in the understanding of human social behavior more generally (J. S. Jackson, 1991; J. S. Jackson & Williams, 2003). Therefore, despite the challenges of a less-than-supportive environment initially, lack of a well-trained cadre of social scientists, lack of consistent funding sources and streams, and some (especially early) resistance to a team science framework, the PRBA has been a successful long-term experiment in social psychological collaborative research.

■ REFERENCES ■

Allen, R. L., & Hatchett, S. J. (1986). The media and social reality effects: Self and system orientations of Blacks. *Communication Research, 13*, 97–123.

Bowman, P. J. (1983). Significant involvement and functional relevance: Challenge to survey research. *Social Work Research, 19*, 21–27.

Bowman, P. J. (1984). Provider role strain, coping resources, and life happiness: A national study of Black fathers. In A. W. Boykin (Ed.), *Empirical research in Black psychology* (pp. 9–19). Rochester, MI: Oakland University.

Bowman, P. J., Gurin, G., & Howard C. (1984). *A longitudinal study of Black youth: Issues, scope, and findings.* Ann Arbor Institute for Social Research, University of Michigan.

Bowman, P. J., & Howard, C. (1985). Race-related socialization, motivation, and academic achievement: A study of youth in three generation families. *Journal of the American Academy of Child Psychiatry, 24*, 134–141.

Bowman, P. J., Jackson, J. S., Hatchett, S. J., & Gurin, G. (1982, Autumn). Joblessness and discouragement among Black Americans. *Economic Outlook USA*, pp. 85–88.

Boyack, K. W., Klavans, R., & Borner, K. (2005). Mapping the backbone of science. *Scientometrics, 64*, 351–374.

Cacioppo, J. T. (2007). The rise in collaborative psychological science. *APS Observer, 20*(9). Retrieved from http://www.psycholologicalscience.org/observer/getArticle.cfm?id=2228

Campbell, D. T., & Fiske, D. W. (1959). Convergent and discriminant validation by the multitrait-multimethod matrix. *Psychological Bulletin, 56*(2), 81–105.

Chatters, L. M., Taylor, R. J., & Jackson, J. S. (1985). Aged Blacks' choices for an informal helper network. *Journal of Gerontology, 41*, 94–100.

Cooke, N. J., & Hilton, M. L. (Eds.). (2015). *Enhancing the effectiveness of team science.* Washington, DC: National Research Council.

Farley, R. (1996). *The new American reality: Who we are, how we got here, where we are going.* New York, NY: Russell Sage Foundation.

Frey, W. H. (2015). *Diversity explosion: How new racial demographics are remaking America.* Washington, DC: The Brookings Institution.

Gurin, P., Hatchett, S. J., & Jackson, J. S. (1989). *Hope and independence: Blacks' response to electoral and party politics.* New York, NY: Russell Sage Foundation.

Hatchett, S. J., & Jackson, J. S. (1993). African-American extended kin systems: An assessment. In H. P. McAdoo (Ed.), *Family ethnicity: Strengths in diversity* (pp. 90–108). Newbury Park, CA: Sage Publications.

Hatchett, S. J., & Nacoste, R. W. (1984). *Exposure to desegregated schooling: Profiling the experience of Black Americans* (Unpublished manuscript). Ann Arbor Institute for Social Research, University of Michigan.

Hess, I. (1985). *Sampling for social research surveys, 1947–1980.* Ann Arbor, MI: Institute for Social Research, University of Michigan.

Hunter, A. G. (1997). Living arrangements of African-American adults: Variations by age, gender, and family status. In R. J. Taylor, J. S. Jackson, & L. M. Chatters (Eds.), *Family life in Black America* (pp. 262–276). Thousand Oaks, CA: Sage Publications.

Jackson, Jr., J. L. (2015, January 26). What it feels like to be a Black professor. *Chronicle of Higher Education: The Chronicle Review.* Retrieved from http://chronicle.com/article/What-It-Feels-Like-to-Be-a/151323/

Jackson, J. S. (Ed.). (1991). *Life in Black America.* Newbury Park, CA: Sage Publications.

Jackson, J. S. (Ed.). (2000). *New directions: African Americans in a diversifying nation.* Washington, DC: National Policy Association.

Jackson, J. S. (2001). Changes over the life-course in productive activities: Black and White comparisons. In N. Morrow-Howell, J. Hinterlong, & M. Sherraden (Eds.), *Productive aging: Perspectives and research directions* (pp. 214–241). Baltimore, MD: Johns Hopkins University Press.

Jackson, J. S., Caldwell, C. H., & Sellers, S. (Eds.) (2012). *Researching Black communities: A methodological guide.* Ann Arbor University of Michigan Press.

Jackson, J. S., Chatters, L. M., & Neighbors, H. W. (1982). The mental health status of older Black Americans: A national study. *Black Scholar, 13*, 21–35.

Jackson, J. S., & Gibson, R. (1985). Work and retirement among Black elderly. In Z. Blau (Ed.), *Work, leisure, retirement and social policy* (pp. 193–222). New York, NY: JAI Press.

Jackson, J. S., Gurin, P., & Hatchett, S. J. (1984). *The National Black Election Study* (Unpublished manuscript). Ann Arbor: University of Michigan.

Jackson, J. S., & Hatchett, S. J. (1986). Intergenerational research: Methodological considerations. In N. Datan, A. L. Greene, & H. W. Reese (Eds.), *Intergenerational relations* (pp. 51–76). Hillsdale, NJ: Erlbaum Associates.

Jackson, J. S., Hutchings, V., Wong, C., Brown, R., & Elms, L. (2008). *Results from the national minority election study: Race and ethnic variation in political participation.* New York, NY: Carnegie Corporation.

Jackson, J. S., Keiper, S., Brown, K. T., Brown, T. N., & Manuel, W. J. (2002). Athletic identity, racial attitudes, and aggression in first-year Black and White intercollegiate athletes. In S. Ball-Rokeach, M. Gatz, & M. A. Messner (Eds.), *Paradoxes of youth and sport* (pp. 159–173). New York, NY: SUNY Press.

Jackson, J. S., McCullough, W., & Gurin, G. (1981). Group identity development within Black families. In H. McAdoo (Ed.), *Black families* (pp. 252–263). Beverly Hills, CA: Sage Publications.

Jackson, J. S., Torres, M., Caldwell, C. H., Neighbors, H. W., Nesse, R. M., Taylor, R. J., . . . Williams, D. W. (2004). The National Survey of American Life: A study of racial, ethnic, and cultural influences on mental disorders and mental health. *International Journal of Methods in Psychiatric Research, 13*(4), 196–207.

Jackson, J. S., Tucker, M. B., & Bowman, P. J. (1982). Conceptual and methodological problems in survey research on Black Americans. In W. Liu (Ed.), *Methodological problems in minority research* (pp. 11–40). Chicago: Pacific/Asian American Mental Health Center.

Jackson, J. S., & Williams, D. R. (2003). Surveying the Black American population. In J. S. House, T. Juster, R. L. Kahn, H. Schuman, & E. Singer (Eds.), *Telescope on society: Survey research and social science at the University of Michigan and beyond* (pp. 393–438). Ann Arbor: University of Michigan Press.

Jenkins, A. H. (1984). *The psychology of the Afro-American: A humanistic approach.* New York, NY: Pergamon Press.

Jones, J. M. (1983). The concept of race in social psychology. In L. Wheeler & P. Shaver (Eds.), *Review of personality and social psychology* (Vol. 4, pp. 117–150). Beverly Hills, CA: Sage Publications.

Jones, R. (Ed.). (1980). *Black psychology* (2nd ed.). New York, NY: Harper and Row.

Krieger, N., Williams, D. R., & Moss, N. (1997). Measuring social class in U.S. public health research: Concepts, methodologies, and guidelines. *Annual Review of Public Health, 18*, 341–378.

Neighbors, H. W., & Jackson, J. S. (1984). The use of informal and formal help: Four patterns of illness behavior in the Black community. *American Journal of Community Psychology, 12*, 629–644.

Neighbors, H. W., Jackson, J. S., Bowman, P. J., & Gurin, G. (1983). Stress, coping, and Black mental health: Preliminary findings from a national study. *Prevention in Human Services, 2*, 5–29.

Schuman, H., & Kalton, G. (1985). Survey methods. In G. Lindzey & E. Aronson (Eds.), *Handbook of social psychology* (Vol. 3, pp. 635–697). New York, NY: Wiley.

Stokols, D., Shalini, M., Moser, R. P., Hall, K. L., Taylor, B. K. (2008). The ecology of team science: Understanding contextual influences on transdisciplinary collaboration. *American Journal of Preventive Medicine, 35*(2S): S96–S115.

Taylor, R. J. (1986). Receipt of support from family among Black Americans: Demographic and familial differences. *Journal of Marriage and the Family, 48*, 67–77.

Taylor, R. J. (1990). Need for support and family involvement among Black Americans. *Journal of Marriage and the Family, 52*, 584–590.

Taylor, R. J., & Chatters, L. M. (1986). Church-based informal support among elderly Blacks. *The Gerontologist, 26*(6), 637–642.

Taylor, R. J., Jackson, J. S., & Quick, A. D. (1982). The frequency of social support among Black Americans: Preliminary findings from the National Surveys of Black Americans. *Urban Research Review, 8*, 1–4.

Taylor, R. J., & Taylor, W. H. (1982). The social and economic status of the Black elderly. *Phylon, 42*, 295–306.

Williams, D. R., & Jackson, J. S. (2000). Race/ethnicity and the 2000 census: Recommendations for African-American and other Black populations in the United States. *American Journal of Public Health, 90*(11), 1728–1730.

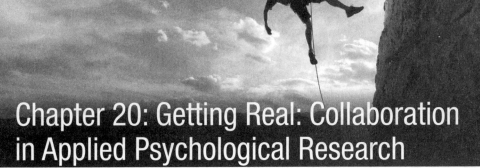

Chapter 20: Getting Real: Collaboration in Applied Psychological Research

Barbara Loken

David C. McFarland Professor of Marketing
Carlson School of Management
University of Minnesota

Deborah Roedder John

Professor and Curtis L. Carlson Chair in Marketing
Carlson School of Management
University of Minnesota

When we sat down to decide what our focus would be for this chapter, our first inclination was to write about our collaborations as coauthors on several papers in marketing journals, which are among our most cited publications. However, as we widened our discussion to include collaborations that each of us had with a whole variety of projects during our careers, we found that some of our best stories involved collaborations undertaken for the purpose of doing applied research. Barbara had extensive experience with applied research in the public health area, focusing on issues such as heart health and tobacco interventions. Debbie had a range of experiences with applied research sponsored by nonprofits and business organizations, working in diverse areas such as increasing milk consumption among children and developing better ways to measure brand images. Together, we had worked with collaborators from very different fields, including public health, medicine, food science, economics, and psychology. And we had worked with an array of funding agencies, companies, and industry groups.

Applied research is important work. It is different than the theoretical research that is the focus of many of our careers. The nature of the questions being asked often requires the researcher to translate the applied problem into more conceptual terms and to draw upon one's expertise to help answer the problem. But applied research also differs in the nature of the collaborators and interactions during the project. Many times, it involves a large team from very different academic areas of expertise, brought together for the purposes of leveraging that expertise for large-scale funded projects. Often, one has little or no history working with some of the research collaborators, and the personal relationships that sustain collaborations are not well developed. Having collaborators from different fields or areas of expertise means that the team members may not speak the same language, may not be familiar with the same methods and statistical tools, and may have different expectations and preferences regarding outcomes, including publication outlets. Yet little is written about how these collaborations take place, what the experience of applied research is like, and how it is different from the research that most of us have been trained to do.

So, in the end, we decided to write about our collaboration experiences in applied research. Our aim is to provide a better sense of the challenges and opportunities of applied research and, specifically, how to advance the applied question while at the same time meeting academic goals. It is not always possible to do both. The collaboration stories that we have chosen highlight the features, obstacles, and challenges of the collaborative effort and guide our understanding of the collaborative process in applied research. Barbara contributed stories about collaborations in public health research, Debbie contributed stories about collaborations with business organizations, and our final story describes a joint collaboration.

After relaying these stories, we conclude with a synthesis of some of the lessons that we learned from our experiences. In brief, we found our collaboration experiences to be more rewarding, more successful, and less frustrating when we:

■ Are less dependent on publication outcomes during posttenure rather than pretenure years

■ Choose academic partners with a common perspective

■ Have empathy for the applied academic perspective and appreciation for the applied researcher's approach to problems

■ Have someone on board to interpret conceptual language differences between academic areas

■ Have a smaller set of "core" collaborators in extremely large collaborative teams

■ Have prior familiarity with collaboration colleagues

■ Have upfront answers to questions about release of data by sponsoring agencies

We also learned that collaborations reap future rewards: They increase our network of colleagues and can lead to unexpected future connections and opportunities.

While we are both professors in a school of management, we believe that these lessons are equally applicable to researchers in psychology departments, who often are called upon to work on grants pertaining to applied issues (e.g., in areas of public health, medicine, and political messaging), with government agencies (e.g., in areas of product safety, health monographs, and product testimony), on legal cases (e.g., expert witness testimony), and with companies (e.g., in product design or advertising messages). We hope that our stories illuminate the nature of collaboration in the arena of applied research and the lessons that we have learned from them.

Collaborations in Public Health Research

Research on Heart Health Promotion

One of the projects that launched me (Barbara) into public health research in the 1980s was an immense communitywide campaign designed to reduce risk factors associated with heart disease. The Minnesota Heart Health Project was funded by the National Institutes of Health (NIH) and tripled the size of the University of Minnesota's department of epidemiology. The project's evaluation team solicited my help with survey design and project evaluation of the many short-term campaigns conducted within the broader heart disease campaign objectives. My expertise in psychological research and some limited laboratory research on tobacco warnings were the impetuses behind the request for my services.

I ended up taking a 5-year, half-time appointment, splitting my time between marketing (my home department) and epidemiology. I worked with a number of psychologists interested in applied issues of health promotion, as well as other public health and media communications researchers. We worked in teams of about four or five people, and these teams varied in composition depending on whether the focus was tobacco control, nutrition, physical activity, or overall impact of communications on campaign (brand) awareness.

My life became filled with meetings. Larger federally funded health projects often depend on collaborations such as these, and they are common in the public health discipline, where field research of health campaigns is highly valued. My interactions with my colleagues, some of which have continued to the present, and the applied field research experience, were career-changing (and I also reduced my consumption of junk food a bit). But this project was in some ways unsatisfying due to certain barriers.

What were they? The key challenges for me, a third-year assistant professor working toward tenure at a major university, were how to add a theoretical focus to cross-disciplinary research and where to publish it. My goal was to apply my theoretical interests in attitude theory and persuasion to heart health promotion and somehow come away with research that was publishable in leading journals of marketing or psychology. The topic of preventive health was not off-limits in these leading marketing journals, although at the time, it was more marginal than in the current academic culture. Publishing in public health and applied psychology journals was also not off-limits (and papers in them "counted"), but when my colleagues in the school considered whether my overall research record was tenurable, I knew that publication in these journals would not be sufficient to obtain tenure.

As a newbie to public health research, I diligently worked to incorporate my psychological theory and research interests with those of my public health colleagues, whose primary objective was, understandably, to assess applied campaign objectives. Finding compelling results for theories was difficult, and my inflated expectations were thwarted. Our goal in developing surveys (and we produced about 25 per year) was to make them short and punchy so that response rates could be maximized and results generalizable to the communities we were studying.

As I think back on the briefings with our highly trained survey team, who carefully reported back to us after they pretested our survey questions ("It's too long; people will drop out"), I recall being persuaded to reduce the number of multi-item measures of constructs. Multi-item scales lengthened our telephone surveys and made it difficult to maintain response rates above 90%, the project target. Similarly, I had hoped to include survey measures for components of the Fishbein–Ajzen theory of reasoned action (Martin Fishbein was my graduate school mentor), but these measures, too, were numerous and sounded repetitious to respondents. Three measures of attitude toward eating low-fat foods and three measures of intention to eat low-fat foods were too many for respondents, who viewed them as all the same. *Brevity* and *novelty* were the watchwords.

I also sought to conduct small, randomized experimental field studies with the media team. One of the studies that I conducted with public health professor John Finnegan and one of his students, Vish Viswanath, was a direct mail persuasion experiment in which we varied the degree to which heart-healthy messages were framed as favorable (focusing on the benefits of reducing heart disease risk factors) or unfavorable (focusing on the risks of not changing one's behavior), somewhat analogous to a promotion-focused versus prevention-focused message. Professional media pieces were developed and mailed to randomly selected sets of respondents in the community. We followed up a week later with a brief telephone survey. Our data analyses yielded a few interesting results, but because of our pared-down survey questions and single-item measures, we ultimately settled on a second-tier publication outlet for the paper.

Small-scale studies such as these, using the program infrastructure to complete the research (but often also giving it a dual purpose), resulted in disappointing outcomes. Certainly, in developing a tenurable record of publication, I found that theory-based laboratory experiments with theory-minded collaborators were far easier to design, implement, and frame for publication than the field research that resulted from this collaboration. Despite the inherent value of field research in public health, my experience involved compromises to reflect the team focus, and these collaborations, with multiple goals, were time-consuming.

However, all was not lost. For example, applied program research on the outcomes of a smoking cessation program resulted in a high-quality journal publication (Lando, Loken, Howard-Pitney, & Pechacek, 1990). This publication was not a small-scale, theory-based study but, rather, research that examined the effectiveness of a communitywide tobacco cessation program. The experience that I gained from working on this project increased my appreciation for the importance of population-based research and enhanced my understanding of the applied perspective.

In writing this chapter, I found myself wondering if I should have been more insistent that theory needed to be tested as part of the field research goals in order for me to join this team. The answer, I've decided, is no. The health project publications did not make or break my tenurable record of research (I had other publications in marketing and psychology independent of this project), and my home department regarded the real-world focus of the publications as an asset. Also, if I had made theory-based research a requirement early on, the team could not have met my expectations, and perhaps the collaboration would have ended. If that had happened, it would have been a great loss for me, both professionally and personally. Another important point is that the experience contributed to my interest in the area of preventive health, leading to my developing future collaborations with remarkable colleagues.

Lancet/NCI Monograph Projects

As a more mature researcher in the 2000s, I collaborated with colleagues on two publications: one was a monograph on the role of media in promoting and reducing tobacco use, for the National Cancer Institute (NCI), and the second was an integrative research review of mass media campaigns published in the medical journal *Lancet*. These experiences were the best that collaboration has to offer. At this point in my career, I was receptive to focusing on and enjoying the applied (rather than theory-testing) aspects of the projects. Also, my collaborators on both projects were seasoned researchers, and we all shared a common goal. Interestingly, it was Vish Viswanath, the PhD student who had collaborated with me years earlier on the heart health project and who now held a position at NCI, who recommended me for the NCI project. Collaborations shape our future, and our fortuitous connection to others often lead to future possibilities. When collaborations are successful, our network of colleagues widens, and this increases further interaction in subsequent years.

My colleagues included experts in the fields of public health, medicine, and communications. Our goals for both projects were to integrate evidentiary research and draw conclusions from the findings. While the research that we reviewed was a mixture of theoretically based and applied findings, and the evidence base included thousands (if not tens of thousands) of empirical studies, the goal was singular in focus.

In the NIH Monograph collaboration, we had five academic coeditors, who were leaders in contributing areas, and an academic representative from NCI. After drafting an outline of the monograph chapters (e.g., "Tobacco Companies' Public Relations Efforts: Corporate Sponsorship" and "Role of Entertainment Media in Promoting or Discouraging Tobacco Use"), we solicited chapter authors who were leaders in their respective areas. After the chapters were drafted, we had more than 50 scholars review drafts. Based on these reviews, the editors (sometimes, but not always, with the assistance of the original authors) revised the chapters.

Our team held conference calls once or twice a month for several years. We also had two gatherings in Chicago—the first to hash out chapter outlines with authors and the second with our editorial team to revise chapter drafts to address reviewers' comments and improve the overall integrated product. As a result of these many phone calls and two face-to-face gatherings, we developed a high degree of collegiality. We were good friends by the time of publication. Our leader, Ron Davis (who also served as president of the American Medical Association for a year during this period), took photos of our gatherings, kept us on track, was a great role model in collegiality, and organized for us a press release at the National Press Club in Washington, but tragically, he died of pancreatic cancer in the midst of this project. His death left a stronger bond among others on the team, and these connections led to future partnerships.

The editorial collaboration was satisfying in part because, as a seasoned researcher, my expectations were now more in line with reality. I expected to attain a high-quality review of the evidence on specific applied issues. As a tenured professor, my concern in finding an underlying theoretical focus was muted, and the publication was a known outcome (Davis, Gilpin, Loken, Viswanath, & Wakefield, 2008). In addition, my satisfaction stemmed from interacting with esteemed, fun colleagues and knowing that we were doing important work.

The project that led to publication in the *Lancet* began when I attended a World Conference on Tobacco and Health in Mumbai, at which three coeditors of the *NCI Monograph*, Vish, Melanie Wakefield (a tobacco control researcher), and I presented our findings in a plenary session. During the conference, I spent some time with Melanie, who suggested that we combine our different skills to write a paper on public health campaigns for the *Lancet*. She also asked Bob Hornik, an expert in communications and public health campaigns, to join us. This project (Wakefield, Loken, & Hornik, 2010) succeeded, largely due to the same factors described in the *NCI Monograph* collaboration. My coauthors and I had a common goal—to examine and review the evidence on the effectiveness of mass media campaigns in reducing health risks. We had the leadership of an esteemed colleague in public health and another proven coauthor who was a leading expert in media communications and health campaigns. And while I still had some outside pressure to publish a certain type of research, as I described earlier, I felt less pressure to do so than I had felt in my earlier, pretenure years.

For both the *NCI Monograph* and the *Lancet* projects, the collaborative teams distributed the work equitably to produce the best possible product. We kept on track in terms of deadlines, and all of us were motivated to contribute our fair share. On the NCI project, we maintained a public health perspective throughout, but we brought to bear our respective areas of expertise where appropriate. For example, my role was, in part, to oversee, revise, and write sections that described research findings on the use of public relations by tobacco companies to improve brand image, the use of tobacco marketing and brand management principles to sell tobacco products, depictions of tobacco in movies, and the variety of types of psychological theories used in developing tobacco-control research.

On the *Lancet* project, we all had expertise in the areas of mass media campaigns and were familiar with the related research literature, but we approached the problem from different angles, including marketing, communications, and public health. Our division of tasks and writing reflected our areas of expertise (cardiovascular health, nutrition, and physical activity campaigns, in my case), but since we broadened our focus to include all mass media campaigns, we also were able to learn about new areas that had not been our prior focus (for instance, I found out more about road safety, organ donation, and other topics).

Collaborations on Business Issues

Increasing Milk Consumption

My first joint research collaboration with business began when I (Debbie) was an assistant professor at the University of Wisconsin. At the time, my primary research stream was children's consumer behavior. My work sought to shed light on debates about whether young children were able to process and critically evaluate advertising messages, and whether advertising adversely influenced their product preferences and choices. My dissertation, for example, showed that television advertising shifted product choices more for younger than older children, which implied that younger children were more influenced by advertising than were their older peers. I was interested in theory-based research, and I had decided, as a matter of principle, not to collaborate or consult with companies marketing to children.

I made an exception, however, to collaborate with a nonprofit called the Wisconsin Milk Marketing Board (WMMB), an organization funded by dairy farmers to promote Wisconsin cheese and dairy products. They had been working with food scientists to develop different varieties of milk beverages—such as fruit-flavored milk—that would appeal to children and encourage them to consume more milk. Their goal was that by introducing more varieties of milk-flavored beverages, sales of milk products would increase and take market share from other beverage categories such as packaged juice drinks and soft drinks. However, they had not conducted consumer research with children, and they were concerned that children would simply substitute a new flavored milk beverage for another milk beverage, such as 2% milk, resulting in no overall increase in milk consumption. They hoped to see that children would substitute a new flavored milk for a packaged juice drink, which would increase milk sales. But they had no idea how to design an experiment to test this, and no expertise to formulate choice models to estimate the effects of interest.

I was a natural choice to work on this project, given my expertise in children's consumer behavior. In addition, I had a colleague in the marketing department, Ramesh Lakshmi-Ratan, who was a quantitative choice modeler with expertise in modeling consumer choice from sets of options. His expertise seemed a perfect fit for this project, so we joined forces and applied for WMMB funding to develop research that could provide useful information to WMMB on the likely success of flavored milk varieties for children of different ages, and contribute to theory-based research showing whether or not certain axioms from choice theory would apply to children of different ages (based on their categorization abilities). This seemed like a "marriage made in heaven," as the saying goes, and it seemed that our joint expertise would yield something far more interesting than either of us would be able to do alone.

Like a lot of marriages, this collaboration had some bumpy spots. We spent a huge amount of time trying to design a study that would serve the dual purpose of answering WMMB's questions and allowing us to publish results in a top marketing journal. I was surprised how hard it was to serve two taskmasters, the sponsoring organization (WMMB) and academic marketing journals. It would have been much easier to design a simple applied study to answer the question: If we make more milk varieties available, will children's total milk consumption increase? This, of course, would not be publishable in a top journal, and both Ramesh and I were assistant professors on the "publish or perish" track. So we decided to incorporate a more theoretical question into the project: If children pick a new product (such as flavored milk) when it is introduced into their choice set, will they consume less of similar products (milk beverages) or dissimilar products (packaged juice drinks)—and will this behavior vary by age?

This issue is central to an axiom from choice theory (independence of irrelevant alternatives), and we reasoned that older children would be more likely to choose the new option as a substitute for similar products (milk beverages) due to their awareness of product categories, thereby reducing the possibility that a new flavored milk beverage would increase overall milk consumption. In contrast, younger children, who are less aware of product categories, would be more likely to choose the new option as a substitute for other beverages without regard to whether it was a milk or juice product, thus increasing the possibility that a new, flavored milk beverage could increase overall milk consumption. Our collaboration needed to kill two birds with one stone—answer the applied question for WMMB and produce research worthy of publication in a top journal—and this dual objective added both time and complexity to the project.

As the project unfolded, there were difficulties in our collaboration. Surprisingly, the locus of the problems was not our sponsoring organization; rather, it was Ramesh and I. Although we were in the same department, we were worlds apart when it came to theories, research approaches, and data analysis expertise. In fact, he had never designed and implemented an experiment because he worked mainly with existing data sets. I didn't totally understand the data requirements for running the type of sophisticated choice models that he was going to employ. I can still remember one meeting when we were discussing experimental design, and I had come up with a switching replication design—and he had no idea what that was. Then, when we started talking about data analysis, I asked him how he would account for repeated measures in the logit analysis that he was going to do—and he didn't know what a repeated measures design was. My shortcomings were also on display quite frequently. He would have to patiently explain the utility functions he was using for the choice model analysis—over and over again.

Finally, the only way that the project got finished and published was through the help of an "interpreter"—someone who understood enough about the work I did, knew experimental design, and knew the quantitative choice modeling area. This happened to be my husband, who also served in the marketing department with me. We often hear about the challenges of working with collaborators outside one's area, but I found it difficult to collaborate with someone in my own department! Marketing departments are eclectic groups of academics, with degrees and expertise in diverse areas such as economics, psychology, sociology, and the like. Applied research that spans these areas is exciting, but as I found out, it can also be difficult, as each individual tries to bring their area of expertise into a joint project.

As I look back, I learned a lot from this project. I learned about how difficult it can be to design a project that meets the needs of a business partner, while at the same time trying to infuse a theoretical overlay so the results are publishable in an academic journal. In fact, I think we were lucky to combine an applied and theoretical focus in one project—the chances of this happening are probably less than many of us would like to admit—and as it turned out, we were able to publish our work in a top marketing journal (John & Lakshmi-Ratan, 1992). It's exciting to think that your theoretical perspective can illuminate real applied problems. But expecting that you will move the needle on important theoretical issues at the same time is optimistic at best, naïve at worst.

Research With the Mayo Clinic

Years later, another opportunity to collaborate with an organization presented itself. By this time, I had moved to the University of Minnesota as a full professor. Since my days of research for the WMMB, I had discussed a few joint research projects with companies, but nothing emerged from those talks. I had decided that I needed to focus on theoretical research, and if applied questions emerged with companies, that I should approach those engagements as pure consulting jobs. With two children, hockey camps, and birthday parties, and PhD students needing my attention, I felt it was too risky and time-consuming to pull off another theoretical research plus applied research coup. I figured there were only so many balls I could juggle in the air, and applied research was a ball that was too slippery to put into the mix.

Then, along came the chance to work with the Mayo Clinic, which could weave together both theory and application. Barbara and I had become acquainted with the director of marketing at the Mayo Clinic a year earlier. He was interested in our research examining consumer perceptions of a brand's reputation. We discussed how these perceptions could be measured, and he asked us to look at the research conducted by the Mayo Clinic and recommend additional study that would be informative. As a result of these informal discussions, Barbara and I were invited to submit a research proposal when the Mayo Clinic decided to invest in more research to better understand how different segments of the population (i.e., patients and nonpatients) perceived their brand's reputation.

The Mayo Clinic had conducted consumer research on this topic for years, but they now wanted a much more sophisticated understanding of consumer perceptions. They knew, for example, that many consumers held strong beliefs that the Mayo Clinic had the "best patient care in the world" and performed "advanced medical research." After some initial discussions with our Mayo Clinic collaborators, Barbara and I prepared a list of five topics that we thought would have an interesting theoretical angle but also address their question. From this list, they chose the option of learning how all the Mayo Clinic beliefs were linked, forming something akin to a spreading activation network. They wanted answers to questions such as: Which beliefs are most important to their reputation and which are less important? What beliefs are connected to each other—for example, is "advanced medical research" connected to having the "best patient care in the world"? Standard marketing research techniques could not answer these questions, and they wanted us to develop a measurement technique that could produce a networklike picture of consumer beliefs about the Mayo Clinic.

Barbara and I found the challenge to be exciting. Barbara came to the project with expertise in attitude–belief measurement techniques, and I had expertise in practitioner research for measuring brand reputations (also called "brand equity"). Given our existing relationship with our Mayo Clinic collaborators, we were given free rein to explore measurement options and decide on the one that we felt was best suited for the applied question. We researched a variety of techniques, and we decided to use a concept-mapping methodology. Concept maps are a known method for eliciting an individual's knowledge about some substantive domain, such as photosynthesis or atom structures. However, no technique was available for aggregating a set of individual concept maps into one consensus picture of the substantive area, which is what we needed for our picture of the Mayo Clinic. We needed to design a new way for people to construct their concept maps that would facilitate data aggregation, and we needed new analysis techniques for actually aggregating these maps.

This project was certainly challenging and took Barbara and me almost two years to complete. Yet the experience was far smoother than my prior business collaboration. Comparing the two, there were important differences in the Mayo Clinic project. First, and foremost, I had a collaborator, Barbara, with whom I shared a common language, research approach, and prior history of working together. Although we brought different strengths to the project, we didn't need someone to interpret for one another our views and suggestions. Second, we had an existing relationship with people at the Mayo Clinic, which enabled us to have productive discussions about the methodology and final product. They were very supportive in funding the research, but more than that, they appreciated our expertise and what we could bring to the project. The Mayo Clinic partners also generated academic research, so they understood what we meant when we needed to do things to enhance our chances of publishing the results in an academic journal. Finally, both Barbara and I were tenured full professors, and we were able to devote the time necessary to developing the project with our outside partners. We were also able to take the risk that we might not be able to publish this type of research technique in journals in our field, which typically published articles that used very different types of research methods. In the end, we were able to place the work in one of our best marketing journals

(John, Loken, Kim, & Monga, 2006)—appropriately enough, in a special issue devoted to joint academic-practitioner research!

A Synthesis of Lessons Learned

In this discussion, we've presented several stories of our collaborations in applied research. Each story is unique in terms of the research area, our collaborators, and the ups and downs of conducting this type of study. However, as we considered our individual stories, we also thought about some lessons we've learned about what made these collaborations more effective, more personally satisfying, and more compatible with our goals as academic researchers. Here are some of the lessons learned from our applied research collaborations:

- **Timing:** Applied research can be challenging and very rewarding, but it also can be time-consuming and risky. While getting our feet wet in applied research had many advantages pretenure, the real satisfaction with applied partnerships (at least for us) came posttenure, when we were more established in our academic careers. We felt more comfortable focusing on applied research questions, without the pressure to combine the applied question with a theoretical angle that would be a more certain path to publication. We also could enjoy the challenges of working on applied questions, which can be more time-consuming and uncertain in terms of outcomes.

- **Academic collaborators:** Applied research was more challenging for us when our outside partners (nonprofits, companies, sponsoring agencies, etc.) had different goals, spoke a different language, and had differing expectations. Given these potential difficulties, choosing your academic partners can ease the burdens—if you choose well. We have both found that choosing academic partners with a common perspective (either a common theoretical perspective or a common applied one) made our collaborations easier.

- **Empathy for applied academic perspectives:** We have found partnerships more rewarding when we are able to develop empathy for the applied academic perspective and understand its importance from the perspective of the applied academic partner. Spending time with colleagues and developing connections through seminars and conferences can contribute to a broader understanding and appreciation of how the applied academic researcher tackles problems.

- **Bridge collaborators:** Many applied projects bring together academics from different areas to take advantage of the expertise that each person can bring to a problem. While the potential synergies are exciting, sometimes the most important collaborator is someone who can bridge the different areas to explain concepts and language that differ among academic areas. These interpreters are critical when the academic team is from disparate areas.

- **Core collaborators:** Applied research projects can involve large teams of researchers, in which single collaborators have less control over decision making. It can be challenging to hone research ideas and reach consensus on project planning and execution. In this case, having a smaller set of core collaborators can be critical to the success of the team and project. These core collaborators may represent different academic areas (e.g., epidemiology, health communications, and community health) or be key players in designing and implementing the research. Someone has to be in charge to carry out applied research projects with larger teams, and core collaborators are the key.

- **Outside collaborators:** Working with a company or nonprofit involves getting to know a different culture, with varying expectations and goals. Having a prior history, knowledge, and familiarity with the individuals with whom you will be working is an important advantage in applied research. Our experience with the Mayo Clinic brought this advantage to the forefront. Due to prior work we had done together, there was already a degree of familiarity and trust as we began our research collaboration. Of course, one doesn't always have the choice of working with an outside partner with shared history. But if the opportunity presents itself, the experience can be much smoother and more satisfying.

- **Deliverables:** Although applied research often has more structure than pure academic research, due to written grants submitted to the sponsoring agency or business entity, there is still the question of defining deliverables from the project. When, early in the project, we and our collaborators knew the answers to questions such as the type of report and presentation that was to be delivered to the sponsoring organization, who would oversee the writing, and what academic articles were planned to publish the results, the process of collaborating was made easier. In the case of business entities, we have also found that one needs to answer upfront whether the results or data will be released by the sponsoring organization for publication in academic journals. Our stories involved applied research where the ability to publish was never in question. However, some organizations may not be comfortable with the total release of data that some academic journals require. These matters must be ironed out early in the collaboration process, before contracts are signed for the project.

- **Long-lasting returns:** Collaborations often bring fortuitous connections that reap later rewards. Even when an applied collaboration does not meet academic publication expectations, less tangible outcomes may arise. Some of our early collaborations with colleagues resulted in requests for future collaborations that were unexpected and highly successful, as well as leading to enduring friendships.

We hope that a few of these lessons prove helpful as you consider participating in applied psychological research. Applied research has been an interesting and gratifying part of our careers, and we hope that the lessons we have learned will make it an even better experience for you.

■ REFERENCES ■

Davis, R., Gilpin, B., Loken, B., Viswanath, K., & Wakefield, M. (Eds.) (2008). *The Role of the Media in Promoting and Reducing Tobacco Use* (National Cancer Institute Monograph 19). Rockville, MD: National Cancer Institute.

John, D. R., & Lakshmi-Ratan, R. (1992). Age differences in children's choice behavior: The impact of available alternatives. *Journal of Marketing Research, 29,* 216–226.

John, D. R., Loken, B., Kim, K., & Monga, A. B. (2006). Brand concept maps: A methodology for identifying brand association networks. *Journal of Marketing Research, 43,* 549–563.

Lando, H. A., Loken, B., Howard-Pitney, B., & Pechacek, T. (1990). Community impact of a localized smoking cessation contest. *American Journal of Public Health, 80,* 601–603.

Wakefield, M. A., Loken, B., & Hornik, R. C. (2010). Use of mass media campaigns to change health behavior. *The Lancet, 375*(9748), 1261–1271.

Chapter 21: Finding the Sweet Spot: What Makes for Successful Collaboration?[1]

Mark Snyder

McKnight Presidential Chair in Psychology
University of Minnesota

Allen M. Omoto

Professor of Psychology
School of Social Science, Policy, and Evaluation
Claremont Graduate University

Every year, throughout the world, millions of people volunteer substantial amounts of time and energy to help other people, their communities, and society at large. In the United States, the Corporation for National and Community Service estimates that in 2012, roughly 64.5 million adults served as volunteers, providing some 7.9 billion hours of service that could be valued at over $175 billion (Corporation for National and Community Service, 2013). In our collaborative research—a partnership that now spans well over two decades—we have studied the psychology of volunteerism and attempted to answer questions about what motivates people to seek out opportunities to volunteer, what sustains them in their volunteer efforts, how are they affected by their service, and what impact they have on other people and the communities in which they live.

In our theorizing and research, we view volunteerism as one form of social action in which people attempt to address social issues and concerns (other forms of social action include charitable giving, political participation, and social movements; see Snyder & Omoto, 2007). Volunteerism is also a distinctive form of helping, marked by several features that set it apart from other

[1] Our collaborative research on volunteerism has been supported by funding from the University of Minnesota, the American Foundation for AIDS Research, and the National Institute of Mental Health.

forms of helping that have been studied by psychologists. Specifically, and as we have detailed elsewhere and expand on below, we have identified six conceptually important, if not heuristically useful, characteristics of volunteerism (Snyder & Omoto, 2008). First, volunteerism involves actions performed on the basis of the actor's free will, without bonds of obligation or coercion. Although volunteers may develop personal relationships with other people through their work (and thereby come to feel obligated to continue to help), the initial impetus for their involvement typically does not stem from feelings of personal obligation or expectations borne of preexisting relationships. Second, volunteerism usually involves some amount of deliberation or decision making; in this way, it is different from reflexive acts of assistance or "emergency helping." Third, rather than onetime special events or activities, volunteerism extends over a period of time, such as weeks, months, or even years. Fourth, the decision to volunteer derives from a person's own goals and desires, without expectation of reward or punishment. Thus, we exclude employment and other activities that people do in order to receive pay or to avoid punishment or censure. Fifth, volunteering involves serving people who need and want help, or assisting causes and movements in their efforts to achieve their aims. That is, the services provided by volunteers are typically and willingly sought out or accepted by recipients. Finally, volunteerism is performed on behalf of people or causes, and commonly through agencies or organizations. An important distinction here is between simple acts of helping or "neighboring" (informal helping) and volunteerism performed through the auspices of or in conjunction with organizations. (For other related definitions of volunteerism, see Musick & Wilson, 2008; Penner, 2004; Wilson, 2000).

In psychology, helping has long been studied in terms of brief, low-cost, generally spontaneous assistance provided by strangers (i.e., bystander intervention) or, more recently, in terms of care provided to chronically sick or severely debilitated family members (e.g., Manning, Levine, & Collins, 2007; Penner, Dovidio, Piliavin, & Schroeder, 2005; Piliavin & Charng, 1990). However, a careful consideration of the features of volunteerism makes it clear that it is a hybrid form of helping that incorporates aspects of both emergency assistance and caregiving (Omoto & Snyder, 1995; Snyder, Clary, & Stukas, 2000).

Our Collaborative Research

Because of its defining and characteristic features, volunteerism is something of a curious phenomenon. For a variety of reasons, it simply should not occur. There is no press of circumstances, nor are there bonds of obligation. Volunteerism can be hard work and presents opportunity costs to volunteers. For example, people may forego other activities and social relations to make time for their volunteer activities, which in turn may introduce additional social costs and possible rejection (Snyder, Omoto, & Crain, 1999). Yet people do seek out opportunities to volunteer, and they do sustain their volunteer efforts over extended periods of time.

The ubiquity of volunteerism alone seems sufficient reason for the topic to garner theoretical and empirical attention. It is perhaps surprising, therefore, that psychologists had not conducted much work on this phenomenon at the time that we initiated our investigations. In addition, and as we have articulated in some of our papers, there is considerable conceptual value in studying volunteerism for broadening the understanding of the nature of helping and being helped. Also, volunteerism is one key way in which individuals work to address social problems of all sorts; hence, research on volunteerism has the potential to offer many practical lessons. Taken together, these reasons offer compelling justification for basic and applied scientific inquiry on volunteerism.

Central to our collaborative efforts has been a commitment to draw broadly and deeply on relevant theories in psychology and related social sciences, to conduct research in "real-world" settings (i.e., community-based service organizations) with actual volunteers engaged in real acts of volunteerism. Thus, we have conducted a coordinated series of cross-sectional, longitudinal, and intervention studies to examine the processes of volunteerism. Although we believe that our approach and findings are applicable to many, if not most forms of volunteerism, much of our empirical research has focused on volunteer service programs and organizations that have emerged in the United States in response to the HIV epidemic.

There can be no disputing that HIV disease, including AIDS, has had and continues to have major medical, economic, social, and societal impact across the globe. A critical component of the societal response to this epidemic in the United States was the development of community-based organizations of volunteers who provided care and support services for people living with HIV or AIDS (PWAs), as well as public education about HIV prevention and PWAs. Although the importance and prevalence of volunteers and some of their specific roles have changed over the course of the epidemic and with changes in medical treatments and government support, volunteer efforts continue to be important in shaping HIV services and education. They remain at the heart of community-based responses to HIV and testify to the power of ordinary citizens to take action in confronting societal problems.

We have also endeavored to conduct the research in ways that it would, at one and the same time, advance the state of theoretical understanding of the nature of helping and prosocial action and generate knowledge of practical relevance, especially for the development of scientifically informed approaches to optimizing volunteer efforts. As such, we view our work as falling within the action-oriented research tradition within the social sciences (Lewin, 1948/1997). The research simultaneously addresses both basic and applied scientific concerns, and it does so in synergistic ways that mutually reinforce and enhance each other.

Elsewhere, we have addressed and reviewed key issues in theory, research, and application to volunteerism (e.g., Snyder & Omoto, 2007, 2008). Instead of revisiting these issues, our task here is to address the nature of the collaboration—or really, collaborations—that made it possible for us to develop our theoretical work on volunteerism, conduct research on the dynamics of volunteer processes, and articulate social issues and policy implications of rigorous scientific research on volunteerism.

We begin by noting that there are actually three partners in our collaboration—the two of us as investigators and the community-based volunteer service organizations that have cooperated with us for data collection and provided access to volunteers and programs. Accordingly, in this chapter, we focus on our collaboration with each other as researchers, as well as on our joint partnerships with community-based service organizations and their volunteers, staff, and clients.

Moreover, we also attempt to detail part of the larger context in which our collaboration developed. Perhaps as a hazard of our social psychological propensities, we identify the substantial influence of circumstances and timing on the causes and course of our collaboration. Along the way, we will describe what we knew going in, what we learned along the way, and what we now know thanks to the wisdom of experience and the benefit of hindsight. Our interests are not just in the specifics of our own collaboration, but also in the ways in which our experiences (adventures?) are potentially illustrative of broader points, warnings, and opportunities for other researchers interested in collaboration, including with community-based organizations or other nonacademic partners.

In organizing our thoughts and memories for this chapter, we have been mindful of the observations of the 19th-century Danish philosopher Søren Kierkegaard, who cautioned, "Life can only be understood backwards; but it must be lived forwards." Although our collaboration was (of necessity) lived forward, we are now in the position to look back at it in hindsight to identify where and how we were just plain lucky, to note what we perceive were important influences in our success, and, finally, to offer some suggestions for others.

Features of Our Collaboration

There are many ways that collaborations come about. Sometimes the collaborators bring together different and complementary perspectives to look at a common problem (e.g., a psychologist and a political scientist collaborating to study voting behavior, with the psychologist offering a micro or individual-level perspective and the political scientist working from a macro or societal-level perspective). Other times, collaborators bring together different methods in the hope of elucidating a phenomenon (e.g., in the aforementioned hypothetical collaborative study of voting, an investigator skilled in experimental methods and a researcher adept at survey work might join forces to conduct research that embeds experiments within surveys). Collaborations also can be intentional, as in the assembly of a research team that ensures that the appropriate expertise and experiences are brought to bear for the research questions of interest. And they can result simply from happenstance and accidents of association, or simply because people enjoy spending time together.

In our case, we came to our collaborative enterprise with shared disciplinary perspectives (both of us are psychologists hovering around the interfaces of social psychology and personality psychology) and similar methodological skill sets (prior to our collaboration, we had each worked primarily within laboratory settings and primarily with undergraduates as research participants). Thus, rather than bringing differences and complementarities of perspective and methodology, we brought similarities of conceptual and investigative orientation to our collaborative enterprise. But, as we discovered, our collaboration led us to broaden and expand our conceptual horizons and to add new methodological skills to our investigative toolkits.

In many ways, we were underprepared, not only to conduct research on the topic of volunteerism but also to do it in the way that we did. That is, although we shared disciplinary and methodological perspectives, we also shared only a scant history of research on topics that have sat at the core of our collaboration. Prior to our collaboration, neither of us had focused on helping behavior or volunteerism as a central part of our research interests, or for that matter, even on other forms of social action. We also had very limited experience with some of the research methods and participant populations that have been central to our collaborative efforts. For example, prior to launching our collaboration, neither of us had done much in the way of research in field settings, nor had we worked with community-based organizations and volunteers.

So, what did we bring to our collaboration, if not complementarity of perspectives and methods or relevant background and prior research experience, which appear to characterize many if not most successful collaborations? We had a shared interest and fascination with problems of social action, and especially of volunteerism as a curious phenomenon. Volunteerism appears essential to the functioning of our society, but it is a phenomenon for which it is generally easier to come up with reasons for why it should *not* occur than for its widespread occurrence. We also both had concerns about HIV/AIDS and how the government and society were responding to it. We started our work, after all, in the late 1980s; at that time, and with our political leanings and awareness being what they were, it was hard not to be concerned about the HIV epidemic.

Moreover, as concerned societal observers, we could not help but notice the emergence of community-based, grassroots volunteer organizations that were springing up to support and assist people infected with HIV, to provide education about HIV disease and its social and economic challenges, and to agitate for political and institutional action to confront the emerging epidemic productively. Even without a history of prior research, we could see within this landscape a wide range of psychological theories that we thought were relevant to understanding volunteerism, and also to the specific context of volunteerism as it was emerging in response to HIV and AIDS. In short, we saw a "real-world laboratory" primed for action-oriented research and, importantly, an opportunity for psychological science to play a role in the societal response to HIV.

Not incidentally, we also were both independently involved on the ground in community and institutional responses to HIV (one of us on a university task force on scientific responses to HIV, the other working to develop a community-based AIDS service organization). These involvements heightened the salience, urgency, and desire to do something specifically about the HIV epidemic. Combining all of this with a spirit of adventure, a willingness to learn along the way, and the (false?) confidence that in collaboration, we could or would do what neither of us could or would do alone, our collaboration was born.

Contributors to the Success of Our Collaboration

Looking back, it seems that there were at least as many reasons not to embark on our collaboration as there were to go forward. Yet go forward we did, and we proceeded to enlist the cooperation and partnership of community-based AIDS service organizations in recruiting their volunteers for our research. Over the years, we have conducted cross-sectional surveys of volunteer motivations, attitudes, and experiences, in addition to longitudinal studies in which we have tracked volunteers over the course of their active service in attempting to learn not just why people volunteer, but also what sustains them over time, accounts for their satisfaction and effectiveness, and predicts their eventual decision to stop serving. We also have expanded our focus beyond volunteers, studying the effects of volunteer service on the recipients of volunteer services, members of their social networks, and their communities and society at large (e.g., Dwyer, Snyder, & Omoto, 2013; Omoto, Snyder, & Hackett, 2010, 2012; Omoto, Snyder, & Martino, 2000; Snyder & Omoto, 2007; Snyder, Omoto, & Dwyer, 2016; Snyder, Omoto, & Smith, 2009).

As can probably be surmised from our description of what we brought to our collaboration, we had to learn a lot (a whole lot!) along the way. We worked to become well acquainted with the relevant research literature (on the dynamics of volunteerism, much of it in disciplines removed from our own), acquire and refine methodological skills (learning such things as effective ways of combating attrition in longitudinal research), and figure out how to work with our partner organizations (whose reasons for existence did not include our research). And (perhaps it goes without saying) we had to seek and secure funding for our research for, as we learned very quickly, field research with real people can be substantially more costly than laboratory research with college students. In fact, truth be told, we did not intend at the outset to start an entire program of research, and certainly not one that we would pursue for decades. As we learned more and delved deeper into the theoretical and practical issues related to volunteerism, however, we identified additional and (what we found to be) intriguing questions in need of empirical exploration, and also increasingly derived satisfaction from collecting data outside the lab that had immediate relevance and utility.

Before turning to some of the lessons that we learned in each of these domains, we pause to acknowledge some aspects of ourselves as *persons* that, we believe, have also contributed to our success as collaborators. From the very beginning, we have always felt that what we did in collaboration, we would not (and could not) have done as individuals. And this is not simply a matter of division of labor. To be sure, two people can do more than one. But there's more;

as we discovered, there has been a certain emboldening that emerged with our collaboration. Working together, we were more willing to go forward, to do new things, and to do hard and even unexpected things.

Our collaboration, and indeed probably most of them, also came with accountability. Working alone, it is relatively easy to let schedules slip or sometimes to overlook important details. As part of a collaborative enterprise, however, we have felt a strong commitment to (if not fear of) not letting each other down. Thus, we've tried to get things done and to honor timelines and scheduling agreements. In addition, with two sets of eyes on our work, we've felt more confident that we have crossed the t's and dotting the i's in attending to details and doing things right. We also get along well and enjoy spending time together; it has been more fun to work together than to work alone. Long hours working on research won't necessarily go by faster when they are shared (although sometimes they seem to), but they do generate more satisfaction and pride of accomplishment. We are pretty sure that our ability to get along has helped smooth our collaborative efforts and, no doubt, has been important in our ability to sustain our collaboration over many years. Finally, it certainly has helped that we value and respect each other's intellectual contributions, share similar perspectives on what makes for scientifically important and practically meaningful research, and can appreciate each other's (sometimes divergent) lenses on research and how to do it well.

In addition to this list of collaboration facilitators, we are well aware of the value of compatible work styles, and our work styles mesh well. As those who know us can attest, and those who don't know us will now know thanks to our confessing this, we both have a stubbornly perfectionist streak and are also very detail oriented. We try to be careful about writing and presenting ideas, and by this time, can (and do) pretty much complete each other's sentences and write "on the same wavelength." We also both work intensely and in a focused way. Sometimes we have worked this way out of necessity (as in when we are trying to meet an impending grant application deadline); other times, this just has seemed to be an easier way to get our collaborative work done.

All of these attributes lead to, and reinforce, a commitment to doing things carefully and what we considered to be the right way. In the case of our research, this also more often than not meant doing it in a harder way (such as collecting data from actual volunteers rather than students). These characteristics also fostered the endurance and stamina necessary to follow through on our research commitments, to not cut corners, and to not take easier roads. At the same time, we have learned through experience that these similar tendencies have a way of getting magnified and accentuated when working together. This magnification and accentuation can be strengths, but also occasionally weaknesses, as when our similar tendencies end up reducing efficiency or distracting from the bigger picture of what we may be trying to accomplish in a given paper or data collection.

Of course, even with the constellation of shared interests and personal attributes, there have been challenges and issues that we had to learn to manage. Over the entire course of our collaboration, for example, we have been at different academic institutions some distance apart (Mark, at the University of Minnesota; Allen, first at the University of Kansas and now at Claremont Graduate University). Being at different universities has presented logistical challenges (e.g., scheduling "face time" to work together) and also meant having to negotiate the differing expectations and capacities of our respective institutions (e.g., our universities vary greatly in the extent of their support and regulation of grant activity and institutional review board policies). In addition, over the decades of collaboration, we have had to work around various leaves and sabbaticals that have taken one or both of us away from our home institutions or even out of the country, adding further practical complexities to our working together.

Being at different stages of our careers has also meant walking a delicate line during our collaboration and setting an agenda that respected those different stages (e.g., deciding authorship and the timing for our pipeline of papers and other scholarly work). In addition, we have tried to be mindful of and sensitive to the managing of public perceptions so that the world would know that our work is a truly full and equal collaboration (which it always has been and always will be), with both partners essential and indispensable; quite simply, without collaboration, there would be no research. Relevant to the matter of public perception, the fact that our collaboration was a new enterprise for both of us has also proven helpful in that the research could not be seen as really the work of only one of us.

Working With Community Organizations

So far, we have commented extensively on our history of collaboration, our motivations and preparation for our work, and also a bit on our own personal characteristics and how we work together. As we noted at the outset, however, our collaboration has involved three partners. In this section, therefore, we turn our attention to discussing how we have worked with our third partner—community organizations whose *raison d'être* is to provide service rather than conducting theoretically relevant research, but who nonetheless cooperated with us in our research.

There are many different models of collaboration with community organizations and people, including much of what goes by the name *action research* (see Chein, Cook, & Harding, 1948; Lewin, 1948/1997; Omoto & Snyder, 1990; Snyder & Omoto, 2007). Our working model is different from many of these models, however, and makes for a distinctive type of partnership with our community partners.

In some program evaluation work and participatory action research endeavors, community members are enlisted as part of the research team (e.g., Fetterman & Wandersman, 2005; Whyte, 1991; Whyte, Greenwood, & Lazes, 1989). They may help identify community needs and goals, even to the point of framing the research questions that are asked and the agenda for a study or program of research. In other related versions of this type of scholarship, community members are empowered to participate actively in the research process, including by setting some of the terms and types of data to be collected, as well as being involved with analyses and the crafting of recommendations derived from the results. At a minimum, they bring local expertise and lived experience with a problem or concern that complements and sometimes guides the work of a researcher or investigative team.

Our work with community-based organizations differed from this model, however. We partnered with community-based organizations in many essential and cooperative ways, including in ways that could help them meet some of their own pressing needs. However, they were not involved in developing our research agenda, nor did they provide research questions and hypotheses that we investigated. Their local knowledge and community credibility was critical for the success of our research, but they did not bring theoretical or methodological grounding that shaped our work in substantive ways. Instead of a shared agenda for action or a common set of research questions, we and our organizational partners had different (but complementary) roles and goals. As scientists, we were interested in conducting rigorous, theoretically relevant psychological research that had relevance for the day-to-day functioning and programming of our partner organizations. Our partner organizations could easily work toward meeting their missions without our involvement, but we did our best to convince them that partnering with us could benefit them, as well as other organizations working on the front lines of the HIV epidemic.

These partnerships were intentional and strategic on our part. We sought out specific organizations to work with in the hope of gaining entry in order to conduct our research. We had a specific set of questions about AIDS volunteerism—questions grounded in psychological theory—and we sought to study the people and organizations that were engaged in this work.

This approach, we note, is reminiscent of a common strategy adopted by personality psychologists in studying traits or characteristics. In order to truly understand a trait and its intricacies, personality psychologists often find it advisable to critically examine the individuals who possess the trait of interest. Thus, although some of our initial research focused on assessing people's perceptions of AIDS volunteers (and was a form of stereotyping research), we quickly moved to attempting to understand AIDS volunteerism from the inside out, by querying the people who developed and staffed AIDS service organizations and the volunteers who worked to deliver the lion's share of their educational and care and assistance programming.

This type of partnership presented several challenges for us, as, understandably but disappointingly, AIDS service organizations initially were not eager to give us open access to their clients and volunteers, or even to get involved with psychological researchers. They were staffed by busy people playing catch-up on a health crisis that was out of control, and they were generally operating on shoestring budgets. In short, these people did not have the time or inclination to take on research activities, especially ones for which they did not perceive any direct benefit to them or their organizations.

They also did not know us from Adam. We may have hoped that our academic credentials and affiliations would carry more weight, and maybe they were important, but the organizations needed to be convinced that our interests were genuine, nonexploitive, and sustainable. As is perhaps endemic to organizations that provide services to or assist vulnerable populations, they have reputations to develop and uphold; the effectiveness of their services depend in many ways on their earning the trust of their clients. Allowing a third party— us—unfettered access would be unthinkable and could result in disastrous consequences for both the organization and its clients. In our experience, it is difficult to overestimate the importance of establishing credibility and transparency with organizations and their staff members through deeds and not merely words, degrees, or affiliations.

Moreover, we wanted to develop ongoing research partnerships with these AIDS service organizations, not just to gain access to clients or volunteers for a onetime study. This desire for continuing contact and cooperation is quite different from the requests entertained by many organizations (AIDS-oriented and otherwise) to assist with a course project, senior thesis, or dissertation study. The demands placed on them by an ongoing partnership are greater, to be sure, but at the same time, there may be a greater sense of security for entering the partnership because the researcher is also making a longer-term and more substantial commitment. For all of these reasons, we could not begrudge our partner organizations for wanting to vet us thoroughly before agreeing to work with us.

For our part, we developed an informal "recipe" for approaching and working with community organization partners; we came to refer to this set of procedures and considerations as the "care and feeding" of our community partners. We started by doing extensive work of our own to learn about our potential partner organizations. We sought to find out how many clients they served, how many volunteers they utilized and in what capacities, what their main sources of funding were, and about their organizational structure and the names of key staff members. Central to our concerns was the question: Did the organization have a paid position responsible for volunteer oversight? Most commonly, responsibility for volunteers was located in the client services branch of the AIDS service organizations and was handled by a case manager or a volunteer coordinator in charge of volunteer services.

We made it a point to have face-to-face meetings with the individuals responsible for volunteers and to discuss with them not only what we hoped to study in our research, but also what they might get out of our research partnership. At the time that we started our work, these organizations had little capacity or proclivity to collect information on their clients or services beyond simple counts of client intakes, volunteers trained, and service hours rendered. However, they knew, or could readily appreciate when we made the point to them, that reliable and evaluative data of this sort would help them become more efficient, responsive, and attractive to funding sources. In exchange for helping us collect data relevant to our research questions, we offered to help them obtain this type of information. In some cases, this was as simple as surveying volunteers about their knowledge and perceptions of service programs administered by the organization, whereas in other cases, it involved devising ways to get potentially more sensitive information about perceived organizational priorities, satisfaction with programs, and gaps in services. In fact, we did our best to honor these requests, at our own expense and on our own time. We wrote survey items, collected relevant data, summarized findings, and provided product reports to our partner organizations. These reports are not part of our professional publications or any other lines of our résumés. Instead, we consider them as part of our cost of forging partnerships with AIDS service organizations.

Furthermore, we attempted to integrate our research projects into our organizational partners' ongoing activities and programs. We wrote articles about our research for organizational newsletters and made ourselves available for public talks and for meetings with organization staff. We also tried to be as "low maintenance" as possible, in that we asked our partner organizations to take on only tasks that had limited time demands and were easy to do.

For example, in one study in which we sought to randomly assign volunteers to versions of a survey in which items were counterbalanced, we explained the necessity of our procedural detail to our organizational contact and provided sealed envelopes of questionnaires that had been randomly sequenced. The task for our partner organization was reduced to simply sending out packets to individuals who indicated interest in volunteering that included these materials, in this prearranged order, along with their usual orientation materials. We also typically sought input from staff members at our partner organizations about the content and wording of items in questionnaires that we developed for our research. In this way, we utilized the expertise that they possessed and also attempted to ensure that our measures were valid—or at least that the things we asked about and the language that we used were "real" and relevant for our research participants (i.e., primarily the organization's volunteers).

It is important to note that we did not pay our cooperating organizations; indeed, this is one of the reasons why we assert that they were a third partner in our research enterprise. However, we did generally offer compensation to our research participants for their time and responses. In every study we conducted, though, we gave research participants the opportunity to donate their compensation to our partner organization. This was not a request, but simply an opportunity, and one that many participants took advantage of. From a wider perspective, it was another small way for us to underscore the fact that we really were working on the same page and in concert with our partner organizations. If we could help the organization, we would. They were, after all, providing invaluable assistance and access to us and to our program of research.

In summary, our relationship with our partner organizations was a form of collaboration, but not like what is commonly espoused among advocates of participatory research or "engaged" scholarship. We had a research agenda and brought research skills and psychological theories to the collaboration, and our partner organizations represented a real-world laboratory for the work. However, they were more than just a laboratory. Through considerable recognizance work and ongoing communication, they helped us to refine our research measures and also suggested new and practically focused questions for us to ponder and explore. We provided information to them that they could use immediately to improve their programs (e.g., through a survey of volunteers about their satisfaction with the organization's operations and communications), and also provided lay-language descriptions of our research that they could use in newsletters and their future planning and program development.

In fact, we developed many of our instruments and procedures with the context of our partner organizations in mind. In our most recent work, for example, we developed and tested an intervention aimed at improving the short- and longer-term functioning of people (e.g., clients and volunteers) associated with AIDS service organizations (see Omoto & Snyder, 2010). Our intervention, which focused on enhancing a psychological sense of community, was created in a way that it could be implemented inexpensively and with the resources available in AIDS service organizations similar to our partner organizations (i.e., it did not require extensive staff or unusual expertise).

In working with our partner organizations, we respected their limits and goals and attended to the dynamics of our relationship with them. We never wanted to be a bother to them, so we worked hard to create a win–win situation for us and for them. Indeed, as most theories of interpersonal relationships would suggest, partnerships are more satisfying and stable when both parties contribute by putting in resources of value. This is precisely what we did with our community partners. We obtained valuable information for them at the same time that they were providing important access for us. For readers interested in developing research partnerships with organizations, especially community-based service organizations, we offer some advice based on our experience: in approaching organizations, be sure that you are well informed about them, that you are honest about your goals and needs, that you are straightforward in what you can provide for them, and that you keep your promises.

Finally, in the actual conduct of our research, we sought to ensure that research participants (e.g., volunteers and clients at our partner organizations) recognized that we were a separate entity, but that we were, indeed, working with our partner organization. We believe that we have showed, although only anecdotally, that making this connection clear helped participants feel greater trust and commitment to our research, as well as probably having the salutary effect of helping to reduce attrition from our studies.

Our Collaboration in Context

Our discussion of how we approached and worked with AIDS service organizations is a reminder that no research occurs in a vacuum. However, the organizational context of our partner organizations is but one facet of the larger context in which our collaboration has operated. Before concluding, therefore, we reflect on, in turn, three other facets of context—the funding agencies that have supported our efforts, the academic institutions in which we have worked, and the larger social and historical contexts in which our efforts have taken place.

It may go (almost) without saying, but research costs money, especially the kind of research that we have done. Following volunteers over the course of their time in service, collecting data at multiple points in time, and coordinating the information collected from participants and from their volunteer service organizations are, singly and together, very labor-intensive activities. To perform them, and especially according to the rigorous standards required for our studies, requires considerable time and effort—time and effort that have been supported by the generous investment of a series of funding agencies. In fact, our studies of AIDS volunteerism have been supported, in successive time periods, by our universities (with seed grants from the University of Minnesota), from the American Foundation for AIDS Research (which supported our initial studies of AIDS volunteers), and the National Institute of Mental Health (which has provided major, continuous funding of our research for over 15 years). This funding has permitted us to do our research in the ways that we thought it should be done, and more expeditiously and more efficiently than if we had not had these resources (although, necessity being the parent of invention, we suspect that we might have found ways to do some of our research even without funding). However, with funding has come the necessity of learning new skills—and not necessarily of the research variety. Working at different institutions has required us to learn, among other things, the intricacies of how funding agencies make awards to separate institutions for a common research program and how institutions negotiate cost-sharing arrangements.

Moreover, the complexities of dealing with funding agencies supporting studies conducted by researchers affiliated with different universities and directing research sites in different states has had its counterparts in dealing with our universities. As complex, and at times trying, as dealing with the bureaucracy of one university can be, it seems simple in contrast to dealing with the bureaucracies of different universities simultaneously. Our universities have different views of issues such as how to set up and administer subcontracts, the role of cost sharing in funded projects, indirect cost rates and bases for calculation, and overhead return policies, to name a few. They are generally well equipped for working with faculty at home and less adept at playing well together. Our skills as go-betweens and negotiators of bureaucracy have been refined, to say the least.

But the context represented by our universities goes beyond offices of research support and administration. As we have learned, universities aren't necessarily well prepared to recognize and support collaborative efforts. For example, on more than one occasion, we have found ourselves explaining to colleagues and administrators that collaboration is not a way to work less (no ... when we collaborate, we don't each work 50%; rather, we each work 100%) and that, at times, collaborating actually takes more time than working solo. And, when the collaboration involves doing research that extends over years (as our longitudinal work did), we have had to explain that data collections that take many years to complete cannot be expected to produce publications in the first year. By analogy, that would be like planting a seedling apple tree in the spring and expecting it to bear fruit in its first fall.

Finally, we recognize the critical role that social and historical contexts played in the development of our collaborative research. Our decision to focus our empirical efforts on the social and psychological aspects of AIDS volunteerism was conditioned, in large measure, by the times in which we began our work—namely, the late 1980s, when society was just becoming aware of the challenges posed by the epidemic of HIV and AIDS. Grassroots organizations of volunteers were but one facet of society's response to HIV and AIDS and, for reasons that we have already articulated, proved to be an inviting real-world laboratory for research for theoretical, practical, and policy reasons.

Had we started our research at a different time, we very well might have focused on a different form of volunteerism—one that would have allowed us to test the same theories of the social and psychological foundations of volunteerism and other forms of social action, and one that might have afforded the same opportunities to conduct research with the potential to speak to social and public policy issues. It is also possible that our collaboration would not have occurred at all, or at least not in such an extensive form. At minimum, we are certain that our collaboration would have taken on a very different set of contours and emphases.

Lessons Learned

As we look back over our almost two-decade collaboration, we are struck by, trite as it is to say, all that we know now that we didn't know then. We surely did not know in advance all the skills, potholes, and serendipity in timing that have been important in our collaborative success. But, with apologies for contorting Kierkegaard's observation, we lived our collaboration forward and are only now attempting to understand it looking backward.

Perhaps more than anything, we are struck by how good our timing was in terms of the life history of the organizations with which we worked, which were relatively early in their development. They were finding their own way, which may have made them more open and receptive to partnering with us, especially because we approached them with offers of assistance that were useful to their functioning. In addition, our timing was good in terms of opportunities for funding, with the American Foundation for AIDS Research just beginning their program of grants for scientific research related to all facets of the AIDS epidemic just as we were starting up, and the National Institute for Mental Health starting its Office on AIDS just as we began to seek funding for larger and longitudinal studies as part of our program of research. We were interested in trying to do something about the HIV epidemic, and at a time when HIV was being recognized as a health crisis to which new funding was being directed. We were, quite simply and fortunately, if not fortuitously, in the right place at the right time (with, perhaps, the right idea).

Not only that, but we have also been fortunate to have been able to learn and self-teach the skills we needed to conduct our research, solve problems as they arose, and work around obstacles and roadblocks as they got in our way. It is perhaps remarkable that we have been able to sustain our collaboration all the way through, still enjoying and compatibly working together. (It is no exaggeration that we are, at this very moment, sitting in the same room at separate tables tapping away on separate computers writing separate sections of this chapter, but with the faith that we are also still completing each other's sentences ...)

Conclusions

Finally, here is the great reveal—the secret to our collaboration. We have been lucky—lucky with our timing, lucky in solving problems, lucky in funding availability, and probably most important of all, lucky to have been collaborating with each other. To underscore a point that we made earlier in this chapter, without our collaboration, it is unlikely that we would have conducted the research that we did. Said another way, without our collaboration, we would not have been in a position to take advantage of the luck that we were so fortunate to encounter. So, here's our advice to others just beginning their collaborative journey: keep your eyes open to what is interesting in the world around you, do your best to be prepared, be willing to take a chance when an opportunity presents itself, and persevere, without being afraid of a few missteps and course corrections along the way. And, in all of this, it helps to have a collaborator!

■ REFERENCES ■

Chein, I., Cook, S. W., & Harding, J. (1948). The field of action research. *American Psychologist, 3*, 43–50.

Corporation for National and Community Service (2013). *Volunteering and civic life in America 2012.* Retrieved July 15, 2014, at http://www.volunteeringinamerica.gov/

Dwyer, P. C., Snyder, M., & Omoto, A. M. (2013). When stigma-by-association threatens, self-esteem helps: Self-esteem protects volunteers in stigmatizing contexts. *Basic and Applied Social Psychology, 35*, 88–97.

Fetterman, D. M., & Wandersman, A. (2005). *Empowerment evaluation principles in practice.* New York, NY: Guilford.

Lewin, K. (1997). Action research and minority problems. In G. W. Lewin (Ed.), *Resolving social conflicts and field theory in social science* (pp. 143–152). Washington, DC: American Psychological Association. (Original work published 1948)

Manning, R., Levine, M., & Collins, A. (2007). The Kitty Genovese murder and the social psychology of helping. *American Psychologist, 62*, 555–562.

Musick, M. A., & Wilson, J. (2008). *Volunteers: A social profile.* Bloomington: Indiana University Press.

Omoto, A. M., & Snyder, M. (1990). Basic research in action: Volunteerism and society's response to AIDS. *Personality and Social Psychology Bulletin, 16*, 152–165.

Omoto, A. M., & Snyder, M. (1995). Sustained helping without obligation: Motivation, longevity of service, and perceived attitude change among AIDS volunteers. *Journal of Personality and Social Psychology, 68*, 671–686.

Omoto, A. M., & Snyder, M. (2010). Influences of psychological sense of community on voluntary helping and prosocial action. In S. Stürmer & M. Snyder (Eds.), *The psychology of prosocial behavior: Group processes, intergroup relations, and helping* (pp. 223–243). Oxford, England: Blackwell.

Omoto, A. M., Snyder, M., & Hackett, J. D. (2010). Personality and motivational antecedents of activism and civic engagement. *Journal of Personality, 78*, 1703–1734.

Omoto, A. M., Snyder, M., & Hackett, J. D. (2012). Everyday helping and responses to crises: A model for understanding volunteerism. In K. Jonas & T. Morton (Eds.), *Restoring civil societies: The psychology of intervention and engagement following crisis* (pp. 98–118). Malden, MA: Wiley-Blackwell.

Omoto, A. M., Snyder, M., & Martino, S. C. (2000). Volunteerism and the life course: Investigating age-related agendas for action. *Basic and Applied Social Psychology, 22*, 181–198.

Penner, L. A. (2004). Volunteerism and social problems: Making things better or worse? *Journal of Social Issues, 60*, 645–666.

Penner, L. A., Dovidio, J. F., Piliavin, J. A., & Schroeder, D. A. (2005). Prosocial behavior: Multilevel perspectives. *Annual Review of Psychology, 56*, 365–392.

Piliavin, J. A., & Charng, H. (1990). Altruism: A review of recent theory and research. *Annual Review of Sociology, 16*, 27–65.

Snyder, M., & Omoto, A. M. (2007). Social action. In A. W. Kruglanski, & E. T. Higgins (Eds.), *Social psychology: A handbook of basic principles* (2nd ed., pp. 940–961). New York, NY: Guilford.

Snyder, M., & Omoto, A. M. (2008). Volunteerism: Social issues perspectives and social policy implications. *Social Issues and Policy Review, 2*, 1–36.

Snyder, M., Clary, E. G., & Stukas, A. A. (2000). The functional approach to volunteerism. In G. R. Maio & J. M. Olson (Eds.), *Why we evaluate: Functions of attitudes* (pp. 365–393). Hillsdale, NJ: Lawrence Erlbaum Associates.

Snyder, M., Omoto, A. M., & Crain, A. L. (1999). Punished for their good deeds: The stigmatization of AIDS volunteers. *American Behavioral Scientist, 42*, 1175–1192.

Snyder, M., Omoto, A. M., & Dwyer, P. C. (2016). Volunteerism: Multiple perspectives on benefits and costs. In A. G. Miller (Ed.), *The social psychology of good and evil* (2nd ed., pp. 467–493). New York, NY: Guilford Publications.

Snyder, M., Omoto, A. M., & Smith, D. M. (2009). The role of persuasion strategies in motivating individual and collective action. In E. Borgida, C. Federico, & J. L. Sullivan (Eds.), *The political psychology of democratic citizenship* (pp. 125–150). New York, NY: Oxford University Press.

Whyte, W. F. (1991). *Participatory action research*. Newbury Park, CA: Sage Publications.

Whyte, W. F., Greenwood, D. J., & Lazes, P. (1989). Participatory action research: Through practice to science in social research. *American Behavioral Scientist, 32*, 513–551. doi: 10.1177/0002764289032005003.

Wilson, J. (2000). Volunteering. *Annual Review of Sociology, 26*, 215–240.

PART V

Conclusion: Best Practices in Collaboration in Psychological Science

Eugene Borgida

Professor of Psychology and Law
Morse-Alumni Distinguished Professor of Psychology
University of Minnesota

Richard L. Zweigenhaft

Charles A. Dana Professor of Psychology
Guilford College

The authors in this collection have addressed many important issues related to the process of collaboration. In some cases, there are now clear (or at least tentative) guidelines for students, faculty, and institutions of higher learning. In other cases, there is little consensus, and it is likely to be a while before systems are in place that establish best practices when it comes to collaboration. However, there does seem to be agreement about just which issues are especially important to think about. In addition to what the contributors have addressed in this book, there is emerging literature on the topic of academic collaboration. Statistics documenting the surge of collaborative research and team science abound, but we like to think that this collection is one of the first to look at this topic in depth, as it applies to the work of psychological scientists. What follows in this discussion are some of the key issues that contributors have identified, some issues that we have culled from the collaboration literature, and our thoughts about the integration of the two. Specifically, we identify several themes that we suggest constitute best practices when it comes to collaboration in psychological science:

- Share the data.
- Beware of social loafing.
- Be crystal clear about who does what.
- Establish the order of authorship early.
- Reward collaboration.
- Maintain open lines of communication.
- Use collaboration as a social support.
- Value mentoring as a form of collaboration

Share the Data, and Other Ethical Practices

In April 2013, *The New York Times Magazine* ran an article that profiled the sad tale of Diederik Stapel, a Dutch social psychologist (Bhattacharjee, 2013). Like some scientists before him (see, e.g., Hearnshaw, 1979), Stapel had been caught fabricating data, and his career was destroyed as a result. Scientific fraud and its origins certainly have attracted the most media attention. We were especially interested in the many issues related to collaboration that are part of Stapel's story. He not only had committed fraud in at least 55 published papers (many with coauthors), but he also had supervised 10 PhD dissertations in which his students used data that Stapel had made up. It was only after many years of such deception and publication that two graduate students accused him of research fraud, and Stapel, at the time the dean of the School of Social and Behavioral Sciences at Tilburg University, was fired.

One has to admire the two graduate students who finally blew the whistle, for to do so they had to challenge someone who clearly had considerable power over their careers. Stapel's graduate students, like graduate students everywhere, depended on him as their faculty advisor to approve their dissertation research, to help them publish their work, and to write letters of recommendation for them when they applied for postdocs or teaching positions. It is not clear how many more of his graduate students over the years suspected that Stapel had made up data that they used in their dissertations or in articles that they had coauthored with him; according to the *New York Times* account (Bhattacharjee, 2013, p. 52), the final report concluded that "the students . . . were not culpable, even though their work was now tarnished." When one coauthor has such power over another, how can the less powerful coauthor make sure that he or she is not taken advantage of or otherwise professionally undermined? What are the best practices that institutions and individuals might follow to protect collaborators from one another?

In our view, one of the most striking and surprising revelations was that Stapel had maintained control of many of the data sets, and the people he worked with apparently did not have access to them. He, therefore, was able to make up or alter the data without them double-checking his work. Allowing all collaborators access to all the data should go without saying. In fact, in psychological science, as in other disciplines, researchers are encouraged to share their data with all interested legitimate researchers (protecting confidentiality when necessary, of course). The importance of transparency and reproducibility has grown considerably in the research community (Open Science Collaboration, 2015). Therefore, our first suggestion when it comes to best practices in team science is one that we shouldn't have to include: share the data.

This suggestion has been promoted more formally in a document entitled "Badges to Acknowledge Open Practices," written by a team of 11 researchers (Blohowiak et al., 2016). The researchers propose awarding symbolic "badges" for "making publicly available the digitally-shareable data necessary to reproduce the reported result." In January 2014, this policy was adopted by the journal *Psychological Science*. Articles that also make publicly available the components of their methodology that will allow others to reproduce the study, as well as those that have preregistered plans for the design and analysis of the data, will receive these badges (Eich, 2014).

Sharing the data, however, is only the most obvious accountability step to take to ensure that one's collaborators behave ethically. As the number of collaborative projects increases, and with it the number of collaborators, accompanied by what can be intense pressure to publish, the potential for unethical behavior is likely to increase as well. Barbara Stanley, a professor of medical psychology at Columbia University, recently wrote that she was involved in a project that includes several sites across the country:

> Although I know the investigators at each of the sites, I have never set foot in the institutions where the data are being collected. How do I know that the study participants are being informed adequately about the research? How do I know that the data are appropriately safeguarded to protect the confidentiality of the participants? How do I know that the data are not fabricated or altered?

She went on to point out:

In response to the growth in team research, many guidebooks and toolkits are rapidly emerging on the science of team science. But this new material tends to focus on team management, conflict resolution and fairness with respect to budgeting and publications. We don't see, in the world of publications, how to ensure that our research partners are performing ethically, responsibly and competently. (Stanley, 2014, p. 45)

More recently, it was discovered that a study about the effect of a survey interviewer's sexual orientation on attitudes toward gay marriage that appeared in the December 2014 issue of *Science* may have been based on flawed methods and fraudulent data. In this case, Michael J. LaCour, a political science graduate student at the University of California, Los Angeles (UCLA), working with Donald P. Green, an eminent political scientist at Columbia University, apparently falsified data. In addition to questions about the legitimacy of the findings, the source of funding for the study, whether participants were paid or not, and the accuracy of claims about the response rate were called into question. It was only after the study was challenged by other colleagues seeking the data set and more study details that Green asked to see the raw data. He was told by LaCour that he had erased them months ago "to protect those who answered the survey." A few days after the story broke in a front-page *New York Times* article (Carey & Belluck, 2015), *Science* retracted the paper at Green's request (Carey, 2015).

Despite the retraction, the interesting ideas that motivated the LaCour and Green study were subsequently pursued by two of the scholars who originally challenged LaCour. David Broockman, a political scientist at Stanford, and Joshua Kalla, a graduate student in political science at Berkeley, found that 10-minute front-door conversations with trained volunteers about shared discrimination experiences led to changed attitudes toward transgender people— attitude changes that persisted three months later (Broockman & Kalla, 2016).

Whereas in the case of Diederik Stapel, it was the faculty member who deceived his students, in this more recent case, the student deceived his faculty coauthor, as well as his doctoral dissertation advisor at UCLA. Both cases demonstrate the importance of open communication in collaborative contexts as a form of scientific checks and balances. Sharing the data, as well as the importance of faculty members and students having open access to each step in the process of gathering and analyzing data, cannot be overstated (Carey & Belluck, 2015). Collaboration per se is not the antidote to scientific fraud.

Beware of Social Loafing, Especially When the Collaboration Is Heterogeneous—and Capitalize on Team Cognition

Research indicates that as groups increase in size, so does the likelihood of individuals doing less than their share of the work—a process that Latané and his colleagues have called "social loafing" (Latané, Williams, & Harkins, 1979).

In the era of Big Data, instead of two or three people working on a project (as has been the case for many of those who have written chapters for this volume), some collaborations now are done by teams, some of which can be quite large. As research teams become bigger and bigger, the risks of diminished individual involvement potentially increases, which can include diminished motivation to closely monitor the work being done. This problem is compounded when the participants in a collaborative project are from multiple disciplines, typically with different knowledge bases. As a result, such collaborations are less likely to be characterized by a shared academic vocabulary (and in many cases, collaborators may not even speak the same language). For example, in a longitudinal study of the publication and citation productivity of 549 research groups who received National Science Foundation (NSF) grants from 2000 to 2004, Cummings, Kiesler, Zadeh, and Balakrishnan (2013) found that research teams that were larger (a metric defined by the number of principal investigators) and heterogeneous (defined by the number of academic disciplines of the researchers on the team and the number of institutions with which they were affiliated) were, over the next 5 to 9 years, *less* productive in terms of publications and citations. Based on interviews that they conducted with a sample of the principal investigators, the authors encouraged such groups to have regular meetings, with clear expectations laid out. They also encouraged a balance of expertise among the various disciplines represented on research teams, rather than the token presence of an outlier or unconnected experts (Cummings et al., 2013, p. 888). For more thoughts on avoiding the dangers of social loafing in the context of collaboration, see Chapter 6 in this volume.

On the other hand, as Cooke (2015) and colleagues (Cooke, Gorman, Myers, & Duran, 2013) have demonstrated in a series of empirical studies, if one pays attention not to the amount of shared knowledge that each collaborator brings to the project, but to the dynamic nature of the interactions among the various collaborators as they make decisions, one can enhance what is referred to as "interactive team cognition." Teams and team leaders who pay attention to these interactions in the form of explicit communications are more likely to generate new knowledge and integrate ideas that take advantage of team members cognitively coordinating with each other, as opposed to succumbing to social loafing and poorer team performance. In other words, thinking about team cognition in this way can serve as an antidote to social loafing tendencies in larger collaborative teams.

Be as Clear as Possible About Who Will Do What and How Decisions Will Be Made

Academic collaborations include more than one person contributing to the many tasks that lead to the final intellectual product. These tasks can include research design, the gathering of data, data analysis, interpretation of the meaning of the findings, and, of course, writing and revising. Different academic disciplines, and different institutions within these disciplines, have their own guidelines about who should be a coauthor and who should not and about the order in which authors are listed. This means that there is great potential for misunderstandings and disputes, especially when it comes to interdisciplinary projects. As many of the chapters in this volume have demonstrated, at the very outset of a project, collaborators should discuss who will contribute, in what ways, and what the expected order of authorship will be (see, e.g., Chapters 5 and 14). If things do not go as planned—as very often they do not—collaborators may need to revisit these topics throughout the project.

Some journals now ask authors to explain who did what in a section at the end of the article titled "Author Contributions." Consider this example, from an article in *Psychological Science* with six coauthors (Bleidorn et al., 2013):

> W. Bleidorn developed the study concept. S. D. Gosling, P. J. Rentfrow, and J. Potter collected the data. W. Bleidorn analyzed the data, and T. A. Klimstra and J. J. A. Denissen helped with interpreting the results. W. Bleidorn drafted the manuscript and S. D. Gosling, P. J. Rentfrow, J. J. A. Denisson, and T. A. Klimstra provided critical revisions. All authors approved the final version of the manuscript for submission.

As Greenberg, Pyszczynski, and Solomon emphasize in Chapter 5, as do various other authors of chapters in this volume (e.g., see Chapters 6 and 14), it is important to assign a team leader for each project. In their terms, it is important "to have a lead dog for each particular project, preferably a dog very open to input from team members, but also driven to keep the project moving forward in bold, creative directions" (p. 58). This decision—who is the team leader—is likely to be part of yet another important issue: Who will be the first author?

Be as Clear as Possible, as Early as Possible, About the Order of Authorship

For some projects in some disciplines, as well as for some interdisciplinary projects, team members decide to list the names of the authors in alphabetical order. In economics, for example, authors are listed alphabetically, but recent research suggests that this can have the unintended consequences of bias against women who coauthor with men—consequences that may contribute to the fact that women in this field are less likely to receive tenure (Wolfers, 2016). Christopher Stubbs, a physicist at the University of Washington, wrote the following about one interdisciplinary project in which he participated: "After considerable debate, we decided early on to use alphabetical author-ship, because it may be awful, but it's better than the alternatives (most of which seem to involve hand-to-hand combat between alleged colleagues). We have not been able to devise a scheme that is 'fairer,' despite considerable creative effort" (Stubbs, 1997, p. 320).

For multiple authorships in some disciplines, like biology, the name of the principal investigator traditionally is listed last, but in others, like organic chemistry, that person is listed first. In order to decrease the inevitable ambiguity that occurs with such different traditions in different scientific disciplines, Helen Pearson, a geneticist who writes for *Nature*, has encouraged scientists to explain the contributions of the various collaborators by addressing this issue in the body of the work: "One way to avoid ambiguity is for each author to spell out their contribution in the paper. Many medical journals, including JAMA [the *Journal of the American Medical Association*], require this" (Pearson, 2006, p. 592; see also Gaeta, 1999; Strange, 2008; Smith & William-Jones, 2011). As noted previously, some journals now require this in a section, footnote, or end note titled "Author Contributions."

In the social sciences, the general rule is that the order of authorship should reflect the relative contributions of the collaborators (see, e.g., the guidelines published in 2009 by the American Psychological Association [APA], as well as the APA's 2006 "A Graduate Student's Guide to Determining Authorship Credit and Authorship Order," a report prepared by the APA Science Student Council). Various graduate programs provide systems by which the order of authorship can be determined and, typically, the ways that disputes are to be settled. There are even online templates that allow collaborators to list the various tasks involved in the project (e.g., literature review, data analysis) and to estimate the relative contributions of each of the coauthors for each (weighted) task, thus creating an overall score that determines the order of authorship (see, e.g., the online template "authororder" at http://www.authorder.com/index.php?option=com_content&view=article&id=18&Itemid=29). Determining the order of authorship is difficult enough for colleagues, and it is even more complicated for faculty-student collaborations (see Fine & Kurdeck, 1993; Thompson, 1994; Zanna & Darley, 2004). Whatever procedure is employed, and whatever the status of the collaborators, we encourage participants, if at all possible, to agree on these at the outset and, if the need arises, to revisit what Zanna and Darley (2004, p. 124) correctly refer to as "this highly complex and emotion-laden issue."

Reward Collaboration When It Comes to Tenure and Promotion

Several contributors to this volume have addressed questions related to tenure and promotion. As many have noted, there are risks involved in choosing to collaborate, but there are also potential benefits (see, e.g., Chapters 3, 13, and 18). As we have stated, however, more and more research is collaborative, and more and more of the most frequently cited research is collaborative. Therefore, colleges and universities (especially those who create the guidelines used by tenure committees) have had to acknowledge and determine how to value the role that collaborative research plays in psychological science today. This, of course, is easier said than done. As Cantor and Englot point out in

Chapter 17, even at Syracuse (where, at the time, Cantor was chancellor), "it took more than 4 years to get agreement from the university senate for a relatively small revision in the faculty manual to recognize collaborative and publicly engaged scholarship in tenure and promotion" (p. 209).

Unfortunately, many universities have a long way to go on this issue. As Cohen and Garcia note in Chapter 18, one of them was told by a member of the tenure committee at his university, "At some point, if the junior faculty member is serious, they have to stop all this collaboration and get down to work" (p. 226). We are concerned that this view is still quite widespread and that there is still a gap at some institutions between the rhetoric in support of collaborative scholarship and the reality that collaborative work poses evaluative challenges.

Perhaps in part as a response to such negative attitudes about collaboration when it comes to tenure and promotion, a number of the contributors to this volume have noted (see Chapters 3 and 10), or emphasized (see Chapter 7), that in addition to the long-term collaborations with other people, they have continued to do solo research to reinforce their bona fides as independent scholars. And they also have collaborated with multiple partners. We agree that there is much to be gained from long-term collaborations, but we also encourage those in such relationships to be cautious about limiting themselves to only these collaborations because change in the academic realm moves at a slow pace.

We are convinced that many graduate students and young faculty members want to collaborate, but they worry that it will hurt their careers if they do so. They are concerned that even if they act as full partners in collaborative research, they will not receive full credit for their contributions. We very much hope that academic institutions in general, and those disciplines or subdisciplines in particular that are especially recalcitrant on this issue, will come to reward collaboration more fully. However, as we have indicated, despite the tendency of some colleges and universities and some departments to talk the collaboration talk, not as many walk the walk. In the meantime, we can only encourage those who are early in their academic careers to try to find a balance between collaborative work and work that they are primarily responsible for (which, when published, will either be solo-authored or will list them as the primary author). In the latter instance, there will be less ambiguity as to who should get credit for the published work.

Allocating credit for collaborative effort is not just problematic in the context of promotion and tenure decisions. It is also problematic when it comes time to determine who should be rewarded and given awards for collaborative research. Consider two long-term collaborators whose work gains prominence. Imagine that they are considered for an academic honor, such as selection to the National Academy of Sciences (NAS). There are at least three outcomes, two of which are not likely to make them both happy or reward them both for their work: (1) both are selected, as the collaboration is seen as genuinely collaborative; (2) only one of the two is selected, as selection bias assumes that only one of the collaborators could possibly have been the driving force behind the research; or (3) neither is selected because the task of determining who did what was deemed impossible. As researchers move along their career paths, and legacy becomes more and more of an issue, the outcome of such award deliberations may feel more consequential.

Action Research Lives On

Several chapters in this collection have mentioned Kurt Lewin, the social psychologist who championed action research ("there's nothing as practical as a good theory"), and who is often referred to as the father of modern social psychology. In Chapter 17, Cantor and Englot point out in their opening paragraph that they work in "the best traditions of action research," as do others in this collection, some of whom cite Lewin, and others of whom do not (see, e.g., Chapters 1, 9, 18, and 21). As we read these engaging chapters, we were struck by the number of roads that lead to Lewin (or, put another way, many are on the roads they are on because of roads previously taken by Lewin).

In Chapter 9, Nisbett and Ross recall being graduate students at Columbia, where their advisor was Stanley Schachter, whom they describe as the "intellectual grandson" of Kurt Lewin (the father, in between, was Leon Festinger). Lewin, therefore, not only was the intellectual grandfather of Stanley Schachter, but the intellectual great-grandfather of both Nisbett and Ross, and, since Nisbett was the dissertation advisor to one of the editors of this collection, we can also note that Lewin was the intellectual great-great-grandfather of Gene Borgida.

In the past few decades, Participatory Action Research (PAR), a distinctive form of collaboration that includes a commitment to social justice, has become more widely used than Lewin's model in some academic fields (e.g., Howard, Polimeno, & Wheeler, 2014; Stoudt, 2009; Tandon, 1996). These collaborations are in some ways similar to the action research projects described by several authors in this collection who have worked with community partners (for instance, see Chapters 17, 18, and 21), but those employing PAR place more emphasis on the involvement of people in the community (including those who are being studied) in both designing and carrying out the research. For example, in one recent PAR study, a faculty member working with a team of graduate students at the University of Pennsylvania met with students of color at an elite boarding school. They asked these students what they considered to be the key issues at their school. The faculty member, the graduate students, and the secondary students worked together to design a study to explore racial stereotypes and discrimination at the school, and then took the findings to the powers that be at the school, calling for changes in policy (Kuriloff & Carl, 2015). Although much PAR, inspired by the work of Paolo Freire and allied with feminist theory, critical race theory, and indigenous theory, has been in the field of education studies, it has been embraced by academics in other disciplines as well, including community studies (e.g., Giles, 2014) and psychology (e.g., Fine, Roberts, Torre, & Upegui, 2001; Fine & Torre, 2004).

PAR as a form of academic collaboration raises many of the same issues identified throughout this book. For example, if the research leads to a publication, who among the many participants should be given credit as the authors, and what should be the order of authorship? Will engaging in such collaborative research enhance, or detract from, the likelihood of a faculty member receiving tenure or promotion? Who has control over the data and whether or not they should be shared?

The contributors to this collection also have identified some of the features that can enhance, or detract from, successful collaboration. As the next section suggests, among these are personal styles when it comes to meeting deadlines, organizational skills, and effective use of the Internet.

Timing May Not Be Everything, but It Is Vital When It Comes to Collaboration

It is clearly important for collaborators to find a rhythm of communication that works for them. Some of the contributors identify the failure to find such a rhythm as potentially problematic (see, for example, the description in Chapter 4 of "Dr. Quick and Dr. Slow," who "drive each other crazy"). In Chapter 14, Wells provides a painful example of how the failure of some participants to get their work done in a reasonable amount of time actually led to the abandonment of a collaborative project. Many of the writers in this collection have described how successful collaborators find their ways to reciprocal timing patterns that work for them. In Chapter 15, for example, Zweigenhaft writes that he and Bill Domhoff have maintained a cross-country collaborative relationship for 40 years—one that depended for a long time on the U.S. mail and occasional phone calls, but now allows Domhoff to send e-mails late at night (Pacific Coast time), for Zweigenhaft to read them the next morning (East Coast time), to work for a few hours, and then send e-mails back to Domhoff that arrive before Domhoff wakes up. Similarly, crossing many more time zones, Shaver (in CA) and Mikulincer (in Israel) have figured out how best to overcome the many time zones between them, as they describe in Chapter 10. In fact, as they explain, not only have they overcome this potential obstacle, they use it as an advantage:

> It is advantageous that we live in different time zones, 10 hours apart. One of us can send the other part of a draft or comments on a draft, and the other can work on it while the sender sleeps. One of us is always awake, and this allows us to accomplish more than if we both slept at the same times. When one of us is eating breakfast and checking e-mail, the other is checking e-mail before going to sleep for the night. Almost nothing gets put off for more than a day. As in a relay race, one of us hands the baton to the other and rests. (p. 122)

Dovidio and Gaertner also note in Chapter 3 the potential increase in productivity that the Internet allows when working internationally with people in different time zones. They are among the many who stress that the Internet has very much improved the way people collaborate:

> In addition, developments in computer-mediated communication greatly facilitated our collaborative connections with international scholars. Whereas working with people from time zones 5 to 7 hours apart had been a major obstacle to sustaining collaborative relationships internationally by phone, the Internet made it a strength. A collaborator in Europe could work on a manuscript for several hours and send it to us at the end of the day, and it would arrive as we began our workday, doubling the amount of time devoted to a manuscript in a 24-hour period. (pp. 40–41)

There is yet another aspect to timing that some of our contributors have emphasized: the need for patience, especially when one is collaborating with people or institutions in the community. Cohen and Garcia make this point quite nicely in Chapter 18, in their discussion of the work that they did in the public school system: "When it comes to cultivating relationships with institutions, the conclusion that we came to as a consequence of our collaboration was 'Don't rush it.' Because of professional pressures, such as the push to publish, patience can be undervalued" (p. 221). Snyder and Omoto make a similar point in Chapter 21 based on their work with a variety of AIDS/HIV service organizations.

Collaboration, Emboldening, and Social Support

Many of the chapters in this collection make clear that although collaboration can be frustrating, it also allows one to do things that one could not do otherwise. It also provides one with interested and supportive colleagues who not only share the load, but who can embolden each other. "Collaboration is a kind of intimacy," says MIT scholar Sherry Turkle. "You don't just get more information. You get different information" (Turkle, 2015). As Snyder and Omoto put it in their chapter, "Working together, we were more willing to go forward, to do new things, and to do hard and even unexpected things" (p. 265; see also Chapters 7, 12, and 14). This may be especially true, and especially valued, when the collaborators see themselves and are seen by others as professional outliers, and perhaps when perceiving oneself as an outlier is irritating (as Markus and Kitayama put it in Chapter 8, p. 95, "We heeded Bob Zajonc's claim that good work often begins with irritation"). And for some outliers—women in settings where they are very much outnumbered by men, or for psychologists of color in settings where they are very much in the minority—the choice to collaborate may provide invaluable social support (see, e.g., see Chapters 1 and 19).

Moreover, as Wells points out in his chapter, in addition to the fact that a well-selected collaboration team that draws on people with complementary interests can lead to higher-quality work, it can help if and when the work is critiqued in peer review (or elsewhere), and certain team members with specific expertise can be especially helpful in challenging the critiques.

Mentoring Is a Form of Collaboration

Finally, as we noted in the preface of this book, one source of inspiration for this collection was when Richie Zweigenhaft read a book titled *Mentor: A Memoir* (Grimes, 2010). While reading it, he realized that his graduate school mentor (Domhoff) had become a collaborator over many decades, and he found himself wondering how their collaboration was similar to, and different from, the work of the many other social science collaborators that he had read and admired for many years. Although this volume, as it took shape, focuses on collaboration, the topic of mentoring weaves its way through several of the chapters. A number of the contributors emphasize the importance of the mentoring that they received from faculty when they were undergraduates (see Chapter 4) or graduate students (see, especially, Greenberg, Pyszczynski, and Solomon's comments about Jack Brehm at Kansas, Nisbett and Ross's comments about Stanley Schachter at Columbia, and Elaine Hatfield's comments about Leon Festinger at Stanford). In his chapter, James Jackson notes that in the collaborative work that he has done, especially with the Program for Research on Black Americans (PRBA), "because of the lack of racial and ethnic minority researchers in the social and behavioral sciences, we attempted to provide a training vehicle for the production of social scientists" (p. 239). Many others in this volume have emphasized the mentoring they have done as faculty members. In Chapter 7, Judd and Park gratefully acknowledge the mentoring that they received from their students over the years. And in Chapter 11, Sullivan and Borgida placed mentoring at the heart of their collaborative enterprise in political psychology. As Greenberg, Pyszczynski, and Solomon point out, "[t]he training of new scientists involves mentoring, which we view very much as another form of collaboration" (p. 58). We could not agree more.

Collaboration in Psychological Science and Beyond

As we and many of the contributors to this volume have pointed out, the lessons to be learned from collaboration in psychological science extend far beyond the field of psychology. The chapters in this collection draw primarily on the collaborative work of social psychologists, which, on the surface, might seem to constrain the scope and generalizability of our best practices. However, and significantly, the features and characteristics of their work bear a remarkable resemblance to the attributes that define collaboration in business, where collaboration and teams are thriving, and in scientific fields outside psychological science. Strong relationships that build trust and make it more likely that conflicts will be well managed, for example, are essential in both business and academic collaboration (see, for example, McDaniel, 2016a, and McDaniel, 2016b). As the editors of the *Harvard Business Review* assert, making the very same arguments about the business world that we have made about collaboration in psychological science:

> The word "collaboration" pops up a lot in business these days—and for good reason. Companies increasingly rely on internal, cross-group cooperation as well as external partnerships to create and sustain their portfolio of products and services. Managers and their employees need to know how to exchange ideas and work together effectively to put those concepts into action. Done well, such as when diverse teams build strong relationships and an atmosphere of trust that encourages healthy debate, collaboration can lead to wonderful outcomes. ("Collaboration That Works," 2014, p. 1)

In biomedical research, some key features of scientific teams are critical to success, and many, if not most, of these features overlap with the set of best practices derived from the chapters in our collection. Bennett and Gadlin (2012) conducted in-depth interviews with researchers at the National Institutes of Health (NIH) who were on diverse teams that experienced success, on teams that did not experience much success, or on teams that folded because of conflict. Perhaps the most important feature critical to the effectiveness of teams is trust among team members. Trust is crucial to the development of interdependence among team members with diverse personal and scientific backgrounds. But other features matter a great deal as well: open communication and a willingness to listen to and learn from other team members, defined roles and responsibilities, sharing authorship and credit, managing conflict, having fun, and challenging each other without the associated conflict becoming personal and undermining the team dynamic.

If these attributes of successful scientific teams at NIH ring a bell for you, then we hope that it is due in part to the salience of the best practices described in this volume. Successful scientific collaborations, as with successful business teams, are mindful of these fundamental elements. We hope that this volume singing the praises and warning of the pitfalls of collaboration will be a useful guide to anyone interested in understanding why collaboration and team science have become such defining features of professional life in the 21st century.

▦ REFERENCES ▦

American Psychological Association. (2006). *A Graduate Student's Guide to Determining Authorship Credit and Authorship Order*. (Report prepared by the APA Science Student Council). Washington, DC: Author.

American Psychological Association. (2009). *Publication manual of the American Psychological Association* (6th ed.). Washington, DC: Author.

Bennett, L. M., & Gadlin, H. 2012. Collaboration and team science: From theory to practice. *Journal of Investigative Medicine*, 60(5), 768–775.

Bhattacharjee, Y. (2013, April 26). The mind of a con man. *The New York Times Magazine*, pp. 44–52.

Bleidorn, W., Klimstra, T. A., Denissen, J. J. A., Rentfrow, P. J., Potter, J., & Gosling, S. D. (2013). Personality maturation around the world: A cross-cultural examination of social-investment theory. *Psychological Science, 24*(12), 2530–2540.

Blohowiak, B. B., Cohoon, J., de-Wit, L., Eich, E., Farach, F. J., Hasselman, F., . . . Mellor, D. (2016). Badges to acknowledge open practices. Retrieved from https:// osciencesframework.org/project/TVyXZ/

Broockman, D., & Kalla, J. (2016). Durably reducing transphobia: A field experiment on door-to-door canvassing. *Science, 352*(6282), 220–224.

Carey, B. (2015, May 28). Journal retracts study on changing attitudes on same-sex marriage. *New York Times*, p. A16.

Carey, B., & Belluck, P. (2015, May 26). Maligned study on gay unions is shaking trust. *New York Times*, p. A1.

Collaboration that works. (2014, Spring). *Harvard Business Review: OnPoint.*

Cooke, N. J. (2015). Team cognition as interaction. *Current Directions in Psychological Science, 24*(6), 415–419.

Cooke, N. J., Gorman, J. C., Myers, C. W., & Duran, J. L. (2013). Interactive team cognition. *Cognitive Science, 37*, 255–285; doi:10.1111/cogs.12009

Cummings, J. N., Kiesler, S., Zadeh, R. B., & Balakrishnan, A. D. (2013). Group heterogeneity increases the risks of large group size: A longitudinal study of productivity in research groups. *Psychological Science, 24*(6), 880–890.

Eich, E. (2014). Business not as usual. *Psychological Science, 25*(1), 3–6.

Fine, M., Roberts, R. A., Torre, M. E., & Upegui, D. (2001). Participatory action research behind bars. *International Journal of Critical Psychology, 2*, 145–157.

Fine, M., & Torre, M. E. (2004). Re-membering exclusions: Participatory action research in public institutions. *Qualitative Research in Psychology, 1*(1), 15–37.

Fine, M. A., & Kurdek, L. A. (1993). Reflections on determining authorship credit and authorship order on faculty-student collaborations. *American Psychologist, 48*, 1141–1147.

Gaeta, T. J. (1999). Authorship: "Law" and order. *Academic Emergency Medicine, 6*(4), 297–301.

Giles, H. C. (2014). Risky epistemology: Connecting with others and dissonance in community-based research. *Michigan Journal of Community Service Learning 20*(2), 65–78.

Grimes, Tom (2010). *Mentor: A Memoir*. Portland, OR and New York, NY: Tin House Books.

Hearnshaw, L. S. (1979). *Cyril Burt, Psychologist*. Ithaca, NY: Cornell University Press.

Howard, A., Polimeno, A., & Wheeler, B. (2014). *Negotiating privilege and identity in educational contexts*. New York, NY: Routledge.

Kuriloff. P., & Carl, N. M. (2015, June). *Studying with, not on: Addressing the challenges of excavating the hidden curricula of power in the elite schools*. Paper delivered at Researching Elite Education Conference, Ontario Institute for Studies in Education (OISE), Toronto, Canada.

Latané, B., Williams, K. D., & Harkins, S. (1979). Many hands make light the work: The causes and consequences of social loafing. *Journal of Personality and Social Psychology, 37*, 822–832.

McDaniel, S. H. (2016a). The collaborative habit. *Monitor on Psychology, 47* (2), 5.

McDaniel, S. H. (2016b). Why teamwork surpasses the individual approach. *Monitor on Psychology, 47* (5), 5.

Open Science Collaboration (2015). Estimating the reproducibility of psychological science. *Science, 349*(6251). doi:10.1126/science.aac4716

Pearson, H. (2006). Credit where credit's due. *Nature*, *440*, 591–592.

Smith, E., & Williams-Jones, B. (2012). Authorship and responsibility in health sciences research: A review of procedures for fairly allocating authorship in multi-author studies. *Science and Engineering Ethics*, *18*, 199–212. doi:10.1007/s11948-011-9263-5

Stanley, Barbara. (2014, July/August). Team science: A matter of trust? *Monitor on Psychology*, 44–45.

Stoudt, B. G. (2009). The role of language and discourse in the investigation of privilege: Using participatory action research to discuss theory, develop methodology, and interrupt power. *Urban Review*, *41*, 7–28.

Strange, K. (2008). Authorship: Why not just toss a coin? *American Journal of Physiology*, *295*, C567–C575.

Stubbs, C. (1997). The serious business of listing authors. *Nature*, *388*(6640), 320.

Tandon, R. (1996). The historical roots and contemporary tendencies in participatory research: Implications for health care. In K. De Koning, & M. Martin (Eds.), *Participatory research in health: Issues and experiences* (pp. 19–26), London: Zed Books.

Thompson, B. (1994). The big picture(s) in deciding authorship order. *American Psychologist*, *49*, 1095–1096.

Turkle, S. (2015, October 2). How to teach in an age of distraction. *The Chronicle Review*. Accessed April 16, 2016, from http://chronicle.com/article/How-to-teach-in-an-age-of/233515?cid.

Wolfers, J. (2016, January 8). When teamwork doesn't work for women. The Upshot. *New York Times*. Retrieved from http://www.nytimes.com/2016/01/10/upshot/when-teamwork-doesnt-work-for-women.html?_r=0

Yang, Y-J., & Chiu, C-Y. (2009). Mapping the structure and dynamics of psychological knowledge: Forty years of APA journal citations (1970–2009). *Review of General Psychology*, *13*, 349–356. doi:10.1037/a0017195

Zanna, M. P., & Darley, J. M. (2004). Mentoring: Managing the faculty-graduate student relationship. In J. M. Darley, M. P. Zanna, & H. L. Roediger III (Eds.), *The compleat academic: a career guide* (2nd ed., pp. 117–132). Washington, DC: American Psychological Association.

Name Index

291

Subject Index